The Inner Life of Catholic Reform

# The Inner Life of Catholic Reform

*From the Council of Trent to the Enlightenment*

ULRICH L. LEHNER

# OXFORD
## UNIVERSITY PRESS

Oxford University Press is a department of the University of Oxford. It furthers
the University's objective of excellence in research, scholarship, and education
by publishing worldwide. Oxford is a registered trade mark of Oxford University
Press in the UK and certain other countries.

Published in the United States of America by Oxford University Press
198 Madison Avenue, New York, NY 10016, United States of America.

Library of Congress Cataloging-in-Publication Data
Names: Lehner, Ulrich L., 1976– author.
Title: The inner life of Catholic reform : from the Council of
Trent to the Enlightenment / Ulrich L. Lehner.
Description: New York, NY, United States of America : Oxford University Press, [2022] |
Includes bibliographical references and index.
Identifiers: LCCN 2021059023 (print) | LCCN 2021059024 (ebook) |
ISBN 9780197620601 (hardback) | ISBN 9780197620625 (epub)
Subjects: LCSH: Church renewal—Catholic Church. |
Catholic Church—History.
Classification: LCC BX1746 .L4325 2022 (print) | LCC BX1746 (ebook) |
DDC 262/.02—dc23/eng/20220121
LC record available at https://lccn.loc.gov/2021059023
LC ebook record available at https://lccn.loc.gov/2021059024

DOI: 10.1093/oso/9780197620601.001.0001

1 3 5 7 9 8 6 4 2

Printed by Integrated Books International, United States of America

*To*
*Notre Dame du Lac*
*—ora pro nobis—*

# Contents

# Preface

I began this book after I had finished several works on the history of the *Catholic Enlightenment*.[1] The term describes not a movement with a unified agenda or group cohesion, but rather "a variety of actors within the fold of Catholicism united by their engagement, in one way or another, with Enlightenment culture for the sake of ecclesial and societal reform."[2] In these works I argued that Catholic Enlightenment continues with its call for church reform, crucial ideas of the *Catholic Reform*[3] in the sixteenth and seventeenth century. For these Enlightenment authors, not only institutions had to change but also the faithful had to be liberated from superstition and become enlightened. Thus, much of their agenda focused on how persons could transform aspects of their inner life such as sentiments, piety, and ethical principles. As baptized Christians, they believed they were children of God, who had to constantly convert in the struggle against sin. Only by reforming their soul, aligning it with the will of God, could they become holy and grow in spiritual perfection. Such *reform* meant bringing the inner life back to a state of grace and to strengthen it for daily challenges. Wondering what such *inner reform* looked like a few hundred years before the Enlightenment, I investigated the reforms initiated in the sixteenth and seventeenth centuries. To my surprise, most works about the *Catholic Reform* that tried to rejuvenate the faith after the Council of Trent, never defined what "reform" meant and how it was understood. Moreover, they did not spend much time—if any at all—on inner reform, on practices and beliefs that would spiritually transform the individual, but rather on institutions and politics. This book aims at filling this lacuna. By sidestepping questions about the importance of the Council of Trent or the papacy, the cohesion of reform ideas or the reform movement, I am focusing here *entirely* on the means of spiritual reform. Such an emphasis allows to see better the roots of early modern religious zeal in late medieval piety and reform. Consequently, I analyze the spiritual resources early modern Catholics possessed, where they encountered them, and how they were used for inner transformation.

Soon it became clear to me that Catholic thinkers not only *in*formed the faithful but *formed* them by instilling in them a vivid religious imagination.

The normative texts and practices, usually produced by clergy, members of religious orders, confraternities, and in some cases laypersons, were, however, not blindly received. Reception and inner formation depended on the willingness of the individuals involved, the compatibility of religious expectations with social norms, and of course personal preferences.[4] Moreover, reception always entailed a personal interpretation of what had been heard or seen or read. The religious demands and pious suggestions were thus often renegotiated and adapted. The COVID pandemic, however, made my plan to research the reception history impossible, and so I decided to focus on presenting the normative resources for religious renewal of the time. Among these resources was of course Holy Scripture, most often filtered through homilies, prayer books and the arrangement of psalms in the breviary, and of course art. Thus, biblical imagery was ubiquitous but did not rest on a widespread culture of reading common among Protestants. Moreover, the lack of research on the history of Catholic exegesis, Catholic Bible translations, and the use of Scripture in different religious orders, despite praiseworthy recent efforts, does not seem to allow just yet a judgment about how the text of Scripture was used for spiritual reform. Therefore the reader will not find a chapter dealing with the "Bible" as might be expected.

Focusing on the spiritual life after the Council of Trent is warranted because "reform" was not something that occurred merely through institutional changes, new laws, and tight social control, as historiographic works sometimes seem to suggest. Understanding early modern societies means taking their religious commitments seriously and trying to understand them on their own terms. The core message of *Catholic Reform* regarding the "salvation of souls" cannot be downplayed to a trivial sideshow. The historian must instead illustrate how this idea influenced thinking, feeling, imagination, and behavior. Thus, the question for me was: What did Catholics do to obtain such salvation, to make themselves pleasing to God? For early modern Catholics, *church reform* began with *personal reform* and by trying to live and remain in a state of grace. They developed ways of changing their behavior and guiding their imagination. Sophisticated tools such as emblems or prayer techniques helped them to mold "new selves" that were "pleasing to God," or at least allowed them access to such resources if they decided to use them. I followed these authors up to the end of the eighteenth century, when the spiritual culture began to shift. Thus, this work presents a *longue durée* of spiritual theology, spanning a little over two hundred years. The scope of the project made it necessary to leave out various things. Controversies that rocked Catholicism are mentioned but not treated in detail, because there was simply no space. This, however, should serve as a reminder that the book is meant to complement other historical approaches—that illuminate social discipline, theological controversy, culture, and institutional history—not to replace them.

Moreover, since I strongly believe that books should be read and not just consulted, my aim was to write a book of moderate length. Omitting early modern authors and works, information about popes, religious orders, the Holy Inquisition, or paradigms such as "social disciplining" and "confessionalization" was therefore necessary. Every author must make choices. Mine was to tell as coherently and accurately as possible what early modern Catholics believed about spiritual transformation and how to go about it. Thus, I took only a small bag of pearls from the treasury and left the rest untouched.

I could not ask for better colleagues and friends than Brad S. Gregory and Don Stelluto, who through a Director's Fellowship at the Notre Dame Institute of Advanced Study in 2018 helped set this book on its course. At Notre Dame, Dean Sarah Mustillo of the College of Arts and Letters and the chair of the theology department, Timothy Matovina, have provided me with generous support, without which my research would never have been possible. My colleagues and friends in the department have inspired me, by their academic rigor and dedication, to aim *ad astra*. I especially thank those friends who helped me along the way by reading drafts of this book, including Shaun Blanchard, Alkuin Schachenmayer O.Cist., Brad Gregory, Robin Jensen, C. J. Jones, Michael Maher S. J., Robert Fastiggi, and Joachim Werz. I thank Alison Britton as well for her careful copyediting.

# 1

# The Dynamics of Reform

Church Reform is necessary[1]

—Cardinal of Lorraine, June 1561

The Reformation changed not only the world but also the religion it tried to alter, namely Catholicism. It motivated Catholics not only to purge their church of abuses and better articulate their faith but also to battle the new religious competition. The actions taken by Catholics to counter the Protestant Reformation have therefore been summarized under the umbrella term "Counter-Reformation."[2] While this term is quite useful and appropriate, especially when it describes the political or polemical behavior of the time, it conveys the impression that *every* Catholic reform was a response to Protestantism. This, however, obscures the common medieval roots of both reform movements. Consequently, historians have enlarged their vocabulary by adding the term "Catholic Reform." It is understood as focusing on the *inner* renewal of the church, often independent of Protestant challenges. Far from identifying a homogeneous movement, the term suggests a wide horizon of ambitions and plans centered around the rejuvenation of Catholicism. Yet, most studies of Catholic Reform have emphasized how new institutions, new forms of discipline, and some major figures brought about ecclesial improvement, but generally left out the spiritual motives for their actions—namely, the inner transformation of the believer.

This book rediscovers this neglected perspective by shedding light on the forms and methods early modern Catholics used to "reform" themselves and achieve spiritual progress. As a result, the reader will better understand why certain institutions and disciplinary forms were initiated, and how early modern Catholics lived and understood their faith. Consequently, the famous theologians of the era as well as popes and bishops are only of secondary concern, while the main focus remains on how and for what purpose the ordinary faithful internalized practices of faith.

*The Inner Life of Catholic Reform*. Ulrich L. Lehner, Oxford University Press. © Oxford University Press 2022.
DOI: 10.1093/oso/9780197620601.003.0001

This strategy also underscores that Catholic Reform and Protestant Reformation understood the reality of reform differently. While Catholics believed that methods and practices existed that helped them to grow in faith and holiness (*sanctification*), Protestants placed their trust in faith alone (*sola fides*). As a consequence, for Protestants reform meant the reestablishment of the church Christ had intended, freed from the errors with which Catholics had disfigured her. The Christian was simultaneously sinful and justified in the eyes of God, but there was no inner reform beyond accepting the word of God in faith. Catholics, however, believed that through the assistance of divine grace one could be truly transformed into a new creature that was pleasing to God. Reform meant the conversion and sanctification of the sinful self, and church reform a return to God by rejecting abuses and aiding the growth of spiritual progress.[3]

By giving one's life a new direction, an early modern Catholic desired to leave sin behind, cling to Christ, and follow the divine and ecclesiastical laws. A person who chose this new life received divine assistance (grace) and began the way of inner transformation. The foundation for this makeover had already been given in the sacrament of baptism when one received the indelible mark of being chosen by God. When sin destroyed friendship with God and deprived a person of grace, it could be restored in the sacrament of confession. Sincere prayer, almsgiving, and mortification amplified grace, helped the will to abandon self-interest, and formed one's will according to God's commands. This process of sanctification was the core idea of Catholic Reform. Certainly, it was nothing new, but the intensity with which Catholics now pursued it was. Sanctification became an ideal for every baptized Catholic and not just for the super-zealous.

## The Terminology of Reform

The intellectual roots of linking personal holiness and church emendation can be found in late medieval reform movements.[4] Many of these grew out of monastic orders, where discipline had decayed. Reforming an order, however, not only expressed the desire to return to a better, normative past (*ecclesia primitiva*), but also acknowledged that the past could not be resuscitated.[5] Instead, one had to find *new* ways to reestablish moral and spiritual discipline while staying faithful to the past.[6] Rejuvenation of order and church was therefore believed to come about through a spiritual renewal but not through an overhaul of church teachings. This characteristic also shaped the Catholic Reform from the sixteenth century onward. It never intended to overthrow an existing system of teaching, but instead desired to recenter Catholic life around Christ.[7] With the outbreak of the Reformation, however, for Catholics the reform of the church became a question of survival. The Council of Trent gave it a loose framework, while inspirational saints provided the driving ideas for leading believers to personal transformation. This Catholic Reform continued well into the eighteenth century, when it overlapped with ideas of the Catholic Enlightenment but also clashed with it on a number of issues.

By focusing on the inner life of Catholic Reform, this book must exclude much. It cannot discuss the forms of suppression, intimidation, and disciplining of Catholics and members of other faiths (as well as atheists), nor the affinities between church and politics, which led to the condoning of colonialism, slavery, nationalism, and confessionalism. Writing the history of transformative spiritual methods and actions of early modern Catholics does not deny these dimensions and does *not* seek to replace them, but rather *complements* and elucidates them.

## The Misunderstood Council

Catholic Reform is often identified with the Council of Trent (1545–1563).[8] Sixteenth-century cardinals of the Roman Curia would delight in such praise, because they worked hard to give it this appearance. Certainly, the council addressed the substantial theological crisis of the Protestant Reformation by reiterating traditional doctrine while at the same time anathematizing dissenters and stopping abuses within the church's own ranks. After all, such was the traditional business of a council. Thus, a contemporary described Trent: "Whoever studies this council can say that he knows all past councils, because they are all summarized and entailed in it."[9] Although it passed a remarkable number of reform decrees, implemented new norms and laws,[10] and demanded that seminaries for priests should be built, it never articulated a passionate vision of reform.[11] Their universal implementation of its reform decrees took almost two hundred years.[12]

What then gave Trent the nimbus of being the origin of reform? Most likely it was its character as a multinational meeting of bishops to address a crisis.[13] It indicated that the entire church began to take pastoral care and the

sanctification of the "people of God" seriously. As a *symbol* of this development, the *image* of the council could inspire where its texts could not. The
adjective *Tridentine* therefore became synonymous with reform and was attached to activities that were accomplished decades after the council. The result of identifying post-conciliar reform with the council itself, however, was
that the texts of Trent became an increasingly *vague* reference point, whose
symbolic meaning outweighed their literal influence. While some named this
development the "myth of Trent,"[14] it is perhaps better and closer to sixteenth-
and seventeenth-century understanding to call it the "spirit of Trent."[15] This
term not only encapsulates the symbolic importance of the council and
reminds us that Catholics believed it to have been directed by the third person
of God, the Holy Spirit, but also describes the flexibility with which Catholic
Reform operated.[16] It did not have to cling to the letter of the council, but often
creatively renegotiated its meaning according to local customs and expectations, whether in Europe, Asia, Africa, or the Americas. The "spirit" allowed
on the one side for devotions to be curtailed and centered around normative expectations but left on the other enough space for ambiguity.[17] Another
reason to prefer "spirit" instead of "myth" becomes clear when one considers
how the actions of the Roman Curia at the beginning of the seventeenth century throttled the success of reforms. It is much easier to explain how a "spirit"
as a guiding motive was crushed or stifled rather than a "myth."[18]

The Roman Curia's curtailing of reforms has been called "Tridentinism."
While this term is helpful in describing the resistance to institutional and
theological change, applying it to the spiritual side of reform would be problematic. After all, Tridentinists relied on the same spiritual resources as
reformers,[19] and even actions aimed at blocking reforms could bring about
and aid the spiritual ends of Catholic Reform. A few examples hopefully
illustrate this: a new law could give the Roman Curia more oversight and influence in a religious order, but that did not mean that such a change smoth-
ered the order's spiritual rejuvenation. Often such a curial intervention,
even if undertaken out of political motivations, allowed reforms to finally
take root because it eliminated negative local and individual influences.
Likewise, even discouraging diocesan and provincial synods, which the
council fathers had envisioned as an important tool of continuing reform,
is not necessarily tantamount to blocking reform. Certainly, it was a curbing
of the conciliar spirit, but one should remember that throughout the seventeenth century, even reformers supporting bishops and clergy became

increasingly frustrated by the task of organizing synods they regarded as superfluous. Lastly, the Curia's framing of confession as an act of judicial penance could be interpreted as contradicting the pastoral intentions of the reformers. Yet, by building a legal structure around the sacrament, the Curia ensured that both penitent and priest were protected by law, felt secure, and could engage in an honest dialogue. Thus, even actions that were motivated by political intentions did not *necessarily* impede spiritual reform, although they sometimes really did. This shows, however, that for the history of how early modern Catholics attempted to change their lives and seek holiness, "Tridentinism" is not a helpful term.

## What's in a Reform?

Catholic Reform informed a theology that attempted to be considerate of contemporary challenges, faithful to tradition, and innovative. Such faithfulness included, as the sixteenth-century Pope Julius II stated, not only the purging of the church but also the aim of reestablishing virtue in her.[20] Reform therefore had to recover what had been lost and find orientation in a normative, unblemished past. It was a *reformatio in pristinum*.[21] That is the reason why dictionaries of the sixteenth and seventeenth centuries explain the verb *reformare* as the reshaping of an already existing entity, expunging its deformations and recovering its pristine beauty.[22] What Protestants had done with their rejection of central tenets of doctrine, was therefore for Catholics not a re-formation but a "de-formation." [23]

Dictionaries, however, also listed a second meaning of reform that is usually overlooked. It was the emendation of something by finding orientation in a normative future and was called *reformatio ad melius*.[24] This second meaning of reform necessarily included innovation, as the fifteenth-century Dominican Johannes Nider conceded. For him every reform of discipline, whether in the church or in a religious community, had to be innovative, but this did not pertain to doctrine:[25] the reformer was like a clockmaker, who removed the impediments to a machine to running properly; or like a cither player, who readjusted the strings on her instrument; or a physician who restored the fluids of the body back to their original harmony.[26] Nider's imagery demonstrates that besides creativity and knowledge, prudence was especially needed for a successful reform.[27]

Taking *reformatio in pristinum* as well as *reformatio ad melius* seriously uncovers a flaw in the historiography of Catholic Reform. Most historians have characterized Catholic reformers as "backward-looking"[28] or "conservative" based on a Protestant understanding of reform, infused with anachronistic political vocabulary from the nineteenth century. Unsurprisingly, such a view misunderstands the project of restoring, reviving, recalling, correcting, and cleansing, invoked by the Catholic reformers.[29] Even more troubling is the fact that because of this unacknowledged perspective, these historians also failed to understand the rhetoric of Catholic reform: it certainly professed a "fear of novelty," but that did not reject innovation per se, as the case of Johannes Nider demonstrates. By disallowing *doctrinal* innovation, the Catholic reformer merely affirmed orthodoxy, but did not exclude novelty in questions of discipline or catechesis. Early modern discussions about the morale in religious orders can elucidate this aspect. On the one side, monastic reformers lamented that their orders had deviated from the strict ways of the past and desired to return to "ancient observance"; yet on the other side, these reformers knew that one could not merely return to the past without adaptations.[30] The seventeenth-century historian Louis Thomassin summarized this attitude by asserting that discipline—unlike faith—constantly changes[31] and therefore needs frequent updating.[32] This rhetoric only changed significantly in the second half of the eighteenth century, when Catholic Enlighteners became less afraid of being called out as modernizers.[33]

This sufficiently clarifies that Catholic reformers did not understand their task as resuscitating the past. Striving to restore aspects of a normative history meant for them the adaptation of old ideals to new circumstances, and therefore required prudence and innovation.[34]

## Reform and Eschatology

Fifteenth-century church reform was heavily influenced by the idea of restoring the Holy Roman Empire to its previous power. Yet, it is often overlooked that this politico-theological vision was inherently eschatological—restoring something decayed was not sentimentalist but was done for the sake of the future.[35] When, for example, the Council of Constance expressed its desire for peace (*redintegrare, unire*), thereby rejecting the revolutionary change for which Jan Hus stood, it simultaneously voiced the eschatological longing for the heavenly Jerusalem as a model for reform. Just like the city built by God in the Heavens, so a renewed church and empire would be infused with the presence of the divine.[36] Consequently, Giles of Viterbo admonished his contemporaries that only by returning to the normative past and its pristine purity, could the church be well prepared for the day of Judgment.[37] Likewise, Thomas de Vio Cajetan, who addressed the Fifth Lateran Council in 1512, used eschatological language to describe reform: that which was distorted had to be corrected and brought into "conformity with the perfect virtue of the New Jerusalem."[38] Closely connected with the imagery of correction was that of reconsecration, of restoring the sacredness of things, places, and persons by purification (*purgere*). Such purging was predominantly the task of the bishops, who were also called to bring illumination and perfection (*purgatio, illuminatio, perfectio*) to their flock. These three hierarchical actions, borrowed from the sixth-century writer Pseudo-Dionysius, were considered the antidotes to the diseases (*turbatio, confusio, enervatio*) that corrupted the church. All three councils—Constance, Lateran V, and Trent—therefore saw it as the bishop's responsibility to lead his flock to eschatological perfection by constantly rejuvenating the faith, and thus enact reform.[39] The bishop would bring the believers together, and as a *vir divinum*, a godly man, "set ablaze by the divine name" (*virum divinum; divino nomine afflamatum*) serve as a role model for all.[40]

## Reform and Freedom of Discernment

Church reform attempted to imbue the faithful with good behavior. This undertaking, however, made it necessary to reflect more deeply on *what* good customs were, what tradition was, and where canon law had possibly distorted the faith. From Jean Gerson in the late Middle Ages to Ludovico Muratori in the Catholic Enlightenment, such discernment was the core of prudential religious decision-making.[41] Consequently, early modern Catholicism developed practices of judgment (*ars critica*) that helped to separate sacred from human, abuse from norm. Using these skills, theologians studied the normative texts of the past and applied them to contemporaneous challenges. Consequently, they began to differentiate between theological expression and truth of faith: while one could not freely discuss whether this or that dogma should be embraced, the way dogmas were explained (*modus explicandi*) and the arguments by which they were explained (*rationes*) could. Such differentiation also established freedom of interpretation for those passages of scripture, of the Church Fathers or the councils, which were ambiguous or unclear. Discernment allowed a theologian to interpret such texts according to one's *recta ratio*, but always in coherence with the "spirit of the church."[42] Moreover, at least in principle, this method protected the faithful from "hardheaded" (*morosi*) fanatics, who denied a hierarchy of truths. Such extremists were for Muratori "flatterers" and "teachers of a pernicious piety," because they declared their favorite theological ideas as church teaching: "The person, who orders to believe things, which are *not* to be believed, is to be considered a tyrant, and the person, who mixes fables under truths, a teacher of error and lies."[43] By leveling the normative differences of ecclesial texts such as breviaries, bulls, conciliar documents, and so forth, and declaring every church document authoritative, the zealot deprived himself of prudential judgment. His obedience was blind and irrational instead of being reasonable as St. Paul had commanded.[44] Such "indiscriminate zeal" not only robbed church reformers of freedom—the foundation of discernment—but also led the proponents on a dangerous path of self-righteousness and pride.

Discernment was also the key for a successful restitution of monastic observance. After all, a reformer had to diligently take time, place, and local traditions into consideration in order to form a prudential judgment of how to rejuvenate discipline.[45] A one-size-fits-all attitude would be not only shortsighted but also as useless as the prescription of the same medicine for all diseases.[46] Zeger Bernhard Van Espen, one of the most celebrated canonists of the eighteenth century, summarized this stance when he spoke of a "prudent economy in the business of reform" (*prudenti oeconomia in reformationis negotio*).[47]

Lastly, discernment also demanded sincere introspection and the acknowledgment of complicity in sin, scandal, and abuse. Nobody made this point better than a participant in the Council of Trent, Cardinal Reginald Pole. In his *De Concilio*, he emphasized that the pope and bishops had to accept responsibility for the disastrous state of the church. Merely transferring guilt to others would only lead to more sin, while honest self-accusation would demonstrate the healing presence of the Holy Spirit.[48]

## Reform and Devotion

Catholic Reform aimed at the *cura animarum*, the welfare of souls, and was thus interested in overcoming the bifurcation between theological erudition and lived faith. The idea of bringing theology out of its ivory tower to the pews was rooted in late medieval reform.[49] The locus for this type of theology, which is often called *devotional theology*, was, however, not the treatise or the disputation, but rather the catechism, the homily, the prayer book, and the hymn. These are therefore also the main sources for this study. Devotional theology avoided speculation and focused on methods and motives to make the faith livable. It allowed countless authors to use their creativity to explain the faith in nonscholastic jargon, and empowered laypersons to create a self-determined prayer life.[50] A good example of this approach are the works of the seventeenth-century Dutch priest Jacques Marchand. They demonstrate an admirable ability to condense the world of theology for the needs of a parish priest without sacrificing depth.[51] Devotional theology also grappled with the difficulty of disseminating the faith in a largely illiterate society, and therefore emphasized mnemonic methods, recognized the importance of apprenticeship learning, and celebrated theological imagery. Nevertheless, like all normative sources such texts lead to the question of to what degree their ideals were being implemented. Their availability in translation and cheap editions, however, serves as an indicator that many readers approved of them and at least partially tried to accept their methods.

Yet devotional theology was a global phenomenon. Missionaries brought the ideals of church reform to every corner of the world, where they were creatively renegotiated, adapted, and assimilated. This was, however, no one-way street: through encounters with Asia, Africa, and the Americas, European Catholics learned to rethink much of their theology and piety, but also infused new questions into the theological discussion. The encounter with Chinese chronology, for example, motivated European scholars to study this tradition more thoroughly, and consequently also the historical claims of the Bible. Even new forms of religious life, which were started in Europe, found global imitation and adaptation: *beatas*, uncloistered religious women (see chapter 6), roamed the streets of Peru and Japan just as much as those in Milan or Madrid. Likewise, European devotions spread. New saints such as Charles Borromeo or Teresa of Avila were presented as role models and intercessors for the faithful in India as well as in Austria. By venerating their relics, sent as gifts from Europe, Christians in Asia or the Americas participated in the rituals of the vibrant post-Reformation Catholic church, and simultaneously asserted that it was resolutely Roman and pope-interested in character.[52]

## Reform and Self-Transformation

Catholic Reform hinged on the conviction that a member of the church could receive supernatural graces and thus be transformed into a person who pleased God.[53] The believer received not just admonition and advice from the clergy but was also taught by them, their parents, and teachers to use a variety of tools to strengthen the will, intellect, and imagination. Catechisms and prayer books conveyed not only new expectations about social norms but also ways to enrich one's prayer life, overcome the passions, and conform the will to divine laws. Especially the Jesuit sodalities were successful in molding sizable segments of the population into the type of devoted Catholics that could impact society.[54]

The most important practice of self-transformation was arguably the sacrament of penance or reconciliation. A sinner could come to church, confess her sins, and receive from the priest absolution in the name of Christ. Its effect was a cleansing of all sin and a restoration to the baptismal state of grace. The only necessary requirement for receiving it was that one earnestly regretted past sins, confessed honestly, and did the restitution or penance that the confessor assigned. Early modern Catholics were required to confess at least once a year, because they had to receive communion on Easter. Yet confession became for many a frequent ritual that consoled and liberated their souls. Some spiritual teachers, especially St. Ignatius of Loyola and his order, the Jesuits, even recommended a once-in-a-lifetime "general confession" covering one's entire biography. This emphasized in the recipients the experience of "a total severing" from their sinful past and the beginning of a "new life."[55] As a powerful means of self-transformation, general confessions played an influential role in the Americas just as in Europe, demonstrating that the search for spiritual perfection was a global phenomenon.[56]

Catholic reform was about individual and communal progress in sanctification, and therefore never revolutionary. Instead, it desired to renew the faith, rejuvenate it with creative elements, and adjust it prudently to the demands of the time. Such an endeavor initiated a major rethinking of the role of the priesthood (chapter 2). The clergy were no longer part of the faithful but visibly separated from them. As special emissaries of the divine, they were increasingly expected to be virtuous role models. The Catholic Reform also stressed the importance of homilies for church reform (chapter 3). In different styles and methods, priests offered believers a wide display of allegorical, typological, and metaphorical bridges to the mysteries of faith. Rhetoric handbooks taught the clergy not only to acquire the proper speech but also methods to shape emotions, intellect, and will (chapter 4). Nevertheless, not only priests but also the laity engaged in the spiritual transformation of Catholics (chapter 5). The most important place where such formation took place was the family, which the post-Trent theology recognized as the center of all church reform. Husband and wife were to live as companions creating an atmosphere of harmony in which both could spiritually progress. The many lay movements such as confraternities and sodalities, were another locus for the teaching and application of methods of self-improvement (chapter 6). The most important sacraments for bringing about inner change were the Eucharist and confession (chapter 7). Unlike the Middle Ages, early modernity encouraged their frequent use and deepened their theological reflection. Additionally, a great variety of new prayer forms and methods were presented to the many faithful seeking spiritual perfection (chapter 8). These practices also cherished the "love for the dead" in Purgatory, which in turn emphasized the importance of individual decisions during one's lifetime and the necessity of exercising the virtues. Not only a variety of texts served Catholic Reform, but also church bells, paintings, and architecture. All senses were invited to follow the theological program of the artists and lifted up the souls of the faithful to contemplation (chapter 9). Of all images, early modern Catholics preferred especially those of the angels, Mary, and St. Joseph. Each of them articulated the reform message that everybody was called to holiness and that God was good and merciful (chapter 10). Such mercy was part of the dialectic of fear and clemency with which the church preached the faith, and which also celebrated a salvific egalitarianism that transcended social and ethnic boundaries.

# 2

# The Varying Theologies of the Priesthood

As important as the Tridentine reform decrees were for the behavior of the clergy in reestablishing discipline, it was a new understanding of the priesthood and its duties that shaped the Catholic Reform from Trent well into the eighteenth century. Trent's indecisive theology of the priesthood, which oscillated between a Pseudo-Dionyisian view of the priest as mediator for the divine and that of a Gersonian shepherd, created the need for a more coherent theological profile. Therefore, during the sixteenth and seventeenth centuries several theologies of the priesthood came into being, which despite their differences all addressed the status, dignity, and duties of the priest.[1]

Already before the Reformation, Catholic theologians such as the members of the Italian *spirituali* movement realized that the priest had to be more than merely the officiator at the Mass. He represented Christ, and his life should resemble his vocation.[2] Educating priests about their mission and duties was therefore seen as a crucial requirement for any change among the clergy. One instrument for such education were books outlining the vices and virtues of a priest, so called mirrors, as well as apologetic treatises such as Pedro de Soto's *On the Institution of the Priesthood*. Given the meager quality of theological priestly education, such tomes were indispensable for anybody who took his vocation seriously.[3]

Although the Council of Trent had already demanded in 1563 that all dioceses build seminaries for the formation of the clergy, in many countries such houses were not opened until two generations later. Moreover, the seminaries were far from being adequate institutions of education until the end of the seventeenth and sometimes into the eighteenth century. Compared to the strict nineteenth- or twentieth-century seminaries they had the name in common, but almost nothing else.[4] Most candidates for ordination attended such establishments for ten or fifteen months. Only bigger cities and rich dioceses offered a better theological education. Attending a university, however, was a rarity among the clergy well into the eighteenth century. In the early 1600s, only about 8 percent of the priests in the region of Vechta in

*The Inner Life of Catholic Reform.* Ulrich L. Lehner, Oxford University Press. © Oxford University Press 2022.
DOI: 10.1093/oso/9780197620601.003.0002

Germany had attended a school of higher learning.[5] Even the seminaries offered only a rudimentary training, focusing on some central truths of faith, the sacraments, and moral theology. After all, the seminarians had to learn to envision themselves not just as "mediators" between God and faithful but also as "doctors and judges in persona Christi, . . . shepherds and physicians of the souls . . . and dispensers of the heavenly treasures."[6] It would be their "fatherly" duty to help their parishioners on the way to sanctification, wherefore parish priests were increasingly addressed as "Father."[7]

A priest in the era after Trent was expected to have a fervent love for the souls entrusted to his care (*zelus animarum*). Such zeal was considered one of the highest forms of love (*caritas*) because, as the scholastic theologians explained, it did not desire a union with the beloved. Therefore, the priest's love for his flock was an act of "heroic charity."[8] Bishops and religious superiors who failed in this virtue lacked a normative characteristic.[9]

Episcopal visitations were a means to encourage such zeal and remind pastors of this expectation.[10] Although such visitations could address problems and mandate changes, they were largely ineffective as a means of discipline.[11] The visit of a superior has never converted a spiritually "blind" pastor, a famous contemporary writer confessed.[12] Nevertheless, the visitation also had an overlooked spiritual dimension. It was the symbolic display of the bishop's care even for a remote and poor parish, and empowered parishioners to express their spiritual demands, particularly to their clergy. For example, seventeenth-century Italian parishioners desired a virtuous, especially chaste clergy,[13] just as much as Catholics in Central or South America. Thus, it is not surprising that at the end of the sixteenth century provincial councils in Peru insisted that only saintly priests could be impactful missionaries. Priests, however, who neglected their duties such as attending the dying, or who harassed the natives, put their divine calling to shame.[14] Once the archbishop of Lima burst out to his fellow priests: "Remember that you are shepherds, not butchers! You are to treat the *indios* not as slaves, but rather as free people and vassals of the King."[15] Similar problems bothered the provincial council of Mexico in 1555, where priests engaged in gambling and took no effort to translate their homilies for the natives.[16] By their interrogation of parish members, visitations allowed the faithful to gain a voice. Parishioners could demand that the authorities take action against bad clergy and were often successful. Nevertheless, the rural clergy in South and Central America did not substantially improve until the seventeenth century.[17] Although priestly negligence was considered a grave sin, it seems that a large number of clergymen did not feel guilt or remorse. This was a serious theological challenge, as critics of Catholicism argued that a church whose own clergy did not live up to its doctrines could not be true.[18]

## The Role Model of Carlo Borromeo

What inspired moral improvement and provided spiritual uplift for early modern Catholics, clergy and laity alike, was the experience of saintly reformers such as Carlo Borromeo. The sixteenth-century archbishop of Milan embodied the new ideal of the priest as a shepherd tending to his flock, defending it, and living with it in exemplary austerity. Most importantly, however, he embodied the ideal Tridentine bishop, present in his diocese and actively working for reform.[19] Soon after his death in 1584 he was invoked as a saint, and the Roman Curia wisely tapped into the euphoria about Borromeo that portrayed him as an executor of Roman reforms rather than the strong-willed individual fighter he had been.[20] This was achieved by careful control over Borromean iconography: while he always was depicted within his own archdiocese as a bishop wearing the *pallium*, outside Milan he was usually pictured in the traditional red robe of a cardinal, which insinuated that all of his reforms had their origin in the college of cardinals in Rome.[21]

Borromean ideals had already spread globally before his canonization in 1610, with the first translations of his works dating to 1575.[22] The texts of the diocesan synods he chaired attracted most of the attention, and they were reprinted continuously for the next two hundred years. In these texts the archbishop not only endorsed institutional changes but also set out a program of personal reform that he prescribed to his clergy and religious; and in adapted form to his entire flock.[23] He inspired others not only because of his integrity but also because he combined personal holiness and pragmatic prudence in administrative decisions. It was this set of characteristics that early modern Catholics longed for in their own pastors. The presence of such charismatic figures, however, made a thorough theological discussion of the office of bishop an unnecessary task. After all, why reflect on something if all that was needed was to emulate these reformers? Consequently, there was little theological examination of the office of bishop, while judicial questions of his authority were debated at length. Even rarer were bishops who wrote profoundly about their office such as the Carmelite Giuseppe Sebastiani, who considered it an unbloody martyrdom.[24]

The tool Borromeo recommended most fervently for the spiritual trans-formation of his flock was the sacrament of confession. Yet, convincing the laity to make frequent use of this sacrament depended on elevating the moral state of the priesthood. After all, many felt uncomfortable confessing sins to men living in debauchery and hypocrisy. Women feared they could be assaulted or raped by such priests, while men dreaded being possibly forced into paying a bribe for receiving absolution. Simply asserting that even a morally corrupt priest could validly absolve from sins did not address this "crisis of credibility."[25] The priests themselves had to change and realize that they were chosen to administer consolation and liberation from sins to their parishioners. They had to arrive at an understanding of confession as a gateway to spiritual progress that was intrinsically linked to their priestly of-fice. Borromeo's guidelines for confessors, published in 1574, reminded the clergy that by fulfilling this task they became "agents of mass conversion."[26]

This pastoral dimension of the confessional has been widely neglected by historians, who viewed it as a tool of social discipline and clerical dom-ination. Such a perspective, however, exaggerated (as was the case with visitations) the effectiveness of penance for discipline. After all, *confession* was conducted as a dialogue "rather than a mere list of misdeeds imparted to a priest while he dozed behind the lattice screen."[27] Since this dialogue was intended to help penitents form their conscience, it had—despite the authority of the priest as a "judge"—a limited potential for social discipline. It would be a gross mischaracterization to view the priest's questions to the penitent as interrogation. The priest was expected to advise the peni-tent in how to avoid vices. He therefore asked for clarifications and infor-mation to form a judgment, but he had to avoid the impression of being nosy and was admonished to always remain tactful and gentle. If he failed, parishioners rebelled against such pastors and often forced them to retire.[28] Additionally, the strict privacy in which confession took place, and the pos-sibility that parishioners could fulfill their confessional duty with a more le-nient priest outside their parish, restricted the sacrament's effectiveness as discipline. The unavailability of confession in many colonies and European rural areas furthermore constrained its usefulness for behavioral control. After all, how could a mere three hundred priests during the seventeenth century have a significant impact on half a million Filipino parishioners?[29] It also seems that in many colonized territories, the indigenous population accepted confession as part of their new Catholic identity and did not re-gard it as a tool of oppression. When, however, like natives in Mexico who previously had access to confessors speaking their language, they were suddenly expected to confess in the language of their cultural oppressors, they complained to the authorities. As full members of the church, they invoked the right to confess in a language they understood—hardly the reaction one would expect if the sacrament would have been identified *only* (!) with colonial control.[30]

Borromeo compared the confessor to a physician. Only if the doctor knew the ailments of his patients could he give sound advice. He thus recommended that every Catholic have a regular confessor, who would also be consulted as spiritual advisor outside the confessional box. This idea underscored not only his belief in everyone's call to holiness but also his conviction that priests had to be personally involved in everyone's lives if a rejuvenation of the church was to be achieved. Such immersion can be analyzed from the perspective of behavioral control, but that neglects its spiritual motivation. Although spiritual guidance intended that the penitents conform their wills to the expectations of the church, such expectations were also identified with the will of God. The directives the laity received from the clergy left them enough space and ambiguity to create their own spiritual identity, as the circles of the *devotés* in seventeenth-century France show.[31] The priest's closeness to the laity, however, also made it necessary that he could be trusted. Therefore, chastity became one of the most important and desired characteristics of the early modern clergyman.[32]

Borromeo's own lifestyle echoed the expectations of generations of Catholics. Although not a member of a religious order, he lived without indulging in luxury, excelled in sexual continence and virtue, and subdued his body in a routine of austere mortification. Borromeo shared with his friend St. Philipp Neri, founder of the Italian Oratorians, these ideals of self-denial and mortification, which through both these leaders became desired characteristics of the early modern priest. A widely popular handbook for priests, written by the Oratorian Giuseppe Mansi (1607–1694)[33] explained, following the ideas of Borromeo and Neri, that a priest had to mortify all his senses for divine grace to transform him. Should he fail and give in to his passion, he would drag Christ's face into the "sewer."[34] Thus, school students already thinking about the priesthood should learn the importance of self-control: "For nothing is more difficult for an adolescent than to moderate immoderate affections."[35] Already ordained ministers could strengthen their mindset in regular meetings with peers and also encounter there a priestly culture of virtue.[36]

Such Borromean ideals were propagated throughout the Catholic world by writers such as Jacques Marchand of Couvin (c. 1585–1648) in the Spanish Netherlands. By avoiding scholastic jargon, his writing achieved a clarity and attractiveness that gained him a wide readership. Unsurprisingly, a number of seminaries even adopted his works as textbooks.[37] Marchand's three-volume *Garden of Pastors* (1626/7) contained everything a priest had to know. It gave a thorough exposition of Catholic doctrine and moral theology, but also pastoral advice, a crash course in homiletics, and a guide to personal holiness. Instead of difficult theological questions, he focused on those a priest would most likely encounter in a parish.[38] Like Berulle, Marchand saw in the priest's own holiness the key for successful pastoral work. The priest had to be a man of faith before he could teach others about it.[39]

## The Berullian Concept of Priesthood

Contemporaries regarded Cardinal Berulle (1575–1629) as Borromeo's seventeenth-century counterpart. By founding a religious order, the French Oratorians, he secured a lasting impact on early modern Catholics.[40] Contemporaries saw in his work a renewal (*renouvelée*) of the church, "the spirit of religion, the supreme cult of adoration and reverence due to God."[41]

The Oratorian priests lived in a community of prayer without the constraints of monastic or mendicant life. By following heroic ideals, the Oratorians were to renew the French priesthood, whose reputation had suffered in the previous centuries.[42] Internalizing their values through a formation in charity also made authoritarian supervision superfluent. "We live," as the eighteenth-century Oratorian Lamy explained, "here in honest liberty, but not libertinage."[43] Condren summarized the community's achievement as such:

> We owe it to the Oratory that the priesthood was raised [*relevé*] from the mire and the dust. These Joshuas have rebuilt [*rebasty*] the altar, making firm the foundations thereof. . . . these Hezekaiahs have re-established [*remis*] the functions of priest and Levite. . . . The laity [*Laïques*] have been dazzled [*éblouies*] by the splendor of the sacred vestments; the respect of Christians for their priest, as for their fathers, has been aroused. . . . Each acknowledges that to bring back life to souls is better than to grant favors to criminals meriting bodily punishments; that to wreck the demon's empire

by a few words and to bring calm to the spirit is a power surpassing that of generals and their armies; that to produce the Body of Jesus Christ and to present it to God as a veritable Gift for the peace of consciences . . . , to be able to give to men the Living God [*donner aux hommes le Dieu vivant*]. . . that is the *chef d'ouvre* of the Church's miracles.[44]

At the center of their founder's theology stood the love of God. "True Christians" should not, he argued, worship God as a guarantor of benefits, but because he was love itself.[45] Acknowledging one's own "nothingness" led the faithful to adore this grandeur of God.[46] The human will could best adhere to God by uniting itself to the Word Incarnate, Jesus Christ.[47] This aspect brought him the title of "Apostle of the Incarnate Word."[48] Priests, however, had through their office an even deeper relationship to Christ. They were sanctified through a special union with him. This union came about through the priest's self-annihilation, the sacrifice of his own will and intellect. Christ himself, whom Berulle also called "the great and primitive sacrament,"[49] filled this void with his presence and thus somewhat established a new personality.[50] Only such holy priests, Berulle was convinced, could reform the church, because they would manifest Christ and his authority among the faithful.[51] Although this theology demanded much of the clergy, it also brought higher esteem from the laity.[52] Nevertheless, the novel idea of a special union of priest and Christ also helped establish a clerical authority above any reproach. After all, how could a layperson question the actions of a priest who was in union with Christ himself?[53] A good example of such a view is Louis Cresol's *Mystagogus de Sacrorum Disciplina* (1629), which the Jesuit dedicated to the Cardinal Berulle. The priest was described as a substitute for God's angels, and his service at the altar qualified him to be called an "altar soldier."[54]

Berulle's theology was buttressed by the education the Oratorians offered in their seminaries. Their love for the sciences and humanities produced what Henri Bremond described as a humanism (*humanisme séparé*) centered on the love for the crucified Christ.[55] It taught the control of human passions by grace and reason, not by austere mortification as was the case with Borromeo or Neri. For the Oratorians, spiritual transformation happened through the virtue of charity. Therefore, the Oratorian Jean Saunault's *The Use of Passions*[56] identified Christianity as the one moral philosophy able to transform the human person through love.[57] By directing such love and thus the affective side of the human person to God, one escaped the pitfalls of creaturely love.[58] The humanist side of Oratorian education also stressed refined manners. Courtesy (*politesse*), for example, was considered by Bernard Lamy an important characteristic of every priest. After all, courtesy was a bond connecting members of society, and good manners therefore the key for discerning what may please or hurt others. Consequently, courtesy was seen as analogous to piety, which never permitted dissimulation (*personne d'une piète reconnue ne ... dissimuler*).[59]

## The Sulpician and Jesuit Concept of Priesthood

The Oratorians in France were, despite their aspirations, not very successful with their seminaries, although they still did better than diocesan institutions. St. Vincent de Paul recognized this reality and was candid enough to call the French Tridentine seminary in 1644 an utter failure. Nevertheless, this diagnosis paved the way for recovery, because not only de Paul's Lazarists began seminary formation but also the Sulpicians, whose model was soon adopted globally. While de Paul preferred a pragmatic, pastoral education, the Sulpician seminaries excelled in forming the future clergy in spirituality.[60]

The Sulpicians, founded by Jean-Jacques Olier and Louis Tronson, were like the Oratorians a community of priests without the strict regime of the orders. The founders were convinced that priestly seminaries had to be reinvented, and the priests who did not "carry the spirit of Christ within"[61] converted if any church reform was to be successful. Olier believed that a clergyman had to do frequent penance for his sins and regain through such a constant "laborious baptism," as he called it, the state of grace.[62] Yet unlike Berulle, he preferred a simpler, emotionless faith. In his eyes, the opposite was dangerous because it could easily degrade God to an object of one's own wishful thinking. Like the Oratorians, the Sulpicians preferred educating seminarians in friendship with God, in charity, and marginalized bodily mortification.[63] Yet, only if a priest was a friend of Christ, kept his promises, and lived honorably and chastely could he convincingly teach others about it.[64] Accordingly, the Sulpicians made priestly teaching the "sacred science,"[65] an essential characteristic of the ordained minister.[66] For Boudon it was more important than any pastoral work apart from administering the sacraments, and no priest had a justifiable excuse to avoid it.[67] After all, a good teacher could by converting a person "steal a soul away from the Devil" and thus gain eternal glory, as the Spanish canonist Augustin Barbosa commented.[68]

Louis Tronson, the third superior of St. Sulpice, summarized the community's motto of reanimating piety (*ranimer la piété*) by forming holy and educated priests in his short book *The Profile of the Clergyman* (1669).[69] He suggested basic rules for the life of a priest, because "without rule, one lives disorderly."[70] He gave such counsel by providing short texts from the Church Fathers and saints, so that the future priest could imagine himself not only as in their line of succession but also as their direct student.[71] This strategic linking of the present with the patristic time was also used by other authors; for example, the Spanish Carthusian Anthony Molina (1560–1619) in his *Instructions for Priests* (1608).[72]

The Jesuits, who had been papally approved in 1540, also manifested a new ideal of priesthood, which they disseminated not only through their many publications, but also their institutions of learning. This new religious order, however, had a strict hierarchical regime and emphasized obedience much more than the Oratorians and Sulpicians. Already by the end of the sixteenth century, the Society of Jesus was entrusted with most university education in Catholic countries. Like the Dominicans, the Jesuits aspired to be an order of practical pastoral outreach that brought the word of God to every corner of the world. Yet, unlike traditional orders, the Jesuits refrained from mendicant or monastic habits in order to have a greater pastoral impact. Only if the Society was exempted from singing the psalms together and other community regulations could its members work successfully for the spiritual progress of souls, its founder St. Ignatius reasoned.

Moreover, every Jesuit underwent obligatory thirty-day *Spiritual Exercises*, which according to St. Ignatius initiated a life-changing conversion experience. During these *Exercises* one encountered being called by God to special service to his Word. The Jesuits therefore understood preaching and instruction as one of their most important charisms. The service to the "Word" did not aim at a mere intellectual reception of theological truths but rather at an increase in the divine virtues of hope, faith, and love among Catholics. Instilling these virtues entailed helping Catholics to overcome despair about their salvation. Consequently, the order adopted probabilism as its official doctrine in moral theology in order to free Catholics from scruples and desolation. Probabilism permitted ambiguity in moral actions and thus enabled timid Catholics to receive communion, which was believed to be the key to spiritual transformation. The Jesuit embrace of attrition or imperfect contrition as the requirement for absolution instead of the more demanding perfect contrition, applied the pastoral vision of St. Ignatius to the confessional.[73]

## The Changing Expectations of Priestly Life

Over the sixteenth and seventeenth centuries the laity increasingly began to expect their priests to be uncorrupted by the vices they wrestled with. They were to manifest a lifestyle different from their own, one without sexual deviance, violence, and greed, but rather filled with the pursuit of holiness. This trend has led many historians to interpret complaints about parish priests in early modernity as personal grievances. Such a view is, however, incomplete and therefore leads to faulty conclusions: when parishioners complained about a priest's lifestyle—for example, that he was a drunk or a sexually lascivious man—they certainly identified him as an immoral "individual." Nevertheless, these accusations also included community aspects, such as the priest not fulfilling the community's expectations or his disregard for local customs. The priest's actions therefore not only undermined priestly moral standards, but also ethical community standards. For example, if a priest tried to forbid his flock to confess outside his parish, the community's complaint to the bishop was mainly about the priest's disregard for the local custom that allowed such a practice.[74] Even accusations of sexual missteps were fabricated if priests violated such community standards, because they usually forced the bishop's hand to intervene in a parish.[75]

Reformer bishops also tried to dissuade men from becoming priests whose eyes were set on a good salary but not a spiritual life. Thus, since the middle of the sixteenth century, candidates for ordination were increasingly examined about their suitability for the profession. Consisting originally of only a few questions, the exam became over the next two centuries quite rigorous, growing with the expectations of laity and bishops. Men who desired to become priests were admonished to scrutinize their soul about their calling.[76] Most popular for such soul searching were guidebooks that offered a condensed, eight-day-long form of the *Spiritual Exercises* of St. Ignatius of Loyola: with the assistance of a priest, the candidate was admonished to eclipse all personal desires and open his soul for divine illumination. In such a state of enlightenment, the candidate would be able to discern the movements of his soul and identify in them the influence of good or evil spirits. The good spirits were from God and had to be followed, while the bad ones were not. According to this spiritual logic one could find out whether one was called by God to the priesthood or merely projecting one's own desires onto the clerical state. Nevertheless, since these spiritual exercises were short, they almost exclusively included Ignatius's meditations from the first week of the *Exercises*, and thus centered mainly on one's personal sins and the forgiveness God offered. Even the Jesuit seminary for diocesan priests in Rome, the *Germanicum et Hungaricum*, only used this shorter form.[77] It therefore seems that even the Jesuits themselves saw penance and the experience of forgiveness as the most important character traits of a diocesan priest. After all, in a parish he would have to call on others to acknowledge their sins, but also dispense the forgiveness and mercy he had received, too. The short *Exercises* anchored the experience of sinfulness and forgiveness in the candidate's memory. Later on, this memory could be retrieved in order to fight temptation and despair, the authors of these guidebooks explained. While Borromeo had required such condensed spiritual exercises since 1576, the pope's own diocese of Rome only made them obligatory in 1662.[78] Even orders in fierce competition with the Jesuits recognized the value of the *Exercises* and adopted them for their own novitiates. One of the most popular of these was *De discretione spirituum liber* (1672) of the Cistercian Cardinal Giovanni Bona.[79]

A candidate for the priesthood was also expected to gain control over his feelings. With the guidance of reason, feelings contributed to moral flourishing, but without it they led a person down the road to perdition. Men guided by emotions were therefore considered unable to discern reasonably. The German Oratorian Bartholomew Holzhauser even labeled them "effeminate"[80] and demanded their immediate expulsion from a seminary. The ideal "masculine" priest had instead control over his emotions and thus demonstrated his virtuous, spiritual virility. To view self-control as a gendered male characteristic was commonplace in early modern spiritual writing. Therefore, female saints who espoused such self-control were considered "spiritually male." Francisco de Ribera, the biographer of Teresa of Avila, wrote of them: "Those women who conquer their passions through strength and subject themselves to God are to be called men, and men who are conquered by their passions are called women. This is not a result of bodily differences, but of a strength of the soul."[81] Discernment, however, was not over after one's ordination or taking vows. It was a tool for continuous self-introspection that led to finding divine guidance in everyday situations. In a religious community, for example, one had to diligently discern with whom one could "converse trustingly"[82] and those whose influence could be harmful,[83] but also how to avoid them without giving offense.[84] Thus, discernment practices empowered priests and religious, men and women alike, to frequently self-evaluate their choices, but also to develop the skills to create a safe space for their spiritual progress.[85]

Discernment led to wise spiritual choices and was thus largely identical with the virtue of prudence. Without it, one's actions were either vicious or foolish. If a reform of the priesthood was to be successful, much depended on educating priests in this virtue. This was all the more important because lack of prudence caused division in parishes and dioceses. Applied to devotion, a lack of prudence manifested itself in religious fanaticism. Many manuals and episcopal directives regularly denounced fanaticism as either *zelus indiscreta* or *inconsultus ardor*: it was "indiscreet" or "unwise" because it lacked the ability to discern what was a matter of faith and what was not. Moreover, such fanaticism easily turned pious devotions into superstitions and thus came into proximity with heresy. A fanatic, for example, could insist that only those who pray the rosary would be saved, or that if one failed to pray daily to one's guardian angel one would not persevere in the hour of death and thus go to Hell. Enlighteners like Ludovico Muratori stressed that this mindset was responsible for the spirit of intolerance and persecution in the church. Whenever somebody offered a theological argument contradicting an opinion of this or that famous saint, or correcting a pious yet superstitious practice, these zealots would decry it as heresy. Without discernment, the fanatics considered ideas that were mere school opinions to be a matter of faith, and thus burdened the faithful with undue demands. Often, such a mindset stemmed from traditionalism, which contemporaries called the "prejudice of antiquity."[86]

Contemporaries knew about the dangers of following false spirits from a number of scandals about false mystics, whom the church censured and prosecuted. The Quietism of Miguel de Molinos and Madame Guyon was especially considered precarious. Molinos's most threatening claim was that the mystic reached a point in which she or he no longer controlled his actions but was a mere tool in the hands of God. His or her soul was "quiet" (therefore Quietism) and merely acted on God's behalf, and thus free from any restraints of codified divine or human law. This, however, enabled a Quietist to legitimize crimes such as sexual abuse, as actions of God for which one was not accountable.[87] Moreover, since Quietists also claimed that human laws did not apply to them, they neglected to recite the obligatory prayers for priests and religious. The Holy Inquisition therefore regarded any reluctance to fulfill this duty as possible evidence for Quietism.[88] Nevertheless,

Molinos's spirituality was still deeply attractive to many, since it promised to easily achieve intimacy with God, which many aspired to. A good example of diocesan clergy falling victim to it was the Cologne priest Johann Jakob Heimbach, who assembled a group of followers whom he taught about the "inner life."[89] Even one of the auxiliary bishops joined his company. Rumors that the small assembly was Quietist made an official investigation necessary. The commissioners found robust parallels between Molinos, Pietism, and the teachings of Heimbach. After a long trial, the priest also confessed to the violation of clerical norms, including chastity, and was imprisoned for a number of years before being released into the care of his mother.[90]

The ideal of the post-Tridentine priest as a constantly praying pastor had unmistakable parallels with the demands of monastic and mendicant life. Nevertheless, the parish priest was not a recluse but lived among his parishioners and was expected to assist them in their spiritual needs. Therefore, he had to espouse knowledge of the world, good manners, and amicability, while at the same avoiding the demands of kinship. By entering the religious state, the priest left behind all affections for his family and agreed not to treat them more favorably than other parishioners.[91] Mary's request to Jesus at the wedding of Cana (John 2:1–11) and her rebuke was understood as manifesting this truth of *salvific egalitarianism*, of treating all the faithful equally. Guidebooks took special pains to warn priests and religious about the dangers of inheritance and money. One could, for example, easily be tempted to steal from the church if one's siblings were in financial trouble, or lose sight of spiritual perfection if one received a large inheritance.[92] Bourdoise therefore advised: "I do not think a clergyman can go to paradise if he lives next to his parents . . . if you have taken the tonsure and your relatives ask you to help with their affairs . . . say boldly to them: I am dead, I can do nothing for you."[93] Such warnings did of course also protect the reputation of the church and tried to avoid potential scandal. A good example is the case of the pastor of Kirchzell near Würzburg in 1771. He allowed his sick cousin to stay in the rectory. When her womb began to swell as in a pregnancy, the rumor spread that he had impregnated her. The bishop's investigator, however, found out that she had suffered from intense bleeding and probably a tumor, which a physician confirmed.[94] According to the guidebooks of the time, the pastor should have declined to have a young relative under the same roof.

The Council of Trent's teaching on marriage, which forbade secret, clandestine marriages and instead required the exchange of vows to be witnessed by a priest, also had repercussions for the clergy. Since pastors were expected to live celibately, their clandestine marriages or partnerships were now considered illicit concubinages. Such living arrangements caused increasing scandal because they demonstrated that the priest contradicted his vow of continence. The ascetic ideal of the priesthood did not allow him to be like other men having a wife, because he represented Christ, who was unmarried himself. Celibacy therefore became a major characteristic of the priesthood. By the end of the seventeenth century the expectation of priestly continence was so widely accepted that previously condoned affairs with unmarried women would cause scandal. The family that a medieval priest could still have, changed in early modernity into the community of the rectory, often consisting of older housekeepers and other priests.[95]

By the eighteenth century, the reputation of the clergy was so exalted that a Benedictine preacher could say in 1729 that a "priest was much more powerful than St. Joseph or the Angels" because it was the clergy whom Jesus had asked to sit to his right and judge the nations on the Last Day.[96] The celibate clergyman, however, needed a concrete role model. Naturally one could point to Christ or Mary, who were both believed to have lived in perfect continence, but one was divine and the other miraculously protected from all sin from her very first moment as a human being. Therefore, St. Joseph, Jesus's foster-father, was given this role. According to the texts of the Gospels he was a just man, but otherwise a human being like everyone else, and could therefore be emulated more easily. St. Vincent de Paul especially recommended St. Joseph as a role model for priests, and the ardent veneration among the clergy confirms that his function was crucial in instilling the desire for chastity. Just as St. Joseph held the Christchild in his virtuous hands, so the chaste hands of the priest would elevate the host at consecration, theologians commented. Like St. Joseph, priests were expected to live in integrity.[97] Moreover, St. Joseph also embodied the new motto of the post-Trent priesthood, the zeal for souls (*zelus animarum*), because his protection of the Holy Family was interpreted as such zeal.[98] Pedro de Morales even went so far as to claim that with the Eucharist the faithful also received a spiritual communion with Jesus's foster-father. He stressed that after Mary, the carpenter was the primary guide to a fruitful reception of communion because he had lived with the Word Incarnate, Christ, and nourished him in his childhood. That the miracle of the Eucharist even existed was therefore, he explained, also owed to St. Joseph.[99]

With the elevation of his dignity the diocesan priest also received more duties, such as regular preaching and catechetical instruction. Adrien

Bourdoise, however, realized that these easily overwhelmed the clergy. Only if it were possible for priests to find enough support for their own spiritual needs, could they be successful agents of parish renewal. He therefore founded the community of St. Nicholas, which enabled priests to live together and support each other. Unlike most theologians of the time, who did not theoretically reflect on the nature of the parish, Bourdoise did. He coined the phrase *la paroisse vivante*—the living parish, which signified that this unit was the "seedbed" for the sanctification of Catholics.[100] After all, the parish was the primary place to receive the sacraments and was therefore "the matrix of religion, the cradle of Christian . . . where they were sanctified."[101] The parish thus became the place where all church reform and rejuvenation originated.

In the second half of the eighteenth century, Catholic Enlighteners slightly changed the expectations about priestly life. While the priest was still seen as a mediator of the Divine, the service for the word of God that the Jesuits had stressed was replaced with service for the welfare of the community. In the so-called general seminaries in the Habsburg lands under Joseph II in the last decade of the eighteenth century, men like Augustin Zippe marginalized the sacraments and envisioned the parish priest predominantly as a teacher of moral philosophy.[102] The priest's homilies were to arouse in the listener a "profound feeling, which penetrates the heart."[103] The priest was now more like a teacher of ethics than a guide to Divine mysteries.

## The Ideal of Priestly Poverty

Although diocesan priests did not take a vow of poverty, the expectation laid out in the literature of the time was that they live a life of moderation and champion also the poverty of Christ. The Acts of the Diocesan Synod of Milan, which were a blueprint for church reform worldwide, stressed that a priest should never waste money on luxury goods, but rather give his surplus to the poor.[104] Nevertheless, it was a group of Franciscans that personified such modesty. The Capuchins, founded in 1525, attracted many followers through their extreme poverty, also among the secular clergy.

The Capuchin friars understood themselves as a radical reform movement of Franciscans and considered the Rule of St. Francis as a "little mirror of the Gospel, from which evangelical perfection radiates."[105] By emphasizing personal and institutional poverty they tried to avoid the corruption and pride that money usually created. Consequently, the order's first constitution of 1536 placed the community at the bottom of the church (I, 7), aiming at servitude for all and avoiding ecclesial privileges.[106] The Capuchin beard, which became a characteristic, expressed this desire. It represented that one was like a poor man, "rough, despicable and austere," and did not care for outward appearances.[107] A Capuchin friar chose the life of a beggar (II, 15) within the church.[108] Even the clothes for their habits were to be solicited and of the poorest quality. Shoes were forbidden, and travel permitted only on foot. Food and drink, which also had to be collected by begging, were hardly ever nourishing. Wine at the table was always diluted, and spices avoided.[109] Likewise, the liturgy in a Capuchin church was much simpler—the friars did not have richly decorated vestments nor splendid high Masses, and even the breviary hours were not sung but recited in a penitential, subdued tone.[110] Unsurprisingly, the architecture of Capuchin churches also mirrored this fixation on simplicity.[111] Yet the ideal of begging for daily food became impossible once the order grew. In the seventeenth century, in the Rhenian province in Germany alone, only nine out of thirty-six monasteries could provide the daily bread by begging.[112] The proscription to never save money nor invest it, but merely trust in divine providence, also proved to be an enormous challenge for an order running monasteries worldwide.[113]

Following their charism, the Capuchins were initially not allowed to hear confessions of the laity unless they had a dispensation. Only over the course of the seventeenth century did the friars gain this privilege and were soon known for their superb spiritual advice.[114] Likewise, the order became famous for its homilies only in the second half of the seventeenth century. In the first decades of the order's existence, only a few Capuchins possessed permission to preach. The order had in 1596 about 7,268 members, of which 3,332 were priests. Of these, only 716 had preaching faculties. Almost a hundred years later, in 1671, the order already had 25,365 members, and while the number of priests had quadrupled, the number of preachers had increased tenfold. By the eighteenth century the Capuchins had enormous influence in the Catholic world. In 1761 the order counted 34,029 members, including 22,022 priests, of which 15,863 had preaching faculties. In 1782, due to laws restricting the number of novices and strong Enlightenment criticism, the number of members fell to 28,598, but one counted now 19,005 priests, of which 15,284 had permission to preach. These numbers tell a very straightforward story: while in the late sixteenth century only 20 percent of Capuchins engaged in sermons, by the end of the eighteenth century it was

80 percent. Such an enormous increase was only possible because the order itself had substantially improved the academic education of their friars. After all, without having undergone serious instruction and study, no Capuchin was allowed to climb into a pulpit.[115]

The Capuchins embodied the zeal of Catholic Reform also by internalizing its ideas. At least twice a week, a friar was to go to confession and take communion at least every two weeks, during Advent and Lent even every Sunday.[116] During the eighteenth century, Enlighteners predominantly mocked Capuchin homilies because of their alleged preoccupation with Purgatory and Hell. Yet, if one consults their published texts a different image emerges. Their sermons did not emphasize Purgatory or Hell more than others but followed the order's motto to preach Christ "crucified" in simplicity and directness, inspiring penance among the listeners. Thus, a Capuchin homily certainly talked about the real possibility of the sinner facing damnation, but also laid out forgiveness and salvation. After all, the audience should hear Jesus and not a friar from the pulpit![117] Alphonsus Lobo (also called *Lupus*), hailed in the 1570s as one of the greatest homilists, once told the young friars in his monastery: "In homiletics it is important to remember these things: It is our business to study before we walk up the pulpit. And it is God's business, once we have entered the pulpit, to direct our tongue."[118]

Capuchin friaries also seem to have had few serious problems with discipline. If transgressions happened, however, they were secretly dealt with to avoid public scandal. Egregious affairs, such as disobedience, theft, or sexual deviance were punished rigorously. Until the eighteenth century, the order therefore did not have a printed handbook outlining the criminal prosecution of friars but only hand-copied tomes. They obviously feared that otherwise the order's reputation would be questioned.[119] The rule of secrecy, though, also gave monastic superiors tyrannical powers, which they sometimes exercised over their brethren. In the eighteenth century, the friars were even commanded to lie to government authorities investigating claims of physical and sexual abuse in order to protect the reputation of the Capuchins.[120] Overall, however, the Capuchins lived their ideals to a great extent, which helped them overcome even the apostasy of some of their most prominent members.[121]

New ideals and expectations elevated the clergy much more than in the Middle Ages. The anointed clergyman had always been a mediator of the divine; Berullians now described him as being mystically united with Christ.

A saintly lifestyle was considered special confirmation of his extraordinary vocation. Continence and chastity, but also pastoral zeal, became therefore essential attributes of the priesthood. Thus, the diocesan priest of the Catholic Reform became more like a monk or a friar, who resembled for his flock an "earthly God."[122] The new image of the priest did not allow much ambiguity and thus fit into the overall early modern trend of reducing complexity and eliminating ambiguity.[123] While in the Middle Ages a priest with concubine was condoned, by the seventeenth century he had to unambiguously comply with celibacy standards.

The specific and demanding norms for the clergy made it a separate class with its own tools of self-improvement and self-transformation.[124] This, however, allowed the faithful to unburden themselves of parts of their religious obligations because they expected priests and *virtuosi* like the Capuchins to fulfill them in abundance.[125]

# 3

# The Homily

The Catholic Reform stressed the importance of the homily as an indispensable part of the pastoral care of souls. Borromeo's late sixteenth-century synod in Milan proclaimed that the rationale for a sermon was to proclaim the glory of God *and* bring others to salvation.[1] Unfortunately, this aspect has been largely neglected in scholarship on the Catholic Reform.

In the theology of the time, the preaching priest was a prophet, who communicated God's commands to the faithful and reminded them of their duties. He was expected "to preach Christ" and not his own ideas. Although the Council of Trent admonished pastors to preach *at least* on Sundays and feast days—besides funerals—the new norm had to overcome two major hurdles.[2] On the one hand, most priests were never trained to give a sermon, while on the other many were resistant to taking on another unpaid and rather burdensome duty. To overcome both was a challenge for reformer bishops. Many of them soon realized that it was better not to have a sermon at all than have an unlearned priest climb the pulpit, who might cause scandal, and still better to have a clergyman read from the catechism rather than spread heresy.[3]

Nevertheless, not only unlearned and unwilling priests were a problem; in some areas it was the plain physical absence of the clergy, either due to the Protestant Reformation or their idleness. If a priest was not in residence in his parish, he could not preach on Sundays. Therefore, attempts to demand strict residence requirements after the Council of Trent must be seen not only as acts of disciplining clergy but also in the interest of securing the sanctification of parishioners. After all, the priest's presence was not only necessary for administering the sacraments, in particular to the dying, but also for teaching the locals about faith and morals. Only if he lived nearby could he have reliable knowledge about the problems and vices in his parish, which he had to address from the pulpit. A diligent fulfillment of this function quickly became a standard expectation. Noncomplying priests were perceived not only as "lazy" (*otiosus non operans*) but also as committing a mortal sin through neglecting their duties.[4]

*The Inner Life of Catholic Reform.* Ulrich L. Lehner, Oxford University Press. © Oxford University Press 2022.
DOI: 10.1093/oso/9780197620601.003.0003

By the late fifteenth century, homilies were regularly offered in some rural areas of Europe, mostly on Sundays and feast days; however, often by wandering mendicants rather than parish priests. By the sixteenth century, however, parishioners seem to have come to demand and expect more from their local priest. In many parishes around this time, both epistle and Gospel readings were read in the vernacular, in addition to their Latin text. Since the liturgical calendar repeated these readings annually, many believers were able to become well acquainted with these texts and memorized them despite being illiterate. A 1559 account testifies: "During my youth I saw and knew old, gray-haired folks, simple laypersons, and peasants who could wonderfully repeat the Sunday and feast day Gospel readings aloud and, along with that, tell you upon which Sunday this or that Gospel fell."[5] One should, however, not take such anecdotal evidence as grounds for generalizations. After all, the availability of vernacular readings as well as of good homilies varied depending on the region. Borromeo's archdiocese of Milan provides a good example: the typical homily of the pastor of Santa Justina in 1570 consisted of a translation of the Latin Gospel, a few allegorical interpretations, and a brief exhortation, altogether lasting about fifteen minutes. This was far from what the reformer bishop of Milan had envisioned. For Borromeo, a good homily was a *detailed* interpretation of the readings, filled with catechesis and moral guidance, and thus about an hour long. In order to educate his priests in homiletics, the archbishop institutionalized a kind of peer review system for sermons. A *vicarius foraneus*, a rural vicar, gathered the clergy of his region monthly and screened their homilies. Invited guest speakers then shared their ideas about best practices for the pulpit, gave example homilies, and educated their listeners about how to address delicate matters. At such conferences, as well as in clergy confraternities, the priests also exchanged theological and homiletic books they considered helpful and inspiring.[6]

## The Sermon as Prophetic Proclamation

The homily's liturgical place differed according to local customs. Most often it was given together with official announcements *after* a Mass, but in the missal for the archdiocese of Trier it was placed after the creed *within* the Mass.[7] Placing it after Mass did not diminish the audience, because most stayed not just for the religious edification but also for the official community announcements the priest proclaimed. Nevertheless, this delivery of the homily made it appear as a liturgical action separate from the Mass.[8]

The pulpit (cathedra) was the physical place from which a priest gave a homily. In many baroque churches it was designed to appear as if floating into the church nave, signifying the entry of the word of God into the world of the listeners.[9] Moreover, due to its elevated position in the church the pulpit forced the audience to raise their eyes, and thus allegorically toward the heavenly proclamations.[10] Above the preacher, usually on the inside of the pulpit's ceiling, was a depiction of the Holy Spirit as a dove, which reminded the priest that he was the mouthpiece of God and should trust in divine assistance. Visibly to the flock, the illustration prompted the laity to pay attention to the preacher speaking with divine authority.[11]

A great variety of such allegories either invited interpreting the priest's presence as representing the Holy Spirit or was intended to influence the priest's own imagination. On Dutch whale pulpits from the seventeenth and eighteenth centuries, the priest appeared like a second Jonah preaching repentance.[12] A priest entering the much less extravagant pulpit in the famous St. Michael's Church in Munich would face the altar of Saints Peter and Paul, reminding him of faithfulness to both saints, and thus to the pope in Rome—a fitting iconography for a Jesuit church! In Irsee in Swabia the pulpit looked like a ship, so that the priest personified the fishers of men Jesus talked about (Mt 4:19).[13] Whatever the artistic program of the church, the theological symbolism remained the same: the priest represented Christ and the Apostles in the sermon, which in turn required the audience to identify with their followers. Even the theatrical use of a handkerchief could be justified as imitating St. Peter.[14] The different readings during the church year, together with varying liturgical vestments, allowed for slight modifications of this representation. On Pentecost the priest became the "fiery canon" of the Holy Spirit, a "flame" to enlighten the faithful and spark the love for God in them—a "light to the world" and their guiding "star"; while on the feast of the Guardian Angels he became an angel of God; and on a Sunday with a Gospel reading about a healing miracle he was the divinely appointed physician, and so forth.[15]

The lack of good vernacular Catholic homiletic resources in the early sixteenth century led many priests to peruse Martin Luther's postils for their sermons, until Catholic scholars realized the lacuna and began publishing similar works. The Franciscan Johann Wild from Mainz, who based all his sermons on a detailed exegesis of biblical text, was widely popular but later censored. Soon these Catholic postils caught up with their Protestant competition so that between 1530 and 1555 about 132,000 complete sets of Catholic postils had been put into circulation in Germany alone. They were read and reread not only by the clergy but also by the laity and thus possessed a remarkable longevity—especially if one considers that these books were handed on to several subsequent generations of readers.[16] Interestingly, though, not only clergy authored sermon books, but also laypeople, like the sixteenth-century schoolteacher Bartholomew Wagner in Augsburg.[17]

For the pastor of a parish, printed homilies became indispensable resources. After all, until the middle of the seventeenth century the average priest did not receive a thorough enough education to write good sermons himself. Nevertheless, the book collections of most of these pastors were much smaller and less sophisticated than those of their Protestant peers. One set of homily books often had to suffice for a rural priest with little income. Monasteries, however, were in the lucky position of being able to gather large libraries of such works for their members. Thus, a collection of printed homily books was an essential tool helping the pastor create some of the up to two hundred homilies needed throughout the year, of which the shortest would be half an hour, the longest one hour. The priest not only had to speak freely and thus know large parts of Holy Scripture by heart, but also use his entire body to convey his message. Gesticulating with his arms, moving back and forth with his hips, speaking in a loud, "flexible, fiery tongue, and with a clear and distinct voice," made preaching not only an intellectual but also a physical challenge.[18] It was no rarity that agitated priests suffered a stroke in the pulpit or broke into a sweat in a cold church and developed a deadly pneumonia. Unsurprisingly, these demands discouraged many clergy from emphasizing preaching.[19]

Despite a great variety of themes and approaches, Catholic sermons from the sixteenth to the eighteenth century shared several common characteristics. Most importantly, a homily was supposed to bring official church teaching alive for the faithful in a powerful way. It could be either a catechism lesson *or* an explanation of the liturgical readings.[20] The success of the homily relied to a great extent on rhetoric, which aroused feelings (*passiones*) of fear, joy, or consolation in the listener.[21] The successful preacher enabled his listeners to identify with figures of his narrative, and thus to encounter the mysteries of their faith and the methods for inner transformation in their imagination.[22] Of course, the steering of people's imagination also had an undeniable social and disciplinary aspect, which we, however, do not analyze in this book.

Influencing the emotions and imagination of the parishioners was achieved by using an allegorical and typological interpretation of the liturgical readings.[23] The preacher extracted a mystical/spiritual sense from the literal meaning of the text and thus opened for his listeners an inexhaustible warehouse of images. He would describe them with great vivacity and colorfulness.[24] For example, in a parish in which everybody owned a dog, and where stray canines were common, a homilist could give an entire sermon on the animal symbolizing his parishioners, while another could compare them to bees producing "supernatural honey."[25]

The theology of the sermons was therefore primarily "pictorial"[26] as it created images in the minds of the audience and shaped their narrative literacy. Although many Catholics could not read and few read biblical texts, they could remember the liturgical readings through the help of memory bridges provided by the images in a sermon. This mnemotechny allowed the parishioner to acquire a knowledge of biblical narratives stored and regularly refreshed in images and accompanying emotions. The priest, who conveyed them, was therefore seen as "feeding" his parishioners, which explains why so many homily books had titles like *Food Storage*, *Spiritual Banquet*, or even *Samsonian Honey-Cake for the Sweet-Tooth Children of Adam*.[27] The preacher was cook and supernatural "restaurant keeper" who prepared the words of Scripture in the "kitchen" of his heart before serving them like delicious dishes to his flock![28]

## Transforming the Affects of the Audience

The enormous importance erudite clergymen attributed to the public speaking of priests is reflected not only in homiletic books but also in treatises that attempted to elucidate the complicated world of human feelings. The massive, three-volume treatise *The Arousing and Taming of Human Affects* by the Italian Theatine Cajetan Felix Veranus can serve as a good example. Widely accepted as a reliable guide to the topic, Veranus maintained, in the Aristotelian-Thomistic tradition, that reason had to control human passions.[29] This could, however, only be accomplished if pride, vanity, and other vices were eradicated.[30] The most effective way of pushing back against vices and steering affects into the right direction was the "school of death": one described the possibility of eternal damnation for a life of vice and laid out the road to forgiveness.[31]

The sphere of feeling and emotion was differentiated in passion and affect. For Catholic philosophers of the time, active intellectual self-movement was morally more valuable than mere passivity. Passions were involuntary and overwhelmed the rational soul (intellect and will) by appealing to the lower, *sensitive appetite* by desiring sensory objects. Consequently, spiritual formation had to focus on making the active intellect the dominant force of the soul because it could control the passions. Without such direction, the passions led to sin. Once they were under control, however, they became resources for a virtuous life as they transformed into movements of the will.[32] Such voluntary movements of will and intellect were called *affects*. Their objects appealed to the higher *intellectual appetite*. They still "affected" the soul, but in a way that allowed voluntary choice of goods and making them part of one's moral vision. Thus, the affects allowed, if trained, the choice of the proper things that affected one's soul and avoidance of the improper ones.[33] Among these affects, those that focused on the divine, such as God's attributes, were of the highest value because they gave a person the right orientation, drew the will away from worldly desires, and focused it on the highest good.[34] These affects were "all part of a perfect love, a well-ordered love, a love from God for God."[35]

Yet, in order to stimulate affects appropriately,[36] the homilist had to possess a profound knowledge of human emotions (*cognitio animorum*) and their causes, be they internal (organs, temperament) or external (nutrition, music, etc.).[37] His expertise should, however, not end there but also include the life circumstances of his listeners. In the seventeenth and eighteenth centuries, this meant chiefly a decent knowledge of the economic and societal challenges people experienced.[38] Only after careful preparation could the preacher determine what affects he needed to elicit in a sermon, since arousing the wrong ones could have a negative effect.[39]

The pedagogically most important affect was fear. As a *stimulus* it awakened parishioners by confronting them with the possibility of eternal damnation or the pains of Purgatory, but also reminded them of the supernatural goal they were created for—communion with God in Heaven. After fear, the preacher tried to instill awe, which brought the soul into a state of content tranquility and joy, helping to sustain the faith. The elicited affects illuminated the faith and anchored it in one's mind so that they could be activated later to steer clear of vices and aim at the virtues. The homilist was therefore

not just the prophet of doom, who terrified his listeners about Hell and damnation, but also the physician, teacher, and *paterfamilias* responsible for
instilling the love of God (*accendere*) in the faithful.[40] He fulfilled these roles
not just in the pulpit, but especially by living an exemplary life and gently
addressing his parishioners in conversation (*conversatio apostolica*).[41]

Since listeners expected directly applicable, allegorical lessons from
homilies, many priests projected their ideas *into* the text. In order to battle
the exaggerated use of allegory, the sixteenth-century Jesuit Alphonsus
Salmeron reminded his readers that not *every* scripture verse contained a
spiritual meaning. In many cases a text *only* had a literal sense. A priest who
disregarded this violated the integrity of the text and demonstrated careless-
ness, Salmeron argued. Nevertheless, he believed that the preacher was not
limited to spiritual interpretations that Church Fathers or medieval authorities had sanctioned. He could, under the assistance of the Holy Spirit, use
the needs of his flock as a hermeneutic key to explain the text. If he followed
this advice diligently, he would produce something "new" (*novo sensu*)
and useful. However, there were still many priests in the seventeenth century who disregarded such recommendations. The Jesuit Albert de Albertis
complained in 1613 that many preachers were corrupted by the "insane desire to find metaphors" (*inventio*) to arouse the feelings of their listeners.
Most often their images were not based on a thorough knowledge of the text
and thus disguised its meaning. This practice, probably also due to a lack of
education in sacred languages, remained a global phenomenon in Catholic
churches until the late eighteenth century.[42] A particularly amusing example
comes from the homily of a Bavarian Capuchin from 1703. While during
Lent the consumption of meat was generally forbidden, it was allowed on the
Sundays of Lent until the Sunday *Laetare*, which in Bavaria was an occasion
to serve a traditional dish, a calf head. Adalbert of Munich used the image of
this dish to explain the Four Last Things (death, judgment, Heaven, Hell).
The description of a cook carving the meat not only made the mouths of his
audience water, but most certainly also his own. After all, the Capuchins were
notoriously underfed. After the preacher had figuratively removed meat and
eyes from the calf head, all that remained was a skull. Now the listeners were
invited to connect the Gospel readings of the day to the skull in their imagination. It was a reminder of death, and of the passing of all earthly goods.
Many might have even lost their appetite to ever eat a calf's head again.[43]

Different orders nevertheless had different preaching methods. These were
prominently on display during parish missions. Jesuit and Redemptorist

missions were known for priests powerfully gesticulating in the pulpit, using every ounce of their training in rhetoric to stir up emotions. Therefore, they often looked like theatrical performances. Thus, St. Peter Canisius famously remarked that his sermons were meant not to enlighten the mind but to ignite the heart (*ad affectus religiose concitandos adferre*).[44] Such "ignition" sometimes turned into a literal wake-up call as some Catholics had the habit of dozing off during a homily. Even Princess Liselotte von der Pfalz confessed to being among the so-called church sleepers, for whom the homilies were more natural than supernatural tranquilizers.[45] Overall, behavior during a homily must have been much less restrictive than in the nineteenth century because numerous accounts exist of loud chatter, children playing, or even animals making noise.[46]

## Eradicating Avarice and Greed through the Sermon

The inner reform of the human person demanded a reorientation of the soul toward God and thus the elimination of vices. Among these, sexual sins were important, yet avarice and greed received the greatest attention. This is understandable because the acquisitiveness of the population, the boom in trade, and widespread usury had become problems that threatened the survival of society.

Priests as well as bishops faced the difficult question of where legitimate profit seeking ended and greed began.[47] The priest also had to address this issue in a parish, yet walk a fine line between criticizing the rich and inviting them to donate to the church. The pastor could carefully distinguish between the individual vice of greed and regular, profit-seeking business. Nevertheless, the mindset of accumulating riches for the sake of riches was branded universally as causing societal discord, negligence of one's duties for the poor, and the loss of God's grace. Such greed was a "social crime" motivated by selfishness, making a citizen a "traitor to humanity."[48] In France, the Oratorian Julien Loriot therefore reminded his listeners that St. Paul did not recognize a difference between robber, thief, and an avaricious person, because the person desiring riches lacked virtues, especially love for the poor.[49] Greedy merchants and usurers, the listeners were told, had plunged countless people into misery. "How many who have tried to make gold, but have distilled away their brain and mind," complained a priest.[50] Likewise, the Palatine Jesuit John Boddler called the riches of this world a "deceiving dream,"[51] which motivated acquisitiveness and deprived the poor of their bread. Only fighting against such a "disordered desire for temporal goods" by focusing on the eternity of Heaven, could save the rich and bring justice to the poor.[52] Not even a powerful listener such as King Louis XIV of France was safe from getting an earful. His court preacher exclaimed boldly that avarice distorted human sociability and the desire for true good. It perverted this longing into something selfish and was therefore the root of injustice.[53] "Once one has been taken by the idea of 'gain,' one finds the same kick wherever gain can be made. Your money and the money of your neighbor have the same smell."[54] A greedy heart, the court preacher continued, had no mercy because it had extinguished justice. It would destroy all natural social bonds of humanity.[55]

Preaching about avarice and demanding alms and charity of those who had enough was one thing, but *empowering* the poor was another. The priest, who for example preached on Jesus's blessing for the poor in spirit (Mt 5:3), not only condemned avarice but *simultaneously* tried to console the poor and give them the assurance of being wanted in church. Such solace did not beautify the appalling aspects of poverty but rather accurately described the poor as having neither advocate nor physician in society, which consequently deprived them of rights and health. Mendicant orders, especially the Capuchins, emphasized God's blessing for these marginalized members of society. The poor should know, Prokop Templin exclaimed, that despite their misery God had not abandoned them. He suggested that the poor could see their poverty as an anticipation of Purgatory, which would make a post-mortem cleansing redundant. Therefore, the poor should not lose faith but stand firm: "While the rich have here a paradise . . . we the poor have here Purgatory, and perhaps we have Hell on the other side after all!"[56] Templin's "theodicy" made clear that poverty did not excuse idleness or lethargy, because all humans were judged by the standard of faith and virtue. Yet, by explaining that poverty was not a sign of having fallen out of God's favor, he reiterated the message of mercy that smoothed the post-Tridentine teaching of predestination.[57] He thereby clarified that Catholics did *not* believe the poor were in their dismal state because they were forsaken by God! Poverty was for Catholic homilists a part of the unchangeable structure of society, which inspired hard work and competition but also made radical changes undesirable.[58] Such a mindset was partially responsible for the stabilization of feudal systems, which radical Enlighteners criticized. The poor were only spiritually empowered, yet their status at the bottom of society was neither questioned nor changed.

## The Shift toward the "French Style" and the Enlightenment

The Lazarists of St. Vincent de Paul preferred a calmer, less rhetorically charged approach in their homilies, particularly in their parish missions. A Lazarist missionary was admonished to be mindful of four points:

> (1) state and explain with clarity what you want to convince the people of;
> (2) talk on those of its themes which are most perceptible to and in keeping with the capabilities of those to whom you are speaking; (3) give specific and easy means of developing or doing it; (4) never neglect to anticipate the objections which could be made, nor ever say anything confusing which might leave the simple people in some error or doubt.[59]

What differentiated the two basic types of mission preaching, however, was that one, dominated by Jesuits and Capuchins, focused on a powerful yet short impact that shook people emotionally, while the Vincentian model sought a subtle yet long-lasting change of heart. This was accomplished not just by the Lazarists' different rhetoric but also by their decision to stay much longer in a parish than their peers. It seems that parish priests emulated the models they encountered in their parish, through their education or the books they read. Thus, it seems reasonable to assume that in parishes where the pastor used a Jesuit approach, his flock would be less shaken by a Jesuit parish mission because it was already acquainted with such a style, while a member of a parish with a rhetorically challenged priest or one following the gentle Vincentian method, would probably be more stirred emotionally.

Especially since the late seventeenth century, many preachers became uncomfortable with the pompous rhetoric of earlier generations and began preferring a simpler style. In their estimation, homilies had become a place to show off one's erudition.[60] Instead, they argued, the sermons should be simple and direct.[61] In France this new style (see also chapters 2 and 4) was favored by the Lazarists and Oratorians. It also had strong proponents in Italy and Spain.[62] Even in South America a return to simplicity occurred, as Antonio Vieira's works testify.[63] He remarked in 1655: "It is actions that give the preacher his being. To have the name of preacher, or to be a preacher by name, means nothing. Actions, way of life, example, and works are what convert the world."[64] The eighteenth century continued the trend toward simplicity and subdued rhetoric, as the popular books of Abbé N. Girard show.[65]

The Catholic Enlightenment—although hardly a homogeneous movement—marked a shift in homiletics. Its proponents tended to eliminate the figurative identification of the priest with an angel, herald, physician, or healer. Instead, the preaching pastor was predominantly seen as the teacher of his flock.[66] Favoring the French style, a 1787 German collection of sermons explained that it was time to eradicate traditional piety. The "old barbarism" and its "prejudices" prevented "self-thinking"[67] and therefore had to be abandoned. In order to overcome these impediments, the faithful had to be taught more reason and a theology that was cleansed from allegory and symbols. Once endowed with these resources, the faithful could follow the message of the Gospel and morally improve. This optimism about human abilities of course went hand in hand with downplaying the importance of Original Sin.[68]

It is therefore not an overstatement to say that the traditional dialectic of fear and mercy disappeared among these authors.[69] Instead of terrifying listeners into changing their behavior, many Catholic Enlightener priests believed that improving the sensibilities of the faithful would be key to changing their behavior.[70] Awe-inspiring miracles and fabulous stories about the saints or adventurous allegorical exegesis were banned because they were associated with the obscurantism of previous generations and their uncultivated "barbarism." What the world needed was not more darkness, but rather "more light," they argued.[71] This light was not only found in conceptual clarity, but especially in an active and welfare-driven faith. Prayer in this framework was tantamount to having a "good will to always fulfill one's duties" and thus to "work toward one's perfection," but was largely vacated of any dialogue with God.[72]

Early modern Catholic authorities realized the importance of the sermon for the faith life of the parish. Bishops therefore created structures that enabled the clergy to deliver orthodox homilies that engaged the whole person, emotionally and intellectually. The homily, however, not only elucidated a text from Holy Scripture or a teaching of faith, but most importantly elicited the right "emotional responses," especially fear and joy.[73] The priest who delivered it was therefore not merely a teacher but assumed the role of Christ and the Apostles or that of a prophet: he informed, admonished, and encouraged. Fear of God's punishment was used to motivate listeners to scrutinize their life choices, while at the same time forgiveness and mercy were offered for those with a contrite heart.

# 4

# Teaching the Faith in a Parish

Religious education was not a priority of the medieval church. The Catholic Reform after the Council of Trent, however, made it one. Such instruction was to instill adherence to the normative expectations in questions of faith and morality in the faithful. These initiatives certainly disciplined the masses and created a culture in which confessional differences became identity markers. Focusing on these aspects, however, has largely ignored the reality that religious instruction also had a spiritual dimension. Learning about the expectations of the church made the faithful aware not only of what they had to know to be saved but also of how to live their faith and transform their lives. For Catholic Reformers, the church could only renew itself if its members were more dedicated, overcame sin, and molded new selves with the help of grace, which was impossible without a decent knowledge of the faith. This conviction allowed a remarkable spiritual dialectic to emerge. On the one hand, it encouraged the individual to find appropriate means for self-transformation and self-reflection, but on the other it kept individual religious experience anchored in the community of both parish and family. After all, it was in the local church and among one's kin that one learned about the normative expectations of the church and began living according to them. Consequently, parish and family became focal points of post-Tridentine pastoral work. The balance between these two poles encompassing individuality and community was the key to the success of post-Trent spirituality.[1]

## The Theological Dimension of the Parish

The parish provided the sacraments of baptism, confession, Eucharist, confirmation, the anointing of the sick, and the ritual framework for two spouses to administer to each other the sacrament of marriage. By keeping records of baptisms and marriages, the parish priest not only provided documentation for the authorities but also security for the faithful. Such a document could, for example, prove that a person had been baptized and was not burdened

*The Inner Life of Catholic Reform*. Ulrich L. Lehner, Oxford University Press. © Oxford University Press 2022.
DOI: 10.1093/oso/9780197620601.003.0004

with any obstacles to entering a marriage, or that a matrimonial ceremony had been performed in front of named witnesses. Before Trent, clandestine marriages were common, but left the female partner without any protection. Also, deaths were now meticulously recorded. This "bureaucratization" of the sacraments showed the importance the Council of Trent attributed to the parish. It desired that the parish become the major place of spiritual formation. This meant, however, that obstacles both among laity and clergy had to be overcome.

Many priests were appointed not by the bishop but a local patron, who often did not have the same zeal for reform as the ecclesial superior. Moreover, priests who received their salary from such a patron easily dismissed additional demands of the bishops to "enliven" the parish by frequent preaching and teaching. These sixteenth-century priests invoked traditional privileges to spare themselves from more unpaid labor. Such behavior should, however, not lead the historian to brand these clergymen as greedy or disinterested in the salvation of souls. Rather, they were wedged in a traditional mindset according to which a parish priest performed a limited range of services, which were remunerated.[2] When bishops or their delegates visited these parishes, they assessed their orthodoxy, discipline, and quality of religious life, yet hardly ever caused a priest to fall in love with reform (see chapter 2). Parishioners used such visitations to complain about problems in the parish. Historians have largely ignored the rhetoric of such grievances. Very often these were actions of protest against priests who had violated community standards and expectations. By expressing their criticisms, parishioners could vent their grievances to a higher-ranking member of the diocesan clergy and experience that the local parish belonged to a larger whole under the guidance of a bishop. The episcopal visitator therefore not only embodied the "eyes" of his bishop but also represented the Apostle being sent to a particular community to ensure the alignment of faith and morals.[3] Thus, the visitation was more than a disciplinary action. It embodied, as the Franciscan Bartholomew of the Martyrs stated, the "soul of the bishop's governance" over his diocese, where he—like Christ—purged, illuminated, and perfected the community.[4] The reference to these three hierarchical acts is not only an echo of Pseudo-Dionysian mysticism, but also a direct reference to the Council of Trent's theology of the bishop (chapter 2).[5] Illuminating others required, however, that one was already "enlightened" by faith, and thus the office of teaching made it necessary for a bishop to know the faith. Likewise, perfecting presupposed that the bishop was "on fire" for the Gospels. Only then could he be a "sun" for his diocese[6] that burned away vices.[7]

The parish priest, however, had to meet not only the increasing expectations of his bishop, such as living in celibacy, praying the breviary, attending to his flock, and more, but also those of his community. Parishes had their own traditions and privileges, and parishioners were aware and proud of them. When bishops disregarded them, a local priest who merely obeyed his superior's orders easily got into trouble with his flock. After all, disregard for local customs was seen as an abuse of priestly power! A good example for the normative conflicts between bishop and parish were the clashes over the distribution of blessed, fermented breads (*eulogias fermentatas*) in France.[8] These were not consecrated, but parishioners often considered them equivalent to the Eucharist, bringing them home and venerating them. However, such behavior was idolatry because the *eulogias* were merely *sacramentals*.[9] As such, they led to the sacraments and echoed them, but were not intrinsic carriers of grace. It is understandable that reform-minded bishops desired to put an end to practices that bordered on superstition or watered down the Catholic doctrine of the Eucharist, but they overlooked that the bread was also a symbol for peace in the community.[10] By abolishing it, they also eliminated an important community ritual. Pastors sometimes accordingly had to face angry crowds, who insisted on the tradition. While in Spain and England the custom was eradicated relatively easily, some areas of France and Belgium successfully defended the *pain bénit* until the twentieth century.[11] This example also shows that reform was never a one-way street, and certainly not a top-down reality. Its success depended on the reception of reforms, which could be renegotiated or even ignored. Strengthening the identity of the priest as a "little Christ" allowed the clergy to circumvent such renegotiations and over time establish a more uniform liturgical and moral discipline. The consequence was that the laity focused more and more on the priest and his leadership and less on their local customs.[12]

Enlivening a parish was also the purpose of parish missions. Priests who acted as missionaries understood it as their duty to instill zeal during a short period of time in which they visited a parish. Invited to a parish, the priests' sermons were well known for portraying death and Hell as means to elicit remorse. This message was followed by a depiction of God as merciful, particularly in the confessional. The missions somewhat mirrored therefore the first week of St. Ignatius of Loyola's *Spiritual Exercises*. They were to drive the penitents to feel sorrow for their sins and begin to transform their lives.

While this was a silent and introspective exercise, the missions were an extroverted appeal to the masses. In order to achieve the same emotional responses, Jesuits and Capuchins therefore used extraordinary tools such as theatrical events that agitated the audience. A report of 1697 described a number of adults who were disguised and instructed to impersonate the dead in Hell and be questioned by children from the parish.

> When the procession arrived at that place the living began to question the damned. The whole audience was moved by their questions, which interested all. But the gloomy voices, expressing the tortures of the damned, which emerged from under the stage, as though from the bottom of the abyss, frightened this great crowd of more than four thousand persons so much that everyone beat his breast and made new resolutions to repent and avoid sin.[13]

The Catholic faith insisted that only the living could do penance and ask for God's forgiveness. Dying in a state of mortal sin meant eternal damnation. Missionaries therefore admonished the faithful to be mindful of a well-prepared death. Nevertheless, since one's own demise could come rather quickly and unexpectedly, the missionary drama stimulated real fear. One could die at any moment, and that moment counted for all eternity. Missionaries used every trick they had learned in their rhetorical training to emotionally engage their listeners, because their stay in the parish was short. Moreover, as visitors they did not have to mince their words as carefully as the local pastor, who dealt with his parishioners all year long. It is hard to imagine that a parish priest would have had recourse to the same drastic gestures that the Jesuit Paolo Segneri used. He yelled from the pulpit with a rope in one hand, and a human skull in the other. The rope symbolized eternal punishment in Hell. It would, however, be a mistake to think that all missionaries were cut from the same cloth. While both Jesuits and Capuchins preferred dramatic, short parish missions, the Lazarists of St. Vincent de Paul not only rejected the theatrics but preferred longer stays during which they preached in a subtler manner.[14]

The Capuchins saw the work of the parish mission as a service of prayer, but also as one of penance, particularly because of its physical and intellectual strains. Missionary friars took on the role of "prophets" fulfilling the will of Christ.[15] As such, they were called not only to provoke fear and terror, but also to create real *desire* for the faith. The goal was to reach not just the sophisticated elite but also the uneducated masses. After all, "God is pleased to communicate Himself to the simplest of souls," as a seventeenth-century missionary stated.[16] This *salvific egalitarianism*, which emphasized that all Christians were facing the same judgment according to faith and morals, regardless of wealth and status, was also a common topic in Jesuit homilies. Nevertheless, a missionary had to mention that this did not mean that groups did not also have specific duties to fulfill. Children had duties toward their parents, lawyers toward their clients, and innkeepers toward their guests, as Nicholas Cusanus's *Christian School* (1623), reprinted at least eighteen times until 1758, explained.[17]

An effective parish mission reached many parishioners. The missionaries ensured that their listeners would hear what the church regarded as necessary knowledge for salvation (*fides explicita*). If they did not accept it and died, both the missionaries and the parish priest could feel free from any responsibility for their fate. Thus, the mission also served as a spiritual unburdening for the local priest. The biggest problem was that the target group of "public sinners" or those too busy with work did not show up for the mission events, and probably also missed the regular Sunday homilies of their pastor. Thus, Bourdoise suggested that the parish priest had to realize that the pulpit had only limited success. "Two priests," he suggested, "must proceed from house to house in the districts assigned to them and remain in each place as long as they think necessary for instructing the rough people and teaching them to receive properly the sacraments."[18] This model of door-to-door evangelizing did not, however, become a widespread custom. It would have overwhelmed the already timeworn rural priests and was deemed impossible.

Until the eighteenth century there existed many rural areas in Catholic Europe that had never seen a parish mission. In the Italian countryside, especially the poor seem to have been largely unaffected by missions. In order to fill this need, the newly founded Redemptorists of St. Alphonsus of Liguori responded to this pastoral challenge. The Redemptorists, however, did not continue the Jesuit/Capuchin dialectic of fear and mercy but adopted the Lazarist model of gentle persuasion. They became a force against aggressive rigorism.[19] Thus, they implicitly addressed the mounting criticism of missions by Catholic Enlighteners. Their vexations on guilt had become a special target of mockery. The Spanish Benedictine Benito Feijoo believed that many missionaries blew the sins of their audience out of proportion and needlessly induced anxiety. Fear of Hell, he believed, was neither a good motivator for conversion nor left a lasting impression.

Therefore, Feijoo put the preaching of God's love at the center of his theology: "It is good to introduce them to the fear of God, but better and safer to make them fall in love with God."[20]

## Forming Princes and Nobility

Catechizing and forming the average parishioner was one task, educating future leaders another. Especially the Jesuits realized the importance of forming a leader's conscience according to the new expectations and norms. Chosen by God, a prince was believed to be guided by the Holy Spirit, but it was his confessor who made sure that he did not act against the divine counsel.[21]

The seven gifts of the Holy Spirit were supposed to transform and shape the ruler, echoing the understanding of the sacrament of confirmation. Wisdom as gift included, a seventeenth-century Augustinian wrote, also the wisdom of dissimulation or the ability to be tacit about certain political matters in a conversation.[22] Such a view was not unproblematic, because the morality of dissimulation or the withholding of information was hotly debated. The Jesuits defended it as a necessity in politics: a king could not always speak the exact truth, because otherwise he and his country could be taken advantage of. Considering dissimulation as a gift of divine wisdom was only possible if one embedded it in a broader theology of princely formation according to the gifts of the Holy Spirit. The gift of wisdom taught the prince to rule justly and to subject his passions to a higher good. The gift of understanding enabled him to see the goods in their proper hierarchy and made him magnanimous.[23] The gift of counsel enabled the prince to be a good judge and to acquire integrity,[24] while the gift of fortitude encouraged him to work tirelessly for the well-being of the realm.[25] The gift of knowledge allowed the prince to gain introspection and recognize his own vocation as well as his shortcomings, while the gift of piety assured his protection of the true faith. The gift of the fear of God made sure that he submitted his will always to God.[26]

A widely read account of personal transformation for the nobility was the *Holy Court* by the Jesuit Nicolas Caussin.[27] According to Caussin, the members of a noble family were obliged to pursue spiritual perfection according to their state and profession. Recognizing the conflicts between courtly and ecclesiastical expectations, Caussin set out to show that one did not have to abandon one's position of power to achieve such perfection.[28]

Nevertheless, one had to infuse societal norms with new spiritual meaning. For example, Caussin acknowledged that an aristocrat could not abandon all riches or stop taking care of his outward appearance. Yet, instead of attaching vanity or selfishness to these goods, the spiritual prince should use them as opportunities to thank God for the gifts he has received.[29] Also, a number of courtly virtues such as courage could be redirected toward personal sanctification: with the same bravery a nobleman would fight in a war, he should pursue his religious goals, admonished Caussin, because otherwise the many temptations at court would surely ruin his soul.[30] After all, living at court meant living in the constant fear of losing the king's favor and being the object of countless temptations. One was a "poor miserable creature" thrown into "an ocean of calamities."[31] Only if the aristocrat became a "spiritual man" could he find a way to Heaven:

> The spiritual man is a man covetous of eternity, prodigal of life, little careful of the present, certain of the future. A man who seems no longer to have commerce with the world, and who hath nothing so familiar as a life that is as if were buried in death, and who flieth above sepulchres like an Angel who holdeth not of the earth, but by the slender root of natural necessities, *and already toucheth heaven with a finger.*[32]

Caussin's message was one of hope, promising that gentry could achieve salvation (*toucheth heaven with a finger*), if they just molded new Christian selves.[33] While the educators and confessors of princes often varied in their approaches—some being more rigorous; others, such as Louis XIV's preacher Charles Boileau, more lenient[34]—they had a fundamental belief in common. They all asserted that noble families had specific duties they had to fulfill without withdrawing from their "God-given" place in society.

The formation of leaders did not only happen in spiritual counseling, confession, catechism lessons, or the reading of academic theology, but also in and through philosophy *and* the sciences. Both helped reason to reach its full potential and enabled it to arrive at the "natural knowledge" of God, and thereby contributed to the character formation of the student. The increasing emphasis on science and mathematics in the curriculum of early modern Catholic schools should therefore not be seen as a concession to "secular" values, but rather as the deliberate introduction of lessons to help the mind in its search for absolute truth, which was tantamount to God.[35] The sciences were also for Descartes "tools for cultivating truer forms of spiritual and mental nobility,"[36] and thus aimed at inner self-transformation. After all, for Descartes true wisdom came from a somewhat meditative thinking that formed intellectual habits. Descartes believed that these would lead the mind to live the virtues.[37] Perhaps, then, one has to reassess Cartesian handbooks under this perspective of formation and place them within—but at the fringes of—the intellectual landscape of Catholic Reform? Works like those of Bernard Lamy would justify this classification: for the Oratorian, logic and mathematics were indispensable in the honest search for God[38] —an idea he shared with the Jansenists of Port Royal. For the latter, however, mathematics also provided the necessary filter to correct our sensory appetites and work as a tool of asceticism:

> Only grace and the exercises of piety . . . can cure it [sensory appetites] truly; but among the human exercises that can serve the most to diminish it and to dispose the mind to receive the Christian truths with less opposition and disgust, it seems that there are hardly any more appropriate than the study of geometry.[39]

## Forming Parishioners through Catechisms

Beginning in the sixteenth century, catechisms, often written in the form of question and answer, became popular all over the Catholic world. The *Roman Catechism*, redacted by St. Carlo Borromeo, had a place of special authority that had come about with a papal endorsement in 1566. Yet also those of St. Peter Canisius and St. Robert Bellarmine were popular and reprinted well into the eighteenth century.[40] These catechisms aimed at teaching not only the necessary knowledge to obtain salvation (*fides explicita*) but also practices of prayer and methods of cultivating virtues. In a world that had an increasing number of conflicting norms, catechisms provided orientation. For example, in the late sixteenth century, soldiers who had become enthusiastic about their faith began to wonder whether they could reconcile the prohibition of murder with their duty to kill an enemy. Forming consciences was therefore a major concern for the authors of catechisms.[41]

Church authorities believed that a certain *explicit knowledge of faith* was necessary to obtain salvation. One had to know and understand these truths, and so catechesis attempted to make them intelligible.[42] However, the amount of what was considered necessary increased over the seventeenth and eighteenth centuries, as the size of the catechisms (particularly in France) show.[43] Theologians were expected to believe in a more explicit mode, because they had been trained to study doctrine, while a regular Catholic layperson was not. For the laity it was sufficient to have for the rest *implicit faith* in what the church taught, because in her the fullness of explicit faith was always present. Such assent to the church required obedience and trust. It is therefore not surprising that the Holy Spirit's guidance of the church, particularly of pope and bishops, was increasingly emphasized. It made her appear not as an authoritarian institution but rather as a divinely guided community of believers, which held with assurance that which Christ commanded her to believe. Implicit faith, however, also wanted to unburden the believer and give the faithful peace of mind that they did not have to know every doctrinal teaching to be saved.[44] After all, implicit faith only required the *assent of the will*, but not an act of the intellect.[45]

The catechetical books explained not only the Christian creed but also basic prayers (such as the *Our Father*) and the seven sacraments. In Latin America, Africa, or Asia, catechetical instruction was often in the hands of the laity who spoke—unlike many clergymen—local dialects. Missionaries used a wide variety of approaches to gain the attention of their listeners. Some emphasized the fear of Hell for the unbaptized, while sixteenth-century Augustinians in Mexico seem to have stressed the message of a merciful God: "He hates no one, despises no one; there is nothing evil in him. He . . . is the deep well of all good things; He is the essence of love, compassion and mercy."[46] Overall, however, missionaries seem to have relied rather on state pressure and spiritual oppression to achieve their goals.[47]

Yet it would be a serious shortcoming to view a catechism only as a tool of indoctrination and social discipline. Such an approach would not only eclipse its intention of sanctifying the faithful but also misunderstand its normative force. After all, parishioners did not blindly accept the lessons they were given but also adapted them according to their own community standards. A Dominican catechism of 1548 for the Nahuatl population in Mexico can serve as an example. Viewing it merely as a document of behavioral control lets the historian miss its spiritual depths, when it explains faith in the Holy Spirit:

> I believe in the *spiritu sancto*, who entirely consecrates and makes entirely righteous the assembly of all Christians, called *sancta yglesia*, for the *spiritu sancto* entirely governs it, entirely guards it, and our savior Jesus Christ,

indeed true *Dios*, indeed is made the head of *sancta yglesia*, for He is indeed our head, and we are his joints.[48]

Certainly, the text calls the faithful to submission to the church's authority because she is "governed" by the Holy Spirit. Yet it also teaches that the natives were "consecrated" by the Spirit, just as all the other members of the worldwide church. Thus, the text allows the students to see themselves as participating in the Godhead together with all other Catholics. The native Nahuatl were members of the mystical body of Christ just as much as the Spanish conquistadors. The catechism thus expresses the already mentioned *salvific egalitarianism*, assuring believers that there was no societal, ethnic, or racial difference in questions of salvation, but limits such equality to the supernatural world. In fact, in missionary territories the rhetoric of spiritual egalitarianism was often used to justify, promote, or condone the oppression of natives in society. A very similar catechetical and rhetorical program can be found in the earliest Chinese catechism, translated by the Jesuit Joao da Rocha.[49]

Traditionally, parents were responsible for the religious education of their children, because the local priest would mostly not provide such services. Since the end of the sixteenth century, however, religious education became a primary obligation of the clergy. The pastors held weekly catechism classes for children in church on Sundays and feast days but also gave lessons for adults. This professionalization of religious instruction ensured that children would receive an orthodox explanation of the faith, but it did not eliminate the obligation of the parents to continue the formation at home. In missionary territories, laypersons often assumed the role of teachers because they spoke the local dialects better than the priest.[50] It was, however, not only the bishops who wished the priest to undertake the role of an educator but also especially the parents themselves. Realizing their own limitations, they desired their children to learn as much as they could for the sake of their salvation *and* moral formation. When they perceived a lack of quality, they would complain to the bishop, as these parents from Perthes in France in 1769:

[D]uring the seasons . . . it is very rare that we can enjoy listening to the catechism classes. . . . [T]he rain, snow, and the frost are constant obstacles, and what is even more lamentable is that our children cannot stay for catechism. . . . For you know, Monseigneur, that the children are ignorant of the religion, and that it is sad to see us abandoned to ourselves, deprived of the most precious advantages of religion.[51]

These parents appreciated catechism classes but complained about their scheduling. The children of the poor could not stay because they had to work at home, and thus the parents reminded the bishop of the salvific egalitarianism they had learned about. Inflexibility of the pastor left them "abandoned," although they had the same ecclesial rights as the rich.

The teaching of the catechism's content to a mostly illiterate community was, however, a major challenge. In Europe as well as in the Americas, it depended largely on instructing listeners to memorize short sentences they heard. Therefore, the question-and-answer format was adequate. In addition, catechism teachers also used printed or painted images to explain the faith. Nevertheless, it seems that although many Catholics knew the right catechism answers, they did not understand their meaning. Many repeated them "like parrots," Bishop Ennemond Alleman de Montmartin of Grenoble complained in 1712:

> Faith, without which it is impossible to please God, does not consist, said St. Augustine, in the sound of syllables, nor in the pronunciation of certain words that one learns by heart: it consists in the understanding of the things signified by the words. However, those who take pains to interrogate the *petit peuple* in the confessional or elsewhere, find that the majority only know the words, and are in a state of profound ignorance of the truths that these words signify.[52]

Lay readers with money often acquired catechisms and also homily books, which they perused as spiritual readings. Homilies not only edified but also entertained, using myths, legends, and example stories.[53] Prayer books often imitated the hours of the breviary, albeit in the vernacular, and enabled the lay reader to "feel" like a monastic. This way they could sanctify their daily routine and imitate the religious superachievers behind the monastery walls.[54] Spiritual books often also focused on the needs of particular groups, such as Martin von Cochem addressing only women in his bestselling *Golden Key to Heaven* (1695).[55] Hymnals and the legends of the Saints were also enormously popular. Since vernacular religious songs had almost universally replaced Gregorian chant by the seventeenth century, such hymnals, whose content varied from region to region, were a primary resource for the spiritual formation of a family. What was learned in a catechism lesson could be augmented by easy-to-memorize hymns.[56] Given these different tastes in reading, it is likely that devoted and educated Catholic families had a variety of several such books in their households, where they could be used for private or common prayer.[57]

From the sixteenth century onward, religious education was increasingly outsourced to professionals, be it priests or specially trained catechists. This guaranteed that the students encountered officially sanctioned doctrine. In these lessons the faithful also learned about the acquisition of virtues and the avoidance of vices. Religious education gave them a number of tools and resources to transform their character. By making the parish the center of spiritual formation, the church ensured that such transformational practices were universally known. Although the parish itself did not become a focus of theological reflection, it successfully claimed the center of people's religious life. Other places of professionalized formation included private tutoring, especially for princes and nobility, and schools.

# 5

# The Spiritual Formation of the Family

## The Place and Value of the Family

Renaissance humanism and the Reformation were at times credited with establishing marriage as a bond of love and companionship.[1] Recent research, however, suggests that this view grew from medieval roots, which already taught "mutual help and comfort" as the "third end" of marriage.[2] The same medieval sources that attracted humanists also shaped the Catholic Reform and consequently its views on marriage.[3] Nevertheless, the Catholic world of early modernity faced diverse challenges and therefore approached marriage and family differently. While sixteenth-century Europeans could build on centuries-old traditions to ruminate about gender relations, the mission territories in the Americas, Africa, and Asia struggled with more rudimentary problems, such as establishing marriage as a monogamous relationship.[4] A first step toward a more complex treatment of marital vocation in the missions was the 1592 Japanese Catechism.[5]

The theology of the diverse Catholic Reform recognized the nuclear family as a pillar of church renewal. In a family the children learned to pray and follow the commandments of God. It produced future vocations to the priesthood, and populated Heaven with holy souls through procreation. The resources that the church poured into families were massive. Religious education was offered on a large scale for children and adults, as were homilies and the sacrament of confession. Likewise, attendance at Sunday Mass became a family undertaking and therefore part of its spiritual formation. These offerings were accepted or rejected by individuals, and therefore historians have often interpreted them not as pastoral care for the *family* but rather for *individuals*. This is, however, a bit shortsighted, because a close reading of the normative texts shows that the goal was to sanctify the whole family *through* the sanctification of each member. By becoming a holier mother, the whole family became saintlier. By embracing the virtues, a husband contributed to the formation of his children and employees, and so forth. The spiritual aspect of marriage as a sacrament embodied this: the two spouses ascertained

*The Inner Life of Catholic Reform*. Ulrich L. Lehner, Oxford University Press. © Oxford University Press 2022.
DOI: 10.1093/oso/9780197620601.003.0005

for each other the grace of the sacrament and each thus led the other to salvation.[6]

In catechesis and art, the image of the Holy Family, which originated in the fifteenth century and thus in the heyday of late medieval Catholic Reform, illustrated the hope for sanctification. Joseph, Mary, and the Christ child demonstrated to the onlooker that faith grew and flourished in the household. In sermons the family was even used as an analogy to the Holy Trinity. To this family also belonged the parents of Mary, Joachim and Anne. Although their veneration initially decreased after the Reformation, mainly because it was rooted in apocryphal traditions, the cult of St. Anne underwent a revitalization during the seventeenth century. The emphasis on the immaculate conception of Mary in Anne's womb gave her maternal relationship an elevated position. This was portrayed by artists when they depicted St. Anne as teaching Mary how to read, alluding to the *Logos* or Word of God that would become incarnate in her. St. Anne and St. Joachim became the role models for good earthly parents, but also for grandparents. While earlier theologians had assumed Anne had been married three times, late sixteenth- and seventeenth-century devotion insisted that she remained after the death of Joachim a chaste widow. Consequently, in post-Trent devotion, the extended family of St. Anne, "holy kinship," disappeared. In line with the Christocentrism of the reform movement, it was only her relation to Mary that counted, and not that she might have also been the grandmother of the apostles. Likewise, the emphasis on one marital bond seems to suggest that the cult was also used to reinforce the Tridentine message about sacramental, indissoluble marriage.[7]

Although the catechesis of spouses in their preparation for marriage followed largely traditional patterns, its availability on the insistence of bishops in every parish was something new.[8] After all, the Council of Trent had enshrined the importance of marriage by confirming the indissolubility of valid and consummated marriages.[9] It was the priest's duty to educate the partners about their lifelong commitment and prepare them for the exchange of their vows. In order to ascertain that neither partner was encumbered from entering into matrimony, the two fiancées were publicly announced to the community several weeks in advance of the festivities. After the wedding, however, the spiritual growth of the partners was largely dependent on *their* initiative in seeking spiritual counsel, beyond the standard advice received in the confessional and from the pulpit. Prayer life within the family was self-determined and without clerical supervision. Priests sometimes wondered how closely families followed their recommendations, and at times expressed suspicions.[10] If a pastor did not respect this traditional sphere of self-determination,[11] he could—just like a priest who asked too many questions in the confessional—be accused of disrespectful nosiness, which often led to official complaints to the bishop. Only for serious reasons, such as rumors about scandal or mortal sin, or if a family member reached out to him, could the pastor safely undertake an inquiry and initiate a pastoral visit.[12]

Many spiritual writers such as St. John of Avila, St. Teresa of Avila, and St. Francis de Sales recommended that married people have a spiritual advisor. This was not a sign of distrust, because members of religious orders also had such advisors. Rather, these authors realized that daily chores in a family made it difficult to find moments of prayerful reflection and that married people should not be left alone in their spiritual struggles. A spiritual advisor, who was usually a priest or a nun, suggested customized ways to live either married or single life as a religious vocation.[13]

The Catholic tradition esteemed celibate life more highly than married life, but normative texts articulated this differently: Medieval texts for the laity tended to praise the married state, while homilies for a monastic audience celebrated celibacy.[14] In early modernity, this separation faded away. After all, the audience for printed vernacular sermons was mixed. Priests read them to prepare their own homilies and laypeople read them for edification. Consequently, one finds in them both a praise of marital unions and also a celebration of the celibate lifestyle. A good example is the Capuchin preacher Prokop of Templin from the 1660s. He explained that both states were blessed by God and grounded in Holy Scripture. Yet, while marriage was the *ordinary* vocation for all, the call to celibate life was directed to a few and thus an *extraordinary* vocation. This, however, did not mean scorn for marriage: "Only because I consider gold as more valuable than silver, it does not follow that I despise silver."[15]

## Preaching and Reading about Marriage

In addition to regular catechism classes for children and optional meetings for adults, the liturgical readings at Mass provided a steady number of opportunities to address marriage and children in homilies. Already in the sixteenth century, such sermons encouraged fiancées to discern their future well and to avoid the wrong motivations for marriage, such as lust or money.[16]

If both spouses worked well together, they could establish peace and harmony in their family, which was considered the basis of companionship and
success. Nevertheless, marriage was presented as hierarchically structured,
giving the husband much authority over his wife.[17]

Homilies about the duties of the partners continued medieval traditions.
Available handbooks contained the summaries of centuries-old discussions,
which made the clergy aware of the problems that arose in marriages. This
historical awareness contributed greatly to the longevity of marital values
and duties.[18] Even medieval rhetorical tools continued to be used, such as
addressing husbands and wives separately. Whenever the preacher focused
on the men, their duties were highlighted as the most important; whenever
the wife was at the center of his attention, then her obligations were the most
significant.[19] While the wife was expected to be obedient to her husband, the
husband was admonished to love her as Christ loved the church, not even
preferring his own parents to her. Only if *both* fulfilled their duties and "took
care of each other, and *gave in* according to the best of their ability," would
their union be joyful.[20] Despite the strong emphasis on happiness, homilists
also described the importance of matrimony for church and society. Since
a marriage was a mirror of the love of Christ for his church, an adulterous
partner not only "lacked a heart" but also committed a grave sin against
Christ, the entire church, and society. Adultery was a sin that damaged the
community and sowed confusion.[21]

The *primary* end of marriage was believed to be raising children, the *second*
the taming of lust, the *third* mutual help and assistance.[22] The numbering of
these ends, however, varied greatly in the literature of the time. Marchant,
for example, mentioned companionship first, but added as the "second and
even more important end the procreation of children."[23] The public setting
of a sermon, however, was not the place to talk about details of marital intimacy—that happened in the confessional. "Decency" prevented the priest
from giving more than a few hints about the marital "debt," the sexual act.[24]
The faithful nevertheless learned in catechesis that pleasurable sex between
spouses was a venial sin. According to traditional authors like St. Thomas
Aquinas, pleasure in intercourse was something animalic and "irrational,"
and thus immoral. Nevertheless, the same theologians also emphasized the
ideal of married love and understood chastity not merely as abstinence but as
"internal and dynamic modification of sexuality to make it participate in the
profound human love."[25] A more positive evaluation of sexual pleasure, as
long as it only accompanied the act and was not the primary end, was given in

the seventeenth century by the Jesuit Thomas Sanchez. In his estimation, the spouses did not have to have the explicit intention to regard sex as a remedy for fornication or desire to procreate—agreeing virtually with such teaching was sufficient. A couple that loves God, "seeks intercourse because they are married . . . if they are in a state of grace, and enter into intercourse . . . they do well. The virtual intention is sufficient."[26] He was also among the first to encourage touches and kisses as expressions of marital love, even if they were arousing: "There is an urgent cause for touches of this kind to show and foster mutual love among spouses, and it would be great austerity, and love would be much diminished, if they abstained from touches of this sort."[27]

Every church year, the readings for the two Sundays after Epiphany allowed the priest to talk at length about marriage.[28] Homily books mostly contained such standard sermons about marriage and family, while specialized books on marriage were quite rare. This was also a clear confessional difference, because printed wedding sermons were quite common among Protestants. For the churches of the Reformation, a wedding was the opportunity to explain in detail why marriage was no sacrament but nevertheless a school of virtue. For Catholics one could presuppose a general knowledge that the sacraments sanctified those who engaged in them, and that marriage was a particular instance of these. Moreover, given the emphasis in catechesis, the pastor could also expect the spouses to know that the effects of the sacrament were infallibly brought about by Christ through the exchange of vows, regardless of the spouses' defects in virtue or charity. Consequently, Catholic weddings did not emphasize the homily but the exchange of the vows, which constituted the sacrament. These vows, called *copulatio*, could be exchanged *before* a Mass (*missa pro sponso et sponsa*), ending with a solemn blessing for the bride (*benedictio nuptialis*), or completely outside the context of the Eucharist.[29] Within a nuptial Mass the priest would not give a sermon unless it was a Sunday or feast day, and would then preach about the gospel of the day. The only marriage-specific address at a wedding was at the *end* of a solemn *copulatio*, when the priest would say a few words about the duties and expectations of the marital state. Such a speech was usually only a few minutes long and based on the *Roman Catechism*. In the archdiocese of Toledo in Spain, however, the betrothed received such a short admonition *during* the ceremony, which shows that the celebration varied according to local customs.[30]

Solemn marriages could not be celebrated on just any day of the year. The *Rituale Romanum* of 1614 forbade them for the penitential seasons (Lent and Advent). In addition, many dioceses also added the octaves of Epiphany, Pentecost, Corpus Christi, and All Souls. Thus, spouses could obtain the solemn blessing only during a relatively narrow window in the church's calendar. Moreover, a woman could receive it only at her first betrothal, not at subsequent ones. Simple weddings, however, were possible during the entire church year with the exception of a few Sundays. Thus, the question of why there were so few Catholic marriage sermons is easily explained by the liturgical and theological tradition of the church. Moreover, since the homily books for the liturgical year already contained texts on matrimony, insufficiently paid and undereducated priests would have most likely avoided spending money on expensive tomes they would never use. For this reason, the few Catholic marriage sermon books are all the more remarkable and deserve close scrutiny.

One of these was a collection of talks by the Bohemian priest Balthasar Ziegler, published in 1698. He claimed as motive for the publication the desire of couples to hear a more personalized message at their nuptials, as well as the inability of the clergy to provide these. Complying with the wish for a customized style, Ziegler based each speech on the baptismal name of the bridegroom. Thus, for a groom named Anthony the priest gave a popular, tongue-in-cheek etymology of the name, which he then connected to the sacrament of marriage. Anthony, he insisted, meant "in tune," which allowed him to talk about harmony in music, and then within marriage. Throughout the address the priest kept repeating this etymology to ensure that it would be anchored in the audience's memory. Another example was the groom's name Christopher. In iconography St. Christopher was depicted as a giant with a rod, carrying the Christ child. This imagery allowed the priest to reflect on the duties of a husband. He should not use the wood in his hand to mistreat his wife but rather be like a palm tree in whose shadow she can rest: "I wish both of you that you flower and green together until you reach the heavenly, paradisiacal garden, the tree of life in God the Father, the Son and the Holy Spirit."[31] While these short marriage speeches were certainly memorable, it is not known how widespread this practice was.

The general sermons about marriage during the church year, as well as these speeches, admonished the partners to seek spiritual transformation together. Quite regularly, husbands were admonished to never treat their wives like slaves or "whores," thus sexually exploiting them.[32] If they did, they failed to love, cherish, and nourish (amare, fovere, nutrire) her as a partner (sociam).[33] Due to the indissolubility of marriage in Catholicism, the

innocent partner in such an abusive marriage was a "captive" in a "permanent prison." Often this included the endurance of physical violence, which
preachers did not shy away from addressing. A monk therefore once yelled
from the pulpit:[34] "Rough men! . . . Fear the God, who will revenge your
wives!"[35] Many women, for example in Spain, endured such mistreatment
with the messianic zeal to improve their lives by changing their husbands.[36]
The actions of these wives indicated that they aimed at restoring the moral
and spiritual leadership of their husbands.

For marriage as the "common and general vocation of all the faithful,"[37]
love was not a requirement but it ensured that the partners took their vocation seriously. Beginning especially in the seventeenth century, the importance of marital love and tenderness was emphasized in spiritual writings.[38]
Such love for each other, however, had to be subordinated to the love of God,
otherwise it was considered disordered. Therefore, Henri Boudon stated in
his *Dieu Seul* (1666)[39] that nothing must ever be done to dishonor God, not
even obeying a spouse's wishes.[40] If both fulfilled this command and continuously exchanged "gifts of respect," they would shine like the bright colors
of a rainbow in a gray sky.[41] Another writer envisioned marital love as a fire
that never faded because it was continuously restoked by acts of kindness and
devotion.[42]

The new emphasis on mutual love and respect did not, however, challenge
the husband's headship, which was envisioned by many as one of love and patience and not of power. One regularly recommended practice for fostering
mutual love was to "invite" Christ into the marriage. This could be achieved
either through the formation of a pure intention to be open to receiving children, so that the "number of saints would be multiplied,"[43] or by cultivating
other acts of mutual love and prayer.[44] Only such an intentional invitation
of God would, as the Catholic Enlightener Beda Mayr explained, enable the
partners to transform their "animalic sexual desire" into a service for the
glory of God, making them regard each other as partners on the road to salvation.[45] This demonstrates that behavioral rules were intended not merely
to discipline sex but also to cultivate spiritual transformation.

Likewise, other gender-specific duties were spiritually framed and
presented as requisites for a harmonious marriage.[46] If these were reversed,
a "sex change" occurred, as Prokop von Templin called it, which resulted in
marital distress.[47] Since Eve had been created out of Adam's rib, both spouses
"knew that one was as good as the other, and that one should not consider
himself better than the other," insisted Templin, and thus emphasized the

equal dignity of both spouses.[48] Nevertheless, the husband was the head of the household and therefore obliged to begin "the Reformation of his house with himself, and after he has brought good order in his soul, has tamed his passions and evil inclinations, his shortcomings and defects, then he can begin leading wife, children and servants towards improvement."[49]

## Apprenticeship and Care for Children

The outsourcing of theological education to the priest did not diminish the predominant role parents played in the religious formation of their offspring. Priests regularly reminded them of this duty. After all, a child could not only fall into mortal sin but also apostatize from the church.[50] The parents were thus much more than role models presented for imitation. They were a child's first "masters," while children were their "apprentices." Such an approach had an advantage over a mere role model relationship. After all, the latter did not entail a personal relationship: one could imitate a hero from afar without ever meeting that individual in person. The apprentice–master relationship, however, presupposed a close bond. The master teaches the apprentice step by step, and leads him or her to maturity in the faith. For early modern parents such responsibility also extended to servants, who like their children were to be taught to love God, to pray, fast, and thus become fully participating Catholics, notwithstanding regular disciplinary efforts.[51] Most of all, children and servants would learn from them the reality of marriage as a mutual giving of oneself to the other.[52] Despite daily struggles and conflicts, they were meant to glimpse the "first" wedding feast in which, as a Capuchin preacher pointed out, God himself led Eve "under heavenly music" to the altar.[53]

The apprenticeship, which also included the godparents, helped "form and purify" the desires and temperaments of the next generation.[54] Additionally, regular confession by the whole family led to a spiritual cleansing comparable to a "good spa,"[55] a contemporary advised. Much depended of course on the confessor. If he had pastoral compassion, he could contribute to his parishioners' spiritual rebirth, assuming the role of the physician or midwife (*obstetricante manu*).[56] Nevertheless, it was the parents who had to show their children that it was matrimony "in which God has set up his tent, and . . . that when both come together with pure conscience . . . they do so in his name."[57] It was from them that they learned the importance of discernment, so that they would not marry the wrong spouse and live together like "the damned in Hell [who] torture and curse each other for all eternity."[58]

Catechesis of adults also involved basic information about medical facts, such as the danger of suffocating babies by placing them in the marital bed or the risks of miscarriage.[59] Given the high child mortality rate during those days, consoling the grieving was a common task for the priest. A homilist described the pain he witnessed: "You pull your hair from your head—you cry, you yell, you scratch with your nails your face every time a child of yours dies—you act in despair!"[60] For many parents whose children died before the age of seven, the assurance that they would immediately be received into Heaven would have been a real consolation. Unbaptized children of this age group, however, were believed by most theologians to go after their death to Limbo, a place of eternal contentedness, although some argued they would go to Heaven.[61]

In order to ensure that most children were baptized right after birth and for the priests to be aware of problems that could occur in pregnancies, a number of textbooks were published, the most famous perhaps being Francesco Cangiamila's Sacred Embryology of 1751. It not only outlined the duties of priests and doctors for both pregnant women and their children but also informed the clergyman what a miscarriage was and how it could occur. After all, it was the priest who would hear about it in the confessional and had to judge the responsibility of the parents or warn them of risky behavior if he witnessed it. Such rudimentary education was necessary because a priest would not have known much about either female anatomy or biology. Cangiamila's book taught him to be alert when seeing a pregnant woman fast or wear a tight dress, both endangering the child she was carrying. In the confessional the priest must have heard countless times women expressing guilt about a natural miscarriage. With the knowledge derived from books like Sacred Embryology, often cited in manuals of moral theology, the priest could counter such self-accusations and assist in spiritual healing. Moreover, he could also reject the popular belief—in some areas—that miscarriages were produced by demons.[62] Nevertheless, embryology correspondingly made the priest aware of the many ways in which abortions were procured. He therefore had to keep his eyes open (apertissimis occulis) for any suspicious activities occurring in his parish, and if necessary, address these from the pulpit.[63]

If a dying child had missed baptism due to either the parents' or the priest's negligence, a spiritual homicide (homicidium spirituale) had been committed.[64] Those responsible were therefore in mortal sin. In order to avoid such tragedies, the priest ensured that somebody else could administer an emergency baptism. In most cases this was done by the midwife. The members of this profession were after all frequently taught about the ritual by the priests and instructed to use the correct baptismal formula.[65]

A more difficult problem posed the question of whether a delivered fetus without recognizable human form should be baptized. Cangiamila answered in the affirmative and recorded the case of a sixteen-day-old, miscarried fetus, who since showing signs of life, was baptized. This practice, though, seems to have terrified women during their menstruation that they might have miscarried.[66] Caring support was also offered if a woman gave birth to malformed children such as in acephalous births, often referred to as "monstrous births" by contemporaries. The pastor was advised to presume the fetus had a soul and thus baptize it like everybody else.[67] Despite the fact that some children died without baptism and thus never entered Heaven, Cangiamila emphasized God's love for the unborn (charitate erga nonnatos). Not only would unbaptized children most likely go to a state of eternal pleasantness, called Limbo, but until the middle of the eighteenth century, church authorities also condoned visits to pilgrimage shrines where stillborn babies were (allegedly) restored for a moment to life, just long enough to be baptized.[68]

## Instilling Virtue and Character in Children

The fact that both parents and clergy desired "obedient and respectful children who would grow up to participate in the sacraments of the church and fulfill their obligations to the community,"[69] made them natural allies. Already in sixteenth-century Italy, volunteers began to teach children doctrine but also rudimentary reading and writing, yet only in the eighteenth century did compulsory schooling become (also because of Enlightenment policies) a pressing concern. The French archbishop Alexandre Talleyrand-Perigord stated in 1788:

> Children are the most precious part of Christianity, the resources of the church and the state; it is in the cultivation of these young plants that a pastor can begin the renewal of his parish, and without attention to the children, the pastor will never complete this work. Scripture and experience confirm this truth and teach us that the first impressions are the most

lasting that a man has; he does not stray from the path that he entered in his youth even in old age. When he has received from his earliest years the principles of integrity and religion, he usually conserves them for all his life. Thus, nothing merits our attention, and the attention of the curés more than the establishment and the conduct of schoolmasters, who are charged in part with the education of children.[70]

Educating children was therefore key to "renew[ing] the whole world" and the church, as the sixteenth-century German pedagogue Matthaeus Tympe stated. Such schooling therefore had to focus on the formation of secular as well as religious virtues.[71] Parents who let their children "grow like trees in the forest" and thus without proper character formation, failed their God-given responsibilities.[72] Only good schooling could immunize children against evil.[73] Such character formation also ensured that children would one day make good, conscientious decisions about marriage or religious life,[74] free from parental pressure or physical force.[75] Parents and teachers should take their roles so seriously that they could imagine themselves as educators of princes.[76]

> When God gives you children, he gives into your responsibility an un-formed mass. You, however, are commanded to bring this flexible matter into form and shape. If you fail, the result will not be a human but a wild and irrational animal, yet if you do what is expected of a good father by God and society, you will make not only a human, but a creature which will find esteem similar to the gods.[77]

Prayer informed the education of children not only because it gave them knowledge about the ends of life and of morality but also because it safeguarded the grace received at baptism so that it would continue to grow in their lives. It ensured that children would grow in virtue and withstand temptation.

One of the most dreaded temptations was illicit sexual behavior. The fear behind this was that an adolescent boy would be incapable of controlling his sexual urges if he did not learn to do so at a young age. Thus, guidebooks emphasized this aspect, in particular books written for the Jesuit Marian student congregations. Philippe Berlaymont's *Paradisus Puerorum* of 1619 can serve as an example. It addressed all teachers of boys and laid out a map of "pastures" where their "souls" could flourish in virtue in sexual purity.[78]

Different in style but similar in aim was Bernardino Rosignoli's treatise, which identified intemperance as an educator's greatest challenge. The teacher therefore had to shield the young from bad sensual influences and emphasize the abhorrence of sexual impurity. For Rosignoli, students were soldiers in a "spiritual war" against the "seeds of vice" within them. Only by imitating the saints could they win in this struggle.[79] Since the Jesuit knew how difficult such a fight was, he advised his readers to better avoid such circumstances altogether. It was much easier to flee them than to withstand them. If one was nevertheless caught up in such a situation, one should fall and genuflect, cry out to the Virgin Mary, and "seal the heart" with the desire for good and holy thoughts. Behind this advice stood the theory that only things, which the mind allowed to enter the heart, could stir up a desire. By closing the heart with the help of the mind one could therefore halt the desire. Consequently, anything that could leave a strong impression on the mind, such as lascivious images, was dangerous because once they entered the mind they were almost impossible to extirpate.[80]

Fleeing and resisting a vice was, however, only half the battle. The other half consisted in a positive formation, attracting the mind toward the Good and the virtues.[81] Supportive communities especially were believed to instill and augment good desires. Accordingly, the motto for Jesuit high schools and student congregations was to "combine virtue and knowledge."[82] There, a young man could encounter a group of chaste and smart peers, who supported each other's aspirations for virtue.[83] Chastity was so valuable, Rosignoli explained, because it tamed one of the strongest human yearnings. Consequently, chaste people were a bit like the asexual angels,[84] who were endowed with heroic fortitude and strength.[85]

## The Everlasting Battle with the Passions

Adults were also admonished to keep up their struggle against the passions and presented with methods to channel them. Most important in this contention, contemporary authors insisted, was knowing the depths of one's own soul. Thus, the French priest Charles Gobinet regarded it the "the science of sciences" and the key to spiritual transformation: The better one knew one's passions and desires, the more one could follow virtue and avoid evil.[86] Such evil was found not only in bad intentions and actions but also in *disordered* passions. The Jesuit Johannes Pelecyus,[87] for example, compared such desires to a disease that demanded urgent medical care: "We are born with this fever. It grows with us, we feed it, and it gets stronger over time."[88]

Pelecyus, as well as most other writers, based their system of character formation on the traditional, largely Aristotelian understanding of the soul. They held that the soul had two desires (or appetites), a *sensitive* and an *intellectual* one. The intellectual appetite moved the body through rational acknowledgment of good or evil, while the sensitive appetite of the soul allowed the body *to be* moved by lust or repulsion for sensory goods. Only the latter were properly called *passions* because of their largely receptive character, especially those which tended to overpower the human will easily.

Active intellectual self-movement was morally more valuable than mere passivity. Consequently, formation had to focus on making the intellectual appetite the dominant force of the soul, because it could tame the passions. Without such control they became disordered and led to sin. While the pleasures of the passions are only short-lived, those of the intellect mirror God's attributes and are thus—in principle—infinite. Yet, in a "fallen world," the sensitive appetite is so strong that it subdues reason. Consequently, a human has to constantly fight against it, because it otherwise corrodes the intellectual soul. While passions overwhelmed the will, *affects* became powerful because mind and will chose them voluntarily. They were the pleasures of the intellect. Such "holy affects," (or affections) together with reason, were believed to keep the passions in check.[89]

The early modern Catholic theory of affects and passions is closely intertwined with the renaissance of Stoicism in the sixteenth and seventeenth centuries. Yet for most Catholic thinkers, Stoicism was by itself insufficient to cultivate the passions and bring about a lasting character change. Only the sanctifying grace of Christ could do that, Pelecyus argued.[90] Frequent meditation would ensure the influence of grace on the soul: "The meditation chews the divine dish, cooks it with the heat of love, and then offers it as food to all others."[91] Other means the Jesuit recommended were frequent prayer, which "captures divine grace,"[92] and the mortification of the body. These practices would help to acquire the holy indifference praised by Jesuit writers: "If one does not desire something particular, one cannot be disappointed."[93]

The emphasis on forming one's character in the virtues and taming the passions continued throughout the eighteenth century. Catholic Enlighteners, however, added a new element when they underlined the importance of "good taste" for the moral life. Muratori defined it as the power to understand and *judge* what was defective or good in the sciences and arts. Following the idea that the soul had cognitive and volitional faculties, three powers of the soul affected human engagement with the sciences and arts—namely, intellect, memory, and desire. For memory to work properly, intellect and desire had to be sound: "Neither a vivacious imagination nor a fortunate memory is able to unite with a miserable intellect or an evil desire; neither one nor the other can create heroes of the Republic of Letters."[94] Only a harmonious cooperation of all the soul's faculties would produce scholars with "good taste," who serve the common good.[95] Such focus on the common good enticed Catholic Enlighteners also to increasingly identify "excessive leisure" as the root of poverty and immorality. Being active and productive gained the attention that previous generations had given to sexual purity. Consequently, work began to be seen as influencing the human character just as much as sensory impressions or passions.[96]

Marriage and family were of central concern to church reformers. Although they did not redefine its characteristics, they brought about a successful retrieval of medieval sources that centered around the mutual companionship of the spouses and not just procreation. While clergymen increasingly took over the responsibility of educating children in the faith, parents continued to shape the child's faith formation at home. The virtues of obedience and chastity were especially emphasized in their education. Methods of self-control were taught that intended to prepare the young generation with means for their self-transformation. Parental obedience, however, found its limits when it came to choosing one's vocation. Parents who forced their offspring either into marriage or a monastery committed a mortal sin and thus "spiritual homicide."

# 6

# Lay Movements Transforming the Church

Confraternities or sodalities were no invention of early modernity. They had existed under the patronage of a saint or a religious mystery, such as the Eucharist, for many centuries. Yet while medieval confraternities placed seemingly few demands on a person's spiritual and moral life, the Catholic Reform infused zeal and rigor into these communities.[1]

## Almsgiving and Praying for the Dead in Confraternities

A confraternity possessed a privileged space in the public sphere. This could be observed at its annual feast days, on holidays, and particularly during processions such as those on Corpus Christi, but also in churches or chapels built and sponsored by confraternities. They embodied the belief that society was subservient to supernatural ends. Membership thus often also meant an improvement in social and religious status. In Munich, for example, the confraternity of St. George possessed the most coveted, last place in the Corpus Christi procession—its exclusively aristocratic members walked before the priest, who carried the monstrance.[2] Nevertheless, confraternities did not influence religious life only in Europe: they were a global phenomenon that also responded to local needs. For example, in seventeenth-century French North America, Marguerite Bourgeoys founded the female *Congrégation des Externes* in Montreal in 1658 to support the work of the Congrégation de Notre Dame. In Mexico City in 1750, about one thousand Spanish confraternities existed, of which several dozen were designed for Africans and natives.[3]

Entering a confraternity was mostly a public religious act. New members were usually received in a ceremony. Sometimes even a "vow" was recited in which one promised to keep the confraternity's rules and obligations. Canonically this was merely a promise, because official vows were only those of the evangelical counsels of poverty, chastity, and obedience. Handbooks laid out what religious exercises and behavior were expected from the

*The Inner Life of Catholic Reform*. Ulrich L. Lehner, Oxford University Press. © Oxford University Press 2022.
DOI: 10.1093/oso/9780197620601.003.0006

members. Catholics chose congregations to extend their social networks, but also to find temporal and spiritual support. What role the religious benefits (e.g., indulgences, funerals) of a confraternity played for its membership, or whether spiritual preferences influenced membership decisions, is largely unknown. Yet each confraternity had a specific profile, was dedicated to a saint or a religious mystery, and offered similar but sometimes also substantially different services. The Trinitarian Confraternity in Vienna, for example, raised money for freeing slaves from captivity in North Africa, and practiced unique invocations to the Holy Trinity.[4] The members of the Carmelite Scapular Confraternity imitated the virtues of faith, hope, and love as manifested in their patroness, Our Lady of Mount Carmel.[5] The Dominicans emphasized in their Holy Rosary confraternities the fight against "human viciousness"; while the Franciscan Confraternity of the Cord (confraternitas Chordae) encouraged the radical imitation of St. Francis and permitted its members to wear a belt made out of rope underneath their clothes.[6] The latter also offered their members a plenary indulgence every month if they went to confession, took communion, and partook in a Franciscan procession. Spiritual benefits such as these were quite attractive, because one could not only free one's own soul, but also those of loved ones from the fires of Purgatory.[7]

Besides personal preferences for certain devotions, an established motive for joining a confraternity was the fear of punishment after death. Early modern Catholics believed that if one died in the state of mortal sin, one would go to Hell. Regular confession alleviated this fear,[8] but also the idea of a well-prepared death with prior absolution and reception of the Eucharist. If one died with venial sins, one had to endure the pains of Purgatory but would ultimately enter Heaven. Since Purgatory was a period of cleansing whose final destination was certain, it could be shortened if the living gained indulgences and said prayers for the souls undergoing purification.[9] Confraternities offered such indulgences, prayed for living and dead members, and sponsored Masses for the deceased, which were believed to be of infinite value for the poor souls in Purgatory.[10] Membership also encouraged forming good habits, such as frequent confession. It not only consoled but also kept one's conscience clean:

> Just like a room which you sweep and clean daily will remain long pure, because one brushes away the daily dirt without much effort. Yet, if you sweep only once or twice a year, you will see that the room will be . . . like a

pigsty. . . . Then it has to be cleansed with hot water and iron brushes . . . to make it an honorable room again.[11]

Printed confraternity books presented clear instructions on how to avoid vices, excel in virtues, and grow in faith. Thus, the fulfillment of membership requirements assured the person could *reasonably expect* to be among the elect in Heaven. Especially during the heyday of Jansenism, which taught a rather grim outlook on the salvation of the faithful, such assurance was sorely needed in order to sidestep despair. Moreover, since official Catholic teaching did not acknowledge absolute *certainty* about one's future fate, such indirect, yet powerful assurances were consoling for many. Evidence for being among the chosen was one's remorse over sin, prayer, devotion to Mary, or dedicated engagement in a confraternity. Moreover, these printed texts also disseminated officially approved devotions and thus contributed to the reduction of superstition. The texts aligned the readers more closely with an increasingly "centered" devotional culture.

A confraternity was a society of its own and had different members than one's parish, although they could to some degree overlap. Its norms mirrored those of an "honorable" parish member. Thus, confraternities took on the role of smaller "parishes," intensifying their demand for spiritual renewal. Yet while the dead were quickly forgotten in a parish, a confraternity vowed to pray for their deceased often for generations. Benefits, such as ten or twelve Masses for a dead member, were especially desired: nothing was more effective for easing the pains of Purgatory than participating in the fruits of the Mass. The cost for such services was covered by a small admission fee and an annual gift. Brotherhoods that offered special benefits, such as solemn funerals, often had a tiered membership structure, similar to insurance plans: the more one initially paid, the more ostentatious was one's funeral. Prayers for the dead were, however, not merely a means of acquiring money but also a work of mercy. Many—yet not all—confraternities therefore focused almost exclusively on it and consequently neglected other works of mercy, such as feeding and clothing the poor.[12] For them, "enflaming the members with love" (*charitas*) meant first and foremost having them pray for the dead. Since such a practice, like every other work of mercy, was done out of love for God, it was considered meritorious for one's salvation because it satisfied the debt created by one's sins.[13]

Nevertheless, there were still many confraternities that engaged in social charity, such as giving bread to poor families, visiting prisoners, or providing dowries for poor girls.[14] Endowing such efforts raised one's social profile and allowed especially women a sphere of influence.[15] Such benevolence also had a side effect: it exculpated the giver from doing the charitable works herself.[16] This consequence might also be a key to understanding the increasing focus of late seventeenth- and early eighteenth-century confraternities on prayers for the dead.[17] By donating to them one fulfilled the obligation to give alms. Yet instead of giving alms to the poor and getting nothing in return, in a confraternity one received a reciprocal benefit—namely, securitized prayers. For Catholic Enlighteners like Ludovico Muratori such behavior was hypocritical. Even the Jansenist Pierre Nicole agreed with him: "If one refuses support for the poor from one's abundance, one acts as unjustly as a person who refutes paying his debtor."[18] Yet, unlike Nicole, contemporaries viewed many poor as undeserving. This was a rather new perspective that had gained increasing traction since the late seventeenth century. It differentiated between the poor that deserved help and those that did not. Giving to the latter was immoral, because it kept them idle and thus from pursuing work. This view even motivated an eighteenth-century Mexican bishop's tirade about beggars in his cathedral. For him they were merely "lazy:"

> The lazy person is a sponge that receives in itself all poison, a pump that attracts all filth, a toadstool where all serpents are harbored, wax in which is impressed and sealed all bad judgment. . . . Catholic without religion, Christian in name, and ultimately an obstacle to human life, bothersome to all, useful to none, harmful to himself. He lives mechanically, without aim in his steps, without plan in his activities, and without rationality in his speech.[19]

Problems with charitable work notwithstanding, many confraternities provided exceptional services for their members. The brotherhoods of African slaves in Central and South America, for example, not only provided for the healthcare and burial of their members but also established a space where indigenous traditions could be openly celebrated.[20] In North America, confraternities were founded among the Iroquois, Huron, and Mohawks, and allowed women like St. Kateri Tekakwitha of the Mohawks to create a space of self-determined agency. Kateri and her friends desired to imitate the life of Mary and thus made vows of perpetual virginity. This, however, made them outcasts from their tribal societies. Yet these celibate women proudly advertised their status by marking their bodies like slaves: "They covered themselves with blood by disciplinary stripes with iron, with rods, with thorns, with nettles . . . they put glowing coals between their toes, . . . disfigured themselves . . . in order not to be sought in marriage."[21] Others merged Christian elements with their native religious belief system. Catholic Mayan confraternities, for example, practiced devotion to Mary and the saints by imitating traditional worship of local, protective divinities.[22] Such devotion included food offerings, festive anniversary celebrations, and sometimes even fireworks. Confraternities such as these protected the native population from societal problems and offered them a place where their native values could be preserved.[23] Although the overall trend after the Council of Trent was to put confraternities under clerical control, their traditional supervisory boards and enormous resources made such control often difficult. Instead of strict control, it seems to have been rather rudimentary oversight, which therefore allowed these communities some autonomy.[24]

## Transforming Society through Marian Sodalities

The Society of Jesus founded new confraternities that spread quickly all over the world. They had a distinct profile that allowed considerable lay participation under the leadership of a clergyman. These Marian sodalities successfully co-opted "the restless religious energies" of the male population.[25] Founded in 1563, two hundred years later they counted around 2,500 local chapters. Even more impressive was the number of members: in a major city like Antwerp, which had about 55,000 inhabitants in 1664, the sodality counted 4,000 followers. Some calculations indicate that in major Catholic cities, every family had at least one member in such a sodality. Thus, these congregations played a decisive role in disseminating Catholic piety.[26] The sodalities understood themselves as a peaceful Catholic militia serving church renewal. A contemporary explained it this way:

> The whole Congregation resembled a vast army; each sodality, like a military body, consisted of a dozen legions which were divided between an equal number of districts of the town, with their own leaders and deputies. And if we may continue the comparison, each army corps had its general staff, composed of the chief dignitaries of each sodality, with its meeting place on the premises of the Congregation under the vigilant eye of the chief directors.[27]

For a member of this Marian militia, intellect and will became a "temple of Mary's glory,"[28] in which one desired not only virtuous self-transformation but also the missionary zeal to share this piety with others.[29] Such proselytizing was particularly successful when it was done in one's own social class and profession.[30] Annually, the members participated in abridged *Spiritual Exercises*, which allowed them to further deepen their experience of vocation.[31] The Jesuit sodalities should first and foremost be regarded as achievements of Catholic Reform,[32] providing not only methods of spiritual self-improvement but also the opportunity for profound religious experiences.[33]

All Marian sodalities were local groups of the main sodality in Rome. This created a virtual community with its center in the Society of Jesus, which was also the center of Latin Catholicism. The sodalities shared a common rule, and their success was due to the missionary zeal of their members, who formed a network for spiritual apprenticeship.[34] The members not only prayed together but also engaged in works of mercy, such as feeding the poor and visiting prisoners. Thus, they echoed in zeal and rigor the Third Orders (see following section). For the Society of Jesus, they were so important that St. Peter Canisius proudly called them the means "for a transformation of Christian society in its entirety."[35] Despite a strong lay leadership, the head of a sodality was always a priest (usually a Jesuit), who like a responsible officer ensured that his "soldiers"[36] sanctified their own families and neighborhoods.[37] Besides their veneration of Mary, and a strong Christocentrism, sodalities also engaged in other spiritual practices that contributed to self-awareness and self-transformation. A good example is the practice of imitating every month a different saint and his or her dominant virtue. Beginning in the 1590s, this practice allowed members who were presented a printed image of the saint in the monthly sodality meeting, to imagine themselves as the holy person and imitate his or her virtues. The result was not only a stronger bond with the saint but also an increased awareness of one's own shortcomings. Moreover, devotions such as these helped less educated members, who could not read elaborate tomes about virtue, to learn good habits by example.[38] How successful the self-transformation of sodality members was on a large scale is impossible to assess. Nevertheless, there exists indirect evidence, such as the commitment of members to their congregation. The most impressive example might be the sodalities of Japan. After the expulsion of all Catholic priests from the islands in 1612, the remaining Catholics flocked to the Marian sodalities, which took over the formation of future generations of believers. Sodality members baptized, catechized, heard confessions—albeit not being ordained—buried the faithful, and prepared themselves and others for martyrdom. These "secret Christians" persevered for over two hundred years until priests were again allowed to enter Japan.[39]

Besides the sodalities, the Jesuits also founded a number of other confraternities.[40] The *Compagnia della Grazia* was erected in 1542 to help prostitutes mend their lives and discern a possible religious vocation.[41] The *Compagnia delle Vergine Miserabili* helped the children of "dishonorable" women, sometimes collecting them from the streets. Its house was also run like a monastery, aiming at spiritual transformation:

> Other companies, according to their good statutes either endeavor to heal wounds or nourish and sustain bodies. Yet our company, almost lifting itself higher, not only nourishes the bodies, but conserves the innocence of the bodies, and souls, and secures them from desperate men. Who knows how many scandals, rapes, and almost indefinite sacrilege would be committed if our company did not collect and preserve these young virgins? Other companies, and truly with great merit, will present to the sight of angels of God the human bodies made sound, but ours will present the souls, which are of a higher worth ... the souls that are freed and preserved from innumerable sins and the mouth of the inferno.[42]

## Third Orders as Places for Secular Superachievers

Although already popular in the Middle Ages, Third Orders enjoyed their peak in early modernity. Their decline in numbers toward the end of the eighteenth century does not necessarily mean a sudden aversion to this piety, because state laws in many countries began restricting or discouraging membership.[43]

Third Orders enabled laypeople to participate in the benefits of religious orders, such as indulgences and Mass intentions. The name "Third Order" (or Tertiary Order) differentiated them from the first and second orders of solemnly vowed priests, brothers, and nuns. According to Pope Benedict XIII (r. 1724–1730), one had to distinguish three degrees *within* the Third Order. The bottom included secular persons—married or unmarried—of both sexes; the second, those who lived together in communities without vows; and the third contained those whose communities had simple vows. The official aim of the order was not to improve the morals of society (*mores reformasse*), and thus differed from the sodalities, but to assist those seeking spiritual perfection.[44] While all members understood themselves as doing penance, the term *poenitentes* (*penitents*) was only used for those members living in a *vowed* community, or who had taken vows as individuals. Another name for them was "regulars" because they observed a specific religious rule and did not just consider it a pious suggestion.[45]

Tertiaries sometimes went under many different names (e.g., Mantellati, Corrigati, Pizzocharae, Cordellati) but were laypeople and thus subject to the same canonical rules as all other laypersons.[46] Yet, by being "called" to be "holy in the world," they understood themselves as a tool of Catholic reform, of being witnesses to spiritual perfection in society.[47] Since the members met more often than a usual confraternity and fulfilled a demanding spiritual routine, one must assume that membership was due to both a spiritual attachment to a particular religious order—for example, being transformed into a mirror image of St. Francis[48]—*and* the extraordinary spiritual benefits these orders promised.[49]

Although the communities of Third Orders have received much attention, not so the members living *in* the world, the *seculars*. These were "a middle state,"[50] as some religious writers called them, whose members lived a "God pleasing life of penance so that they would more easily and securely obtain salvation."[51] Married, widowed, or single Catholics could join, and sometimes a member could join a cloistered community as a *donada* (see what follows).[52] An early modern Franciscan explained that the Third Order was preferable to any confraternity, because it was an approved *form of living* (*modus vivendi*) within the church, mirroring a specific religious order and aiming at the transformation of the whole person.[53]

Moreover, only those who had proven themselves worthy during a novitiate and who were thoroughly examined by a priest of the order were allowed to enter the Third Order. The Jesuit Marian sodality also had such a "novitiate." Third Orders were therefore much more exclusive than regular confraternities. After satisfying the demanding membership criteria, one received the "habit" and after a year of probation was allowed to pronounce the "profession." These elements, however, confused many historians.[54] For seculars, the habit was *not* the regular long vestment a friar wore, but merely a large scapular. Members wore it mostly under their clothes. Only in the coffin could they be robed in a full habit.[55] The profession after the novitiate was legally speaking also not a vow, but merely a solemn reiteration of one's baptismal promises,[56] even if some orders added the agreement "to keep the obligations of one's state, and if one is unmarried, to remain in it, or if one is married and becomes widowed not to marry again."[57]

Like friars or monks, seculars were expected to avoid the theater, especially comedies and public dances, not carry weapons, and to fast from meat Mondays, Wednesdays, Fridays, and Saturdays.[58] The expectations for members varied, however, according to their abilities. Seculars with children or sick family members were dispensed from fasting. They were also not expected to come as frequently to confession and communion. Even the daily prayer obligations could be adapted. Nevertheless, a monthly meeting was common to all, usually organized by the monastery of the order, where one listened to a spiritual talk by a priest.

Membership in a Third Order also allowed women who could not follow the standard expectation of a *beata* to promise chastity, poverty, and obedience, a way to obtain spiritual progress. A particularly interesting example is the life of Anna Guerra de Jesús of Guatemala. As an abandoned wife and mother, she was not able to take vows. This, however, did not prevent her from creating her own religious identity, which was particularly challenging due to her poverty and her mixed racial background. Membership in the Third Order of the Franciscans allowed her and other poor, "lost women" to build a relatively self-determined religious life that was accepted by authorities. Anna saw herself as a harbinger of God's mercy and described her vision of God as an eagle, "sheltering his little chicks under his wings . . . and he told her: these are the sinners that have returned to me and you are one of them, see how I take them into my shelter, do not fear, because whoever is protected by my wings, will never be lost."[59] Anna Guerra was one of many. Research suggests that in Spanish America, women made up about two-thirds of the members of confraternities, and most likely the same is true for Third Orders.[60] Often they taught their insights to female followers in very pragmatic ways. St. Rosa of Lima, for example, is recorded as having shown her devotees a printed image of the devil, which she then threw to the ground and fiercely stamped on. Less symbolic was St. Rosa's teaching that women had to find God even in the most mundane actions, such as embroidering. In China, where embroidery was also a traditional Buddhist devotion, Catholics also adopted it and used it for a nationwide charitable network.[61]

Such apprenticeship instruction avoided conflict with male authorities because spiritualized gender-stereotypical practices avoided everything that looked like theological teaching. The women did not appear as teachers and thus did not challenge priestly authority. Instead, they showed themselves as *exemplary* women, worthy of imitation.[62] Other female religious leaders and reformers, such as St. Teresa of Avila, had developed similar niches for their doctrine of self-transformation. The foundress of the Carmelite Reform, however, had to defend her written teachings more robustly than St. Rosa. After all, a papal legate charged her with being a "restless gadabout, a disobedient and contumacious woman, who . . . taught others, against the commands of St. Paul, who had forbidden women to teach."[63] Therefore, St. Teresa adopted a deliberate rhetoric of submissiveness, which exploited contemporary gender stereotypes. She only styled herself as unskilled and uneducated so that the authorities would not charge her with "teaching"![64]

Third Orders also impacted the spiritual life of Catholic women in Tudor England. After the end of organized Catholicism due to the penal laws, it was largely women who preserved the old faith. Third Order practices allowed them to experience a "virtual" community among the dispersed Catholic families on the island as well as in exile. A common rule of life and prayer connected them.[65] Married women like St. Margaret Clitherow, a secular of the Dominican order, or Anne Dacre Howard, recited the breviary hours and thus turned their households into quasi-monastic communities.[66] Also in China, women organized devotional networks and erected domestic convents, which ensured the religious formation of children and families.[67]

At the end of the eighteenth century, however, even the Third Order niche was increasingly distrusted. For the gender-specific norms of that century, the growing number of women who desired to live independent but devout lives disrupted the traditional family structure. Popular sentiment turned even more strongly against them when fears of a demographic collapse increased. Therefore, even the Archbishop of Cologne restricted Third Order membership in 1786: only financially independent women past childbearing age were allowed to become single Third Order members with vows.[68]

## The Devotional Practices of Third Orders

Religious orders published countless guides and handbooks for their Third Orders, either in Latin or the vernacular.[69] Homilies were also often distributed, read, and discussed among the members.[70] Most of these guidebooks paralleled the monastic breviary, but were much shorter.[71] They thus allowed the member to experience participation in the life of the order while living as a layperson. The prayers they contained sanctified the day because they infused every hour with pious thoughts and molded the members into religious superachievers.[72] Yet, despite being caught in the middle between laity and religious life, Third Orders largely avoided creating normative conflicts. For example, while vowed religious lived in perfect continence, a married member was not expected to embrace flawless chastity, but merely what was demanded of every Catholic—namely, to reject lust.[73] Likewise, while rich members or royalty such as Queen Catherine of Aragon were expected to generously give alms, they did not have to abandon all private property like a friar.[74]

The understanding of the Third Order as a way of living penance, and thus of a transformed life, was explained in detail in William Stanney's rules for the Third Order of the English Franciscans of the Strict Obedience (1671).[75] The order, he explained, was called to demonstrate God's "vehement desire" for the love of humanity. Yet, since humans had responded to this call with sin, penance became necessary.[76] Without penance, a sinner could never successfully overcome sinful habits. It was by penance that a Catholic cut ties with the devil. A secular person could not have a better place to live such penance than in the Third Order. There, he or she could gain God's benevolence.[77] Since penitential acts were ridiculed by Protestants, Stanney had to ensure that the members had a proper understanding of penance and did not fuel anti-Catholic sentiments. True penance was motivated by love for God and *not* by the fear of damnation. God asked for a person's heart and not for a superstitious service:

> But if peradventure this demand may seeme to be so hard, that it cannot be fulfilled, for that God demanding our whole heart, demandeth there with all our will, in such fort, that there is nothing left to our owne other affaires.[78]

Another often-recommended method to efficiently fulfill one's obligations was meditation on the passion of Christ. This mystery of faith should be remembered during all seven prayer times of the day. By the help of easy-to-memorize verses, one learned to see one's own prayer as a sacred "sacrifice."[79] For example, at the *prima* one could meditate on the false accusations against Christ and pray especially for the pope and bishops; at the *tertia*, meditate on the flagellation of Christ while praying for all Christian kings to take up arms against the infidels; at the *sexta* remember Christ as the Lamb of God being slaughtered while praying for the order, and so forth.[80]

## Devout Women and the Ideal of "Submission"

After the Council of Trent, women experienced a renaissance of religious fervor.[81] They desired to have a place in the Catholic Reform just as the other members of the laity, of whom Adrien Bourdoise wrote: "God had to raise up the laity . . . to do the work of idle priests."[82] Small groups of such devout, often married women, usually under the direction of a priest, not only began to change their own lives by taking on a rigorous life of penance but also transformed their families and social networks. Some felt so inspired that they founded communities of their own, which catechized or offered services to those in need. The seventeenth-century French nun Mary of the Holy Trinity (Sévin) described her calling this way:

> I felt such a pressing desire for the salvation of all the world that I wished that my sex did not prevent me from going to preach the Kingdom of God to the most barbarous and abandoned people, so as to announce to them the redemption of all.[83]

Apart from the recognition of gender boundaries that impeded women in following their vocation as missionaries, Mary's statement alludes to a solution to her dilemma—she changed the object of her desire. Instead of going to the "most barbarous and abandoned," tantamount to mission territories, she now redefined missionary work as service for others in her immediate neighborhood.

Yet not only women from the higher echelons of society but also the poor desired to change their lives through a more profound participation in the faith. A remarkable example of this is the seventeenth-century French maid Armelle Nicolas. Five years after her death in 1671, an Ursuline from Vennes, Jeanne de la Nativité, published a hagiographic account of her life, which she called a "triumph of love." Armelle's simple piety consisted of giving God preference in everything and submitting to his will, which also meant accepting suffering. She made the claim that if God loved her, a poor chamber maid, and had given her so many graces, then everybody should trust him, whom she invoked as "my Love and my Everything" (*mon amour*

& mon tout).[84] Armelle's love of God was so pure and simple that it predated any deeper theological knowledge. Her statement "Although I do not know you ... I burn with love for you," summarizes this mysticism.[85]

Inspired by religious literature and confirmed in their faith by small prayer groups, devout women also initiated a remarkable change in spirituality. While submissiveness to one's husband had been an established gendered expectation, early seventeenth-century women like Barbe Acarie turned it into a deliberate choice of self-mortification, and thus undermined the prejudice of "feminine weakness."[86] *Intentional submission* now signified strength of will. It embodied the virtue of total obedience to God's will, and often included the patient suffering of an abusive marriage.[87] Despite the fact that this practice did *not* challenge male authority and thus prolonged paternalism, it gave these women a tool of spiritual self-empowerment. One could *choose* to see one's suffering as a good, and thus make sense of one's life. The Capuchin Benoit of Canfield explained how such submission could be learned and lived, and especially what it entailed. He envisioned it as containing three steps. On the first, the soul merely reached conformity with the *exterior* will of God as it was expressed in the laws of state and church; on the second step it reached conformity with God's *interior* will, experienced through prayerful enlightenment. The third and final step was achieved when the soul was finally perfected to conformity with God's *essential* will, and thus was in total union with Christ. Canfield's ideas widely influenced devout women and helped them to articulate self-determined plans for their lives. A good example of this is the *Company of Mary*, which the contemporary of Madame de Acarie, Luisa de Carvajal, modeled after the Jesuits. The female members of her community considered themselves *companions* and not sisters, and thus occupied a place between lay and religious life. The companions assisted Catholic prisoners in London and emphasized in a vow their total *submission* to the will of God, even to the point of martyrdom.[88] Also, married women who were passionate about their faith found Canfield's theology attractive because it energized their passion to work for the church. Their zeal was often so enthusiastic that it raised suspicions of heterodoxy.[89]

In England where Catholicism was officially outlawed, these married women took on leadership positions for the sanctification of their households, because their husbands conformed to the practices of the Church of England. This was also one of the main reasons why in England a wife was permitted to join a Third Order without her husband's permission.[90] The stamina of these women was often described using male adjectives, demonstrating how their strength in faith challenged gender prejudice. Such a woman overcame the "limitations of her sex" and became like St. Teresa of Avila "not only a masculine man but one of the manliest [los mas barbados]."[91] Nevertheless, the practice of linking certain virtues exclusively with males also demonstrates how the practice of submission reinforced gender stereotypes. After all, a woman had to become like a man to merit such descriptors.

Since religious orders could only accept a small number of novices and the number of marriages also decreased, the sixteenth and seventeenth centuries witnessed a swelling number of unmarried women. Many of these were devout (devotae virgines) but did not want to remain maids in their parents' households. Especially in the Netherlands and the German-speaking lands, groups of such women congregated to set up a common life "in the world yet not of the world" (in der welt nit weltlich). Their small communities engaged in charitable work like Beguines or Third Order communities.[92] These devotees, however, showed as a special characteristic an eager desire to imitate Christ by being on pilgrimage in the world (peregrinatio pro Christo). By identifying with this old medieval tradition, they legitimized their active work in society, but also adapted it to the needs of their time.[93] The integrity of these women, soon called beatas in the Spanish-speaking world, captured the attention of the most famous writers of their time, such as St. Francis de Sales or St. Vincent de Paul. St. John of Avila, the famous Spanish reformer, even wrote his celebrated Audi, Filia in the 1530s for a beata. Avila's disciple Diego Perez de Valdivia continued assisting them with a massive 700-page tome.[94]

Avila and Valdivia recommended recogimiento or recollection as the foundation of a beata spirituality (see chapter 8). In this Franciscan devotional exercise, the person placed herself in the presence of God whatever the situation. Missionaries also disseminated this method in South America, where it became a synonym for semireligious penitentiary houses.[95] Nevertheless, the new form of community life threatened conventional norms, as Valdiva acknowledged: "They are women and most of them are young; they have as much freedom as they want; they have no superior; they do not observe enclosure; they do not have a fixed rule; . . . each one is a law unto herself."[96] Despite his criticism, Valdiva did not reject their lifestyle, but insisted that they establish some norms for their community life. Of particular importance for him was that the beatas live "in a secluded and safe fashion,"[97] which fulfilled the societal expectations for "protecting" unmarried women from sexual improprieties. Church authorities had demanded that nuns live in a cloister for very similar reasons. The pressure on the *beatas* to adopt more restrictive norms was therefore an attempt to force them into the self-understanding of a religious "order" and accept the cloister.

After all, their lifestyle did not fit into the existing categories. Even the famous seventeenth-century Jesuit Hermann Busenbaum struggled with the question of how to define their calling. Nevertheless, for him the *devota* stood on a higher level than secular persons. Thus, she should be seen as analogous to the diocesan secular clergy standing above the laity.[98] This view, however, created another normative expectation; namely, that of direct obedience to a local bishop, because the secular clergy were sworn to that. Criticized from all sides, the *beata* communities, such as the *Congregation of Notre Dame*, understandably caved and decided to transform into habited religious orders.[99]

Although one could argue that forcing devout women into the "cloister" was a consequence of the Council of Trent, the history of the notorious 1563 decree on the cloister demands a nuanced interpretation. It certainly prescribed the enclosure for nuns (*moniales*), but *not* for members of a tertiary order (*poenitentes*). Moreover, even cloistered nuns had ways of circumventing the Tridentine rules, and often renegotiated enclosure successfully.[100] In 1566, Pius V clarified that all women who desired to be regarded as *religiosi* had to live within a cloister—also tertiaries. Nevertheless, the pope left a loophole open. Instead of explicitly demanding they live in a cloister he merely "admonished" that it was the better choice. Thus, wherever women found that a cloister would make their charitable work impossible, they could ask the local bishop for a simple dispensation from the pope's vision for them.[101] Not really being monastic and not following the papal precepts, these new communities also had to convince local communities of the integrity of their vocation.

Such a struggle can be seen in the history of the *St. Catherine Sisters*. Founded by Regina Protman of Braunsberg in East Prussia in 1571 as a lay movement, it developed into a community with simple vows but without a habit. The members were dedicated to the care of the sick and therefore could not and did not want to live in the cloister. Nevertheless, the new lifestyle caused distrust. Such suspicion increased more when Protman decided to pen the rules of her community herself. Only the patronage of Cardinal Stanislaus Hosius, himself a participant in the Council of Trent, saved the congregation.[102]

Likewise, the *Company of St. Ursula*, founded by St. Angela of Merici in 1535, was originally not a religious order but a confraternity. Members lived without vows in the world and came together for prayer, meals, and charitable work. Nevertheless, the members insisted on living the evangelical counsels of poverty, obedience, and chastity in the world, similar to tertiaries.[103] St. Angela's rule gave the women guidance in spiritual transformation and for their work serving the Catholic Reform.[104] Although obedience to the local bishop and the confessor was mentioned in her rule, its context suggests that it was secondary to the obedience to the Holy Spirit, which each member experienced individually.[105] Since the Holy Spirit was traditionally understood as the source of wisdom and knowledge, it is not surprising that the Ursulines stressed teaching as their particular charism. They understood it as the extension of their prayer life into the world—*peregrinatio pro Christo* once again. A seventeenth-century Ursuline described their motto thus: "To remove souls from vice and instruct girls in virtue, to teach them Christian doctrine and piety, to engrave in their hearts both the love and fear of God, and to form them to the exercises befitting to their sex."[106] Ursuline independence, however, lasted only until the rule was rewritten in 1582, in which the role of guidance by the Holy Spirit was diminished. The community in France was already forced in 1610 to accept a habit and become a regular religious order.

*Devotas* or *beatas* were, however, not only married women or virgins, but also widows. Living with likeminded females allowed groups like the one founded by Ludovica Torelli in the mid-seventeenth century to live free from the expectation of pleasing a second husband.[107] They valued their freedom immensely, as a widow explained: "Please pardon my frankness, when I tell you, where marriage is concerned, I obeyed once, and in obeying I bound myself to love the world more than Heaven, and vanity more than piety. . . . I shall stay in the freedom that my condition allows me now."[108] By 1532, Torelli's group had moved to Milan, where priests who called themselves Barnabites joined them, while the women named themselves *Angelics*. Both groups stressed conversion to God, dressed simply, and engaged in the display of public penance. In 1537 the women were molded into a second order under the authority of the Barnabites but kept ministering to the sick and marginalized. The prayer life of the Angelics was strict and included the traditional eight breviary hours.[109] Nevertheless, the community was still quite secular insofar as many of the widows had *not* taken the second order vows and had misgivings about the authorities' push to force them into the cloister. Therefore, the boundaries between professed and unprofessed Angelics remained blurry, and thus enclosure could not be enforced.[110] After becoming the spiritual leader of the sisters, Paola Antonia Negri also began to impress the Barnabites. By 1544, she was referred to by both communities as "Divine Mother," to whom God had entrusted authority over their congregations. The Barnabite priests even allowed her to supervise the penitential "guilt chapters" and made her appear as if she had priestly powers to hear confessions and forgive sins.[111] Unsurprisingly, the Inquisition of Milan used this practice to force the Angelics into strict supervision. It imposed the cloister upon all female members and stopped their charitable work. In its eyes, the experiment of open female and unvowed religious life had failed. The rules for female religious communities that the Provincial Councils of Milan under the leadership of St. Carlo Borromeo now developed, however, became the standard for the Catholic World for the next few centuries.[112]

Particularly in France after the 1630s, the influence of penitential, ascetic spirituality was replaced by one focusing on charitable causes.[113] Unlike the Ursulines, some of the newer female communities were able to defend their original character as *filles séculières*, as the *devotas* were called in France. The most successful were the *Daughters of Charity* of St. Vincent de Paul and St. Louise de Marillac.[114] In order to avoid the cloister, the Daughters, who focused on the poor, sick, and needy, only pronounced simple promises, which did not qualify as vows and rejected any categorization as a religious order. One followed the advice that St. Vincent de Paul himself had given in 1645 to Marillac: "We have judged it appropriate to leave you with the name of society or confraternity . . . for fear that, if the title congregation was given to you, people would some day start wanting to turn the house into a cloister."[115] In all conversations Marillac had with bishops, who tried to force her into accepting enclosure, she shrewdly circumvented questions about their religious status and instead specified that they were merely "poor Daughters of Charity . . . given to God for the service of the poor."[116] The enormous success of the Daughters of Charity therefore seemed to lie in an almost tacit challenge to the established criteria of religious life: While new congregations for women sought a modification of the cloister but still had a rigorous community life, the Daughters saw their life as a modification of the secular—though more ordered and more devout. It was this strategy that protected their freedom.[117] The self-understanding of the society was expressed by de Paul as such:

> They should consider that although they do not belong to a religious order, that state not being compatible with the duties of their vocation, yet as they

are much more exposed to the world than nuns; their monastery, being generally no other than the abode of the sick; their cell, a hired room; their chapel, the parish church; their cloister the streets or wards of hospitals; their enclosure, obedience; their grate, the fear of God; and their veil, holy modesty—they are obliged on this account to lead as virtuous a life as if they were professed in a religious order; to conduct themselves wherever they mingle with the world with as much recollection, purity of heart and body, detachment from creatures; and to give as much edification as nuns in the seclusion of their monasteries.[118]

The *Daughters of St. Genevieve* (*Miramionnes*) were another such community, founded in 1660. It disseminated Adrien Bourdoise's ideal of the "living parish." The Daughters understood themselves as more perfect parishioners that tried to positively influence a community, but like the Daughters of Charity not as religious sisters. The Miramionnes set up parish workshops for the poor and needy, decorated churches, and taught children. Unsurprisingly they did not have their own chapel, did not wear uniform clothes, and avoided everything that would distract them from fulfilling their parish duties:

This community esteems and respects the religious profession; nevertheless, having been advised . . . to consecrate itself to the secular state . . . it prefers this state to all others. . . . And the superiors must always reject as temptations all proposals which might be made to quit or cut back these exterior functions.[119]

The endurance of the secular women's movement must also have encouraged many others to imitate their lifestyle. Therefore, priests also tended to individual devout women, who came together for religious events. In published homilies, every once in a while one finds sermons dedicated to such events. In 1696, for example, a Capuchin priest in Cologne compared the transformation of a virgin to a *devotessa* with that of a crawfish into a scorpion. While the crawfish looks fearsome but is harmless, the scorpion looks friendly but bears a deadly thorn on his back. The meaning the priest extracts from this image is one of scornful admonition: devout women often appear kind, but stab others in the back. Then, however, he turns positive when he points to the scorpion's behavior when one lays a ring of fire around him. He will try to escape by looking for an exit. Like the scorpion, the devout women are surrounded by the dangers of the world that try to destroy them. Yet they look in vain for an exit on the ground. Only by acquiring wings through grace can they escape the fire: "And thus, this is the office of the devout: to stand at all time before God in his presence and to be always found close to those things, which are the Father's."[120] An eighteenth-century homilist expressed similar misgivings, albeit about the affability of *devotas* with clergy and laity, hinting at sexual improprieties.[121] It was, as he acknowledged, often priests who abused their position of power to assault devout women seeking spiritual counsel.[122] Nevertheless, the service and witness of the "world-spiritual or spiritual-worldly virgins," as these semireligious were called, was highly valued. With remarkable tenderness, the Capuchin Peter Hofer described the *devotas* as analogous to the hair of Christ. Like hairs are rooted in flesh but are not flesh, the virgins stand in the world but are not of it, and like hair grows from proper nutrition, so they grow through their virtues.[123] Moreover, the hair on one's head is closer to the head than all other body parts and moves closest with the head, who is Christ himself. "Likewise, the pious virgins have to be strongly connected and rooted in Christ and follow him in everything."[124] Growing hair humbly falls down, and likewise the virgins practice humility. Nevertheless, like hair is easily ripped out but becomes strong in a knot, so the virgins find empowerment in a community.[125]

Such self-determined female religious life also became an attractive option in non-European territories. In Japan for example, it allowed the former Buddhist abbess Naito Julia (martyred in 1627) to continue a religious lifestyle, spiritually aided by the Jesuits. A contemporary described the little community she founded as one concerned with spiritual perfection but also missionary outreach: "Usually, she taught non-Christians doctrine, catechizing them so that they would be converted to our holy faith . . . and at the same time, she attended to the teaching of Christians . . . and she was so busy with these holy ministries" that she never found time to undergo the Jesuit *Spiritual Exercises* herself.[126] The strong faith of these *bikuni/beatas* earned them high esteem among the Christian population, and by 1612, the beginning of the end of the *Kirishitan* movement, the 600,000 Japanese Christians provided strong support for them. What attracted these women to Catholic doctrine was probably that unlike Shinto-Buddhism, Catholicism emphasized their self-worth and the love of God. The *beata* lifestyle allowed them an independence they could have never had in traditional Japanese society. It permitted them to form bonds with women of other social classes as well as to obtain leadership positions. Only after 1607, when the *Tokugawa* shogunate began strict gender segregation, did the women's missionary activities decline. After their expulsion, the noble *bikuni* of Miyako resettled in the Philippines in Manila, where they established a cloistered community on their own terms: since there were no more Japanese women to be catechized, their apostolate of teaching had ceased.[127]

Frequently, devout women also lived in cloistered communities without being professed members. They had decided to dedicate their service to the community. In exchange for their work these unmarried *donadas*, as they were called in Spanish, received spiritual counsel from nuns. Often, the *donadas* were members of a Third Order. Ursula de Jesús of Lima, of African descent, had come as a slave into the monastery of St. Clara, Lima, where between 1617 and 1645 about 130 slaves worked and lived. After gaining her freedom in 1645, she offered herself as *donada* to the monastery, where she fulfilled the work of a maid and learned methods of prayer and meditation. Later, she joined the convent as a professed member.[128]

Yet not all pious women who were enthusiastic about their faith wanted to be identified as "devout" because they regarded some of these circles as too indolent and lax. Especially in France, a rigorist countermovement began to spread in the seventeenth century. Its members expressed their dissatisfaction with the church's lack of spiritual care for them.[129] Many of them were sympathetic to Jansenist ideas and preferred intensive mortification of the body to contemplative prayer.[130] These rigorist women often also did not share their practices of self-transformation with their husbands, nor ask for their permission to engage in them. Even in their written correspondence, men are largely absent. Instead, they focused on female friendships and spiritual networks.[131] They manifested a robust emancipation from male authority and the creativity to mold their own spiritual vision for women.[132]

The two hundred years from the Council of Trent to the French Revolution saw a variety of lay movements come into existence and shape the face of Catholicism. Throughout the world, confraternities helped to organize devotional ethnic and social groups in order to carve out spheres of influence and self-determined piety. Yet, such groups also fulfilled regular Christian duties, such as charity, albeit in a more organized way. While most confraternities served only specific groups and had a rather small influence on personal transformation, the Marian sodalities of the Society of Jesus aimed at changing society. By creating local chapters of their sodalities in every major city, they became tools to influence the masses. Focusing on the veneration and imitation of Mary, but also a solid Christocentrism, these congregations manifested a clear confessional profile and provided an arrangement in which members could learn and live the virtues. Third Orders were similar to the Marian sodalities. These communities allowed laypeople living in the world an affiliation with a religious order and its spiritual benefits and enabled them to imitate the monastic lifestyle they venerated within the modest means of their own households. While not geared toward a conversion of the masses, but rather seen as a vocation for few, the Third Orders had enormous influence due to their vast number of members. Apart from these organizations, women also flocked to small circles, often under the guidance of a priest, to intensify their prayer life. Some began small communities without a cloister and explicit vows, but dedicated to a life of service, while others focused on their own spiritual progress. Especially the ideal of the *devota* or *beata*—that is, of a vowed single woman, living a life of prayer and service outside a monastic community—found imitators all around the Catholic world and produced some of the most remarkable mystics of the time.

# 7

# Eucharist and Confession

Even before the Council of Trent, a number of theologians had argued that the faithful should receive communion more often in order to fully grow as members of the church. They considered it a major element of successful church reform because it aided the spiritual transformation of the recipients. But "frequent" communion meant for most Catholics during the sixteenth and seventeenth centuries merely more than once, and thus usually only a few times a year. Weekly or daily communion was rare, St. Francis de Sales explained, although the Jesuits successfully motivated the members of their Marian congregations to receive at least twice a month.[1] It was, however, not just Jesuits who promoted more frequent reception, as the works of sixteenth-century writers Bonsignore Cacciaguerra and Luis de Granada show.[2] For the latter, a Dominican, the communicant should approach the communion rail out of love for God, but never out of "spiritual greediness ... with an appetite to 'feel' God."[3] Only a heart stirred by such love could follow Christ: "We transforme our selves into him, and do make our selves one same thinge with him, by imitation and followinge of his most Holie life."[4] Despite such encouragement, most of the laity received communion only once a year during Easter, when it was obligatory. Such reluctance was mostly due to fear. After all, the faithful were taught that if one consumed the consecrated host in a state of grave sin, one committed a sacrilege that deserved eternal damnation. Contemporary catechesis had emphasized this aspect so heavily that many were terrified of receiving the Eucharist and therefore tried to communicate immediately after confession.

## Preparing for and Receiving the Eucharist

The Council of Trent's desire for more frequent communion by the faithful depended on the frequent use of the confessional because the recipient was to be free from any serious sin. Bishops therefore admonished priests to make themselves available for hearing confessions and to recommend it to

*The Inner Life of Catholic Reform.* Ulrich L. Lehner, Oxford University Press. © Oxford University Press 2022.
DOI: 10.1093/oso/9780197620601.003.0007

their parishioners.[5] Simultaneously, catechists stressed that reception of the Eucharist was the best way to transform the self into a person pleasing to God. Hence, frequent communion was seen as necessary for such a change. It alone had the power to defeat the "rabid temptations of the flesh."[6] Countless books provided help to prepare for communion with prayers and meditations. While most described spiritual transformation through the Eucharist as one of change and growth, Giovanni Battista Novati's *Eucharistici Amores* used erotic imagery, comparing communion with supernatural nuptials.[7] By the eighteenth century, *daily* communion for religious "superachievers" became common. The Italian Cesare Franciotti proposed that such communicants could increase the effectiveness of their prayers by dedicating the fruits of their communion to different intentions. On Mondays one could offer them up for the dead, on Tuesdays for one's penance, and so on.[8] The infinite number of fruits could be stored in a supernatural treasure house, which especially French Eucharistic confraternities emphasized. Nevertheless, they also seem to have contributed to a Catholic mindset of spiritual acquisitiveness. [9]

Growth in virtue, especially in chastity, was considered a clear sign that one had received communion in a state of grace. Consequently, such sexual purity was also expected from the priest who celebrated the Eucharist. Although the validity of the sacraments did not—according to church doctrine—depend on the moral status of a priest, a clergyman's sexual improprieties nevertheless undermined popular belief in their authenticity. A good example is the complaint of a Mayan Catholic from 1774. He doubted that bread and wine would change into the body and blood of Christ if the priests engaged in sexual activity.[10] This widespread attitude raises the question whether parishioners expected to experience a change in their own sexual attitudes after receiving the Eucharist or became disillusioned if they did not. Apart from certain sexual behavior, other actions were also considered sinful. Often, however, the faithful did not know enough about the norms for receiving the Eucharist and in fear of committing a serious sin either refrained from acting, ignored church teachings, or gave in to scruples. While rigorists claimed one could only act in full knowledge of the norms, Jesuit moral theologians realized such an approach overburdened the faithful. They could not be expected to analyze business transactions or interpersonal behavior with the depth of an ethicist. Therefore, Jesuit probabilism provided a way out by contextualizing sin and culpability. It gave people more freedom for their actions. If a good reason (*probabilis opinio*) for action existed and one was uncertain about a norm, one could follow such a reasonable choice of action. Rigorists, on the other hand, allowed only actions which known norms prescribed or permitted.[11]

Jansenists, however, found the practice of frequent communion problematic because they did not believe that most recipients were in a state of grace. Their most prominent voice, the seventeenth-century theologian Antoine Arnauld, therefore asserted that frequent communion could *only* be spiritually fruitful if the communicant *experienced* an intense love for the Eucharist. If such love was missing, it was sacrilegious.[12] The Jesuits believed Arnauld's demands to be unsatisfiable by most faithful and therefore rejected them. The Jesuits argued that God had merely demanded that communicants be free from serious sin but not that they were perfectly holy, as Arnauld seemed to suggest. After all, for them the Eucharist was not a prize for the virtuous, but a medicine for the sick. The faithful, who were caught in the middle of the conflict between Jansenists and Jesuits, often avoided choosing between sides. Instead, they asked their confessor to recommend how often they should receive communion.[13]

The connection between eucharistic spirituality, moral transformation, and belief in a merciful God also became apparent in the early modern interpretations of psalm 23 (Vulgate, Ps 22), which was included in many communion handbooks: the pastures to which the shepherd led were the remedy for eternal life, the Eucharist. Christ himself converts the soul (Ps 23:3), takes up his dwelling place in her, and renews and revives her through the Holy Eucharist.[14] Since this psalm was also frequently recited in catechism classes, homilies, and hymns, a rudimentary knowledge of its imagery can be presupposed even among the illiterate. Another image that the communicants were given as a help to focus on their inner development was that of the Last Supper, at which the Eucharist was institutionalized. The priest advised his flock to imagine themselves as receiving—like the disciples—the very "first communion" from Jesus's hands, and encouraged them to invite the angels to join their celebration.[15]

An inexhaustible storehouse of imagery existed for the sophisticated reader. Printed emblems with meditations, like those of Louis Richeome, promised to rediscover the sacrament in new depth. Each image was carefully crafted, containing several layers of meaning that the accompanying text patiently peeled away. His first symbol showed the tree of life in paradise. Richemone described water, air, soil, plant, and animal life in order to create a vivid impression. This was followed by a typological interpretation: paradise was a figure for the church, and how the "sacrament of the body of the Son of God was planted on the whole world" and became the source of life.[16] The second image emphasized the priesthood of all believers by invoking the sacrifice of Abel and Cain. Not only should the two brothers be imagined sacrificing, but rather the entire community (including the reader) as they offer their prayers, tears, and joys, since "not only the priests, but every Christian should sacrifice on the altar of his soul, like Abel."[17] Consequently, Melchizedek is the theme of the third image. He was considered to be the prototype of the ministerial priest, sacrificing to God bread and wine.[18] Not surprisingly, the fourth image was that of Abraham offering Isaac, a typology for Christ's death on the cross. The fifth was the Easter lamb, the sixth the manna in the desert.[19] The seventh image was of the bread of presentation in the Jewish temple, which prefigured how Christ offered his life for the world.[20] The eighth image was the offering of the first fruits, the ninth the ash bread of the prophet Elijah.[21] The tenth image brought the reader to the sacrifice of reconciliation in the sanctuary of the Jewish temple (Lev 4), demonstrating that the Eucharist was the one and only sacrifice, superseding and replacing all others.[22] Only the eleventh figure introduced the reader to the world of the New Testament; namely, Jesus's miracle of the five loaves and two fishes (Mt 14).[23] The twelfth was about Jesus's own words about his body in the Gospel of John (ch. 6),[24] the thirteenth about the washing of the feet (John 13).[25] Richeome was one of many who propagated such emblematic eucharistic theology. With its help Catholics encountered throughout their life a vast number of images, which served as associative bridges to doctrines, but also anchored their religious experience in their memory. By hearing repeatedly of such images, singing about them, and perceiving them visually in paintings and frescoes, a believer could acquire a deeper spiritual knowledge of the Eucharist, and reflect on it for inner reform and growth.

Perhaps the greatest pedagogical difficulty an early modern catechist faced was publicizing the Eucharist's power to sanctify the soul, while avoiding making it appear as a superstitious "tool" for moral change.[26] Using the Eucharist in the latter sense was considered sacrilegious, and therefore catechists emphasized the need of Catholics to develop a sincere desire for the Eucharist. It was this desire that Arnauld had exaggerated in his writings. The expression of this yearning was a late medieval practice, called *spiritual communion*, which could replace sacramental communion and then became a *communion of desire*. As a mental act it had the power to transform the will by eliciting a fervent love for God, and consequently establish true remorse (*contrition*).[27] The churches of the Reformation despised this devotional practice, which in turn made it a confessionalized identity marker of Catholics.[28]

Spiritual communion was also somewhat like eucharistic adoration, another medieval devotion that peaked in early modernity. In addition to the mental focus, adoration added visual contact with the object of desire by adoring the exposed host in a monstrance. Although every child was taught this piety in catechism class, not everybody experienced Jesus "strolling through one's soul" and thus an intimate, pleasureful presence of God, which the seventeenth-century Oratorian Francesco Marchese described.[29] Nevertheless, it was a practice appealing to a large audience, including the illiterate, because it was visible and merely demanded attention. Although adoration remained quite popular throughout the eighteenth century, St. Alphonsus of Liguori thought it underutilized as a way to fall in love with God. He therefore published in 1745 an extremely popular booklet, still in print today, in which he showed that this form of prayer was especially suitable for anybody who desired to grow spiritually.[30]

Although the sacrifice of the Mass was offered through an ordained priest, it was considered the actualization of the one and only sacrifice of Christ and not its repetition. Nevertheless, it was licit to view the sacrament under three distinct perspectives. In the first it appeared as the sacrifice of Christ himself; in the second as the sacrifice offered by the priest representing Christ (*in persona Christi*); and in the third it was the sacrifice of all the faithful, representing the body of Christ, the church.[31] This third meaning became crucial in explaining to Catholics their participation in the Mass. The laity was not merely watching an event unfold in the sanctuary but played a role in it: all were called to unite their prayer with the priest. By doing so, they acted with him, and thus "like" a priest. A seventeenth-century homilist therefore advised: "Unite your intention with that of the priest, that is: *sacrifice* with him this holy sacrifice and do it as often as possible."[32] Certainly, lay participation in the Mass was purely a matter of intention, apart from possibly offering a stipend,[33] yet it shared with the priest an important component. Although the clergyman acted liturgically, he was also uniting *his* intentions with another "person"—namely, the whole church. Both priest and laity thus integrated their intentions into a larger whole.

In practical catechesis, however, this theology of participation was usually underdeveloped. One reason was certainly the difficulty in explaining it properly. If one said, like the sixteenth-century Franciscan Johann Wild, that all believers were "priests," one risked being censored for sounding "Lutheran."[34] Even a master pedagogue like St. Peter Canisius avoided it in his catechisms for minors.[35] Instead of giving a clear outline of what lay participation and priesthood of believers meant, most catechists remained elusive like Bossuet, who stated in his children's catechism that the church sacrificed "in the body and blood of Christ . . . the prayer of all the faithful . . . and herself—the head and all members."[36] Bossuet carefully avoided attributing the verb "sacrifice" to the laity and only assigned it to the entire church and the ministerial priest in the following paragraph. Yet by doing so he obscured that all the faithful participated in the priesthood of Christ. Only rarely would a theologian during this time attempt to explain such a teaching.[37] The fear that the laity might confuse it with the Lutheran/Calvinist *universal* priesthood was too great. The seventeenth-century Jesuit Louis Bourdaloue was a rare exception. He encouraged his listeners to see themselves "offer together with the priest the Eucharistic Sacrifice whenever they are present."[38] The priesthood of believers, he explained, meant that every baptized Catholic was God's servant. Yet this office did not make a specialized, ministerial priesthood superfluous.[39]

Individualized devotion and the integration of one's intention into the liturgical prayers ensured preparation not only for communion but also the ritual of the Mass itself. It prescribed at its beginning the penitential act of the *Confiteor*, the acknowledgment of sins and the asking of God's forgiveness. The prayer, which was said by the priest and the Mass servers, who represented the faithful, also had a place in a pious family. Having been taught the vernacular version in catechism classes, the laity recited it at home, before confession, communion, and before receiving last rites on the deathbed. A priest would enunciate it not only at Mass, but also twice daily during praying his breviary hours.

Apart from preparing the person to feel remorse for one's sins and expressing belief in the mercy of God, the *Confiteor* also established a connection to Rome and the papacy. After all, its traditional Roman text was enshrined in the *Missale Romanum* of 1570 as the standard version for the Catholic world. This text, however, invoked not just the Mother of God, but also Sts. Peter and Paul, St. John the Baptist, and St. Michael for their intercession. While Sts. Peter and Paul were the patrons of the papacy as well as the church of Rome, St. John the Baptist was the patron of the Lateran Basilica, considered the "mother" of all Latin Catholic churches. By reciting the text, a Catholic therefore acknowledged Rome as the center of the

Catholic world. Consequently, the Curia only allowed a few alterations to the *Confiteor*; for example, adding St. James in Spain, or St. Augustine in the Augustinian order.[40] The addition of St. Michael demonstrated how intensely one hoped for angelic support against evils, especially what was branded as heresy—Protestantism.

The *Confiteor*, however, also conserved the communal aspect of sin. It not only asked God for forgiveness and the saints for their intercession but invoked *all* fellow Catholics to pray for the individual, too, thus acknowledging that one's sins had offended the entire church, in the world and in Heaven. While French and Spanish Catechisms seem to have implemented the Roman text from early on, some German catechisms failed to mention Sts. Peter, Paul, John, and Michael until the middle of the seventeenth century.[41]

## Healing Scruples with a Message of Hope

The Catholic Reform desired to make the church holier. Seen from the perspective of the French historian Jean Delumeau, this implied imposing a monastic contempt for the world onto all members, thereby overwhelming many. One consequence was the ubiquitous catechesis about Hell and guilt as well as the enumeration of sins in confession. Perhaps therefore the exponential increase in scrupulosity since the late Middle Ages should not surprise the historian. Yet would it be accurate to say that the church "created" this problem? It certainly contributed to it because fear was an accepted and widely recommended pedagogical tool to elicit the beginning of a conversion, but as pointed out before, "terror" was only one part of the dialectical pattern of fear *and* mercy. Nevertheless, most early modern theologians did *not* see the preaching of fear as problematic and therefore condoned tilting the dialectic in its favor. This, however, caused agonizing scruples among mentally volatile parishioners (in the sources characterized as "melancholic") and those with malformed consciences.[42]

Most commentators of the time distinguished three categories of scrupulants. The first obsessively thought about the sins they had *committed* and felt they did not receive or could not receive forgiveness. The members of the second group deliberated obsessively about *avoiding* sins, while the third *exaggerated* them. Priests, many of whom suffered themselves from scruples (including in his early days St. Ignatius of Loyola), addressed this affliction.

Yet as a famous ascetical writer once remarked, it was hard to find a good confessor, because too many were "stupid, and have neither wisdom nor prudence."[43] It is therefore not surprising that the moral theology textbooks of the time, the casuistry manuals, listed numerous scenarios for how a priest could diligently address the issue in confession.[44] Despite these widely available resources, many pastors were negligent and often increased scrupulosity among their parishioners, either by being unavailable for confession, being impatient with penitents, imposing overpowering penances, or by preaching rigorist ideas.

European scrupulosity also made its way abroad and became a global challenge. Already in 1723, an anonymous treatise against scrupulosity was published at the urging of the local ordinary in Mexico. It identified ignorance and "secret pride" (*occulta superbia*), inordinate fear, and physical character as main causes of the disorder. Yet, it also considered the influence of theological books. The laity especially, the text argued, would be driven to scruples by devouring works of moral theology, because they would suddenly identify actions as sins they had never even thought about. Supernatural causes for scrupulosity were for the Mexican author of minimal interest— just as everywhere else.[45] The best remedies were to let go of extreme forms of devotion, clinging instead to "sane and right doctrine," listening to one's confessor and meditating on divine goodness and mercy. Then, the scrupulous person could begin to judge fairly and overcome the illness.[46]

Scrupulosity, however, was far from being a problem merely for the laity. Many priests and members of religious orders suffered from it, too. Nevertheless, a religious usually had a superior who could intervene if he or she observed problematic symptoms. Novices were instructed in how to alleviate scruples by frequent conversation with a spiritual counselor or by objectively charting their sins according to frequency and severity, and to create trust in God.[47] The latter could be achieved by focusing on the presence of God, or as Thomas de Jesu said, to "carry the one and true God present so that you are surrounded by his majesty always."[48] This method, popularized by the seventeenth-century Carmelite Brother Lawrence of the Resurrection, allowed an individual to see all good actions and intentions as participating in the merits of Christ, and thus gain an experience of comfort and consolation.[49] The Jesuit Jerome Gonnelieu also considered it one of the most effective methods for fighting scruples.[50]

Apart from the more general care for scrupulous persons, early modern Catholicism also produced a great number of authors who dealt with the problem of scruples theologically, trying to instill the image of a loving and merciful God that would lead to inner peace. For example, the 1718 book on confidence in the mercy of God by the French bishop Jean-Joseph Languet de Gergy was translated into several languages and frequently reprinted. Of all divine attributes, the bishop lamented, humans knew the least about mercy.[51] Fear of divine justice had led many to give up hope for salvation or saddened their hearts and soured their tender (*tendresse*) love for God. Yet, only in such tender love could the Christian hope to address God as "abba, Father."[52] Consequently, the believer had to leave fear behind and accept love and hope as guides, realizing that the "clement God who could have forced us into his service, has invited us through the sweetness of his love."[53] The Catholic could learn such confidence, Gergy stated, by acknowledging the attribute of divine goodness, a goodness that extended also to the sinner. Such confidence would be meritorious and a means to salvation.[54] The bishop did not deny that divine justice was *terrifying*, but he insisted that God was *more merciful* than just, and that Christ was in fact not just a judge, but also a person's friend and brother.[55] Unlike a secular judge, the divine judge had an interest in the defendant being rewarded—namely with eternal life—and therefore desired to win over the person's heart.[56]

The approach of the Capuchin Ambroise de Lombez was very similar. His treatise on *Inner Peace* (1758) was widely read in German, Italian, and Spanish, and in the nineteenth century also in Dutch and English, with reprints well into the twentieth century. Ambroise avoided aligning himself with any extreme theological position, and instead continued on a course of moderation. Scrupulosity and despair over one's salvation should be addressed, he thought, by leading the person to inner peace. Such peace was the peak of Christian perfection. It strengthened the "Kingdom of God in us," made humans able to participate in the divine life and endowed them with the gift of discernment.[57] The transformation to this inner peace, however, required self-awareness about one's affections, passions, and temperament, and the eradication of anything immoderate, including "impetuous zeal."[58] Scrupulosity was for Ambroise a *natural disease* and therefore he recommended natural remedies. The primary antidote was to convince the scrupulous person to think less about her affairs, and more about the glory of the divine light, which would dispel all fear.[59] The virtues of humility, patience, faithfulness, and moderate zeal would not come about by excessive mortification, because this practice most often led to spiritual defeatism. "God demands nothing from us than giving him preference," and therefore acceptance of his will alone was required.[60] Surprisingly, Ambroise revealed stronger affinities with Jesuit theology than most Capuchins of his time, who praised bodily mortification. To clarify, he did not reject the latter, but emphasized *internal* mortification; that is, of mind and will. Should, for example, passions arise in a person, the believer should subtly reject them so that they dissipate, but not inflict pain on the body to achieve this effect. One should flee to God's mercy and "lock oneself in with God," quietly awaiting his gift of peace. Such waiting (*attendre*) for Christ meant first and foremost giving the Divine preference in all, but also avoiding precipitous actions, such as "walking ahead of God" (*prevenire*).[61] The Capuchin was convinced that the more the human heart loved God, the more its passions would subside and be conformed to the divine will.[62]

The question of why, despite such powerful efforts, scrupulosity still remained a pervasive problem in Catholic parishes until the end of the eighteenth century (and well into the twentieth), becomes all the more interesting. Did use of fear necessarily bring about scruples? Was perhaps the early modern talk about scruples exaggerated? And does the scrupulosity of the nineteenth century have different roots than early modern scruples?

## Distrust, Contrition, and Remorse

For an early modern Catholic, the root of all vices was pride, not only because it was traditionally blamed for the fall of Adam and Eve, but also because it sidetracked even a devout person. In moments of intense prayer, it could suddenly fill one's heart with noxious presumptuousness.[63] Only distrust in one's own powers and abilities could prevent such pride. Such doubt also had an intrinsic connection with penance because the sacrament required contrition for one's sins and the will to abstain from bad deeds in the future. After all, only with supernatural help could the Christian fulfill the commandments in their substance, yet never by natural powers alone.[64]

The possibility of falling into *superbia* was nevertheless ubiquitous and therefore demanded, especially for someone seeking spiritual perfection, decisive steps. The most recommended action was to consider oneself the lowest, a "useless servant," who only fulfilled the commands of God.[65] Such a stance, however, was only possible after defeating the effects of pride—namely vainglory, hypocrisy, and ambition. Vanity was the vice that most easily entangled saintly persons because it tricked them into trusting in their own virtues.[66] Pride produced the desire to be praised for piety, and thus hypocrisy.[67] Ambition resulted from restless discontentment due to a prideful desire for more.[68] Only firm, obedient surrender to God's will could keep pride and its effects in check.[69] For the member of a religious community this advice suggested unquestioned submission to superiors, while laypersons would have been expected to be obedient to their confessor. Trusting in one's own powers was considered tantamount to eclipsing one's own sins,[70] and thus a clear path to Hell.[71]

A consequence of such distrust in one's capabilities was the "virtue of vigilance," which meant the avoidance of the occasion of sin. For a celibate religious this meant, for example, avoiding contact with women, especially eye contact or touching. Nobody was as extreme as the fifth-century Pope Leo I, who allegedly cut off his hand after a woman had kissed it and he had become sexually aroused. Yet, early modern writers praised *perfect* chastity and offered in their manuals advice for countless situations involving one's libido.[72] After all, even theologians frankly admitted that sexual lust overpowered the mind so rapidly, that it was better to avoid situations that could lead to them than to engage in a futile struggle.[73] The strategy pursued by Catholic writers consisted therefore not merely in containing the *eros* and subduing it to reason, but also in avoiding such occasions. Such methods of self-control were buttressed in a religious community by additional surveillance through superiors and peers.[74] The principle of distrust in oneself, enshrined in Lorenzo Scupoli's *Spiritual Combat* (1589), remained the cornerstone of spiritual progress for Catholic self-transformation at least until the end of the eighteenth century. Only then did an increasing number of Catholic Enlighteners question it, because they considered the effects of original sin as less damaging to human nature than had earlier generations.[75]

The image of a spiritual battle conveyed that attention and decisiveness were needed, but also that the way to become a *homo spiritualis* entailed suffering. After all, it was painful to submit all desires to God.[76] Louis de Granada saw the sacrament of penance as one of the best ways to grow in the spirit of submission: by confessing one's sins honestly, one overcame pride, but also showed trust in Christ's mercy and forgiveness. Such forgiveness was real and not an empty phrase. One example might suffice: although nuns could expect severe punishments for breaking their vow of chastity, often they found lenience if they expressed remorse. When, for example, in 1699 a professed nun in Neuwerk near Erfurt in Germany, who had run away with the young organist, became Lutheran and returned nine months later pregnant, she was *reconciled* with the community on the grounds of her sincere confession.[77] This story, however, also shows that early modern Catholic belief demanded a contrite heart to extend such forgiveness. Only those who were sorry for their deeds could be forgiven. Often this was not easy to ascertain, perhaps because one enjoyed the sin or could not find real fault with it. Thus, requesting the *gift* of contrition from God was an important first step, as de Granada explains:

> To come unto Christe is nothinge els, but to love him above all thinges, and to be sorowful for our sinnes more than all other thinges in the worlde: & such love and sorowe no man can have of him selfe. . . . Now for almightie God to graunte this benefite unto a sinner, is the greatest grace, and the greatest benefit that he can possible graunt him. For . . . it is a greater matter to plucke and helpe a man out of sinne, and to sette him in state of grace, than after he is placed in grace, to geve him glorie.[78]

The Dominican maintained that contrition was the prerequisite for receiving absolution but clarified that it was simple to achieve: loving Christ and seeking his forgiveness was sufficient. Both demonstrated that grace was at work in the soul. A second means to elicit contrition consisted in holding "parliament within him selfe." In this exercise the penitent carefully examined his memory to find instances in his life that could provoke repentance.[79] Without such true contrition the roots of sin could not be plucked out and left the Christian vulnerable to evil. Then, however, the believer who should be the "spouse of almightie God has become the harlot of Satan: The temple of the holie Ghost is changed into a denne of theeves. The bridebedde of Christ into a stinckinge puddle of swine: The seate of almightie God into a chaire of pestilence: The sister of Angells into the fellowshippe of devels."[80]

Closely connected with contrition and distrust of oneself was the "fear of God." On the one hand, this very popular term described agony about potential sentencing to the pains of Hell or Purgatory. On the other hand, the theological tradition differentiated very clearly such psychological fear from the fear of God that was considered a work of the Holy Spirit (and was transferred in the sacrament of confirmation). This *holy* fear designated the mindset of keeping the divine commandments and avoiding everything that could offend God. Having such holy fear was a sign of profound love for God, which calmed the soul and gave her, according to St. Teresa of Avila, assurance of being among the saved.[81] Although the sacrament of confirmation was already administered before the Council of Trent, it did not become a widespread sacrament of initiation until early modernity. Preparation for it provided an opportunity to remind Catholics about the "proper" fear of God. In addition, priests were admonished to preach frequently about it in order to disseminate this message.[82]

## Confession as Individualized Pastoral Care

Parishes were responsible for ascertaining that the faithful went to confession before Easter and to communion on Easter. The priests kept records of the number of penitents and communicants. Catholics who preferred a confessor outside their parish could prove the fulfillment of their religious duty by bringing to their pastor a penitence card that they had received. Annual statistics of these events were used by diocesan administrators, especially during a visitation, whether in Lima, India, or Austria, to determine whether a parish priest had fulfilled all his obligations.[83] While neither auricular confession nor the annual obligation to receive it were Tridentine innovations, ensuring that the faithful *actually* went and keeping records was.

Yet, the most radical change of the sacrament pertained to its theological dimension. From the sixteenth century onward, confession focused less on the societal repercussions of sin and more on the individual conversion of the sinner. It became a tool of introspection and spiritual self-transformation, implementing an important insight of the *devotio moderna*.[84] This theological change, however, made it necessary to distance priest from penitent. After all, the penitent disclosed personal information and had to be sure it was not abused. Therefore, the priest was bound by threat of excommunication to remain silent about what had been said in the confessional box (*forum internum*). The increasing veneration of St. John Nepomuk, especially since his official canonization in 1729 as a martyr of the "seal" of the confessional, anchored this belief in the belief of the faithful: a priest would rather die than divulge information from a penitent. If priests broke the seal, they faced serious consequences—but, as Adriano Prosperi has shown, inquisitors especially were often quite lax about keeping these secrets.[85] Beyond such transgressions there was, however, also a legitimate way to intrude on the privacy of the confessional, albeit reserved to the bishop (and in some rare cases the pope). For cases that affected the public (*forum externum*), the *casus reservati* such as clandestine marriages, homicide, and others, the priest could not give absolution unless the bishop had given his permission. Thus, the confessor admonished the penitent to approach the bishop, because the seal would not allow the clergyman to do that. Once the permission was granted, he could absolve the penitent.[86]

This new focus was represented in Borromeo's invention of the closed confessional box. It not only created a distinct space within the church for the sacrament, but also accounted for privacy, and due to a screen also protection from inappropriate sexual advances. Moreover, the box—even an open one—allowed the penitent to confess to the priest without having to directly look at him, keeping him behind the screen in a dark, separate domain. The clergyman's personal features were not perceivable, which reminded the penitent that one confessed to Christ *represented* by the priest, and did not receive absolution from a human, but from God. By pronouncing admonition, advice, and absolution from behind the screen, the penitent could accept the priest's words as if they came from Christ himself. Nevertheless, the privacy of the *forum internum* also allowed the penitent to accommodate the advice he had been given according to his or her own preferences.[87]

Conscience as a person's ability for decision making, the "knowledge of the heart,"[88] was part of the practical intellect. Its decision bound the will to follow the good and avoid evil, but also accused the person if one acted against it. A conscience could be properly formed by natural and divine law, or it could be erroneous or malformed, a scrupulous one counting among the latter. When a Catholic began confessing to a priest she not only accounted for her actions, but also submitted her conscience for review. The priest's role was to judge both conscience and actions in the internal forum of the confessional, deciding whether the penitent correctly identified his or her sins or had an erring conscience. After all, nobody judges one's own sins fairly. The verdict could involve requiring the restitution of goods, demanding that the penitent confess a crime to the authorities, inflicting a censure, or merely giving him or her a penance. All of these aimed at the spiritual healing of the person and inner conversion and were therefore largely categorized as "medicinal." In order to justly assess a penitent's actions, the priest, however, had to be acquainted with the complex horizon of the person's obligations and life situation. While duties in family, church, and society were already often intertwined, the rapidly changing economy and increasingly individualized society complicated things even more. Only a thorough knowledge of secular and canon law could help the clergyman maneuver on the sea of moral dilemmas. Therefore, the Jesuits especially spearheaded the campaign for priestly education about confession, with publications containing a substantial amount of juridical material.

Confession was a hierarchical act between a kneeling penitent and a sitting, listening priest. In principle all penitents were equal in the sight of the divine commandments, regardless of status in the world or church. Everybody confessed to a priest, who represented Christ. Noble or reigning families, however, often had a private court chaplain, who was not only able to spend more time with his clients but was also directly dependent on their benevolence. Thus, these chaplains would at times be more lenient in handing out penances if they wished to retain their position. Clergy likewise went to confession, typically more frequently than a layperson. Members of religious orders confessed about every week.

The penitents were expected to give an account of the number and gravity of their sins, so that the priest could give them adequate penance and advice. This admittance of past transgressions was together with guilt and satisfaction the "matter" of this sacrament.[89] While the handbooks for confessors emphasized the juridical aspects of confession due to the complexities of life, the printed resources that prepared penitents for confession focused on reconciliation with God and spiritual healing. Yet for this transformation to work, it was necessary that the proper "medicine" be assigned, which depended on the priest's role as "judge." His verdict had to be accepted obediently by the penitent, because the priest announced it with the authority of Christ.[90] Even in areas where Catholicism was discriminated against, the sacrament was highly valued despite occasional complaints.[91]

The liturgical rite and the manuals intended *for* confessors show that the sacrament was a rite of spiritual transformation.[92] They demonstrate that the priest was *not* like a secular judge, who after consulting a legal commentary would give a verdict. After all, the pastor did not have his library with him in the dark confessional box. Instead, he knew from his studies what scenarios existed and what a proper response looked like. Thus, during the confession itself he had to rely on his experience and adapt it to a particular case. In uncommon instances he may have withheld absolution in order to consult his handbook, while for the reserved cases (which were all grave crimes such as homicide) he referred to the bishop for permission to absolve the penitent.[93]

Handbooks prompted the priests to pray before hearing confessions. One of the recommended prayers reminded the pastor that God was the author of the sacrament, while he was merely a *conduit* for his grace. It also emphasized his responsibility to make good use of his God-given authority to absolve or

bind. Lastly, it expressed that he was much more than *merely* a judge: "Place
in me the mercy of the father, the experience of the doctor, and the care of the
pastor."[94] This petition illustrates that the sacrament aimed at solace, compassion, and help for the sinner. Admonishing sinners to mend their ways
was included in this task and required the priest to be honest and impartial
like a judge, but the clergyman was also instructed to never insult a penitent or be too harsh. Like a physician, as the texts describe it, the priest was
to prescribe a remedy, but needed to know the exact illness. This permitted
him to ask in the confessional for the exact circumstances of a sin. Yet *every*
manual warned a pastor to avoid appearing nosy or giving the impression of
an interrogation. Such behavior would only intimidate the penitent and keep
the person from honestly confessing the sins. A priest acting against such advice could become the cause of the sinner's damnation and had to bear it as
his own responsibility.[95] A good pastor, however, would gently guide a penitent through questions about sinful behavior or omissions, and elicit in him
the pain of sin (*dolor*) necessary for true repentance. Such remorse was often
elicited by the fear of God's punishment.[96]

A priest had to "apply all his energy and efforts to help the penitent to
have true sorrow for his sins and a determined resolution not to sin again,"
a Mexican manual of 1585 stated.[97] If the pastor did not perceive remorse in
the penitent's words, he was not supposed to absolve. What counted as signs
of true remorse was, however, a disputed theological question. Moreover, remorse was differentiated into two categories. If a sinner experienced it out of
love for God, who had been offended by the sin, it was called perfect *contrition*
(*formata caritate*) and more valuable than the regret experienced because of
the fear of punishment, which was called *attrition*. The debate over which
of these two was necessary to receive absolution spanned almost the entire
time between the Council of Trent and the French Revolution. The council
itself had preferred contrition but also taught that attrition was a gift of the
Holy Spirit that enabled the penitent to receive absolution.[98] Consequently,
the Roman Inquisition censored theologians who argued that contrition was
a necessary requirement. For Thomism, defended mostly by Dominicans,
but also Carmelites and Benedictines, sorrow over one's sins *formed by the
virtue of charity* was already contrition and implied a complete renounce-
ment of sin, while attrition by itself was incomplete. Thus, for this school of
thought it was not so much the *motive* or intention for remorse that was important, but rather the underlying ontological status of the human person;
namely, whether he or she was *formed* by the virtue of charity. Contrition

was redefined and thus allowed more incidences that others may have considered as mere attrition to be subsumed under it.[99] The Jesuits also emphasized the importance of contrition but made clear that even if a penitent only showed attrition, it was no reason to deny absolution, which sometimes happened if the confessor was unsatisfied with the expression of remorse. Such withholding was, however, not seen as a punishment but rather, as Neercassel explained, a wake-up call that should lead the sinner to a rekindling of the love for God. Borromeo had previously recommended it, and in eighteenth-century France Jansenists reprinted his directives approvingly.[100] Nevertheless, this practice left penitents unabsolved and thus in a state of sin. Should they die without absolution, they were believed to face eternal punishment. Contemporaries saw this problem because it was unlikely that somebody could "rekindle" one's love for God *without* the supernatural help of the sacrament. Therefore, most pastoral handbooks advised that if a penitent showed even only signs of disgust for past sins and had the intention to avoid these sins in the future, one should assume that the person's heart was moved by *true contrition*.[101]

The fight over contrition was not limited to Europe. In the American settlements, early sixteenth-century Thomists like de las Casas used it to demand from the conquistadors and *encomenderos* restitution of property to the native population before they could receive absolution. In the Philippines, the Dominican bishop Domingo de Salazar tried to implement the same ideas at the synod of Manila in 1582, but was met with strong resistance.[102] In Mexico, however, where the use of the confessional was quickly adopted by the local population because it had a parallel in their native religion, a fierce dispute broke out over whether the natives showed "enough" contrition.[103] The Franciscans, inspired by the actions of the Jesuit Jose de Acosta in Peru, charged the natives with a lack of moral progress. If they were really living in a state of grace, their social mores would be more European, they reasoned. They therefore concluded that most natives had not received absolution worthily because they never had true contrition, and consequently should have never been given communion. As a consequence, the friars began withholding the Eucharist from them, although the Mexican provincial synod had condemned this custom. Finally, the Augustinian Pedro de Agurto came to the defense of the natives and in 1572 published a treatise refuting de Acosta's idea of the Eucharist as a "reward." The conflict, though, continued in some form or another for the next decades. As late as 1600, the

Franciscan Juan Bautista had to defend the natives against the charge that they did not show "enough" contrition for their past sins.[104]

It is, however, important not to confuse the necessary *experience* of contrition with an affect or emotion. Nothing of the sort was intended by early modern Catholic theologians. Experiencing remorse was an act of intellect *and* will, which *could* be accompanied by affects such as tears, but did not have to be.[105] The Carmelite Juan de Jesu Maria therefore defined contrition as the realization of God's majesty and the simultaneous acknowledgment of one's failures against him, motivated by the desire to never lose the friendship of God again. By giving the penitent a new perspective on life, it had therefore a strong epistemological dimension.[106] Nevertheless, this acknowledgment was accompanied by pain over one's transgressions (*stimulus compunctionis*).[107] Such pain was, however, short-lived because it led to the joy of friendship with God.[108] Juan imagined Jesus speaking within the soul:

> An invaluable treasure is my friendship, dearest son, whom I call to reconciliation and to a desirable peace, which the world can never give. Consider what I am and what I can do, and what a trustworthy friend I am, and how I kept steadily the right to friendship. I am rich in mercy to all, who return to me, but I am not pleased by wicked bowels (of sinners).[109]

For the Carmelite, such an encounter with Christ led the soul back to a path of grace. Every moment of Jesus's life, as narrated in the Gospels, was an invitation to discover the divine "friend" and to embrace his invitation to holiness. Reform of the person begins therefore with a remorseful heart, sensing the loss of God, and leads through mortification of the senses to a transformation of one's interior life (imagination, will, and intellect). Human imagination had to be cleansed, Juan explained, from all distraction so that the mind could form a constant image of God.[110] Yet only if the will surrendered completely was the work of *reform* done. The will must speak to God:

> I will sacrifice you my innermost being [*viscera mea*]. . . . O most powerful and mighty God, overcome me in your charity and renew this will, which wanders through all creation, so that it . . . aims directly to see your precious face. If you will, grant me this wish . . . I will be your lowly slave and signed with the seal of your freedom, not allowing my will any other loves, which distract me from you.[111]

Spiritual writers often ranked the motives for contrition differently. Juan saw as the first motive the immense majesty of God, the second as gratitude for his gifts, the third as the goodness of God, and the fourth as divine clemency. In fifth place he lists the favor a person receives after converting one's heart, and in sixth place God's invitation even to the greatest sinner.[112] Only the seventh motive entailed recognizing the harm one's sins have caused; the eighth the good things one has done with the help of God; while the ninth is the passion and death of Christ, and the tenth and last motive the sacrament of the Eucharist. Since most of Juan's readers were priests or members of religious communities, one wonders whether and how such concepts were disseminated to parishioners. Ultimately it depended on the local priest and whether he followed a balanced theology like Juan Maria's or preferred the rhetorically persuasive writings of Jansenists, who fervently defended contrition as a necessary requirement for absolution.[113] Consequently, a Catholic could be treated quite differently in the confessional: in the church of a sympathizer with Jansenism, he might meet a priest considering his remorse inadequate, while he might find in a monastery a more empathetic confessor.

In general, the confessional seems to have been a dialectic counterpart to the terrifying homily: while the priest would intimidate his flock from the pulpit, he would be consoling and empathetic in the confessional.[114] This, however, demonstrates that labeling early modern catechesis as a "pastoral of fear" (Jean Delumeau) is too one-sided. Delumeau's claim that generations of believers had been taught merely to "fear" God but not to love him, ultimately leading many to abandon their faith in the eighteenth century, has eclipsed too many sources that communicated the exact opposite.[115] A more nuanced view would acknowledge the existence of terror *and* mercy in a dialectical relationship, which was usually tilted toward one of its poles. Moreover, the fact that many Catholics accepted confession as a means of self-reform and as an "accessible and routine means of consolation"[116] shows that frequent recourse to the confessional cannot be reduced to fear of punishment alone. This notwithstanding, many must have regarded even the obligatory annual exercise of penance as psychological torture.

## Imprudence and Sexual Abuse in the Confessional

To be judge, physician, and father was a demanding task for a priest and the increasing expectations of parishioners made it even harder.[117] A priest had to be prudent in inquiring about the circumstances of a sin, what penance he prescribed, and what advice he gave. Every day, a good confessor was supposed to invoke the Holy Spirit to assist him in bringing sinners back and the faithful closer to perfection, yet always with intelligence, modesty, moderation, good humor, benevolence, and great compassion. In short, he had to be not just holy but also erudite and endowed with good judgment.[118]

Priests rejecting advice about moderation and prudence readily found themselves in difficult situations. Since a confessor was expected to inquire carefully if the severity or extent of sins seemed unclear, demanding answers about delicate areas such as sexuality could be seen as overstepping boundaries of decency. It was not uncommon that parishioners boycotted a priest whom they perceived as too inquisitive, or invented accusations against him to get rid of him.[119] At the end of the eighteenth century, when privacy became a societal value, reform-minded Catholics felt increasingly uncomfortable with priests asking even questions such as these: "Have you at times listened to a free spirit or heretic? Have you used make-up . . . to please men?"[120]

Yet, not only imprudent behavior could cause scandal, but also priests who used the confessional to pursue their sexual fantasies. Kissing a penitent in the confessional, touching, or intentionally provoking the libido of the other (either priest or penitent) were actions that were no longer imprudent but outright criminal. They were regarded as *solicitation*. It was one of the gravest crimes in canon law because it abused a sacrament, undermined the people's faith in it and thus led them astray. In order to qualify as solicitation, however, the acts had to be committed in connection with the confessional. Thus, a priest drugging a woman in the confessional box, and raping her later outside the church was guilty, while a priest masturbating in the rectory after a confession in remembrance of what he had heard, was "merely" committing a sacrilege. If found guilty in an ecclesiastical criminal trial (since 1559 prosecuted only by the Roman Inquisition), a priest lost the faculties to hear confessions until he had improved (after at least three years) or was defrocked and sentenced to a galley or prison.[121] Popes Gregory XV and Benedict XIV insisted that every Catholic was obliged to denounce a soliciting confessor to the authorities. Frequent reminders in homilies disseminated the knowledge of this obligation among the faithful. How universally this law was accepted can be seen from seventeenth-century cases in the Americas. The Mayas zealously denounced abusive priests to the authorities.[122] The eighteenth-century Bavarian Eusebius Amort, an erudite Augustinian canon, insisted that solicitation was predominantly a problem in Mediterranean countries but rare "on this side of the Alps." Whether this statement came from actual knowledge or was merely a prejudice could only be verified by intensive archival research. Nevertheless, Amort did not downplay the seriousness of the crime but made clear that not the frequency, but the enormity of the offense should terrify every clergyman![123] Interestingly, Spain is one of the few countries for which solicitation has been meticulously analyzed. For the eighteenth century alone, historians have counted around 660 cases. Among the accused there were hardly any Jesuits but many Franciscans and secular clergy. Since the rise of this crime coincides with the stricter enforcement of celibacy after 1600, many historians began to wonder whether a mutual dependence of the two exists. For a satisfying answer, however, more studies from other countries and continents would be needed.[124]

Jesus's warning against those tempting a child (Mt 18) was understood by early modern exegetes not only as sexual seduction or abuse. Every intentional action that led a child to mortal sin fell under this category, because the adult's actions had then caused the child to choose evil.[125] Cases of priests soliciting either young boys or underage girls were not as frequent as those involving adult women. Curiously enough, though, the scenario of a priest seducing a boy either to "sodomy" (an unclear term at the time)[126] or to a sexual impropriety (*nefariam mollitiem*) remained a standard topic in moral theology handbooks until the end of the eighteenth century. Even a predator's pretenses, such as visiting a boy to give him a holy card, were known and discussed.[127] A major problem in investigating accusations against soliciting priests was, however, that children were not considered reliable witnesses unless several could testify. This practice might have been a contributing factor to the low number of actual criminal trials for this offense.[128]

In order to avoid public scandal, criminal trials against priests were held in secrecy. If they did not involve solicitation, they could be handled by religious orders themselves or a diocesan bishop. Most accusations of irregular sexual behavior were raised against mendicant friars and not parish priests.[129] Orders would therefore have their own trials and lock up the guilty in monastic prisons. Little is known about their spiritual care.[130] Cases that had become public or involved rape or sodomy demanded that the sentenced priest be handed over to the secular powers. Before the clergyman could be sent to a galley as a rower, he was ritually defrocked by one of his superiors (*degradatio*).[131] Only rarely, however, would a priest find himself in the situation of being solicited by the penitent, but such cases did occur. In 1621

Augustina Ruiz was so obsessed with a friar that she began her confession by describing Christ's genitalia and her own sexual arousal in the hope of sparking his libido. The inquisitors sentenced her to three years' imprisonment in a Mexican convent.[132]

One of the biggest changes in early modern piety was how the Eucharist and confession were celebrated. From being a rare, annual occasion in the Middle Ages, communion became a frequent ritual. Since confession was a requirement to receive the consecrated host, it also became a regularly frequented sacrament. Yet instead of admitting one's sins in the open, the confessional box provided privacy and visualized the trend toward perceiving confession as a ritual of individualized self-improvement.

Catholic authorities, however, not only prescribed the reception of these sacraments, but also developed pedagogical tools to connect the faithful with the Eucharist and confession on a deeper spiritual and emotional level. Emblems and metaphors allowed the faithful to grasp that the sacraments were able to transform the self and elevate the person to a God-pleasing level. Moreover, catechisms and prayerbooks articulated the concept of a merciful God, who was interested in a sinner's conversion. Problematic, however, was that such a conversion was assessed by an outsider—the priest. This forced theologians to analyze what outward signs could provide the necessary evidence for the remorse of the penitent (*contrition*) and gave priests the power to also harass the faithful by withholding absolution.

# 8

# Transformation through Prayer

Far from being a harmonious story, the variety of theological approaches engaged in by early modern Catholics often proved contentious. How quiet could, for example, the soul become in a state of contemplation and rest "in" God? Was it possible that human agency all but ceased in such moments? Moreover, was it possible for a human to love God so much that one became disinterested in one's own salvation? While these were some of the questions that drove the debate over Quietism in which Fénelon and Madame Guyon were involved, they were not the only ones.[1] Due to a number of cases of false mysticism, questionable morals, and unusual or heterodox expressions of piety, teachers of prayer techniques were often suspected of heresy.[2] Even St. Ignatius of Loyola had to defend himself for his novel prayer method.[3] These controversies, are, however, outside the scope of a study looking at ecclesially approved, transformative practices. Of the many different forms of prayer, I have chosen merely a representative number that offer an insight into the early modern practice of prayer.

Rejuvenating the faith of church members necessarily included a better formation in prayer. Consequently, post-conciliar norms centered traditional practices around new ideals of spirituality. These orbited around the approved understanding of justification and sanctification.[4] However, one lost the baptismal grace of justification by committing a mortal sin. Only sacramental confession and penance restored it. Yet the necessary preparation for confession was not only an examination of conscience but also sincere prayer. These actions were also indispensable for a person who had remained in a state of grace to grow in holiness.[5] The holier one became, the more one recognized one's own sinfulness and imperfection. Small transgressions began to appear egregious. This was not scrupulosity but the consequence of a logic of love in which saintly persons compared their love to the infinite love of God. Nevertheless, the focus on guilt in early modern spirituality intensified the fear of going to Hell, which was further exacerbated by the Council of Trent's *anathema* against anyone claiming to be among the Elect.[6]

*The Inner Life of Catholic Reform*. Ulrich L. Lehner, Oxford University Press. © Oxford University Press 2022.
DOI: 10.1093/oso/9780197620601.003.0008

Even those who did not fear eternal damnation were unsettled about the likelihood of postmortem pain in Purgatory.

Such fears were nothing new. Medieval Christians were haunted by them, too, but early modern Catholicism intensified them through its pedagogical apparatus. By teaching the faithful in catechism classes, sermons, devotional books, and the confessional, the believer was confronted everywhere with the possibility of Hell and Purgatory. Preachers encouraged their listeners to vividly imagine not just the pleasures of heavenly delight, but also the sufferings of eternal damnation as a real possibility. After all, these images shook the soul to begin the way of inner conversion. According to the belief of the time, every person who had heard about the Gospels was offered the gratuitous gift of grace (*gratia sufficiens*), which needed to be accepted in a free decision. Sermons about fire and brimstone were the tools to overcome inner uncertainties and thus became catalysts for a free embrace of the divine gift.[7] Unsurprisingly, the instrument of fear was widely used, including in parish missions. In addition to homilies, printed images also disseminated such "holy terror." Widely known was the work of the seventeenth-century Jesuit Michel Le Nobletz, whose allegorical maps outlined the roads to salvation and perdition. Among missionaries, fear was used as a strategy for converting listeners: A Jesuit in French North America, for example, thought that such images were particularly well suited to making the Iroquois rethink their lives.[8]

Fear, however, was only a wake-up call for the soul, and led to deepened faith, love, and hope. Faith gained in such sanctification the form of love and became meritorious in the eyes of God. Thus, the goal behind what Jean Delumeau called an "evangelization of fear" was the joy of encountering the gift of salvation. By prayer and conversion, the penitent certainly "pacified the wrath" of God's justice, but only in order to capture divine mercy. A contemporary therefore wrote: "Prayer destroys the doors of Hell, opens the gate of Heaven, and appeases God."[9] It is this dialectic of threat and clemency that shaped early modern Catholic spirituality most substantially.[10]

This dialectic should therefore caution us not to single out the fear of Hell as *the* defining characteristic of early modern Catholicism.[11] Fear was, after all, just one factor that transformed passions into affects, leading to sanctification. None of the great devotional works of the time, from Louis de Granada to Francis de Sales, identify Hell or fear as their main themes, and catechisms placed it always in the context of divine justice.[12] Using fear as a pedagogical tool has to be seen in the context of the church's attempt at inner transformation: integrating *all* affects into prayer allowed for a new closeness with Christ that was also accessible to the laity.[13] Such transformative, devotional theology also overcame racial and ethnic boundaries. Jewish converts in Spain cherished especially the works of St. John of Avila, for whom the soul was wedded by the Holy Spirit in an "intimate marriage" with God, and thus made any prejudice toward newly converted Christians illegitimate.[14]

## Mental Prayer and Divine Presence

Like any other religious action, prayer needed a proper inner disposition. In order to be sincere, it had to go beyond mere vocal expressions. The mind, not just the lips, had to be lifted to God.[15] Prayer required attention. Since highly focused attentiveness was an act of the intellect, it was referred to as *mental* prayer. As the elevation of the mind to God, mental prayer was the "basis and foundation of Christian perfection"[16] and was not restricted to religious superachievers in monasteries.[17]

The method of *recogimiento*, in which the praying individual aimed at becoming aware of the divine presence and incrementally developed this knowledge into a "habitual attention to God"[18] was a widely practiced form of mental prayer. It had been developed in the 1480s by Spanish Franciscans. Francisco de Osuna's writings made it famous, and through him it also influenced St. Teresa of Avila. Osuna believed that the old self had to be annihilated and replaced by the divine will.[19] One achieved this by paying close attention to the presence of God's will in the soul. The praying individual had to "collect" all the senses, calm them, and then focus on the new object, the divine will.[20] Since all that was required for this practice was concentration, it was, as the early sixteenth-century Cardinal Cisneros explained, a simple and easily accessible way of "finding divine love."[21] The simplicity and effectiveness of *recogimiento* allowed for its fast dissemination among religious and laity in Europe and the Americas.[22]

The approach of St. Ignatius of Loyola was similar. He explained in the *Spiritual Exercises* that the believer should use all the powers of imagination for meditation on Scripture.[23] This way, one's attention was focused on the word of God and the reactions these meditations caused in the soul. The person undergoing the *Exercises* learned to *discern* where the movements of the soul originated. Only those that were lastingly peaceful could come from God and deserved to be objects of one's desire, while the delightful yet short-lived pleasures originated either in the world or from Satan and had to be rejected.[24] In the first week of the *Exercises*, the affects of penance and guilt were elicited in order to overshadow all sensitive passions and lead to the desire of God's forgiveness and true contrition (see chapters 2 and 7). In it one faced one's own sins and the possibility of eternal damnation and in this way provoked a fear of Hell. The following weeks guided the penitent to the experience of joy and redemption. Nevertheless, it would be false to describe the *Exercises* as a tool for inducing specific *affects*. Their aim was not so much *what* one experienced but rather to replace the worldly objects of desire with the divine will, making the believer's will conform to God's. The length and intensity of the thirty-day *Exercises* made them one of the most powerful tools of Catholic self-transformation.[25] Most religious orders adopted them in one form or another, and in condensed form they were given during parish missions. Offered to the laity also in retreat houses, Jesuits sometimes relied even on lay directors such as Catherine Francheville. The abbreviated *Exercises* for the laity were, however, also meditations infused with gender expectations; for example, through the selection of meditation images.[26] Nevertheless, Ignatius's open spirituality also created a space for the diverse forms of female religious life in early modernity: women could experience and find God's will even if this often led to tensions with male authorities.[27]

The *Spiritual Exercises* influenced not only priests and members of religious orders but also large segments of society. Popular authors like Luis de la Puente spread St. Ignatius's approach and made it accessible to all. De la Puente, for example, offered short meditation "points" in his popularized version of the *Exercises* for all Gospel readings of the year.[28] By providing images, allegories, and metaphors that led his reader to the desired outcome, he demonstrated that people's individual prayer experiences were to be normatively centered. Because this approach steered a person's imagination in a certain direction, it made the end results more predictable. But the historian can hardly describe Puente as intruding on people's pious imagination. After all, it was the believer who *desired* to be steered and directed by picking up Puente's book. The reader entrusted his or her soul to the spiritual master to obtain help for the transformation of the soul. Moreover, believers also had the freedom to look for other sources of spiritual counsel and of course did not have to follow the "points" to the letter. Certainly, members of Marian congregations, who perhaps had to listen to the reading of Puente's meditations, did not have as much freedom, but as members they had promised to shape their lives according to the Gospels and to follow the spiritual advice of their leaders.

Widely popular, the *Exercises* came under attack in the second half of the eighteenth century. For Catholic Enlighteners they stood for indoctrination and an unhealthy use of imagination. These thinkers preferred a more austere piety that focused on practical outcomes. They still upheld the necessity of mental prayer, but often ridiculed vocal prayer, especially if it was repetitive. Yet by mocking widespread practices, these reformers caused resistance to their ideas. Thus, their plan for an "Enlightenment of the mind in divine things, an improvement of the heart towards Christian perfection,"[29] remained an elitist project.

Countless authors, including Jansenists, praised the value of mental prayer, and emphasized that it was the foundation for *any* reform of the self, because it united the soul with God. Often it was also called a *prayer of the heart* or simply meditation. The quality of mental prayer differed whether it was mainly *acquired* by the strength of a person's faculties or *infused* by divine grace.[30] Nevertheless, it *never* made redundant spoken prayer such as the liturgy of the Church. Only "false" mystics such as Quietists, who claimed infused contemplation, could have disregard for the breviary or other required vocal prayers, Catholic reformers explained.[31] The definitions of what mental prayer exactly was varied greatly, and consequently there was a vivid discourse about its nature.

Since mental prayer allowed for a more intimate relationship with God, laypersons eagerly welcomed the many vernacular instruction books that appeared in print beginning in the late sixteenth century. The laity also did not face the same scrutiny religious would when exercising this devotional technique. While friars or nuns had to be careful not to appear to be neglecting their vocal prayer obligations, laypersons were largely free from such commitments. However, since they were not educated in theology, they (also like lay brothers, lay sisters, and *devotas*) tended to be suspected of ignorance. Immersing oneself in approved books about meditation was thus a way to find direction for one's spiritual life and escape this prejudice. Teachers from many religious orders perceived the potential interior prayer could have for church reform and advertised their works to all those "who love the interior life."[32]

The Discalced Carmelites especially were known as outstanding teachers of prayer. They produced several mystical theologians, who not only systematized the works of St. Teresa of Avila and St. John of the Cross but also immersed them in the theological debates of the time. For example, Thomas a Jesus's compendium on mental prayer, which was translated into several languages,[33] and the works of Miguel de San Agustin, were widely used. They taught in scholastic fashion, infused with mystical sources, that in order "to enjoy God through the light of faith, and to adhere to him in loving familiarity"[34] one had to be purged from selfishness and embrace internal solitude.[35] Only those who were content with God as their only companion and who could avoid needless chatter (*linguosi*) were capable of truly conversing with God in mental prayer.[36]

Since 1583, also the Franciscans admonished all their members, including lay brothers and Third Order members, to practice mental prayer.[37] Religious orders without an emphasis on such prayer could, they were convinced, *not* reform themselves, because vocal prayer alone left the soul "dry and cold in the love for God," as Pedro de Alcantara stated. Only such "interior prayer" would fight evil inclinations and protect from temptations, because it inspired true love. Yet personal, mental prayer was not an exercise without rules. Instead, it followed approved meditation texts. After the meditation, in which intellect and imagination worked together, the soul was called to thank God and offer herself to him.[38]

The rigor recommended for mental prayer varied greatly. While Carmelite writers such as San Agustin had high expectations for the members of their order, they were happy with much less effort from those in other states of life. All writers, however, insisted that mental prayer was shaped by its attentiveness to God. The secular priest Francis Agricola, for example, explained in 1585: "Such attention can be achieved by the uneducated when they pray in Latin but do not understand a word, since it is enough that God, to whom they pray understands, and that the person's heart and mind and desire are stretched towards God and his grace."[39]

Agricola was no exception. Countless confraternities and Marian sodalities (see chapter 6) taught these basics of mental prayer to their members, who in turn passed them on to their families.[40] Their widely disseminated texts provided ample evidence of how far-reaching the attempts were to improve the prayer life and sanctification of *all* church members. These books agreed that praying with one's lips was insufficient not only for salvation but also for one's self-transformation. Prayer had to come from the heart and was offered not merely as a *service* to God but also as an expression of love and friendship for him. St. Teresa of Avila even went so far as to deny that the mere repetition of vocal prayers without an intentional focus on God was prayer at all![41] Since this understanding of spirituality was broadly taught in catechism classes, homilies, confraternities, and prayer books, one can safely assume that by the seventeenth century at the latest, every observant Catholic had encountered this challenge to change their attitude to prayer.[42]

Meditation as an intellectual and discursive exercise[43] led only to a certain level of spiritual achievement. The more advanced would no longer find it fulfilling and aimed, as the contemporary sources explained, to reach the next higher level, namely that of discursive-free *contemplation*. It was first and foremost a divine gift that one could not force by one's own powers. Therefore, the mystical teachers called it "infused."[44] This form of mental prayer, however, had come under scrutiny because heretical groups such as the *alumbrados* claimed it, too. Thus, a skillful defense was necessary to make the difference between church-approved and heretical contemplation visible. A diligent theology of discernment, which showed that friars and nuns followed a strict regimen of introspection, could serve this very purpose.[45] In the Discalced Carmelite Order, Juan de Jesus Maria da Calahorra articulated this approach in his mystical theology. Discernment was for Juan not just the key to the spiritual progress of the mystic, but rather the key to salvation for *everybody*. After all, how could somebody be saved who did not do God's will and lived a life of debauchery? And how could those living close to such depraved people be encouraged in their good choices? Both needed to know what actions and goods they should pursue if they desired to have a chance at avoiding eternal damnation. Thus, Juan's *Art of Living Spiritually* of 1610 was a practical book.[46] It spoke to all those who already loved God and assured them of their salvation, but also made clear that such love had to grow throughout one's life. This progress, however, was not achieved by uttering a few prayers or fasting, but rather by transforming the self into a person who truly loved God and neighbor.[47] Without discerning between spiritual and worldly goods, one could never advance on this road.[48] Yet such practice was an "art," and thus a technique that depended largely on one's perseverance and attention, supported by divine grace.[49]

## Affective Prayer

Some historians have argued that religious traditions used emotion to validate either mystical experiences or doctrine by "fabricating" illusions or "false selves" and constructing an "emotional ideology."[50] Yet, for a contemporary these "false selves" were not false at all, but rather the desired "new creation" they had learned about in catechism classes. Their old, sinful self had to "die" in order to be newly created by grace, which included emotions that were considered "disordered" or "selfish." After all, for an early modern Catholic, emotions were not "spontaneous forms of self-expression, but . . . means of self-interpretation and self-transformation."[51]

Emotions (*passiones, affectus, inclinationes*, etc.) were "motions" or movements of the soul that one "learned to perceive and interpret, stimulate, display, repress or internalize in a methodological way, thereby gaining a stronger sense of self."[52] Beginning in the sixteenth century, theologians systematically engaged them for an "affective spirituality." By reading and meditating one could transform one's passions into spiritual affects. With this technique, the believer severed ties to all worldly things and became attached to God.[53] This liberated the soul and restored in her the desire for the objects of the intellectual appetite. Now, a person could approach God "with pure mind and a heart, purged from all evil."[54] Also the illiterate could adopt this practice by using Scripture quotations as mnemonic triggers for their affects.[55] This method also fostered petitionary prayer, especially if it was spontaneous or accompanied by tears.[56]

One of the most sophisticated attempts to merge scholastic theology with the demands of affective spirituality was Louis Bail's *Theologia Affectiva* (1638). He lamented that despite its intellectual lucidity, scholasticism could not set the heart ablaze for God. After all, theology had to not only "shine" but also "burn," he reasoned, meaning that it must lead to an interior delight in God.[57] Bail's theology therefore exposed the intellectual appetites of the soul to holy affects of wonder, gratitude, fear, and love.[58] Once the soul had learned about the lasting delights of these objects, it would leave earthly desires behind, making painful mortification redundant.[59] "This method is much milder, more humane, more universal, and leads much more easily to its goal."[60] A person who had achieved this state was continuously filled with "holy affects" (*sainte affection*).[61] Very similar to Bail's approach was the widely read *Theology of Mind and Heart* (1681) by the Dominican Vincent Contenson. Like Bail, it followed St. Thomas Aquinas and presented after each chapter a meditation, which elicited "sweet" affects of piety that secured one's "formation" (*formandos*) in the virtues of faith, hope, and love.[62] The *Ignatian Exercises*, which likewise aimed at the integration of the affective side into spirituality, could also be subsumed under this label.

The most famous proponent of affective spirituality was arguably St. Francis de Sales. He not only emphasized that every baptized Catholic was called in freedom to respond to the offer of love from God, but also that those seeking spiritual perfection needed good counsel.[63] Such permanent apprenticeship was necessary because the union with God that enabled a person to overcome temptations[64] was never long-lasting. Instead, humans had to constantly battle with their sinful inclinations.[65] The goal of his affective theology was therefore to reach a state of indifference toward earthly desires and completely surrender to God.[66] One no longer loved the "things" God willed, but his will instead.[67] Such love happened like the "visitation": as the virgin Mary visited, pregnant with Jesus, her cousin Elizabeth (Lk 1:39–56), so the follower of de Sales was called to carry the spirit of the Gospel to others. This subtlety avoided ostentatiousness and instead emulated gentleness (*douceur*) and humility. As Mary had shared in gentleness the secret of her pregnancy with Elizabeth, so a Catholic should share the fruits of affective prayer with others. De Sales's pedagogy of prayer found wide acceptance in Catholic circles and allowed people of different states, religious and lay, to pursue perfection.[68]

François Fénelon was substantially influenced by de Sales and the Carmelite mystics. The archbishop of Cambrai was arguably one of the most gifted reformer bishops and theological writers of the seventeenth century. In his many books, Fénelon taught that a Christian had to unconditionally surrender everything to God out of love. Mere "correctness"—a term that echoes St. Teresa of Avila—would never change a person, and neither would fear. Instead of offering God actions like coins, one should give everything out of love and never expect anything in return. This theology of prayer challenged the popular Catholic view of seeking direct reward for good actions without inner transformation. He therefore stressed what he called "disinterested love" as an ideal for all.[69]

## The Pious "Sigh"

Widely popular among Protestants, the arrow prayer was a short phrase either from scripture or an approved source that one could shout or sigh (*piae aspirationes*; *preces aspirativae*). It was also widely used by Catholic laity and religious.

In the fourth century, St. Augustine already knew the *orationes jaculatoria* or "thrown" prayers. They were compared to "arrows" shot toward God (*sagittas*; cf. Jonathan's arrow in 2 Kings 1:22) because they were fast and short, such as *Dominus meus et Deus meus*. Since they arose spontaneously from the heart, they were considered meritorious.[70] Before the Council of Trent a number of mystical teachers had recommended them, such as St. Bonaventure or Louis Blosius, but the catechetical initiative of the council made them a widely adopted practice.[71]

Not every arrow prayer found acceptance, though. Self-formulated ones especially were discouraged, because church authorities feared that heretical statements could thus take root. Such reservations extended also to the religious, who were instructed to cooperate with divine grace and recite as arrow prayers the words of Scripture, particularly short verses from the psalms. For each moment of the day, a friar or lay brother could find a passage from scripture and use it as a "pious sigh" to sanctify even the most mundane activities, such as washing laundry or cleaning the stables.[72] Because of the alignment of breathing and pronouncing words, this devotion was also often called an *aspiratio*. Its striking similarity with Byzantine traditions did not escape the learned Cistercian Cardinal Giovanni Bona. Convinced of the ancient roots of this method, he claimed that Jesus himself practiced it; for example, when he petitioned the Father in the Garden of Gethsemane (Mk 14:32–36; Mt 26:36–46; Lk 22:39–46).[73]

Misgivings about the arrow prayers had various origins. On the one side fear of heterodox formulas persisted, on the other there was a grave concern that this prayer form might lead to uncontrollable "enthusiasm." After all, since the prayers derived from spontaneous movements (*motus anagogici*) of the soul, church authorities feared that people would try hunting for emotional effects and thus dissimulate piety. Therefore, it is not surprising that apart from warnings to the laity, the monastic manuals of the time also advised young friars to use this method only sparingly, while those advanced in mental prayer could practice it continuously to remain in union with God.[74]

The laity learned these prayers through catechism classes and frequent mentions in homilies. Parents most likely also taught them to their children. Canisius's 1590 catechism contains several sections of such brief prayers. One of them encompasses thirty-three short sighs (each of one sentence) designed to be said during the day when one hears a signal from the church bell tower, and seventeen short prayers for the dying, such as, "Oh my savior Jesus Christ, have mercy on me a poor sinner."[75] By linking the arrow prayer with the bells, church reformers had devised an easy and accessible tool to advance the sanctification of the laity. The short texts also had a variety of other uses. They were recited as preparation for communion or confession and could even be used if one wished to emulate a special saint: memorable aphorisms from the works of St. Teresa of Avila allowed a nun to slip into the skin of her order's reformer and imitate her.[76]

Despite their popularity, church authorities also saw dangers in the use of arrow prayers. They could, after all, be taken from heterodox sources, contain ambiguous doctrinal statements, or even lead some to dismiss official church prayer. The early seventeenth-century Jesuit Antoine Balinghem therefore dedicated an entire tome to this form of prayer. He was convinced that if practiced daily and following church recommendations, aspirations would inscribe themselves with an iron pen on the soul and hold the praying person back from sin. In his eyes the sighs had the ability to contribute to the sanctification of the person and to instill the life of virtue in them.[77] Since this method was simpler than mental prayer, meditation, or the saying of the breviary, Balinghem recommended it widely for the laity and for the physically or psychologically weak.[78]

## Purgatory Piety

As the history of confraternities in chapter 6 showed, a crucial part of the Christian virtue of charity was prayerful love for the dead (*dilectio defunctorum*) in Purgatory.[79] These souls were in a state of purification, but despite their suffering certain to see God face to face one day, unlike the damned in Hell. Prayer for the dead, which ceased to exist in the churches of the Reformation, empowered the living to do something worthwhile for their deceased loved ones.[80]

The most valuable prayer for the dead was offering up holy Mass for them.[81] After Trent, the tendency to emphasize the "fruits of the Mass" (*utilitates missae*) for the souls in Purgatory as well as the living made it easier for priests to receive Mass stipends and for male monasteries to raise funding. Female monasteries also garnered support. They received endowments or gifts to pray for their benefactors, alive or deceased. Moreover, numerous female mystics impressed the faithful with their visions and locutions of the poor souls in Purgatory. They claimed to have received a revelation about which prayers the dead needed and offered them. Among churchgoers, these women and their orders were accordingly held in high esteem. Everywhere, women seemed to engage in this work of charity for the dead, dedicating their prayers to them. It also permitted them to direct their religious zeal to help those who could not afford to have a Mass said for their deceased family members. With the rise in veneration of the Sacred Heart, as propagated by St. Margaret Mary Alacoque, this niche of female agency was strengthened. In her visions the French saint had claimed that the poor souls had asked specifically for prayers to the Sacred Heart to alleviate their suffering. This work for the "redemption of souls" was something laywomen and religious zealously engaged in.[82] It should therefore not surprise us that one of the few apologetical works of the time that can claim female authorship was written in defense of Purgatory. Jane Owen's treatise of 1634 implored Catholics to continue funding female monasteries. This way, poor girls could also enter religious life and become advocates for the redemption of their benefactors.[83] Such magnanimity for the sake of obtaining "eternal friends" was the best "investment" of one's earthly riches, she explained.[84]

The presence of the poor souls in art and liturgy, as well as the propagated methods of using one's imagination in prayer, contributed to widespread speculations about both the sufferings and joys of these souls. The visions of mystics satisfied the popular desire to know more about life after death, and simultaneously assured Catholics of an egalitarianism in salvation: just like a peasant, popes and bishops had to pass through Purgatory on their way to Heaven. The souls in Purgatory, who contacted the living and asked for prayers, were messengers from an invisible world, pleading for relief from their suffering and drawing the living into service for the dead.[85] If such a vision occurred, the priest had to guide the believer in the discernment process of whether the apparition was mere imagination, a vision permitted by God, or a demonic simulation.[86] Much more common than such visionary encounters was simply praying for the dead during the day, and in church and cemetery visits.[87] The devotion to the dead allowed their families to help their loved ones participate in the triumph of the church in Heaven.[88]

The catechetical emphasis on Purgatory and Hell in early modern Catholicism was also needed to counter a popular dualist understanding of God. After all, according to a widespread popular belief, the devil was just as powerful as God and tried to steal souls away from him. Some Catholics even believed that angels and saints could play tricks on humans or do evil things to them! Consequently, priests had to combat such views, which were incompatible with the Christian creed. The catechesis on Heaven, Hell, and Purgatory made clear that not God but human (and angelic) freedom was responsible for the existence of sin. Such preaching also emphasized the power of grace that would be given to everybody cooperating with God's will; for example, by doing works of charity.[89]

Using prayers for the souls in Purgatory for personal transformation arose at the beginning of the sixteenth century, when the "art of dying" (*ars moriendi*) was sluggishly replaced by the art of "proper living." Instead of accentuating a holy death, a moral life preceding it became more important. One began to speculate intensively about what the afterlife of people would look like who did *not* die in a state of mortal sin but merely venial sin. Catholics reflected on the harvest of their lives rather than on the universal judgment over the entire human race on the Last Day. St. Robert Bellarmine, Jacques Suarez de Sainte-Marie, and St. Catherine of Genoa especially shaped this new perspective.[90] By the end of the seventeenth century, the transformation of the *ars moriendi* into an *ars vivendi* was completed. A good death was now presented as the consequence of a good life. This trend, however, also seems to have undermined the message of everlasting punishment in Hell. If the less perfect could obtain salvation, would not most fall into that category rather than into the one that is damned forever?[91]

The emphasis of Purgatory went hand in hand with the liturgical reform of the Roman Ritual concerning pastoral care for the sick, dying, and dead. The clergy were increasingly expected to visit the sick and keep notes about which parishioners were in danger of dying. Likewise, the faithful were admonished that in a severe illness, the clergy should be called to the sickbed. The priest's presence meant that a penitent could confess and receive last rites and communion, all of which led to entry into Heaven. The new *Rituale Romanum* of 1614 also recommended that the priest should be subtle in admonishing the sick "to put their entire trust in God, repent their sins and invoke the mercy of God."[92] Only if a parishioner ignored the danger of death should the minister reveal to him the danger of losing his soul to the devil.[93] After all, death was the "grand moment on which one's eternal fate depended."[94] The Roman liturgy from which these prayers for the dead were taken centered around God as judge, whose wrath had to be appeased, and thus emphasized penance. In the Enlightenment, such fear about judgment was connected with new theories of sentiments that moved the sinner through trembling to action.[95] While the liturgy for the deceased emphasized penance and fear, perhaps more so for the surviving than the dead, the pastoral guidelines for the dying seemed to have stressed clemency instead.[96] Funeral sermons also emphasized hope in the justice and clemency of God more than fear.[97] Despite the assurances of preachers, death remained "a tough piece to chew on, and hard to digest."[98] Beyond the fear of nearing the end of one's life, many faithful were afraid of *how* God would judge their lives. Prokop of Templin explained that such fear could be good "as long as one remained smart and did not give in to lethargy or despair," because the judge will be the merciful Christ. "He will not condemn us if we are not guilty. And if we have something laying on our conscience . . . let's liberate ourselves from it . . . and die every day and every hour . . . so that the judge will not find fault in us."[99]

The love for the dead in Purgatory was also celebrated in the visual arts. These were called the "poor souls." The adjective "poor" indicated their suffering and their inability to do anything by themselves to alleviate their pains or shorten their stay. Moreover, it signified also the enormity of their pains, which were believed to be equal to those in Hell, albeit only temporarily.[100] Depictions of Purgatory were therefore gruesome, as the Theatine Felix Fasso demonstrated: "Imagine, o Christian, what pain and heart break you will feel when you see in Purgatory your own mother, who fed you on her breasts, being roasted in fire?"[101] Such talk encouraged fear in and a commotion of the soul, but on the other hand it was also a message of hope because Purgatory was the threshold of Heaven. Every person in it was saved.[102] Moreover, by explaining to the faithful that their sufferings on earth could, if united with the merits of Christ, count toward the punishments of Purgatory, early modern Catholics were empowered to view their own lives in anticipation of the next. They were given the tools to endure their existence with a positive outlook toward the next life and could, if they were sufficiently transformed and sanctified by good works, escape the postmortem cleansing altogether.[103]

Despite such individualist tendencies, piety concerning Purgatory also contained a powerful communal perspective. The living formed a community of solidarity for the helpless dead and practiced the "beautiful, easy and powerful means to assist the Christian souls which suffer temporal punishment in Purgatory."[104] Yet due to the Protestant rejection of any prayer for the dead, Catholics had to defend its rationale. By the seventeenth century, however, they referred not only to Scripture, the Church Fathers, and philosophy but also to the witness of animals: careful observation of the animal world would teach a person divine wisdom (Proverbs 6:6). As ants collect food for the winter, so the faithful would collect treasures for the afterlife, by accumulating meritorious deeds. Like the fish, which did not devour the corpses of St. Adriano and his four companions, people should show mercy to the dead, and like a faithful dog who would not part from the side of his deceased owner, so the living should not abandon the poor souls. Of course, such remarks echoed the ancient tradition of natural theology that saw divine wisdom mirrored in the world, but its application to Purgatory was seemingly new. Invoking the wisdom of nature, however, allowed Purgatory piety to also receive impulses from the mysticism of nature. It expressed connectedness with the dead and allowed the faithful to see themselves participating in a mystery deeply engrained in the laws of nature.[105]

While theologians had much to say about individual souls in Purgatory, talk about Heaven emphasized the beatific vision. Once a soul arrived there, seeing God face to face meant perpetual joy. Such infinite delight was the supernatural end all humans were created for. The idea of a reunion with loved ones in the afterlife was secondary to that and only began to play a role in the eighteenth century.[106] One reason for this was the belief that only the resurrected bodies could experience the delight of seeing all the other elect in Heaven. Until that Last Day, however, they were merely disembodied souls.[107] A seventeenth-century Capuchin therefore exclaimed in a homily about this day: "Our sight will be filled with immense joy looking at the glorious humanity of Christ but also the bodies of our beloved Lady and of all the elect."[108] Since this joy was a side product of the vision of God, he explained that parents will have a "great *accidental* happiness when they will see their own children in glory, which they helped them to achieve by forming them."[109]

## Mortification of Body and Soul

Prayer, however, was not only a mental operation. In fact, the spiritual teachers of the time were convinced that it had to be sharpened by fasting to prevent it from becoming weak and dull. Moreover, the Council of Trent had explained that through mortification the justified would increase their sanctification and make prayers and good works even more meritorious.[110] The need for these ascetic practices was a direct consequence of the Fall. While the human body was believed to have been divinely designed and honored by the Incarnation, in the Fall its natural powers had become substantially disordered and thus prone to sin. In order to reestablish the intellect's control over the unruly desires of the body for leisure, good food, and sex, they had to be "crucified" or "killed" as one called practices such as fasting, self-flagellation, self-humiliation, and infliction of other bodily hardships. Thus, these passions had to be mortified and brought under the control of reason. Fasting was a particularly popular practice of mortification, also because it was required or expected from every Catholic, numerous times a year. The fasting person therefore not only imposed hardships on the body but also consciously *imitated* the state of innocence in Paradise.[111]

The restrictions on earthly goods, such as food, were seen as a means to suffocate the sinful powers within and strengthen the will to center on cooperating with the divine will. All five senses had to be "mortified" or deprived of the objects they desired and die to the old world, the spiritual writers taught.[112] Visual and tactile experience was especially prone to arouse unwanted desires. Priests were therefore warned not to look at women and avoid their touches. Likewise, the clergy was cautioned not to observe "beautiful boys," indicating fears about homosexuality. Since overcoming one's libido demanded a fight within one's soul, chastity was considered a "male" virtue: nuns excelling in such integrity embodied therefore a male characteristic.[113] Even seemingly harmless delights such as smelling fresh flowers, perfume, or the nonmedicinal use of tobacco were seen as distracting the mind and will, in particular for religious.[114] By "crucifying" the senses, a person took action against them and undermined the possibility of "demonic attacks." Through this practice, female cloistered religious also gained the ability to "reenact the triumph" of early Christian virgin martyrs in their own cells. Here, however, they took on the task of killing undesirable and evil inclinations in their own soul.[115]

While such mortification of all senses was a practice for the spiritually advanced, every Catholic—unless dispensed—was expected to fast during certain times of the year.[116] Since the churches of the Reformation rejected fasting as superstition, the practice also became a confessional identity marker. When in 1556 Pedro Calvo of Avila in Spain was observed eating roasted pigskin during Lent, he had to defend himself against the Inquisition, which suspected him of heterodoxy. While eating pork during Lent showed disrespect for the rules of the church, avoiding it outside that liturgical season could make one appear to be following Jewish or Muslim food laws. Therefore in a number of regions, following food regulations had a performative function signifying one's religious identity.[117] The implication of fasting in a political and confessional discipline made historians somewhat neglect that the Church saw in it first and foremost a penitential practice aimed at *sanctification*. The Capuchin Lawrence of Brindisi demonstrated that since Jesus himself had fasted, it was a practice that enjoyed explicit divine affirmation.

Protestants, however, argued that Jesus did not give a clear commandment that he expected his followers to fast, to which Brindisi responded:

> What command was needed for something so necessary for salvation? You see a fire burning in your house, and do you wait for an order to use water to extinguish it? You have learned you are infected with poison. You have the cure with you—do you wait for a command from the doctor? . . . It is true that Christ does not command us to fast in the Gospel; but Christ explains in the Gospel to the Church how to fast, is it reasonable to believe that he did not want her to fast? Tell me, why does the Doctor order a sick person to follow a diet unless he wants to follow it?[118]

The fasting regimen of early modern Catholicism was far from rigid. Not only did many dioceses grant exceptions and dispensations, but theologians also quarreled about how much fasting was necessary to fulfill one's duties. This is yet another example of how normative claims were often renegotiated on the local or individual level. A particularly interesting example of this was the discussion about whether drinking hot chocolate before Mass would break the Eucharistic fast—being without food or water until the reception of communion. The new habit of mid-seventeenth-century Spanish women of having a cup of chocolate before or even during Mass, made this discussion necessary.[119] Bishop Bernardino de Salazar was so repulsed that he threatened everybody with excommunication who would pass the threshold of his cathedral with a cup of chocolate! Another example of the flexibility of fasting obligations were female monasteries. Originally, many nuns were forbidden to buy luxury products such as chocolate because they undermined their rules of life. Yet by 1729, for its sixty nuns the Franciscan convent of Santa Isabel in Mexico City spent 3,000 pesos on chocolate—half the amount that they spent on meat and bread.[120]

Mortification was considered "reasonable" (rationabile) because it counteracted disordered passions and strengthened the will to do good. Different opinions, however, existed as to how far the crucifixion of the senses should go and how much bodily harm could be done to oneself without committing a sin. Only in the Catholic Enlightenment of the late eighteenth century was the idea of depriving oneself of goods or inflicting bodily harm in such manner (e.g., by wearing a coarse shirt) rejected outright.[121] It stressed instead internal mortification, which aimed at subduing intellect, judgment, memory, will, and passions. Pre-eighteenth-century theologians had already held that such internal mortification was more meritorious, but unlike the Catholic Enlightenment, they saw the distrust of oneself as its core principle (see chapter 7).[122]

In the wake of the Council of Trent, the Catholic Reform produced an impressive number of spiritual writers, both women and men, who developed a multitude of approaches to progress in sanctification. Including laypersons in the catechesis on prayer allowed wide segments of the population to engage in forms of self-improvement, often under the direction of a clergyman.

Praying for the souls in Purgatory was immensely popular, which gave the living the opportunity to still act on behalf of the dead and simultaneously fulfill the expectation to do acts of mercy. While such acts were meritorious, they were believed to be insufficient if not accompanied by sincere mortification of body and mind. Only by taming one's passions and will could a Catholic hope to conform completely to God's commandments. It was new that the laity were also able to receive ample information about the many different means of mortification. Although medieval theologians had already analyzed passions and affects, early modern Catholics systematized these approaches, integrated new knowledge from medicine, anthropology, and rhetoric, and thereby aimed at changing desires and thus molding new selves that were pleasing to God.

# 9

# Symbols and Images

The sacred architecture of early modern Catholicism invited participation and contemplative awe. In a Gothic church the observer's view was raised by the columns to the stained-glass windows rising to the ceiling, manifesting a stairway to Heaven. The holy rituals on the altar, however, were often blocked from view by a rood screen. Renaissance and Baroque churches eliminated the screen and allowed a largely unimpeded view of the altar. One could now perceive the elevation of host and chalice during the Mass, and visually participate in it. The Baroque also developed a new church design: instead of rectangular foundations, architects now preferred the oval. Instead of walking a long nave toward the high altar, when entering one of these new shrines the visitor stepped almost immediately into the center of the church. The divine mysteries no longer seemed to be kept at a distance but rather revealed to the visitor. This was underscored by *putti* lifting heavy curtains that previously hid the glory of Heaven.

Yet the believer would also realize that the opening of the heavenly perspective engaged her in new and surprising ways: as in a theater, she was suddenly on stage with the other actors (in this case the saints in Heaven), integrated into the center and no longer at the bottom as in a Gothic cathedral. The architecture of the Baroque high altar of the Carmelite Church in Straubing, Bavaria, exemplifies this. It is placed in a traditional Gothic church with columns carrying three naves of equal height. The wooden pillars of the high altar, however, parallel the Gothic ones and are continued within the altar painting, so that the observer is integrated into the depicted sacred space. In this case, the viewer becomes an eyewitness to Mary and the Apostles receiving the Holy Spirit at Pentecost. The believer could thus better identify with the images in the church and mirror them and their actions: like Mary, one could patiently await the Holy Spirit; like St. Sebastian, endure being pierced by pain; or like St. Elizabeth, care for the needy. The idea that art encouraged the early modern viewer to such specific actions and thus played a crucial role in the formation and transformation of identity has often been neglected. Moreover, it was not just the art in church, but rather

*The Inner Life of Catholic Reform*. Ulrich L. Lehner, Oxford University Press. © Oxford University Press 2022.
DOI: 10.1093/oso/9780197620601.003.0009

every possible image, material object, sound, or smell that could become a conduit for the divine, thereby eliciting imitation and action.[1]

## Unifying and Dividing Sounds

Early modernity cannot be understood unless one grasps that it largely understood the world, like the Middle Ages before it, as God's creation. Thus, everything mirrored the divine. The world constituted a limitless treasure of symbols, metaphors, and allegories speaking in riddles about the glory of God. The world was, as the seventeenth-century Jesuit Eusebius Nieremberg called it, "God's poetry. I add that this poem is a labyrinth, which . . . gives intimation of, and points to, its author."[2] This *emblematic* worldview, as historians tend to call it, provided the church with an inexhaustible fountain of images and rituals that were used to instill faith. Through their availability, such symbols buttressed the methods of prayer and self-transformation people had been exposed to and gave them a concrete object to anchor their attention. A sign, however, only had meaning if the onlooker understood it. The omnipresence of symbolic language in homilies, prayers, and rituals guaranteed that the faithful could encounter and learn about the transformation of faith and morals. Moreover, this worldview enabled a preacher to bridge the gap between doctrinal message and experience by using images and examples from a parishioner's life. After all, every action or image was fair game, and even the most ordinary task could be given a profound allegorical meaning.[3]

While historians have paid much attention to visible signs, the entirely allegorical *soundscape* of early modern Catholicism has been widely neglected. As we saw earlier in the discussion of confraternities and prayer, a Catholic could understand the hourly bell signs as reminders to perform devotions. Moreover, the frequent bells indicating a forthcoming Mass, the moment of consecration, the sign for the hours, a death in the parish, or a threat, were invitations to pray. At the end of the sixteenth century, Borromeo's Synod of Milan emphasized that hearing a bell calling for Mass was an invitation for listeners to collect their thoughts, become conscious of their mortal sins, feel pain of remorse, and ask God for forgiveness. The bell tower (*campana*) acted as an audible reminder of the importance of personal conversion.[4] Furthermore, ringing the bells also scared demons away and called the angelic forces to assistance, be it in a thunderstorm, a war, or a spiritual struggle.[5]

Although the use of bells was already widespread in the Middle Ages, after the Council of Trent their importance was noticeably elevated. Instead of a single bell, parishes now often acquired sets of them for their newly constructed towers. Parishioners or Mass servers rang them in harmonic motifs and thus carried ancient hymns and prayers throughout the soundscape of cities and villages. These motifs imitated the beginning of hymns such as the *Salve Regina* and could therefore direct the listener to more *specific* actions. A certain motif called for prayer for the dead, another indicated the hour of Jesus's death, while yet another called for a prayer to Mary, and so forth. A sixteenth-century traveler through the Upper Palatinate testified that listeners were able to distinguish the different bells and understood their importance in creating community:

> If one rings the *Salve* bell, then people flock there like hens. . . . There is piping, running around, singing, screeching; people bellow like an ox, howl like wolves. . . . Whoever does not do this is a heretic, even if he is otherwise the godliest of them.[6]

The Marian bell signal to meet at the church, this text shows, not only created a community but also segregated it. Those who would not accept the "invitation" of the bell were branded as "heretics" who scorned the Virgin Mary.[7]

Likewise, hymns had a profound meaning for the self-transformation of the faithful. The expansion of plain, vernacular chant allowed early modern Catholics to recite or sing hymns at home and thereby use them not only as prayer but also as vocalization of the virtues they desired to imitate. In times of distress, it was such hymns, learned by heart, which the faithful chanted to console themselves and others. During the outbreak of the plague in Milan in the late sixteenth century, for example, families sang such hymns in their homes with their windows open. In a time of closed churches, this created an audible community.[8]

A German Catholic song book of 1663 was almost five hundred pages long and included songs for every day, but also for the liturgical seasons and feast days—songs about grace and virtues, against the enemies of Christianity, and of course about death. It proudly claimed that the texts allowed Catholics to learn the truths of faith much more easily, and thus be transformed into singing "paradise birds." The text also gives an indication of how widespread this method was. It claims that priests in Spain, France, Italy, and the Americas had already been using the method of hymnal learning for some time.[9] Since this, as well as most other hymnals, often also offered Latin songs with translations but hardly ever any musical notes, the faithful must have known the melodies from church or earlier instruction.[10] Hymns, however, did not only teach the mysteries of faith, but also the virtues.[11] Their emphasis on conversion, consolation, mercy, and forgiveness provided a curious counterbalance to the emphasis on Purgatory and Hell in many homilies. Verses describing God like this were legion in them: "He is full of patience and clemency: he is full of mercy. His offended spirit is not wrathful all the time. His zeal is appeased, and he judges our sins not as they deserve."[12]

A remarkable series of events in 1731 affirmed the power and influence of hymns. In the fall of that year, the police of Neustadt an der Weinstrasse arrested twenty-one-year-old Esther Grünhagen for infanticide. She was soon joined by two more inmates, who were incarcerated for homosexual acts, Johann Dietrich Schiffer and Philipp Thomas Götz, and another child murderer, Anna Barbara Jacquin (also referred to as Schackin). Although all the prisoners were members of the Reformed Church, Jaquin asked for a priest because she wanted to become Catholic. Fearing that the other prisoners might want to convert, too, the Reformed pastors began visiting them in prison but (allegedly) merely accused them of their past sins, while the Catholic priest extended mercy to them.[13] The Jesuit who gave us this account certainly weaved in confessional polemics in his portrayal of the Reformed, but the curious fact remains that indeed all the prisoners converted to Catholicism before they were executed on January 25, 1732. The two men were burnt at the stake and their ashes thrown into a nearby river. Since they had been reconciled with God, they had beforehand received communion. The priest assured Esther that both "are now with God in Heaven [and] will not cease to pray for you that you will fulfill his divine will exact with his grace and with joy."[14]

The text suggests that the Jesuit author wanted to describe the joy of the converts, thereby paralleling them with ancient martyrs, but at no point does he accuse the city government of wrongdoing for condemning them to death. The condemned were fortified with the Eucharist and thus died a happy death, he explained. The motives present here certainly justify reading this account as a confessional propaganda piece, but besides the polemical rhetoric it nevertheless maintains God's mercy and forgiveness. This theological message is continued in the narrative about the two convicted women. On the way to their execution, they chanted the hymns they had learned during catechism classes in prison.[15] This depicts them as martyrs, and the author claims that even the eyewitnesses to their execution regarded them as such. Both women recited twice the popular song "Whenever I imagine Jesus," the German rendering of a poem by St. Bernard of Clairvaux, which stressed joy about the presence of Jesus and hope in his mercy.[16] "Loving, loving is my Life" was the other hymn both sang with enthusiasm before their beheading. It expressed full abandonment to the divine will in the verse: "May God do what he pleases with me, yet he will be loving to me."[17] Confessional rhetoric emphasized here not only the exemplary Catholic love of God the converts demonstrated, but also their strong belief in an afterlife that would reward them with everlasting joy. Even if we subtract the layers of propaganda and polemic, it remains possible and probable that the two indeed cited or even sung these hymns, which they had just learned and were therefore fresh in their memory. More important, however, these texts demonstrate how hymns could be and were used to calm Catholics in difficult situations and prepare them for the worst, even death. The reader of this account by no means encounters something extraordinary about these women knowing and reciting hymns, but rather is reminded of their exemplary role. Like them, he or she should make ample use of the hymns, keeping them on their minds so that they spring from the lips in challenging moments of life. Hymns could easily be learned and remembered, and by repetition help Catholics mold themselves into different, holy people.

## Material Objects as Supernatural Weaponry

Early modern Catholicism offered countless means for the individual to deal with fear, misfortune, or sickness. Holy images and objects were believed to be supernatural weapons against evil inclinations, but also conduits of divine grace that strengthened the faithful. Catholics call(ed) such sacred objects, which led to the sacraments and somewhat echoed them, *sacramentals*. While the seven sacraments were visible signs instituted by Christ that always delivered the grace they promised (e.g., the supernatural cleansing from original and all other sin through the waters of baptism), sacramentals were of a much lower category, somewhat the remote resonance of a sacrament. A sacramental was merely a sacred *object*, which could be anything from holy water, a holy card, rosary, or scapular, to an amulet or medal. These objects could not communicate divine grace directly but merely helped the person using them. This theological distinction, however, did not deter many from ascribing supernatural powers to the material objects themselves, which church officials condemned as either superstition or as magic if used with spells.[18]

What attracted people to these objects? Since most sacraments were only celebrated in church, sacramentals allowed the faithful to have a tactile and visible conduit of divine presence in their own home. By hanging them on a wall or carrying them in a coat pocket, a Catholic extended the sacred space of the church into the home. Sacramentals continued traditions that were already popular in the Middle Ages. In the early modern period, however, the church began to standardize them and educate the faithful about them.[19] Such standardization also made it necessary to eradicate competing objects, such as pre-Christian magical amulets, which were still in use in large areas of Europe in the seventeenth century, as well as unapproved Catholic sacramentals. Yet instead of merely proscribing these objects, Catholic reformers set out to *convince* believers not only of the dangers of magic but also of the power of the approved sacramentals. The Capuchins in seventeenth-century Freiburg therefore disseminated stories about the miracles their Catholic medals had brought about. The historical sources suggest that the faithful accepted these sacramentals not out of a desire to conform to church norms but because they were considered more powerful. Catholics thus struck a good supernatural "bargain" with them.[20] Women were especially interested in sacramentals that assured them of a safe delivery and healthy children. In China, Marian devotionals, which were handed out by Jesuits, were additionally believed to help conceiving male heirs.[21]

The Capuchins could like other orders rely in their marketing on a large number of printed accounts. Among them, stories such as these were legion: a sixteenth-century Italian woman had broken off a piece of the wax *Agnus Dei* and given it as medicine to her fever-ridden husband, who recovered miraculously. A woman laid the *Agnus Dei* in water and gave it to her sick sister to drink, whose "withered" hand as well as other limbs were immediately healed. In 1593 a soldier's life was saved by the medallion as its silver housing caught a bullet aimed at his heart.[22]

The *Agnus Dei* was made from the previous year's Easter candle, solemnly bathed in chrism by the pope himself, and looked like a little host, usually with the image of a lamb carved on it.[23] Since the Easter candle represented the victory of Christ over death through his resurrection, it also symbolized the ultimate defeat of the powers of evil.[24] Veneration for the *Agnus Dei* derived, however, not only from its noble origin in Rome, but especially from its likeness to a consecrated host. It allowed the faithful to bring something home that looked like the Eucharist and was believed to repel demonic powers.[25] People wore it around the neck, while others kept it in a small box close to their bed or embroidered in a frame on the wall.[26] Baroque churches from India to Poland also made ample use of this sacramental, usually together with relics. The *Agnus Dei* never lost its original meaning as representing the Easter candle. Since it was blessed by the pope in Rome, it often served as a pilgrim's souvenir, allowing the observer to mentally travel to Rome and imaginatively partake in the papal liturgy (*peregrinatio pro Christo*). This piece of the Roman Easter candle thus put a Catholic in a direct relationship with the bishop of Rome, the pope, and visualized his primacy even in his or her own household.[27]

Nevertheless, even approved sacramentals could be maltreated if used superstitiously.[28] This was the case if one gave them undue reverence. To regard an *Agnus Dei* or a scapular as an object possessing divinely infused powers was superstition. Popular practice, however, often came close to such irregular use or even embraced it.[29] Since superstition led away from God and his graces, Catholic reformers catechized about the proper use of sacramentals and fought against their abuse. Their attempts spanned the time from the Council of Trent to the Catholic Enlightenment. The homilies of a Salzburg priest from the 1660s provide a good example. He admonished his parishioners that an *Agnus Dei* or a scapular would not save them from Hell if they had not gone to confession. Carrying a sacramental without living a Christian life was for him a bit like dressing wounds, "as if one put all kinds of ointments on it from the outside while there is pus and infection on the inside."[30] A sacramental would only help in the fight against the devil if one had first reformed one's own heart.

At the end of the eighteenth century, Catholic Enlighteners vehemently criticized sacramentals because they regarded them as superstitious objects. For rejecting the old customs their critics branded them as "libertines."[31] Among the population, however, the sacred objects remained in high demand. In Silesia, for example, in 1796 alone the Dominicans of Schweidnitz produced 32,400 of their popular St. Luke holy cards. Some of these cards were small and thin enough to be swallowed or mixed into food, while those intended as "prayers for good weather" were loaded with gunpowder into rifles.[32]

Although there are countless reports about widespread superstitious handling of sacred objects, the historian should be cautious in assuming that this was the only or even the preferred usage. Such an interpretation presumes that most users rejected their catechetical instruction about sacramentals. In most cases, apart from intentional use for "witchcraft," it seems far more probable to assume instead a *partial* disregard for church norms. Even the unapproved use of an object does not necessarily mean exclusivity: those using an *Agnus Dei* in a superstitious way knew about some of its true meaning. Could they not also have used it appropriately at times according to church norms then? Could not somebody wear an *Agnus Dei* like a magical amulet, but simultaneously cherish it as a memorial of the papal Easter candle? Moreover, one should not assume that the use of such objects was *unchanging*. Could not a person early in life obey the norms, but later—under the duress of pain and distress—be swayed to embrace it superstitiously? After all, the lives of Saints testify to the opposite pattern, from superstition to approved use, so why should it not be possible the other way around? Assuming a petrified stance toward the use of religious objects seems to rest on the assumption that faith is inflexible, which it obviously was not. These questions are extremely difficult to answer, and therefore a hermeneutic of caution is warranted when analyzing archival sources about popular faith practices involving material objects.

## Eliciting Imitation through Images

Much of early modern Catholic art not only attempted to provoke excitement in the soul but also to help detect a likeness between observer and image. The onlooker could find herself in the images painted on church ceilings, printed on holy cards, or presented in flowery narratives. The self could mirror itself in religious images even in cases of extreme duress, as the example of prisoners on death row shows. Confraternity members showed these criminals painted images of the martyrdom of St. John the Baptist and the passion of Christ. The confraternity member would explain the image, relate it to the prisoner's life, and carry it openly the next day to the place of execution. This ritual rested on the assumption that the image would not anger but rather calm the soul of the prisoner. This practice demonstrates that early modern Catholics believed that certain images caused predictable emotional and cognitive outcomes.[33] How this insight was used in meditation we have seen in chapter 7.[34]

Among the new images one encounters in seventeenth-century spirituality is the depiction of the infancy of Jesus. It was based on the visions of the seventeenth-century Carmelite Margaret of Beaune. She claimed that Christ did not dislike becoming incarnate in a child and that this phase of his life revealed the virtues of "holy childlikeness."[35] The image of the Christ child allowed Margaret to see her "inner child" and thus her own weaknesses as expressions of these virtues. The imagery of childhood did not, however, eclipse the reality of suffering because it also called for the imitation of the pains of Jesus's childhood—for example, over the killing of the innocent children of Bethlehem. The imitation of the Christ child gave Margaret of Beaune and others the possibility to see their own lives mirrored in Jesus's existence.[36] This veneration should therefore be seen not only as the result of the rise in parental love toward children but also as an expression of the spiritual needs of those who felt powerless and marginalized, just like children, and knew that they were completely dependent on God's will.[37] Like a child who was unprotected and without means, so the follower of the infant Jesus knew that she was dependent on the unmerited grace and mercy of God. Therefore, an eighteenth-century Benedictine recommended that his fellow monks make the infant the topic of their annual retreat. It would help to become more cognizant of God's mercy and love for humanity. Every Sunday of the year, he argued, can be used to meditate on the infancy of Jesus, and thus to heal intellect and will.[38] The *Infant of Prague*, a wax figurine of the Christ child celebrated on the feast of the Holy Name of Jesus since the 1720s, gave the generic message about Jesus's infancy a concrete image. It was venerated especially in churches of the Jesuit, Carmelite, and Capuchin orders, and spread the message of a "great God, who as a little child without the use of his feet, runs after the sinner."[39] Nevertheless, the Christ child not only invited imitation of the child's virtues but also those of his mother Mary and foster father Joseph. The practitioner of this devotion was thus called to emulate the fear, love, adoration, and praise that Joseph and Mary showed toward the divine child.

Another new image emphasizing the love of God for humanity, and thus focusing on a central theme of Catholic Reform, was that of the Sacred Heart of Jesus. Although of medieval origins, only its propagation by St. Francis de Sales, St. Jeanne de Chantal, and St. Margaret Mary Alacoque made it one of the most widespread devotions in the seventeenth and eighteenth centuries. By concentrating on the heart as disconnected from the rest of the body, Margaret's visions not only legitimized an already existing *emblematic* understanding of the heart as the organ created for love but also raised it to the level of a distinct devotion.[40]

Among the notable pre-Alacoque works on the emblematic understanding of the heart one can mention Francesco Pona's 1645 *Cardiomorphoseos*[41] and the *Schola Cordis* of Benedict van Haeften. The latter, a Dutch Benedictine, saw in the human heart the bride God longed for. Since the human heart was created for the love of God, it had a triangular shape, indicating that only the triune God could satisfy its deepest desires.[42] Once the heart was transformed by grace, it became, as Haeften said, the garden in which lover and bride met.[43] Such theologies of the heart suggest that the image not only elicited the response of acknowledging God's love for humanity but also invited the observer to detect likeness on an emotional level: as the observer's heart was full of desires, so was Jesus's. Facing the image of true love in the Sacred Heart also enabled the believer to examine whether one's own desires were aligned with God's or not. "Where is my heart and what does it beat for?," a person could ask and feel in such a moment.

Emblematic theology like that of the heart "enchanted" the world of early modernity by insisting that there were mysterious symbols carrying secret divine messages.[44] In sophisticated pictorial settings, theologians enshrined doctrinal communications for spiritual and moral reform. Although many of these needed a textual explanation, many *emblemata* could also be understood by the less educated or even illiterate. Popular depictions were printed on holy cards, in prayer books of Marian sodalities, or could be seen in church ornaments. The onlooker knew some of their meaning through parish catechesis, or in the case of Jesuit schools, through explicit lessons on emblems.[45] Of enormous influence was the pictorial theology produced in the Spanish Netherlands, which enjoyed a great popularity throughout the Catholic world. Hermann Hugo's *Pia Desideria*, first published in 1624, went through countless editions and translations, and even influenced Protestant piety. Each of the Jesuit's scenes contained next to the emblem a quotation from Scripture. Image meditation and scriptural meditation were thus intertwined.[46] The emblematic works of other Jesuits also were successful, especially Jan David's *Veridicus Christianus* of 1601 and Antoine Sucquet's *Via Vitae Aeternae* of 1620.[47]

## Angelic Assistance and Imitation

A distinctive feature of early modern Catholic art is the presence of angels. While the archangels had been venerated since antiquity, the Feast of the

Guardian Angels was only added to the Roman liturgical calendar in 1608. Even later, in 1670 it was made an obligatory feast for the whole church. Guardian angels were believed to be spiritual beings whose task it was to watch over humanity. Every human had its own caretaker. The Society of Jesus especially stressed this devotion because it acknowledged in angels the *embodiment of service* for God and humanity.[48]

In Catholic belief the angels had been created good by God. Faced with the decision to serve God or not, some decided in the negative, "fell," and became with their leader Lucifer devils/demons. The angelic decision, theologians reasoned, was final so that no further angelic fall or conversion was possible.[49] Building on an already sophisticated angelology, Francesco Albertini's 1612 treatise on guardian angels reached a large audience due to its popular style. He stressed the continuous support of angels for human efforts at moral and spiritual transformation.[50] Jeremias Drexel, a Jesuit in Munich, elevated his confrere's ideas in his book *The Guardian Angel's Clock*. Drexel envisioned the angels working tirelessly for the good of humanity, interceding for humans and protecting them, but also assisting them in the fight against heresies, for which especially the Archangel St. Michael was invoked.[51] In Spain, the erudite Benedictine Blasco Lanuza identified in a massive treatise twelve offices of the angels, namely "teaching, mediating, avoiding dangers, fighting against the devil, reprimanding, consoling, guiding, reducing temptations, defending, helping people out of predicaments, exhorting to virtue and, finally, lovingly punishing those under their protection."[52]

The image of the angel, however, not only promised assistance but also invited the devout to *imitate* angelic virtues, especially chastity,[53] patience, vigilance, and perseverance. Drexel explained that patience was the foundation of a Christian life. It not only reduced fear but also encouraged perseverance in distress. The angels espoused these virtues through their enduring and tireless assistance. A believer might be helpless on his own, but he could, Drexel admonished, trust patiently in his guardian angels to fight any temptation. The promise of such angelic assistance calmed the minds of the faithful fearing eternal damnation. Through them they gained supernatural assistants who protected them.[54] The bishops of the Catholic Reform were called to imitate such faithfulness, too: instead of abandoning sinners, they should work tirelessly, like the angels, to bring them back to the church.[55]

The imagery of angels also manifested several theological controversies. Jesuits, for example, could continue the controversies on grace and present the angels as an embodiment of divine help, the *auxilium divinum*, which left human freedom intact. Likewise, angelology could be weaponized for the quarrels in moral theology. Jesuit probabilism encouraged humans to make reasonable (*probable*) decisions in morally uncertain areas, while rigorism avoided such choices. Assuring the faithful of *angelic* assistance in their reasoning gave the believer self-confidence in their behavior and liberated them from scruples.[56] Additionally, angelic presence also provided a theodicy. Even if God permitted evil, he had established a spiritual force to assist humanity, thus proving his love and care.[57] A Jesuit angelology also offered the possibility of answering what would happen to the unbaptized. After all, if every human soul received a guardian angel, what was their role for unbelievers? Jesuit theologians argued that angelic help, very similar to the concept of sufficient grace, was available to all humans and gave them a protective shield against doing evil and protected them from the devil. Only the free decision not to accept angelic help could render it ineffective. Such belief also consoled Catholic parents, who entrusted their unbaptized children to the care of the angels until they received the sacrament and gave those who had adult unbaptized family members the ability to invoke angelic assistance for them.[58] Some theologians even argued that the angels had revealed themselves to ancient pagan cultures.[59]

Perhaps the last idea derived from early modern knowledge of ancient art. Beginning in the fifteenth century, the depiction of protective gods such as Cupid served as a role model for a new type of angel, the *putto*. The putti style spread from Italy to the rest of the world. The plump children with wings were seen as guardian angels and considered intermediaries between the divine and the human world.[60] Due to their polytheistic origin, putti were enthusiastically accepted in missionary territories such as Mexico. Already in the sixteenth century, a Nahuatl song written by a Franciscan asserted that at Jesus's death on the cross angels had become the friends of humanity. Missionary catechesis stressed that they were creatures just like humans. Nevertheless, many natives saw in them benign semidivine creatures that permeated nature.[61] Some have argued that the new *putti* style also established the possibility of *commemorating* deceased infants through the symbolic presence of the childlike angels.[62] This did *not* mean that putti represented the deceased children, because a dead, baptized child would never "turn into" an angel. Rather, the putti represented *angels* but through their outward appearance allowed an *association* with the deceased children. In the absence of convincing evidence for this claim, however, it seems much more probable to assume that the putti manifested the pedagogy of the Catholic reform. As naked or barely clothed childlike beings, the putti emanated the message of purity, in particular sexual innocence, which the theology of the time emphasized. Thus, they presented to the onlooker an imitable state of life in which all sensual desires were redeemed by grace and transformed into something pleasing to God's will. Furthermore, the putti testified that God was truly present in the world. Instead of focusing on the presence of God in Scripture, as the churches of the Reformation did, this focus reminded the observer that in the Catholic worldview God had endowed seven signs as sacraments of his grace. All of these were as visible and tangible as the putti in a church. Finally, most putti exercised in art a service for God, be it singing, playing instruments, pulling curtains, or holding columns. They demonstrated that all of creation was destined to serve God and that every part of it had its distinctive duties. Thus, the angels reminded the onlooker of serving God first, and of fulfilling one's duties.

Of all angels it was the Archangel St. Michael who enjoyed the highest veneration. For the high altar (1624) for the cathedral of Freising in Bavaria, Peter Paul Rubens placed St. Michael into a painting of the apocalyptic woman. It depicted the archangel defeating demons and heretics. With it, he articulated the then-popular devotion to invoke the "prince of the angels" for what was seen as the apocalyptic battle with evil, the Protestant Reformation—right in the middle of the Thirty Years' War. Other uses notwithstanding, the veneration of St. Michael and the angels also prevented apostasy in the hour of death.[63] In recusant England, however, Catholics felt uncomfortable with their Jesuit priests talking about the presence of angels at the altar, possibly because their veneration was distinctly Catholic and ridiculed by Anglican neighbors.[64]

Angelology visualized a divine guidance that did not usurp human freedom. With remarkable acuity, theologians clarified that angels never violated this freedom. Therefore, most rejected the idea that an angel could visually or mentally manipulate a person. Only if God permitted it was such action possible. Thus, the angelic beings were just as restricted in their powers as their evil counterparts, the devils. Neither could transform the human will except by persuasion or the arousal of passions and appetites.[65] Talk about good and evil angels often came dangerously close to dualism.[66] Therefore, catechisms made sure the lessons about angels presented an antidualist theism, according to which *only* God was all-powerful:[67] accordingly, both good and fallen angels were creatures of God. While the good angels did what God commanded them to do, the evil angels followed the command of Satan.[68] The fact that Scripture did not contain much about the angels led several theologians to also peruse apocryphal sources. Following these, the Jesuit Andre Serrano, stationed in the Philippines, published in 1699 in Mexico a book propagating devotion to the apocryphal archangels Uriel, Sealthiel, Jehudiel, and Barachiel.[69] This devotion was, however, only practiced in Spain, Portugal, and their colonies, and is perhaps an echo of Jewish mysticism.[70]

One of the most sophisticated treatments of angels was undertaken by the master of late scholasticism, the Jesuit Francisco Suarez. He embodied the early modern victory of Scotus's angelology over that of Aquinas. In his system the angels were described as having a close bond with humanity. Likewise, Franciscans and Capuchins propagated a Scotistic understanding of angels. A telling example of this trend can be found in the homilies of the renowned Capuchin Prokop of Templin. For him, the angels stand "between two fires of love," one representing God, the other humanity.[71] A much more detailed account of such an approach was given by the Jesuit Jacques Coret in his popular *The Guiding Angel*. He saw the angels assisting the faithful in *all* daily chores.[72] This piety intensified throughout subsequent generations, so that by the end of the seventeenth century French Catholics would not only greet another person on the street, but *also* their guardian angel.[73] Such robust and often exaggerated devotion drew heavy criticism at the end of the eighteenth century—Catholic Enlighteners regarded angelology as genuinely problematic. Since Scripture did not say much about angels, they argued that theologians should not engage in wild speculations about them as Suarez had done. Moreover, the Enlighteners did not think that the veneration of angels contributed to moral improvement but had the opposite effect. For them, angelology had become an embarrassment.[74]

Early modern Catholicism is most famous for its exuberant Baroque architecture and art. Their images evoked a variety of emotional responses, which were carefully studied and anticipated by theologians and philosophers. By using a variety of metaphors, the Catholic Reform addressed the senses of the faithful. Yet they not only elicited responses but also invited the viewer to imitate them. The believer therefore became "part" of salvation history, could slip into the role of a saint, and thus experience what a different life (namely one that pleased God) would look like. Such learning by examples was accessible to both the literate and illiterate. New among these images were those of the angels. While they were depicted as distant in the Middle Ages, they now became close companions for humanity.

# 10

# Mary and Joseph

## Images of Hope

Although practiced since antiquity, Marian piety became a confessional characteristic of Catholicism in the sixteenth century after the churches of the Reformation rejected it. In the immediate aftermath of the Council of Trent, which recommended the veneration of sacred images, count-less new images of Mary were placed prominently in churches. When the kings of Portugal and Poland not only dedicated their lands to her protection but also even assigned Mary queenship over their territories, they demon-strated the profound devotion their populations had for the *Theotokos*. After all, honoring her was considered a sign of being among the elect for eternal life, and entrusting a nation to her meant extending her blessing upon it.[1] Theologically, with Marian piety the church emphasized love and mercy. This brought more balance to the dialectic of fear and mercy that we have encountered throughout this book.[2] Here it is not intended to even attempt to adequately present Marian piety of the time (such an endeavor would have to be the topic of a separate monograph), but merely to point to two of the many Marian tools of self-improvement—the rosary and the scapular.[3]

## Transformation through the Rosary

The rosary and its global dissemination after the Council of Trent can serve as a good example for the new Marian self-understanding of Catholicism. In priest-deprived territories like Tudor England, praying the rosary was a substitute for receiving the *viaticum* or confessing to a priest. The reciting person entrusted his or her eternal fate to the intercession of the Blessed Virgin. Since Mary was seen as compassionate and loving, and as a pow-erful intercessor with her son, she alleviated the fear of Hell. Such trust in Mary did not originate in the council but grew out of late medieval piety. At the end of the fifteenth century, the *Ave Maria* (Lk 1:28; 1:42) had been

*The Inner Life of Catholic Reform*. Ulrich L. Lehner, Oxford University Press. © Oxford University Press 2022.
DOI: 10.1093/oso/9780197620601.003.0010

amended with the phrase "Holy Mother of God, pray for us sinners, now and in the hour of our death. Amen," indicating the increased importance assigned to Mary as intercessor. The new phrase was found in Spain by 1534 and in France by 1560, yet it was not officially endorsed until its inclusion in the Roman Breviary in 1568. This addition went beyond the biblical text of the *Ave Maria* and thus explicitly rebuked the Protestant denial of the invocation of the saints.[4]

The rosary was a sacramental recommended for spiritual battles, especially for a good hour of death. St. Peter Canisius also praised its power for protection against heretics and to lead them to conversion. By reciting the *Ave Maria*, he explained, the faithful would step into the role of the Archangel Gabriel congratulating Mary, representing the whole church, and thus bring her immense joy.[5] Unsurprisingly, the rosary also became one of the most cherished devotions in the mission territories. A Chinese manual written around 1620 explained it carefully to the newly baptized: "In a full rosary one recites 150 times the Hail Mary and fifteen times the Our Father. It has three parts. In each part one prays fifty times the Hail Mary and five times the Our Father." It "nourishes the life of the soul" and "preserves virtue," the Chinese catechumens learned.[6] Thus, praying the rosary was much more than a formulaic recital, because the devotion aimed at establishing a genuine dialogue with God through Mary. For example, for the rosary's mystery of finding the twelve-year-old Jesus among the rabbis in the Temple (Lk 2:41ff), one could contemplate: "Today I implore you with faith and respect to plead with your son Jesus when I have difficulties in life, to grant me spiritual consolation. Also enable me at all times and in all things to act in accordance with the holy will. With humility and filial piety, to serve the Lord of Heaven. Amen."[7] The rosary invoked Mary as mother and allowed the praying believer to partake in a filial relationship. This assured Catholics of a benevolent mother in Heaven, who would assist her children—and thus spoke to the needs of Chinese Catholics as well as believers everywhere.

In 1569 the Dominican Pope Pius V strongly urged all Catholics to pray the rosary in the fight against heresies and use it to please God.[8] The prayer beads became now officially a tool of personal transformation and were praised as such in the coming centuries. After all, not only did they invite the faithful to a deeper relationship with God by the repetition of the fifteen stations of salvation history, but they also ensured that the praying person *knew* the faith necessary for salvation (*fides explicita*). Spirituality and catechesis went hand in hand in the devotion of the rosary, and thus it is not surprising that it became a popular present at the baptism of a Catholic, from Austria to Mexico.

When reciting the Hail Mary, a Catholic should "imagine that the sacred Virgin is present," thus taking on the role of the Archangel Gabriel at the annunciation.[9] Immediately after saying morning prayers to the triune God, a devotee should face an image of Our Lady and ask for her benediction for the day. He should imagine Mary raising her blessing hand, thus anchoring this mental image in his soul.[10] Likewise, one could dedicate all daily chores to her, even stitching and sewing. One could associate them with similar stations in the life of Mary, such as her fashioning clothes for the boy Jesus. Mothers were additionally encouraged on the feast of the presentation of Mary in the Temple (November 21) to offer their children to Mary for protection.[11]

The rosary also allowed a Catholic to offer up sufferings as "flowers" to Mary. The Mother of God bore the title of lily and rose, and flowers were the appropriate present to venerate a statue or image of hers. Offering up one's sufferings as metaphorical flowers constituted a profoundly personal act of devotion, entrusting oneself to Mary's motherly love and mercy. One way of assembling such a flower bouquet was by personal mortification in honor of Mary, such as fasting on Saturdays.[12] Another was propagated by the seventeenth-century Italian Jesuit Tommaso Auriemma. He recommended that on Saturdays, devotees share stories about the graces they had received from Mary. This way one's experiences were not only subjected to a benign peer review that discouraged excesses but also reaffirmed the faith of others. This way, one became a missionary of Marian graces. Moreover, these devotees often also studied printed accounts of Marian miracles. By learning about Catholics witnessing such events in India and the Americas, this piety reminded them of their *global* faith community.[13] Miracles facilitated by the rosary were especially popular among readers, such as this one from the Philippines: in 1637 a young man fell into a river; when crocodiles attacked him, he showed them his rosary and was spared.[14]

## Mary as Refuge of Sinners

Trust in divine mercy was highly sought after because many feared eternal damnation.[15] Therefore, pastors recommended the rosary to despondent persons and reminded them that the veneration of Mary was considered a clear sign that one was among the elect, while her rejection was an indicator of reprobation or eternal damnation. The theological opinion that no true devotee of Mary was ever condemned to Hell, because she was the ultimate refuge for sinners (*tutissimum asylum*; *refugium singulare*), certainly boosted Marian zeal.[16] Some theologians even went so far as to claim that *nobody* could hope to obtain salvation unless through the intercession of the *Theotokos*.[17] Although Mary's elevated status certainly confused contemporaries without theological training, official church preaching always pointed out the difference between her veneration (*hyperdulia*) and that of worship reserved for God alone. Even the most excessive veneration of Mary, which tended to marginalize talk about the need of Christ's grace for salvation, expressed an optimistic understanding of predestination: Mary would succeed in swaying the judgment of Christ in the favor of her devotees. Her intervention was accessible to everybody. Even the greatest sinner, who had neglected all duties, could be saved as long as he stretched out his hands to her on his deathbed. A swarm of such near-death conversions were narrated by St. Alphonsus of Liguori in his *Glories of Mary* (1750).[18] Liguori's book, one of the most widely translated religious books of all time, articulated a maximalist Mariology, which for Catholic Enlightenment authors such as Ludovico Muratori seemed to reduce human responsibility and also the centrality of Christ. The Muratorian and Liguorian approaches had different agendas: while Liguori wanted to address religious despair over salvation and preach mercy and forgiveness, Muratori wanted to prune early modern spirituality, teach responsibility, and recenter it on Christ. However, both agreed on the optimistic post-Tridentine approach to predestination, emphasizing God's mercy and forgiveness over his right to reprobate sinners.[19]

Spreading this message of Marian mercy in missionary territories complemented the preaching of anxiety and demonstrated that the dialectic of fear and mercy was a *global* Catholic phenomenon. In many areas, the image of the Virgin and her miraculously born child connected easily to ancient native myths, such as that of the Sky Woman among Mohawks and Iroquois, and was immediately associated with benevolence and love.[20] How quickly Mary was "adopted" by the newly baptized was shown by the remarks of a Huron explaining to a Jesuit in the 1650s that for ten years the Virgin had never refused to answer his prayers: "She it is who gives me patience in the sufferings that I constantly endure; she it is who obtains for me grace to pay little heed to the good things of this life, and not to fear its evils . . . and she does all that I wish, as I desire to do nothing and to wish for nothing except what she wishes."[21]

The widespread Marian congregations founded by the Society of Jesus also propagated the teaching of Mary as the refuge of sinners.[22] The members were encouraged to keep track of the graces they had received from her, and one Jesuit proudly exclaimed: "I wish that the tongues of so many thousand members . . . would be quills," so that all the miracles could be written down that happened due to her intercession.[23] These congregations aimed, as we saw in chapter 6, at a wholesome transformation of their members. In fact, the most successful advertisement for the sodalities was the virtuous behavior of its members.[24] Narratives of their conversion often circulated orally, but were sometimes also collected in print to reinforce the members' desire to obtain such perfection.[25] The dissemination and propagation of the congregation's aims lay mostly in the hands of its lay leaders.[26] Such a position was of course a societal honor, but priests made sure that members elected their leader only after prayerful discernment.[27] After all, such a leader was more than an administrator and had to emulate the Marian virtues of purity and obedience. Together with the priestly superior, he embodied for the members the voice and authority of Mary and Christ, so that an eighteenth-century preacher put these words into the mouth of the Virgin: "Whoever follows me . . . , reveres me, and asks advice from me . . . shall be guided by those whom I set above him as presiders in the congregation."[28]

Marian piety, however, also had a polemical, confessional side. Since the Protestant Reformers had rejected all intercessory prayer to the saints and the veneration of Mary, reciting the rosary or the Lauretanian litany became quite divisive in a religiously split territory. Moreover, since devotees of Mary were assured that they were predilected for Heaven, Marian piety successfully undermined Protestant polemics about the uncertainty over a person's future state. Educating Catholics about this was therefore an easy way to not only dispel fears of Hell, but also diminish the attractiveness of Protestantism, which promised *certainty* about salvation. Although Marian piety reduced perpetual doubt about salvation, Catholic theologians emphasized that such assurance was *not* infallible.[29] Unlike the "fraudulent" Protestant certainty, this Catholic variant, polemicists added, was not presumptuous but rather an act of true *hope*. It therefore inspired a Catholic to spiritually progress in honest humility and charity.[30] Likewise, catechisms did not eliminate the fear of Hell or teach absolute certainty about salvation, but instead encouraged the faithful to have "strong hope" in their eternal glory by following the divine laws and the precepts of the church.

It is important to note that by rejecting infallible knowledge about one's fate, Catholics also implicitly rejected the notion that one could save oneself, even by an act of faith. Salvation for Catholic theology was "worked out" in "fear and trembling" and thus linked to the requirement of becoming a follower of Christ able to participate in his merits. Since no one could know for sure whether one would persevere until death, as a Catholic one could only espouse, as Blosius said, "courageous hope in the benignity and mercy of God."[31]

## The Scapular and the See of Mercy

Apart from the rosary, the most popular Marian devotional object was the scapular. Believed to have been presented to St. Simon Stock by Mary in the thirteenth century, this brown piece of cloth was worn by the Carmelites and later by other orders to symbolize their close relationship with the *Theotokos* (see also chapter 9). The Carmelite tradition promised that a person without mortal sin who wore it in the hour of death would immediately enter paradise. By wearing it, one slipped under Mary's mantle and thus under her special protection, being "covered" by the plentitude of her graces. It is not surprising that the laity aspired to participate in such promises, for which purpose the Carmelites distributed a miniature format of their body-length scapular. Cut into two small squares of about an inch in size, connected by a band, it was worn hanging down the chest and back.[32] The design of the scapular did not only imitate Mary's mantle, but also that of military breast- and backplates. This, together with Mary's reputation for being the "terror of demons," allowed the scapular to be named a shield (*clypeus*) against all attacks of the devil.[33]

Especially during the seventeenth century, when enthusiasm about the Carmelite Reform swept over Europe, veneration of the scapular increased, particularly in Spain. There, it also received a series of royal privileges, until in 1726 the Feast of the Holy Scapular became a solemnity in the calendars of all religious orders. Like other sacramentals, Enlighteners ridiculed the wearing of the cloth as "superstition."[34] Yet the Carmelite friars, discalced and unreformed, as well as other orders, continued to praise it as a unique image of God's mercy and as a "sign of salvation" (*signum salutis*). They successfully propagated this piety in every area they were present, be it India, the Middle East, or the Americas.[35] Other religious orders soon developed their own versions of the scapular. The Servites had a black one, which they introduced to Syrian Catholics in 1727,[36] while the Theatines propagated the blue scapular of the Immaculate Conception, which originated in the visions of Ursula Benincasa.[37]

Unlike the *Agnus Dei*, which had Roman roots, the scapular suggested a miraculous origin in the Holy Land itself. This allowed the carrier to step into the role of a pilgrim to the land where Jesus was born, while wearing Mary's cloak. A place under her mantle guaranteed God's favor. Like a queen who would request mercy from the king for a prisoner, so Mary would intercede for every sinner who fled to her protection. Although all humans were given Mary as mother, the devotees of the scapular assumed the status of favorites, something that many Catholics desired.[38] This devotion manifested that her mercy was as "wide as the Ocean," inexhaustible, and open to everyone.[39] This Carmelite notion of God as "ocean of mercy" parallels Bellarmine's insight that the second highest step in the ascent to God was the meditation on his mercy.[40] Theologians concluded that if any Christian could profit from Mary's mercy through the scapular, then so must the poor souls in Purgatory. There was also belief in the "Sabbatine Privilege" by which Mary would help free souls from Purgatory on the Saturday after their deaths if they wore the Carmelite scapular, observed chastity according to their state in life, and recited the *Little Office of the Blessed Virgin Mary* (or abstained from meat on Wednesdays and Saturdays if they could not read). The Sabbatine Privilege was linked to a papal bull said to have been issued by Pope John XXII on March 3, 1322. Various scholars have questioned the authenticity of this bull, but eight popes between 1530 and 1684 invoked it.[41] Consequently, many Catholics combined their Purgatory piety with the veneration of the scapular. The Carmelite Dominicus a Jesu Maria even claimed that Mary herself instructed him in a vision to recommend the scapular to pray for the dead.[42]

The Trinitarians offered their own version of Mary as See of Mercy and their own scapular. Nevertheless, the Trinitarian scapular was not dedicated to Mary but to the Holy Trinity. The spirituality of the order, dedicated to the liberation of Christian slaves out of Muslim hands, centered on divine mercy. It invoked Mary as "Our Lady of Grace" and "Redeemer of Prisoners" (*redemptrix captivorum*), while the Mercedarians gave her the title "Lady of Mercy." Members of Trinitarian confraternities not only raised money to buy Christians out of slavery but also hoped to be redeemed from the metaphorical "prison of their soul." The captives themselves, men and women who suffered either galley service or demeaning servitude in the Orient or North Africa,[43] were considered part of the same body of Christ, the church, and thus worthy of every feasible assistance. Freeing them physically and spiritually was therefore "the most excellent" work of mercy, the "triumph of mercy."[44]

## The Image and Imitation of St. Joseph

An eighteenth-century Catholic might have been surprised to hear that the ardent veneration of one of the most widely beloved saints in his church was relatively new. Of course, St. Joseph had been present to the Christian imagination since antiquity; after all, he is mentioned in the Gospels of Matthew, Luke, and John, and had been included as *confessor* in the Roman Martyrology since the ninth century,[45] but it was not until the fourteenth and fifteenth centuries that his devotion took off. From then on, he became the patron of new churches more often, as well as ecclesial organizations and confraternities, and a fervently invoked intercessor. Isidor Isolani's *Summa de Donis de s. Joseph* of 1522, dedicated to the reformer pope Hadrian VI, must especially be credited with spreading veneration of the saint as a symbol of personal and ecclesial sanctification. Yet even the seventeenth-century French Jesuit Paul de Barry confessed his bewilderment about why the veneration of St. Joseph developed so late. Most likely though, he reasoned, it was because it would have caused confusion before the consubstantiality of Son and Father, or Mary's virginity, had been dogmatically defined.[46] By the fifteenth century, however, such questions were long settled and thus nothing stood in the way of giving the cult official approval. The addition of St. Joseph's feast day (March 19) to the *Roman Missal* and breviary happened only under Pope Sixtus IV in 1484, and it took another 150 years before it would become a liturgical solemnity (*de praecepto*) in 1621.[47]

St. Joseph's rise fits well into the Catholic Reform method of engaging the faithful not only on a cognitive level but also through the imagination, emotions, and senses. Slipping under the mantle of Mary or imitating the virtues of the great figures of salvation history enabled a Catholic to take ownership of her life and interpret it against the background of an allegorical landscape. One was not merely called to fight against temptations und overcome them, but rather to put on the persona of holy people like King

David and reshape one's life in their image.[48] The celebration of their virtues, however, underscored that all their accomplishments had their origin in the merits of Christ. This was visualized in the art of Tridentine churches: instead of a local patron saint, usually Jesus or Mary occupies the center of a church's high altar. The surrounding saints therefore appear not as independent agents but rather as recipients of the grace that emanates from Christ, the Trinity, or Mary. This iconography grounded the saints on the same level as the believer and made them relatable and imitable role models.

Such a grounding of the saints in salvation history made many accounts of their lives appear as made-up fables. Not only Protestants but also Catholic Reformers criticized invented tales as deceiving the public. In order to put the veneration of the saints on a new and secure footing, in 1603 the Bollandists began to collect historically verifiable accounts of the saints. Two decades earlier, Cesare Baronius had already announced a similar plan for the martyrs of the church in his *Martyrologium Romanum* of 1584. He explained that only "solidly confirmed" accounts of martyrs should be disseminated among the faithful. These would be the source from which artists should draw their inspiration. The depiction of the gory death of a martyr, however, not only terrified the onlooker but also awakened the desire to imitate the saint's per-severance and to anticipate the joy of heavenly glory. Moreover, the historical accounts that Baronius approved articulated that the martyr's heroism had been a gift from Christ and thus in principle available to everyone else, too.[49]

Popular saints like St. Christopher or St. Margaret, whose legends were full of superstitious elements, were for the post-Trent church a growing source of embarrassment. Erasmus had already ridiculed St. Christopher, and Peter Paul Rubens's attempt to counter such criticism by depicting him as a Christian "Hercules" was a rare exception. Most church leaders preferred to emphasize saints that fulfilled the newly established standards of historicity. Consequently, St. Christopher was increasingly replaced as patron of a good death by St. Joseph.[50] The new emphasis on Christ was another profoundly theological reason to transition to the foster father of Jesus. While St. Christopher's interaction with the Christ child was legendary, St. Joseph's was testified to by the Gospels and the entire church tradition. St. Christopher could not compete with St. Joseph's position in the Holy Family. Additionally, St. Joseph personified the connection between a good, virtuous life and a good death—an aspect that was underdeveloped in the legend of St. Christopher. Unsurprisingly, confraternities in honor of St. Joseph began to spread all over the Catholic world. In 1555 he was chosen as a patron for the ecclesiastical provinces in New Spain and Mexico, in 1667 as patron of the China missions, and by the middle of the late seventeenth century it was almost impossible to find a Catholic church anywhere on the globe without an image, altar, or statue of the saint.[51]

For theologians, however, St. Joseph created several problems. Especially his relationship to the Virgin had to be clarified, and his own status as foster father of Jesus. What kind of man, they asked, could have been destined by God to become the caretaker of his Son as well as of the Mother of God? Did he not have to possess similar characteristics to Mary? Did he not have to be predestined in anticipation of the merits of Christ, like her? Most theologians assumed that Joseph never committed a mortal sin because he had been protected by divine grace. With such purity of heart, he could be the perfect caretaker and earthly role model for Jesus. Herein lies perhaps also the appeal of this "new" saint for reformers: St. Joseph embodied the Tridentine discovery of the importance of the family. As the custodian of Jesus, he served as a role model for all men and showed them how to lead a household, educate their offspring, and live a life in which all virtues are perfectly "integrated." He embodied also how a disciplined household functioned without domestic tyranny but instead with love and justice.[52]

In Spain, for example, his veneration was heavily supported by reform orders such as the Capuchins. The friars saw in St. Joseph a powerful device to battle the moral decline of the Spanish empire in the seventeenth century. He was presented as the remedy for a decadent male society, which had stopped following its honor code and needed to rediscover chastity and fortitude. In 1635, the Dominican Francisco de Leon recommended the saint's masculinity to the "effeminate" men of Spain. Especially St. Joseph's faith, the fulfillment of his duties, and his sense of honor and chastity, were seen as the antidote to lascivious behavior. The Franciscan Andres de Soto emphasized St. Joseph as the successful artisan, thereby rejecting the idleness of Spanish men: "He practiced his art and occupation to sustain himself and to live by the work of his hands, occupying himself also in acts of charity and mercy."[53] The custodian of Jesus was thus identified as the embodiment of virtues that had once made Spain successful. This message, however, made it necessary to alter the traditional depiction of St. Joseph as an older male. In the early seventeenth century one can therefore observe the trend of portraying him as a younger and more vigorous, even "virile man."[54] Such virility, however, was paired with wisdom, so that the Mexican Jesuit Pedro Morales called him "God's main advisor" in human things and a representative of the Holy

Spirit.[55] This movement reached a climax when by 1679 Saint Joseph had become the most commonly depicted saint in the Spanish empire, and was officially endorsed as its new protector.[56]

It should therefore not surprise us that the most important authors propagating the cult of St. Joseph came from Spain, namely the sixteenth-century theologians Andres de Soto, a Franciscan, and Jerónimo Gracián, a Carmelite.[57] For Gracián, St. Joseph espoused justice and fortitude:

> [In Joseph] is found the sum of all perfection of the ancient fathers and the virtues of them all: the faith of Abraham, the confidence of Isaac, the charity of Jacob, chastity of Joseph, the meekness of Moses, the fortitude of Gideon, the spirit of Elijah, the devotion of David, and all the excellences of the other fathers.[58]

St. Joseph is furthermore the "angelic man" or "angel on earth," who leads the Holy Family out of harm's way (Herod's soldiers, Mt 2) following the command of God's angel.[59] This theology of St. Joseph spread widely and was enriched over time. A seventeenth-century Carmelite from Brabant, for example, praises him also as the fulfillment of Old Testament typologies:[60] St. Joseph is the perfect "homo faber," who works for his bread, becomes the role model for all artisans and craftsmen to live and die in virtue, and never prefers business over faith.[61] He embodied the sanctification of work and could thus appeal to the somewhat sidelined groups of artisans and the rising bourgeoisie. St. Joseph's role in socially integrating upwardly mobile citizens can also be concluded from his depiction as a man of royal descent, who was committed to physical work. God had chosen him, not one of the rich and vain members of David's lineage, a preacher reasoned. This imagery gave physical work more dignity and boosted the confidence of artisans to identify with St. Joseph. They could see themselves as members of the same "nobility," namely that of the working "class."[62]

Besides his unshakable faith and fortitude, St. Joseph's sexual purity was especially of interest to church reformers. Since Mary was believed to have remained a virgin throughout her life and thus never had sexual relations with him, heroic bodily self-control was attributed to St. Joseph.[63] This virtue was especially desirable in priests. It was the outward sign of a transformed heart, as St. Ignatius of Loyola suggested. For Bellarmine, such purity entailed five stages: in the first stage are those who desire to live chastely but often fail; in the second are those who have a more robust will and undergo fasting and prayer; in the third are those who are proficient and have won many victories over their flesh. The fourth stage is that of a perfect holy life without inner struggle, because one has won victory over the world and the flesh. Yet only a few reached stage five, that of St. Joseph, in which one is absolutely free from all "movements of the flesh."[64] Such chastity was particularly important for confessors because they could easily abuse their position for sexual advantage. A widely popular handbook for new confessors thus spoke very frankly about the "pulsations of the flesh" or the temptation of "luxuria" that could overcome a priest in the confessional. In such moments, the young priest was to immediately invoke Christ and the Virgin Mary but also St. Joseph and St. Aloysius—another patron of purity—for help. He should implore God for the gift of continence and wisdom, submit himself humbly to the divine laws, and abstain from exceedingly good nourishment for the body. Moreover, the priest should tame the senses, avoid idleness, read pious books, frequently confess, mortify his body, and constantly have God on his mind (*ambulante in conspectu Dei*). Countless manuals recommended that St. Joseph, who many believed to have been a "virgin" throughout his life, would be a powerful assistant in these efforts. Some even went so far as to assume that St. Joseph had been sanctified *in utero*—very much like the *Theotokos*.[65]

Nevertheless, the purity attributed to Joseph and Mary was more than mere sexual abstinence. It entailed complete submission to the divine will, and thus the absence of selfishness. Elevating St. Joseph to such heights furthermore made it possible to see his marriage to Mary as one between equals in purity that allowed men a new role model. St. Joseph became the "jewel of a husband," and next to Mary the "King of the Saints," and the most efficacious intercessor.[66] Showing that a sanctified husband could emulate St. Joseph and thus bring about a peaceful, harmonious marriage, made the carpenter also appealing to women, who would ask for his intercession to obtain a good spouse or for his conversion. For the clergy, the cult of St. Joseph helped to give the priesthood the personification of perfect celibacy. The priests with their promise of a chaste life imitated the husband of Mary, whom theologians regarded as the first man in history to take a vow of absolute chastity. Not only did the clergy imitate his virtues, but they were likewise allegorically married to Mary, who symbolized the church, and thus they could live out a more profound identification with these saints.[67]

A now-forgotten title of St. Joseph, one he shared with Mary, was that of "terror of demons." Invoking him as the most powerful saint after Mary assured an early modern Catholic that he addressed his request to the best possible patron for his cause. Since purity meant total faith and love for God, St. Joseph's life terrorized the demons. They perceived that he could instantly repel them by his grace-filled presence. An early modern Catholic therefore reasoned that under his patronage one would be securely protected, like the Christ child himself. It was therefore fitting that some also invoked him in cases of demonic possession. Although the *Rituale Romanum* does not mention him in the *Great Exorcism*, a Jesuit who specialized in exorcising evil spirits, Jean-Joseph Surin, attributed to St. Joseph a more prominent role. The priest, who exorcised the possessed prioress of the Ursuline nuns of Loudun in 1634, used a new (and unapproved) method: He instructed the afflicted person to assist him by remembering and invoking the mercy and love of God, but also by invoking St. Joseph's intercession. By doing so, the possessed person's will and self-control would be strengthened. Once recovered, the soul could reject the demons itself.[68]

Not only love of God terrorized demons, but also the joy of one's faith. This was visualized in the depiction of St. Joseph as "God's own lily" radiating beauty and bliss. Paul du Barry compared St. Joseph's virtues with a blooming garden: "The soul of St. Joseph is a flower bed, in which one can see at all times flowers of virtue, among which humility, chastity and constancy are the most prominent."[69] In typically Jesuit manner, he gave his readers concrete "points" that helped kindle their imagination for meditation. A particularly interesting point is his advice to reflect on the conversations St. Joseph had with Mary and Jesus. These, du Barry explains, were so pleasing to him that St. Joseph avoided all others. He therefore addresses the reader: "Consider whether the conversation you have with them in prayer is as pleasing to you. Will it make you quit all other unnecessary conversations?"[70] Meditating on the joys of St. Joseph, however, did not mean that Catholics ignored his sufferings, as the meditation on St. Joseph's "seven fears" shows.[71] However, the contemplation of the carpenter's death, at which Jesus supposedly closed his eyes, became the most popular meditation..[72] It helped a believer to embrace the inevitable fate of death and be assured of a powerful intercessor. Yet it also encouraged patience in the hour of death, just as St. Joseph had patiently waited in Limbo until Jesus brought him on Easter to heavenly joy.[73]

The theology of St. Joseph tilted the dialectic of fear and mercy heavily toward the latter, just as Mariology had done. Thus, it made perfect sense for the Mexican Jesuit Antonio Peralta to remind his contemporaries that St. Joseph was a symbol of God's love for humanity. If a simple carpenter like him, who heroically fulfilled all his duties, could be chosen by the Holy

Trinity to become Mary's husband as well as the teacher and caretaker of Jesus, and moreover was predilected for Heaven, then other men could become saints, too![74] The Josephist piety therefore eased fears of reprobation, smoothed the harsh theology of predestination, and instead emphasized a merciful yet just God.

Finally, St. Joseph embodied the new type of saint the Council of Trent and the Catholic Reform tried to mold, namely one of heroic virtue. His life had not anything extraordinary in it apart from the supernatural grace within his soul. He did not perform miracles or have visions or receive the stigmata. He rather simply fulfilled with heroic virtue all his duties. He mirrored perfection just like Mary, and therefore some theologians reasoned that God would have assumed him body and soul into Heaven, just like the *Theotokos*. This idea, floated by the Jesuit Pedro Morales, was merely a theological opinion that never received official approval, yet it expresses the gendered desire to have a male role model as equally perfect as Mary.[75]

The Catholic Enlightenment of the eighteenth century tried to curtail the veneration of the saints, including that of St. Joseph. The Prague archbishop and Enlightener Schaffgotsch praised St. Joseph's virtues of fidelity and clemency, which led him to absolute obedience toward God, but was not nearly as afire about the custodian of Jesus as earlier generations.[76] This does not mean, however, that the population had also become unenthusiastic about the saint. Even in the heyday of the Enlightenment, in 1777, we can find in the Silesian city of Grüssau a 400-page book printed that summarized the spiritual expectations of members of the St. Joseph confraternity. The length of the book alone suggests that this devotion must have had a strong following—otherwise the printing costs would have never been feasible. Yet, what is striking about the content is the virtual absence of particularities about St. Joseph. Instead, the book gives a list of the saints of the entire year and presents generic Catholic practices to sanctify the day. Perhaps this is an indicator that rather than being decreased, the devotion to St. Joseph was transformed by eliminating some of its ostentatious focus.[77]

The devotion to Mary the Mother of God and St. Joseph espouses the optimism of post-Trent spirituality—that God loved humanity and offered plentiful ways of salvation. Both devotions contributed to tilting the dialectic of fear and mercy, presented throughout this volume, in favor of the latter. Both also emphasized the unique role of Christ as redeemer, and thus called for an imitation of Christ by imitating the saints. Moreover, St. Joseph presented a new role model for family fathers, artisans, and priests, and thus for societal groups that felt either abandoned or in special need of a connection to Mary and Jesus, which they could gain through the carpenter saint. This also allowed work to be perceived as an opportunity for sanctification, and no longer merely as a collateral of original sin.

# Conclusion

Reform was a difficult business. Not only did it challenge established power structures but it also brought unrest and discomfort. Especially the members of religious orders knew this. Their communities had been reformed countless times despite the grumbling of friars, the resistance of monks, and the intrigues of bishops. Yet, they knew that such efforts were necessary to renew and rejuvenate religious zeal. Institutional and disciplinary change never achieved much if it was not paired with spiritual transformation. True reform, these reformers realized, always began with the conversion of the individual, with a person changing and conforming to the will of God. Nicholas of Cusa described this accordingly: "We, therefore, who wish to reform all Christians, can inevitably propose to them no other form than that they imitate the form of Christ. . . . Those conformed to Him are the blessed children of life, who are called to possess the kingdom of God. Those not conformed . . . are cast down into Gehenna accursed. Therefore, all our zeal ought to be directed to cleansing ourselves by penance and putting on again the form of innocence, which we have received in Christ's baptismal bath."[1] By imitating the "form of Christ," early modern Catholics recovered supernatural grace that informed their lives. Countless methods and tools were available to them to "capture" grace and use its power to mold a new self that conformed to God's will. These spiritual means represented their values and beliefs about their identity.[2] By engaging with them, the historian will uncover how individuals and communities thought about themselves and the world.

The *Catholic Reform*,[3] which originated in the Middle Ages, picked up steam through charismatic personalities such as St. Charles Borromeo and St. Teresa of Avila. The Council of Trent had inspired them, because it demonstrated that change was possible. This was remarkable because the conciliar decrees fell short of the expectations of ardent reformers, were often only implemented with delay, or heavily diluted. Thus, the council served more like a symbol than an actual force of reform. Catholicism after Trent set a "giant educational machine"[4] in motion, which attempted to enforce doctrinal unity in devotional diversity,[5] but also proclaimed that Christian

*The Inner Life of Catholic Reform*. Ulrich L. Lehner, Oxford University Press. © Oxford University Press 2022.
DOI: 10.1093/oso/9780197620601.003.0011

belief had to be "transformative."[6] Social and cultural history has much to say about the time's disciplinary efforts, institutional changes, or what counted as "belief," but little about this transformation, about how Catholics spiritually conformed to the will of God. This is surprising because this inner reform represents core ideas and values of early modern Catholic identity, individually and collectively. By excluding this dimension, the historian not only loses sight of the church's reason for existence—namely, the salvation of souls—but also of the multifaceted religious actions and intentions of the time. The church could achieve her aim only if her members were sanctified.[7] Thus, it needed to educate them about approved methods and tools for the search for individual redemption, but also emphasize its authority as the exclusive and trustworthy warehouse for such means. The efforts that aided the rejuvenation of religious commitment and deepened personal religious experience could of course also be seen from a different perspective as top-down attempts with political and social intentions. This viewpoint, however, is only one aspect; just as the one of this book, which focuses entirely on the spiritual side of reform, is another. Eliminating the latter does not give a more objective view of early modern Catholicism but rather perpetuates a chimerical picture of a religion emptied of everything precious to contemporary believers.

*Inner reform* sought to restore the sinner to a state of grace like a newly baptized child. The adult had, however, the disadvantage of being ensnared in bad habits that led to sin. In order to break free from them and focus on a life in grace, Catholics were presented with many different means of self-transformation. Although these approved tools were usually learned from clergymen, they empowered believers with a dynamic agency and ultimately turned early modern Catholicism into a "genuine religion of action."[8] Of greatest importance were the sacraments, which were holy signs that restored the divine life (grace)[9] in the believer and allowed growth in sanctification. The priest celebrated most of the sacraments, and for the one he did not—matrimony—the Council of Trent codified his required presence and witness. From the pulpit and in catechesis the parish priest educated and admonished his flock, but also on the occasions of weddings, confessions, baptisms, the anointing of the sick, and confirmation. In the Eucharist of the Mass, his ordination enabled him as God's conduit to change bread and wine into the body and blood of Christ, which an increasing number of the faithful consumed more frequently. By elevating the importance of the sacraments, the priest's status as representative of Christ in a local community was also increased. Parishioners expected the priest to be holier than themselves, live an exemplary life of integrity (especially of chastity), which in turn alleviated their own burden of fulfilling ecclesial demands. Seeing the priest mystically united with Christ, however, had a (possibly) unintended consequence. It elevated the priest's status and made him an increasingly unquestionable authority. This paved the way for an inflexible clericalism and seemingly enabled systemic power abuse in the Catholic church.

Priests were also given several new duties. Most prominent among them were preaching and teaching.[10] By explaining the Scriptures from the pulpit, the clergy not only proclaimed the mysteries of faith but also explained them in vivid images and metaphors and admonished their flock to improve their behavior. By arousing the right affects, priests tried to emotionally engage their listeners. Faith was after all the assent not only of the intellect but also of the will. The latter was moved most efficiently by the affects of the soul. By appealing to them, moral behavior was changed because the desires of the audience were subtly shifted from worldly to spiritual goods, often by instrumentalizing the fear of Hell or Purgatory. Although such fear was omnipresent, especially in preaching, so was the church's presentation of a merciful God. Ideally, these two dialectic poles were in balance, but most often tilted to one of the two sides. While the pulpit tended to be a place of preaching fear, the confessional, prayerbook, and pastoral discourse seem to have been the places of mercy and compassion. This dialectic approach also suggests that a normative flexibility existed, which believers expected from their clergy. Thus, the faithful desired a priest who was not an inflexible judge but one who would understand and empathize with them.

Much of the catechesis in a parish was taken over by laypersons. Children's catechisms were printed and parents were instructed how to form their children at home, while professionally delegated laypersons or priests took over the instructional side of religious education. Since proponents of Catholic Reform believed that every level of society had to be "converted," many authors saw the need to engage a variety of audiences. Nobility and aristocracy were addressed by sophisticated works on education, lower classes by parish missions and direct pastoral discourse. Crucial, however, was the claim that God desired the salvation of all and that one could be saved in every honorable profession or state. This *salvific egalitarianism* made it possible to see not only the temporal world as being infused with divine grace but also one's status in it as a place of religious vocation. One could pray as a butcher just as fervently as a merchant, and a courtier could seek God just as sincerely as a monk if one's intentions were focused on the divine. This dynamic broadened the appeal of early modern Catholicism because everybody who wished to engage more profoundly in religious affairs could do so and find a place of preferred intensity. The laity was assured of its ability to achieve salvation and their work received a place of honor. This theological axiom unleashed hitherto unknown activity among church members. These devotional actions were believed to need ecclesiastical approval, which makes the church's bureaucracy in this respect more understandable.[11]

Such egalitarianism can also be found in discourses on marriage and family. During the Catholic Reform, the church poured massive resources into catechizing families about becoming communities where holiness and therefore church reform could grow. The priest's duty to preach on Sundays and feast days made it necessary several times a year to teach about matrimony, in addition to other catechetical events. Often a clergyman would also use this opportunity to denounce violent, abusive husbands, and admonish wives to be obedient. Catholic theology upheld and affirmed traditional gender roles within marriages and called relationships in which the roles were reversed, "disordered." By rediscovering the same late medieval sources that aided Protestant reformers, Catholic reformers likewise praised harmony between spouses, mutual love, and companionship. For Catholic theologians a harmonious marriage was the seedbed of virtue and holiness for children. As the spouses spiritually cared for each other, constantly renewed and rekindled their love, they enabled their children to become apprentices in this "school of virtue" and learn control over their passions. In addition, priests and teachers instructed parents in how to form their children's conscience and religious imagination in accordance with the divine commandments. Depending on how much of such formation one accepted and desired, early modern Catholics had access to a wide variety of religious resources that were also used as pedagogical means.

Lay movements such as confraternities and Marian sodalities harnessed the zeal of the population. Their rules recommended a rigorous prayer schedule, often with detailed instructions for changing one's imagination and conscience and molding a new self with the help of grace. Many lay Catholics, however, were members merely out of fear of Hell or Purgatory and saw in confraternities a way not only to get others to pray for one's soul but also to participate in communal benefits such as requiem Masses or indulgences. The pious practice of "collecting" as many benefits as possible continued well into the nineteenth century and was often deemed superficial. Nevertheless, the historian must ask whether such accumulative behavior does not also presuppose some internal spiritual state. Why would a person engage in such behavior? One answer seems to be that these benefits calmed the mind about postmortem punishment by assuring the believer of peace and tranquility after death, but often failed if pursued superficially or with scruples. Moreover, since the "collector" would try to fulfill confraternity obligations carefully to obtain the benefits, one can assume that membership was for such people a means of transforming the self by subduing their fears, even if only on a superficial level.

Many confraternities did not expect more from their members than did parishes, and thus historians have wondered about their value for spiritual reform. Yet, such a view misses the fact that confraternities tried to make people participate more fully in their faith life, especially in their parish. The perfect confraternity member was a practicing parishioner. Thus, meager religious participation should not surprise at all, because the vision of church reform labored to reach every household and slowly change the faithful. Not everybody was a religious superachiever, who desired to go to monthly or weekly meetings. Many instead sought a group with spiritual benefits, which enticed one to do one's duties as a Catholic but offered an ecclesial home in addition to the parish. Those with strong zeal, however, joined a Third Order or one of the many Jesuit sodalities, which had strict admission and prayer requirements.

The center of early modern Catholic spirituality was the Eucharist. The trend to emphasize the real presence of Christ in the host was visualized in church architecture by moving the tabernacle from the margins to the high altar. Since receiving communion meant the consumption of Christ, it was considered an act of unifying one's soul with the divine. If the recipient was well prepared for this action, the Eucharist could profoundly transform his or her inner self, as early modern theologians believed. The Council of Trent therefore advised more frequent communion and with it more frequent confession as its necessary preparation but had to overcome hesitancy among the faithful. Most Catholics used to commune only once or twice a year and went shortly beforehand to confession. The council's admonition not only changed the workload of pastors, who were now expected to be constantly present in the confessional, but also established the two sacraments as major sources of spiritual renewal and transformation. Frequent confession would lead to the avoidance of sin, heartfelt remorse, and penance, while communion allowed participation in the divine, church leaders reasoned. Emblematic or pictorial theology allowed believers to form their imagination about the consecrated host, while spiritual communion increased the desire for sacramental reception and proper disposition. Scruples over how often one should receive the Eucharist or whether one's sins had properly been forgiven by absolution, nevertheless burdened many Catholics. Numerous methods and approaches were developed to address this illness. Scrupulous persons were therefore encouraged not to read texts that focused on punishment or fear, but rather invited to discover the tender compassion and mercy of God. Likewise, catechesis made increasingly clear that "fear of God" was not emotional *angst*, but rather the loving diligence never to trespass God's commandments. The confessional box itself became a place where such spiritual counsel could be individually given if time and the ability of the priest permitted it. The spiritual transformation of the believer was, however, somewhat endangered by the possibility of the priest withholding absolution if he perceived a lack of true contrition. Leading a Catholic to this feeling of remorse and judging it became a major task of the priest and put a new burden on the penitents. They had to *convincingly* express their remorse and demonstrate their inner change. Did this perhaps encourage a culture that simulated emotional responses in the confessional? If this was the case, did learning methods of dissimulation perhaps also empower those confessing with new abilities of social interaction?

While such dissimilation or even dishonesty was perhaps unintentionally encouraged by the requirement of regular confession, widespread education about prayer techniques could have balanced it. While repetition was a genuine meditative tool, it often deteriorated into mere lip-service among clergy, religious, and laity. Thus, it became crucial to teach techniques that helped to concentrate in prayer, to become attentive to the words and raise them up to the divine. Such intentionality was augmented by the affective side of the human person. Affects were elicited or directed to supernatural ends and thus aimed at replacing worldly desires or goods. This was intrinsically connected with teaching methods of discernment. This enabled the believer to differentiate which "spirits" or nonmaterial motives drove his or her behavior and whether these were of divine, demonic, or worldly origin. Discernment was indispensable if one engaged in "mental prayer," which was for most the habitual attention to God's presence. Some, however, understood it as a nonvocal prayer technique that used written texts merely as a starting point. Such schools of prayer (e.g., Quietists) were therefore suspected of marginalizing Scripture and church authority. Teresa of Avila, however, defined it as the core of all true prayer, whether vocal or nonvocal. The believer focused on the divine, like spending time with a good friend, in whose presence one forgets about oneself because one feels loved.[12] Mental prayer is in her tradition not intellectually discursive, but rather a prayer of the heart, which can differ in intensity and quality, and is in its highest form a supernaturally infused gift. Such mental prayer, which enabled the believer to address God in private speech or silence while acknowledging his or her failures in *recollection*, was taught in a simplified way by confraternities and sodalities. These therefore worked as engines of spiritual formation.

Historians should therefore not underestimate how widespread knowledge of prayer techniques was, albeit the intensity and quality of this knowledge certainly varied greatly. The pious sighs or arrow prayers, which historians have hitherto overlooked and which were disseminated through catechesis, prayerbooks, and confraternities, also served the faithful as an accessible tool for transforming any given time of day into a religious service. These short texts provided help in forming the intention to be attentive to God's will and presence. Prayer could be strengthened through proper ascetic tools for intellect and body: to mortify both meant to fortify them supernaturally. This practice presupposed that one could not trust the self to fulfill God's commandments. After all, the human will was weak and just as easily swayed as the intellect to desire false goods. By subduing the body in *exterior* mortification, all senses were subjected to the rule of reason and thus predisposed to virtue. For *interior* mortification, intellectual and volitional challenges such as pride and acquisitiveness had to be overcome so that the believer's soul would conform solely to God and not the world. The practice of mortification offered Catholics successful means of spiritual self-transformation that were endorsed by church tradition. By applying them, they could achieve progress in molding a new self, provided these actions were repeated with sufficient diligence throughout the course of one's life. Spiritual transformation was not understood as a sudden vertical ascension, but rather as progress by "chicken steps," which often led back to one's starting point.[13]

Spiritual transformation was most visible in prayers for the deceased in Purgatory. These "poor souls" waited at the threshold of Heaven for admission but suffered a process of purification. The living could by prayers and charitable deeds, such as indulgences, either diminish their pain or free them. Thus, the living became agents of transformation for the dead and the devotion of those who prayed also effected their own self-transformation. After all, it allowed the living to deal with their own pain of loss, the acknowledgment of their own failures, and their fear of future pain in purification. Despite such personalized effects, this devotion reinforced their awareness of the church teaching that both the dead and living were members of the same communion of saints.[14]

For early modern Catholics, countless images and symbols reaffirmed that they were on pilgrimage to a heavenly destination. Bell signals filled the soundscape and called to interrupt daily chores with prayer. Material objects, such as the *Agnus Dei* wax carvings or scapulars, gave Catholics a tactile symbolic presence that reminded them of the promises of Christ in their daily prayer. Through them, they could experience the presence of the divine in their own home and on their own body. Hymnals translated the symbolic world of Catholicism into comprehensible prose, which could be learned by heart and recited in every context. Their verses outlined how one was called to imitate Christ and the saints, and to transform one's life. The printing press and the invention of copperplate print enabled early modern Catholics to develop a pictorial theology with the help of emblems. These sophisticated images depicted theological allegories, often combined with quotations from scripture. They not only stirred curiosity by their cryptic messages but also especially invited Catholics to deeper meditation, whether practiced alone or in a community. All these symbols and images conveyed the divine presence in the world of the believer as well as God's interest in the salvation of his people. The image of the angel visualized these ideas. Guardian angels, who protected and assisted the living, exemplified God's presence and help in every situation, but also underlined human freedom and responsibility. Angelic assistance did not interfere with human freedom, but rather reminded believers that they had to transform their lives *themselves*, albeit with the help of grace.

While much of early modern Catholic practice included a culture of fear, the increasing prominence of Mary and Joseph in art and worship emphasized the mercy and love of God. Ardent veneration of the *Mother of God* was considered a trustworthy sign that one belonged to the Elect and did not have to fear Hell. Privileges attached to her veneration, such as the scapular, also decreased the fear of punishment in Purgatory. St. Joseph was invoked as patron of a good death and for a virtuous life. The cult of St. Joseph invited artisans and merchants to consider the work of their hands as dignified and part of a divine vocation. Just as Joseph had worked for his family, so men could by fulfilling their duties toward their families achieve a virtuous life. Like Mary, he embodied a gentle love that would not tire of interceding for the living and dead members of the church. Both saints allowed Catholics to view their faith with less fear and to approach God with the knowledge of his love and merciful justice. Marian maximalism in theology and widespread popular veneration of Mary seem to suggest that this piety addressed a real demand among believers and through its imagery shaped their spiritual transformation. The fact that both Mary and Joseph were merely human beings allowed their cult to become one of personal imitation and not just veneration.

The time after the Council of Trent witnessed a Catholic revival that did not owe much *per se* to this meeting of bishops, but everything to charismatic church reformers. For them, the holiness of the flock was at the heart of church reform. The human person was to be drawn into the divine mysteries by appealing to sentiments and intellect, by teaching prayer and meditation techniques, and also by conveying the content of the faith. Such interests gave rise to developments not only in pedagogy, rhetoric, anthropology, and psychology but also in mystical and sacramental theology. The spirituality that emerged from this time relied heavily on a long tradition but applied it to new challenges and molded it into new forms. Thereby it shaped not just a small set of behavioral actions, but rather the imagination of believers. An "enchanted" Catholic imagination developed that allowed and encouraged a diversity of expression, but nevertheless bridged cultural differences between Europe, Asia, America, and Africa. Without such a spiritual vision of inner reform and self-transformation, Catholicism would not have become a world religion.

# Notes

## Preface

1. Ulrich L. Lehner, *On the Road to Vatican II. German Catholic Enlighteners and Reform of the Church* (Augsburg: Fortress Press, 2016); idem, *The Catholic Enlightenment* (New York: Oxford University Press, 2016); idem (ed.), *Women, Enlightenment and Catholicism. A Transnational Biographical History* (New York: Routledge, 2018); idem (ed.), *Innovation in Early Modern Catholicism* (New York: Routledge, 2022).
2. Ulrich L. Lehner and Shaun Blanchard, "Introduction," in Ulrich L. Lehner and Shaun Blanchard (eds.), *The Catholic Enlightenment. A Global Anthology* (Washington, DC: Catholic University of America Press, 2021), 1–20, at 10–11.
3. See, for example, Carlos Eire, *Reformations. The Early Modern World, 1450–1650* (New Haven: Yale University Press, 2016), 367–522, and Michael A. Mullet, *The Catholic Reformation* (London: Routledge, 1999).
4. Hillard van Thiessen, *Das Zeitalter der Ambiguität. Vom Umgang mit Werten und Normen in der Frühen Neuzeit* (Cologne et al.: Böhlau, 2021), 60–61.

## Chapter 1

1. Cardinal of Lorraine in June 1561, at Henry Outram Evennett, *The Cardinal of Lorraine and the Council of Trent. A Study in the Counter-Reformation* (Cambridge: Cambridge University Press, 1930), 485.
2. Cf. Paolo Prodi, *The Papal Prince. One Body and Two Souls. The Papal Monarchy in Early Modern Europe* [orig.: *Il sovrano pontifice*, 1982] (Cambridge: Cambridge University Press, 1987).
3. Zeger Bernhard van Espen, *Jus Ecclesiasticum Universum Hodiernae Disciplinae Accomodatum*, vol. 1 (Madrid: 1778), pars 1, c. 5, 289. For an example for the Catholic view of inner transformation, see Johannes Eusebius Kendlmayr, *Canonica Reformatio Hominis Veteris per Decem Dies . . .* (Vienna: 1691), 5.
4. Klaus Unterburger, "Reform der ganzen Kirche. Konturen, Ursachen und Wirkungen einer Leitidee und Zwangsvorstellungen im Spätmittelalter," in Andreas Merkt et al. (eds.), *Reformen in der Kirche. Historische Perspektiven* (Freiburg: Herder, 2014), 109–137.
5. Konrad Repgen, "Reform als Leitgedanke kirchlicher Vergangenheit und Gegenwart," *Römische Quartalsschrift* 85 (1989): 5–30. In 1955 Willem A. Visser t'Hooft encouraged historians for the first time to write ecclesiastical history from the point of view

of *reform* (idem, *The Renewal of the Church* [London: Westminster Press, 1956], 67–85). Gerhart Ladner, *The Idea of Reform. Its Impact on Christian Thought and Action in the Age of the Fathers* (Cambridge: Harvard University Press, 1959), 26. Cf. Jacques Maritain, *On the Philosophy of History* (New York: Scribner, 1957).

6. Ladner, *The Idea of Reform*, 35; cf. Gerald Strauss, "Reformatio and Renovatio from the Middle Ages to the Reformation," in Thomas Brady et al. (eds.), *Handbook of European History, 1400–1700*, vol. 2 (Leiden: Brill, 1995), 1–30.

7. Erasmus of Rotterdam, *Ausgewählte Schriften*, ed. Werner Welzig, vol. 1: *Enchiridion Militis Christiani* (Darmstadt: WBG, 1968), 21: "Maneat Christus id quod est, centrum, ambientibus circulis aliquot." Cf., for example, the attempts to frame a Catholic understanding of "reform," see Ferenc Otrokocsi Foris, *Restitutio Israel futura seu Tractatus quo ex tetxtu Hoseae 3v.4.5* (Vienna: 1712), 234, 510; Martin Gerbert, *Principia Theologiae Mysticae ad Renovationem Interiorem et Sanctificationem Christiani Hominis* (St. Blasien: 1758), 9; 277f. John W. O'Malley, *Trent and All That. Renaming Catholicism in the Early Modern Era* (Cambridge: Harvard University Press, 2002), 18ff. Nevertheless, for most Catholic historians the Protestant Reformation was more of a *revolution*, a paradigm shift, than a reform, as Hubert Jedin explained (ibid., 61).

8. Called the "misunderstood council" by Simon Ditchfield, "Tridentine Catholicism," in Alexandra Bamji et al. (eds.), *The Ashgate Research Companion to the Counter-Reformation* (Farnham: Ashgate, 2013), 15–32.

9. Giuseppe Alberigo, "Die Ekklesiologie des Konzils von Trient [1964]," in Remigius Bäumer (ed.), *Concilium Tridentinum. Wege der Forschung* (Darmstadt: WBG, 1976), 278–300, at 280. Cf. Narciso Jubany, "El Concilio de Trento y la renovación de las ordenes inferiores al presbiterado," *Estudios Eclesiásticos* 36 (1961): 127–143.

10. Wolfgang Reinhard, "Mythologie des Konzils von Trient," in Michela Catto and Adriano Prosperi (eds.), *Trent and Beyond. The Council, Other Powers, Other Cultures* (Turnhout: Brepols, 2018), 27–43.

11. Peter Hersche, "Die Marginalisierung der Universitäten im katholischen Europa des Barockzeitalters," in Rainer Schwinges (ed.), *Universität, Religion und Kirchen* (Basel: Schwabe, 2011), 267–276.

12. For the tensions between reformers and reform "blockers," see the magisterial history of the council by Hubert Jedin, *Geschichte des Konzils von Trient*, 4 vols. (Darmstadt: WBG Reprint, 2017). See also Peter Hersche, *Muße und Verschwendung Europäische Gesellschaft und Kultur im Barockzeitalter* (Freiburg: Herder, 2006), vol. 1, 152–213.

13. John W. O'Malley, "The Hermeneutic of Reform. A Historical Analysis," *Theological Studies* 73 (2012): 517–546.

14. Alberigo, "Ekklesiologie."

15. Günther Wassilowsky, "Das Konzil von Trient und die katholische Konfessionskultur," in Peter Walter and Günther Wassilowsky (eds.), *Das Konzil von Trient und die Katholische Konfessionskultur (1563–2013)* (Freiburg: Herder, 2016), 1–30; Wolfgang Reinhard and Peter Hersche, "Wie modern ist der Barockkatholizismus?," in ibid., 587–419.

16. Simon Ditchfield, "Catholic Reformation," in Peter Marshall (ed.), *The Oxford Illustrated History of Christianity. The Reformation* (Oxford: Oxford University Press, 2015), 152–185; John Headley and John Tomaro (eds.), *San Carlo Borromeo. Catholic Reform and Ecclesiastical Politics in the Second Half of the Sixteenth Century* (Washington: Folger Books, 1988); Mariano Delgado and Markus Ries (eds.), *Karl Borromaeus und die katholische Reform* (Stuttgart: Kohlhammer, 2010); Enrico Cattaneo, "La singolare fortuna degli *Acta ecclesiae Mediolanensis*," *Scuola cattolica* 111 (1983): 191–217; Simon Ditchfield, "Decentering the Catholic Reformation. Papacy and Peoples in the Early Modern World," *Archiv für Reformationsgeschichte* 101 (2010): 186–208.

17. Cf. Ditchfield, "Catholic Reformation," 170–171. Berndt Hamm, "Normative Zentrierung im 15. und 16. Jahrhundert," *Zeitschrift für Historische Forschung* 26 (1999): 163–202; Hillard van Thiessen, *Die Kapuziner zwischen Konfessionalisierung und Alltagskultur. Vergleichende Fallstudie am Beispiel Freiburgs und Hildesheims 1599–1750* (Freiburg im Breisgau: Rombach, 2002); Arne Karsten and Hillard van Thiessen (eds.), *Normenkonkurrenz in historischer Perspektive. Zeitschrift für historische Forschung, Beiheft 50* (Berlin: Duncker & Humblot, 2015).

18. Wolfgang Reinhard, "Kirchendisziplin, Sozialdisziplinierung und Verfestigung der konfessionellen Fronten. Das katholische Reformprogramm und seine Auswirkungen," in Stefano Andretta et al. (eds.), *Das Papsttum, die Christenheit und die Staaten Europas, 1592–1605* (Tübingen: Niemeyer, 1994), 1–13; Prodi, *The Papal Prince*, 18. The slow suppression of provincial and diocesan synods, which the Council Fathers had hoped would become the tool to implement their decrees was certainly a curial "achievement": The papal confirmation bull for the council's proceedings, *Benedictus Deus* of January 26, 1564 (published June 30), made no mention of synods. Whereas the Council Fathers had hoped for a flexible implementation of the decrees, based on their episcopal authority, the interpretation of the council lay now only in the hands of the Curia. Reception became equivalent with observance. *Concilium Tridentinum. Diariorum, Actorum, Epistularum, Tractatuum*, vol. 9 (Freiburg: Herder, 1965), 979 (Sessio XXIV, can. 2, November 11, 1563); 1106 (sessio XXV, *De recipiendis et observandis decretis concilii*, December 4, 1563); John Butler Tomaro, *The Papacy and the Implementation of the Council of Trent, 1564–1588* (PhD Thesis: University of North Carolina at Chapel Hill, 1974), 63ff; Daniele Menozzi, "Prospettive sinodali nel Settecento," *Cristianesimo nella Storia* 8 (1987): 115–146, at146; Giuseppe Alberigo, "La réception du Concile de Trente par l'Église catholique romaine," *Irenikon* 58 (1985): 311–337. Nevertheless, it must be said that Catholic states also acted as stumbling blocks for the convening of such synods, as the example of Spain shows (Michele Miele, *Die Provinzialkonzilien Süditaliens in der Neuzeit* [Paderborn: Schöningh, 1997], 130–157).

19. Giuseppe Alberigo, "From the Council of Trent to Tridentinism," in Raymond F. Bulman et al. (eds.), *From Trent to Vatican II. Historical and Theological Investigations* (Aldershot: Ashgate, 2006), 19–37; Reinhard, "Mythologie," 39; Katja Burzer, *San Carlo Borromeo. Konstruktion und Inszenierung eines Heiligenbildes im Spannungsfeld zwischen Mailand und Rom* (Berlin und München: Deutscher Kunstverlag, 2011);

cf. Giuseppe Alberigo, "Carlo Borromeo come modello di vescovo nella cheas post-tridentina," *Rivista storica Italiana* 79 (1967): 1031–1052; Gianluigi Panzeri, "Carlo Borromeo e la figura ideale del vescovo della chiesa tridentina," *Scuola cattolica* 124 (1996): 685–731. One must not forget that Cardinal Bellarmine proposed in 1600/01 convening a *new* council because of the deficient implementation of Trent; yet such a meeting could have proved fatal for papal primacy and was therefore rejected (Robert Bellarmine, *Auctuarium Bellarminianum*, ed. Xavier Le Bachelet [Paris: 1913], 518; cf. Alberigo, "From the Council of Trent to Tridentinism," 26).

20. Nelson Minnich, "Concepts of Reform Proposed at the Fifth Lateran Council," *Archivum Historicum Pontificae* 7 (1969): 163–251, at 164.

21. Ibid., 166.

22. Theodor Mahlmann, "Reformation," *Historisches Wörterbuch der Philosophie*, vol. 8 (Basel: Schwabe, 1992), 416–442; cf. Franz Wagner, *Universae Phraseologiae Latinae Corpus* (Trinava: 1775), s.p. defines "reformare religionem" as "instaurare religiones, ex solutiore disciplina ad veterem sanctimoniam revocare." Basilius Fabri, *Thesaurus Eruditionis Scholasticae. Recensitus ac emendates a Augustum Buchnerum* (Wittenberg and Leipzig: 1655), 396: "instaurare, sive in priorem aut potius meliore formam redigere."

23. Joachim Rapperswilanus O.F.M. Cap., *Reformatio Difformis & Deformis . . .*, vol. 1 (Argentati: 1726), 1. Brocardus a S. Nicolao, *Professio Fidei Catholicae secundum veras verae fidei regulas* (Frankfurt: 1758), vol. 1, 515f: "Ecce praetenti reformatores & reformati adversus Ecclesiam insurrexerunt, eamque non tam reformare, & repurgare, quam impugnare & evertere conati sunt sub praetextu Spricturae." Franciscus Porter, *Palinodia Religionis Praetensae Reformatae . . .* (Rome: 1679), art. 2, 7: "Praetenti reformato ex suis principiis fateantur, necereformato ex suis principiis fateantur, necesse est, veram Christi Ecclesiam apud ipsos inveniri non posse."

24. Hubert Wolf, *Krypta. Unterdrückte Traditionen der Kirchengeschichte* (Munich: C.H. Beck, 2015), 20; Philipp Stump, *The Reforms of the Council of Constance, 1414–1418* (Leiden and Boston: Brill, 1994), 209, 221–226.

25. Johannes Nider, *De reformatione religiosorum libri tres*, ed. Johannes Boucquet (Antwerp: 1611), 126, 217. Cf. Stump, *The Reforms*, 221. The seventeenth-century Dominican reformer Giovanni Paolo Nazari echoes Nider's understanding of healthy innovation in his *Aureus de reformatione Religiosorum Libellus* (Brussels: 1637), 77: "Quia non omnis novitas mala est, multas enim divina Scriptura laudat, promittit ac praecipit novitates."

26. Nider, *De reformatione*, 228–230.

27. Nider, *De reformatione*, 230 and, on innovation, 52: "Novitas enim non semper in malo, sed saepe in Sacra pagina in bono accipitur: imo nullus reformari potest absque inductione novae formae; unde toto nisu cordis studere debent Religiosi, quatenus innoventur spiritu."

28. Minnich, "Concepts of Reform," 228, where M. speaks about the council's "conservatism."

29. Minnich, "Concepts of Reform," 233.

30. Zeger Bernhard van Espen, *Dissertatio canonica de veterum canonum et in eis contentae canonicae disciplinae stabilitate . . .* (Vienna: 1776), 27.

31. Vincentius Ilger, *Observationes in Secula Christiana de disciplina et moribus*, vol. 1 (St. Blasien: 1791), vol. 1, XV.

32. Louis Thomassin, *Vetus et nova ecclesiae disciplina*, vol. 1 (Luca: 1728), preface: "Quod priori Disciplinae deerat, adjecere Concilia, Pontifices, Sancti Patres." Cf. Ilger, *Observationes*, vol. 1, XVf: "disciplina vero alias, aliasque induit facies secundum temporum, locorumque circumstantias."

33. However, due to the polemics of the time, the term "reform" was sometimes used pejoratively to describe the Jansenists (*Janseniana Reformatio*) or Protestants, who were branded as "pretend reformers" ("praetensos reformatores"). See, for example, in Anonymous, *Lamindi Pritanii redivivi Epistola Paraenetica ad patrem Benedictum Plazza SJ* (Venice: 1755). See for example Carolus Sardagna SJ, *Theologia Dogmatico-Polemica . . .*, vol. 5 (Regensburg: 1771), 1–24. Muratori even laments that particularly in moral theology, novelty or development ("novitatem & augmentum") was denied as "impossible," see Ludovico Muratori, *Epistola Paraenetica ad Superiores Religiosorum* (Augsburg: 1765), 15. A good example for innovation is the introduction of Wolffianism into Catholic theology, which according to Brandmeyer would improve scholasticism, see Johann Adam Brandmeyer, *Schema Introductionis in Universam Theologiam Catholicam* (Mannheim: 1780), 34, 39f. Cf. the preface to Muratori, *Epistola*, VIII: ". . . in illo enim Emendatio aut Reformatio locum non habet."

34. For Gerson as well as for others, the more the earthly church imitates the *ecclesia triumphans* the more authentic it becomes. Despite all deformation and decay, the *semen vivificum at reformativum* remained in the church, and in its hierarchical structure. See Louis B. Pascoe, *Jean Gerson. Principles of Church Reform* (Leiden and Boston: Brill, 1973), 17f, 32–46. Visitations are one such innovation. They are often characterized as events of social disciplining, see Angelo Turchini, "Die Visitation als Mittel zur Regierung des Territoriums," in Paolo Prodi and Wolfgang Reinhard (eds.), *Das Konzil von Trient und die Moderne* (Berlin: Duncker and Humblot, 2001), 261–298. Hersche, *Muße*, vol. 1, 185–194, demonstrates, however, how ineffective visitations were in regard to discipline.

35. Stump, *The Reforms*, 207.

36. Stump, *The Reforms*, 207; Gerhart Ladner, "Terms and Ideals of Renewal," in Robert L. Benson and Giles Constable (eds.), *Renaissance and Renewal in the Twelfth Century* (Cambridge: Harvard University Press, 1982), 1–33.

37. Minnich, "Concepts of Reform," 170; John W. O'Malley, *Giles of Viterbo on Church and Reform* (Leiden and Boston: Brill, 1968), 140; Steven Ozment, *The Age of Reform, 1250–1550. An Intellectual and Religious History of Late Medieval and Reformation Europe* (New Haven: Yale University Press, 1980), 401f.

38. Minnich, "Concepts of Reform," 176–177, cf. 179.

39. Stump, *The Reforms*, 211–212; August Reding, *Oecumenici Tridentini Concilii Veritas Inextincta*, vol. 1 (Einsiedeln: 1684), 242. Aghostino Barbosa, *Pastoralis solicitudinis sive de officio et potestate parochi* (Lyon: 1640; 4th ed., 1655), pars 1, tit. 1, c. 1. Cf. Contarini, *On the Office*, 71.

40. Barbosa, *Pastoralis Solicitudinis*, vol. 1, p. 1, t. 1, c. 2, nu. 22.

41. Stump, *The Reforms*, 216–218.

42. Ludovico Muratori, *De Ingeniorum Moderatione in Religionis negotio* (Augsburg: 1779). lib. 1, c. 12, 113.

43. Muratori, *De Ingeniorum*, lib. 1, c. 13, 116: "Deinde ad tyrannidem accedet, qui minime credenda credi jubeat, aut se prodet erroris magistrum, qui in censum veritatis fabulas quasque referat."

44. Lehner, "De Moderatione."

45. Ilger, *Observationes*, vol. 1, XVI.

46. Not just abuse and greed are identified as causes of decay in the church but also historical, geographic, and political context, as the French Jesuit Theophile Raynaud showed already in his 1665 *Heteroclita Spiritualia et Anomala Pietatis*. Theophil Raynaud SJ, *Heteroclita Spiritualia et Anomala Pietatis Terrestrium Spectantium Morales*, Opera Omnia vol. 16 (Lyon: 1665), 386. In vol. 14, see his dissertation on the castration of children for the sake of choir singing.

47. Espen, *Dissertatio canonica*, 33.

48. Dermot Fenlon, *Heresy and Obedience in Tridentine Italy. Cardinal Pole and the Counter Reformation* (Cambridge: Cambridge University Press, 1972), 107.

49. Berndt Hamm, "Frömmigkeitstheologie als Gegenstand theologiegeschichtlicher Forschung," *Theologie und Kirche* 74 (1977): 464–497.

50. Hamm, "Frömmigkeitstheologie," 493.

51. Jacques Marchand, *Hortus pastorum sacræ doctrinæ floribus polymitus. Exemplis selectis adornatus, in lectionum areolas partitus* (Montibus: 1626); idem, *Candelabrum Mysticum* (Montibus: 1630).

52. Allan Greer and Jodi Bilinkoff, *Colonial Saints. Discovering the Holy in the Americas, 1500–1800* (Abingdon: Routledge, 2015); cf. Hamm, "Normative Zentrierung."

53. Espen, *Jus Ecclesiasticum*, pars 1, c. 5, 289. For an example for the Catholic view of inner transformation, one can consult Johannes Eusebius Kendlmayr, *Canonica Reformatio Hominis Veteris per Decem Dies* . . . (Vienna: 1691), 5.

54. Alison Forrestal, *Vincent de Paul, the Lazarist Mission and French Catholic Reform* (Oxford: Oxford University Press, 2017), 31. See the chapter on lay organizations in this volume.

55. Moshe Sluhovsky, *Becoming a New Self. Practices of Belief in Early Modern Catholicism* (Chicago: University of Chicago Press, 2017), 104–105, at 109.

56. Sluhovsky, *Becoming a New Self*, 131f, 143. Such transformation was also a counterexample to the idealistic model of the heroic Saint and thus a model for transforming the masses much more swiftly and economically (Michelle Molina, *To Overcome Oneself. The Jesuit Ethic and Spirit of Global Expansion, 1520–1767* [Berkeley: University of California Press, 2013], 73.).

# Chapter 2

1. Michael Arneth, *Das Ringen um Geist und Form der Priesterbildung im Säkularklerus des 17. Jahrhundert* (Würzburg: Echter, 1970), 162–164; Heinz Finger, "Das Konzil von Trient und die Ausbilung der Säkularkleriker in Priesterseminaren

während der Frühen Neuzeit," in Wim Francois and Violet Soen (eds.), *The Council of Trent. Reform and Controversy in Europe and Beyond (1545–1700)*, vol. 2 (Göttingen: Vandenhoeck & Rupprecht, 2018), 33–60; Werner Freitag, *Pfarrer, Kirche und ländliche Gemeinschaft. Das Dekanat Vechta, 1400–1803* (Bielefeld: Verlag für Regionalgeschichte, 1998), 81.

2. Clare McGrath-Merkle, *Berulle's Spiritual Theology of the Priesthood. A Study on Speculative Mysticism and Applied Metaphysics* (Münster: Aschendorff, 2018), 54ff.

3. Dermot Fenlon, *Heresy and Obedience in Tridentine Italy. Cardinal Pole and the Counter Reformation* (Cambridge: Cambridge University Press, 1972), 19.

4. Pedro de Soto, *Tractatus de institutione sacerdotum* (Antwerp: 1560; 1566); Sebastianus Faciuta, *De Vita & Honestate Clericorum* (Florence: 1576), 13.

5. Hersche, *Muße*, vol. 1, 177–185.

6. Anonymous, *Doctrina Pastoralis. Cum Idea Reformationis Cleri et Populi ad Mentem Concilii Tridentini* . . . (Augsburg: 1802), 13.

7. Theophil Raynaud SJ, *Confiteor Reformatum Dissertatio de Paternitate Spirituali* (Lyon: 1654), 109–124, 125–153.

8. Michael a S. Catharina, *Trinum Perfectum*, vol. 3, par. 611ff, 224ff.

9. Michael a S. Catharina, *Trinum Perfectum*, vol. 3, par. 645, 235. On the ideal of the tridentine bishop in France and the claim of jurisdiction by divine right, see Alison Forrestal, *Fathers, Pastors and Kings. Visions of Episcopacy in Seventeenth-Century France* (Manchester: Manchester University Press, 2004).

10. Ernst Walter Zeeden (ed.), *Die Visitation im Dienst der kirchlichen Reform* (Munster: Aschendorff, 1967); Georges Livet and Iris Heinz (eds.), *Sensibilité religieuse et discipline ecclésiastique. Les visites pastorales en territoires protestants, pays rhénans, comté de Montbéliard, pays de Vaud, XVIe–XVIIIe siècles* (Strasbourg: Libr. Istra, 1973).

11. Cesare Franciotti, *Himmlische Tischreden, oder das grosse Communion-Buch* (Vienna: 1650), vol. 5, 134; cf. on the role of visitations for the dissemination of Catholicism in the mission territories, Jose Pedro Paiva, "Pastoral Visitations in the First World Empires (Spain and Portugal in the 16th and 18th Centuries): A Comparative Approach," *Journal of Early Modern History* 24 (2020): 224–252.

12. Henri Boudon, *La science sacrée du Catéchisme* (Paris: 1678), ch. 10, 123. See also Hersche, *Muße*, vol. 1, 185–194.

13. Celeste McNamara, "Conceptualizing the Priest: Lay and Episcopal Expectations of Clerical Reform in Late Seventeenth-Century Padua," *Archiv für Reformationsgeschichte* 104 (2014): 297–320; idem, *The Bishop's Burden. Reforming the Catholic Church in Early Modern Italy* (Washington, DC: Catholic University of America Press, 2020).

14. Willi Henkel and Josep-Ignasi Saranyana, *Die Konzilien in Lateinamerika, Vol. 2. Lima* (Paderborn: Schöningh, 2010), 176ff; Mary McGlone, "The King's Surprise: The Mission Methodology of Toribio de Mogrovejo," *The Americas* 50 (1993): 65–83.

15. McGlone, "The King's Surprise," 73; cf. José Antonio González García, *Fray Martin de Valencia y Santo Toribio de Mayorga vidas paralelas de dos leoneses preclaros del siglo XVI. Valencia de Don Juan, Mayorga de Campos* (Madrid: Pliega, 2010); Magnus

Lundberg, *Church Life between the Metropolitan and the Local. Parishes, Parishioners and Paris Priests in Seventeenth-Century Mexico* (Orlando, FL: Iberoamericana, 2011), 68; Reynerio Lebroc, "Proyección tridentina en América," *Missionalia Hispánica* 26 (1969): 129–207.

16. Willi Henkel, *Die Konzilien in Lateinamerika. Vol. 1. Mexiko* (Paderborn Schöningh, 1984), 64ff.

17. Philip T. Hoffman, *Church and Community in the Diocese of Lyon, 1500–1789* (New Haven: Yale University Press, 1984), 52f.

18. Augustinus Reding, *Oecumenici Tridentini Concilii Veritas Inextincta* (Einsiedeln: 1684), vol. 1, 151. See ibid., 152, on the criticism that too many lazy and improper candidates were ordained to the priesthood or to the office of bishop: "Angelica solertia petatur ab Angelis in caelo regendo, non ab hominibus in terris administrandis."

19. Katja Burzer, *San Carlo Borromeo. Konstruktion und Inszenierung eines Heiligenbildes im Spannungsfeld zwischen Mailand und Rom* (Munich: Deutscher Kunstverlag, 2011), 36–40, 78–136.

20. Burzer, *San Carolo Borromeo*, 26; Volker Reinhard, "Krieg um Erinnerungs-Hoheit. Die Heiligsprechung Carlo Borromeos," *Schweizerische Zeitschrift für Religions-und Kulturgeschichte* 103 (2009): 63–72.

21. Alberigo, "Carlo Borromeo come modello," 1048; Cf. Christopher F. Black, *Society in Early Modern Italy* (New York: Palgrave Macmillan, 2004), 62–85.

22. John Headley, "Borromean Reform in the Empire? La Strada Rigorosa of Giovanni Francesco Bonomi," in John Headley and John Tomaro (eds.), *San Carlo Borromeo. Catholic Reform and Ecclesiastical Politics in the Second Half of the Sixteenth Century* (Washington, DC: Folger Books, 1988), 228–249. Hadley, however, falsely claims that Borromeo's *Acta* were never published on German soil although they were printed in 1603 in Brixen, which was part of the Holy Roman Empire.

23. Wietse de Boer, *The Conquest of the Soul. Confession, Discipline, and Public Order in Counter-Reformation Milan* (Leiden and Boston: Brill, 2001), 9; Adriano Prosperi, *Tribunali della coscienza* (Turin: Einaudi, 1996).

24. Cf. Forrestal, *Fathers*, 69; Giuseppe Maria Sebastiani, *De consolatione ad episcopos sub analogia episcopatus, et martyrij* (Rome: 1685).

25. de Boer, *The Conquest of the Soul*, 14, 17, 24f. Ditchfield, "Catholic Reformation," 171; Adriano Prosperi, "Die Beichte und das Gericht des Gewissens," in Prodi and Reinhard (eds.), *Das Konzil von Trient und die Moderne*, 175–197; idem, *Tribunali*; Karen Carter, *Creating Catholics. Catechism and Primary Education in Early Modern France* (Notre Dame, IN: University of Notre Dame Press, 2011), 121.

26. de Boer, *The Conquest of the Soul*, 50–53.

27. Nancy M. Farriss, *Tongues of Fire. Language and Evangelization Colonial Mexico* (Oxford: Oxford University Press, 2018), 50.

28. de Boer, *The Conquest of the Soul*, 54; idem, "Boundaries in Early Modern Europe," in Abigail Firey (ed.), *A New History of Penance* (Leiden and Boston: Brill, 2008), 343–346; Christophe Duhamelle, *Die Grenze im Dorf. Katholische Identität im Zeitalter der Aufklärung* (Baden-Baden: Ergon Verlag, 2018).

29. Zeb Tortorici, *Sins against Nature. Sex and Archives in Colonial New Spain* (Durham and London: Duke University Press, 2018), 174f.

30. Tortorici, *Sins*, 174; Johannes N. Brochhagen, *Kirchliche Kontrolle und religiöse Kommunikation im kolonialzeitlichen Andenraum. Die bischöfliche Visitation ländlicher Pfarreien der Diözese La Paz (17.-18. Jahrhundert)* (University of Hamburg/Germany: PhD Thesis, 2017), 107, 111. Peter Gose, *Invaders as Ancestors. On the Intercultural Making and Unmaking of Spanish Colonialism in the Andes* (Toronto: University of Toronto Press, 2008), 205f; A. C. van Oss, *Catholic Colonialism. A Parish History of Guatemala, 1524-1821* (Cambridge: Cambridge University Press, 2002), 141f; Nicholas A. Robins, *Priest-Indian Conflict in Upper Peru. The Generation of Rebellion, 1750-1780* (Syracuse: Syracuse University Press, 2007), 150f.

31. Barbara Diefendorf, *From Penitence to Charity. Pious Women and the Catholic Reformation on Paris* (Oxford: Oxford University Press, 2004), 70.

32. de Boer, *The Conquest of the Soul*, 70–76; cf. 116; 147. On optimism in Counter-Reformation politics and theology, especially that of Francis de Sales, see Damien Tricoire, *Mit Gott rechnen. Katholische Reform und politisches Kalkül in Frankreich, Bayern und Polen-Litauen* (Göttingen: Vandenhoeck & Ruprecht, 2013); Adriano Prosperi, *Infanticide, Secular Justice, and Religious Debate in Early Modern Europe* (Turnhout: Brepols, 2016), 103; cf. idem, *L' Inquisizione Romana. Letture e Ricerche* (Roma: Edizioni di storia e letteratura, 2003), 413–434.

33. Not to be confused with the conciliar historian Giovanni Mansi (1692–1769).

34. Giuseppe Mansi, *Il Vero Ecclesiastico Studioso di Conoscere e di corrispondere alla sua Vocazione* (Rome: 1673; Venice: 10th ed., 1712; last Italian edition, Venice: 1755). Translations into Polish and Latin. I am citing idem, *Verus Ecclesiasticus* (Frankfurt: 1693), 18–34 (on integrity of life and morals), 104: "Si sacerdotium integrum fuerit, tota Ecclesia floret." In the same work, see also 105–114 (on *oculi ecclesiae*); 125ff, 174–196 on sexual continence; and 274–400 on the vices of ambition, avarice, gluttony, and idleness; Mansi's *Bibliotheca Moralis* (Augsburg: 1732), vol. 1, tract 4, on the love of God was censored, and the expurgation of the entire third discourse demanded (*Novissimus Librorum Prohibitorum et Expurgandorum Index Pro Catholicis Hispanicis* [Madrid: 1747], 776).

35. Carlo Borromeo, *Acta Ecclesiae Mediolanensis*, vol. 1 (Lyon: 1683), 36, 875: " . . . cum nihil sit difficilius adolescenti quam immoderatis animi affectionibus per se moderari."

36. Cf. Joseph Bergin, *Church, Society and Religious Change in France, 1580-1730* (New Haven, CT: Yale University Press, 2009), 190ff.

37. Ellen A. Macek, "Advice Manuals and the Formation of English Protestant and Catholic identities, 1560-1660), *Dutch Review of Church History* 85 (2005): 315–331.

38. Marchand, *Hortus*, vol. 1, preface.

39. Cf. Marchand, *Hortus*, vol. 2, 1, and on faith, see 1–110.

40. Arneth, *Das Ringen*, 11.

41. Henri Bremond, *A Literary History of Religious Thought in France* (London: SPCK, 1936), vol. 3, 26; Francois Bourgoing, in *Oeuvres complete de Berulle*, ed. J. Migne (Paris: 1856), 102.

42. Bremond, *A Literary History*, vol. 3, 142; Bernard J. Ganter, *Clerical Attire. A Historical Synopsis and a Commentary* (Washington, DC: Catholic University of America Press, 1955).

43. Lamy, *Entretiens sur les sciences*, ch. 5, 187: "Nous vivons ici avec une honnête liberté, mais on n'y aime pas le libertinage." On Thomassin, see Paul Nordhues, *Der Kirchenbegriff des Louis de Thomassin. in seinem dogmatischen Zusammenhängen und in seiner lebensmässigen Bedeutung* (Leipzig: St. Benno-Verlag, 1958). On the decline of the communal aspects of the sacraments, see Andrew Barnes, *The Social Dimension of Piety* (New York: Paulist Press, 1993); Karen Carter, *Scandal in the Parish. Priests and Parishioners Behaving Badly in Eighteenth-Century France* (Montreal: McGill University Press, 2019).

44. At Bremond, *A Literary History*, vol. 3, 142–143; Denis Amelote, *La Vie du Père Charles de Condren* (Paris: 1643), part 2, 98–100.

45. Bremond, *A Literary History*, vol. 3, 27; Bourgoing, *Oeuvres complete de Berulle*, 103.

46. Arneth, *Das Ringen*, 19f; Kiesler, *Die Struktur des Theozentrismus bei Pierre de Berulle und Charles de Condren* (Berlin: 1934), 49ff.

47. Bremond, *A Literary History*, vol. 3, 108ff.

48. Kiesler, *Die Struktur*, 20; Arneth, *Das Ringen*, 11.

49. Bourgoing, *Oeuvres complet de Berulle*, 98: "La premier chef qui fait un etat de vie et de grâce spécial en l'Eglise, c'est le regard la contemplation et l'adoration de Jesus-Christ Notre-Seigneur en lui-même, en sa personne et en ses états et grandeurs. Car il est en cet objet le grand sacrement de piète, et le sacrément primitive de la religion chrétienne."

50. McGrath-Merkle, *Berulle's*, 39, 136–139.

51. Bremond, *A Literary History*, vol. 3, 30, 63, and also see 39.

52. At Bremond, *A Literary History*, vol. 3, 137; Bourgoing, *Oevres complete de Berulle*, 1474.

53. Merkle, *Berulle's*, 163, 244f, 272ff, 322f, 350.

54. Ludovicus Cresoli, *Mystagogus de Sacrorum Hominum Disciplina* (Paris: 1629), 18, 60, and on the title father, 74–81; on the physician, 81–89; navigator, 89–97; on the beauty of the hierarchy, which the angels admire, 115–119.

55. Arneth, *Das Ringen*, 37; Amelote, *La Vie du Père Charles de Condren*, vol. 2, ch. 8, 104–105.

56. Jean-François Senault, *De l'usage des passions* (Paris: 1641); English translation, idem, *The Use of Passions* (London: 1671), 47: "Passion then is nothing else, but a motion of the sensitive appetite caused by the imagination of an appearing or veritable good, or evil, which changeth the body against the laws of nature."

57. Senault, *The Use*, 197.

58. Senault, *The Use*, 212–213,

59. Bernard Lamy, *Entretiens sur les sciences* (Paris: 1752), ch. 5, 185–186. After all, even if dissimulation was permitted for Catholics in England due to persecution, it backfired and created the impression that Catholic men ought not to be trusted, which led in the eighteenth century to a widespread rejection of equivocation and dissimulation (Lisa McClain, *Divided Loyalties. Pushing the Boundaries of Gender and Lay Roles*

*in the Catholic Church, 1534–1829* [Basingstoke: Palgrave Macmillan, 2018], 98ff, 101ff).

60. Forrestal, *Vincent de Paul*, 123; Arneth, *Das Ringen*, 77–85.

61. Jean-Jacques Olier, *Catechisme chrestien pour la vie interieure* (Paris: 1657), 4. See also Arneth, *Das Ringen*, 11; George Letourneau, *La méthode d'Oraison Mentale du Séminaire de Saint-Sulpice* (Paris: Libraire Victore Lecoffre, 1903). On the reform of the clergy in the diocese of Lyon with the help of Sulpicians and Oratorians, see Hoffman, *Church and Community*, 74–97.

62. Olier, *Catechisme chrestien*, 7: "Bapteme aborieux."

63. Olier, *Catechisme chrestien*, 212: "qu'il ne faut point en vostre interieur de dispositions sensibles"; see also 214–216.

64. Robin Briggs, *Communities of Belief. Cultural and Social Tension in Early Modern France* (Oxford: Clarendon Press, 1989), 45. Barbosa, *Pastoralis*, pars 1, 58–66.

65. Boudon, *La science sacrée*, 1: "Le Catechisme ... est une doctrine qui nous est revelee."

66. Boudon, *La science sacrée*, ch. 3, 15–21, and also 19: "il n'est pas un veritable pasteur, ce sera un cure qui n'en aura que le nom." Cf. Barbosa, *Pastoralis*, pars 1, ch. 14, 113–116; ch. 15, 116–120. Even neglecting one soul was a terrifying burden, see Boudon, *La science sacrée*, ch. 10, 125ff, and also ch. 12, 142: "J'appelle ce compte épouvantable parce qu'il sera compte sur le prix de Ames perdues."

67. Boudon, *La science sacrée*, ch. 4, 22–23.

68. Barbosa, *Pastoralis*, pars 1, ch. 3, 47: "Ante mentis oculos ponat quanta gloria & honore," and also 48: "Cogitet, & ponderet quod etiam negligentes gravissimas Deo daturi sunt poenas." Examples for such enthusiasm at Freitag, *Pfarrer*, 226.

69. English according to Edward Healy Thompson, *The Life of Jean-Jacques Olier* (London: 1886), 418; Jean-Jacques Olier and Etienne-Michel Faillon, *Vie intérieure de la très-sainte Vierge* (s.l.: s.n., 1866), 4; see also, for the full text, Etienne-Michel Faillon, *Vie de M. Olier*, vol. 1 (Le Mans: 1841), 392–393.

70. Louis Tronson, *Forma cleri secundum exemplar quod ecclesiæ sanctisque patribus a Christo domino summo sacerdote demonstratum est* (Paris: 1739), preface, "ad devotos."

71. Tronson, *Forma*, preface.

72. Antonio Molina O.Cart., *Instruccion de sacerdotes* (Burgos: 1608); Latin editions were printed from 1618 to 1898, Italian editions from 1614 until the middle of the eighteenth century, French from 1619 until 1890.

73. Marianne Schlosser, "Den Seelen helfen: Neues und Traditionelles in der Spiritualität des Ignatius von Loyola und der ersten Jesuiten," in Sigrid Müller and Cornelia Schweiger (eds.), *Between Creativity and Norm Making. Tensions in the Later Middle Ages and the Early Modern Era* (Leiden and Boston: 2013), 103–130; Anna Ohlidal and Stefan Samerski (eds.), *Jesuitische Frömmigkeitskulturen. Konfessionelle Interaktion in Ostmitteleuropa 1570–1700* (Stuttgart: Steiner, 2006); Cathleen Comerford, *Reforming Priests and Parishes. Tuscan Dioceses in the First Century of Seminary Education* (Leiden and Boston: Brill, 2006).

74. Duhamelle, *Grenze*.

75. Cf. Carter, *Scandal*, 24ff.

76. Freitag, *Pfarrer*, 82, 169, 191f. Jan van Opstraet, *Quid est theologus?* (Vienna: 1788), 12, on priests who only desire a comfortable life.

77. Klaus Vechtel, "Das Priesterbild des Ignatius und die Priesterbildung heute," *Geist und Leben* 80 (2007): 94–108.

78. E.g., Rupert Presinger OSB, *Neu-angehendes Ordens-Kind des heiligen Ertz-Vatters Benedicti, da es noch in der Welt lebet* . . . (Salzburg: 1737), 10–33; on "many" or "few," see Antonio Molina, *Instructio Sacerdotum ex SS. Patribus* . . . (Antwerp: 1618), 103f, citing St John Chrysostom; on spiritual exercises, see Benedict XIV, *Institutiones Ecclesiasticae*, vol. 3 (Leuven: 1743), 210–224; on the election of suitable candidates, see Cresoli, *Mystagogus*, 261–265.

79. Giovanni Bona, *Opera Omnia* (Venice: 1752), 128–188.

80. Arneth, *Das Ringen*, 210–214.

81. Erin Kathleen Rowe, *Saint and Nation. Santiago, Teresa of Avila, and Plural Identities in Early Modern Spain* (University Park: Pennsylvania State Press, 2011), 51. In Teresa's case, femininity was seen by some as an obstacle to her patronage over Spain because it seemed to undermine the "collective virility" of the country (ibid., 110f).

82. Anselm Fischer OSB and Meinrad Mosmiller OSB, *Das äusserliche Leben mit dem Nächsten oder Geistreiche Unterweisung wie ein Ordens-Geistlicher fromm und gottselig mit seinem Nächsten wanderen könne*, vol. 2 (Augsburg: 1763), 205–331, here at 209.

83. Fischer and Mosmiller, *Das äusserliche Leben*, 218ff, 222f; Anselm Fischer, *Conversatio externa religiosa, modus pie, & religiose vivendi in communitate, & societate hominum* (Constance: 1711), 274: "Denique omnem paene malitiam superat, si remissoris vitae improbus propugnaor pessima sua principia effutiat in prasentia juniorum."

84. The familiarity one builds with one's peers, however, must never degenerate into "private friendships." These can bring unrest and discord into a community in which everybody should be loved the same way, just as Jacob brought discord when he publicly preferred Joseph from among his sons (Gen 37). Fischer and Mosmiller, *Das äusserliche Leben*, 23ff; Fischer, *Conversatio externa*, 289ff. In fact, the Latin original avoids the term friendship altogether (*familiaritas* instead of *amicitia*), while the German translation has it.

85. Sigismud Neudecker, *Schola Religiosa seu Tractatus Asceticus Universalis. Pars Prior, Editio Secunda* (Munich and Ingolstadt: 1757), 19, 21.

86. On the "prejudice of antiquity," see Christoph Matthäus Pfaff, *Dissertatio de Praejudicatis Opinionibus* . . . (Hagen: 1719), 24: "auctoritatis praejudicia vel praecipitantiae." On the importance of prudence and discernment, see also Francois Feuardent, *Epistola Secunda D. Petri Apostolorum Principis* . . . (Paris: 1601), 52. For Jansenists emphasizing these virtues, see Opstraet, *Quid est theologus?*, 227, and also 228: "Ubi vero abest charitas, ibi zelus indiscretus, vel carnalis prudentia regnet necesse est." On heresy hunting, see the Protestant Johann Jacob Zimmermann, *Opuscula Theologici* . . ., vol. 2/2 (Zurich: 1759), "Dissertationis de crimine haeretificationis, ejus causis et remedis," 798–958, at 779–780.

87. Bernardino Llorca, *Die Spanische Inquisition und die Alumbrados, 1509-1667* (Munich: 1934).

88. Emil Pauls, "Zur Geschichte der Censur am Niederrhein bis zum Frühjahr 1816," *Beiträge zur Geschichte des Niederrheins* 15 (1900): 36–117.

89. Landesarchiv Nordrhein-Westfalen, Düsseldorf: KK VIII, 192. Befehl an den Weihbischof zu Köln vom 20. Mai 1771 durch den Erzbischof aus Bonn, fol. 1.

90. Landesarchiv Nordrhein-Westfalen, Düsseldorf: KK VIII, 192, fol. 221. Other parallels were seen to the forbidden book by Antonio de Rojas, *Vida del espiritu para saber tener oracion y union con Dios* . . . (Madrid: 1630) and Jean de Bernières de Louvigny, *Pensées ou Sentimens du chrestien intérieur sur les principaux mystères de la Foi* (Paris: 1676).

91. Karl Joseph Lehner OSB, *Turtur Sacer oder geistliche Turteltaub* (Cologne: 1720), 284; cf. Briggs, *Communities of Belief*, 255, with reference to Adrien Bourdoise.

92. Hoffman, *Church and Community*, 82; Lehner, *Turtur*, 288f, 302, and at 325: "Darumb soll er sorgen, dass er alle affection gegen die Verwandten ablege, dieselbige in Geistliche verwechsle und nur die Liebe zu ihnen trage, welche die ordentliche Lieb erfordert, damit derjenig welcher der Welt und eigener Lieb abgestorben Christo . . . allein lebt, denselbigen anstatt der Elteren, Brüdern und aller Sachen halte."

93. Briggs, *Communities of Belief*, 254.

94. Staatsarchiv Würzburg: Stifte und Klöster 1769.

95. Freitag, *Pfarrer*, 212f.

96. Antje Flüchter, *Der Zölibat zwischen Devianz und Norm. Kirchenpolitik und Gemeindealltag in den Herzogtümern Jülich und Berg im 16. und 17. Jahrhundert* (Cologne et al.: Böhlau, 2006), 40, 82–94, 300ff. Anja Huovinen, "Zwischen Zölibat, Familie und Unzucht. Katholische Geistliche in Andalusien am Ende des Ancien Régime," *L'Homme* 9 (1998): 7–25; Augustin Fischer, *Sacerdotium Infiniti Pretii, Muneris Reverentiae et Dignitatis Deificum* (Krems: 1729), s.pag.

97. See, for example, Benedikt Land, *Land-, Statt- und Schutzpatron S. Joseph* . . . (Amberg: 1730), s.pag.; Georg Iwanek SJ, *Lilium Paradisi Coelestis S. Josephus* . . . (New Prague: 1688), 341. Also, angelic chastity was to be imitated by priests, see Andre Saussay, *Panoplia Sacerdotalis seu de Venerando Sacerdotum habitu* . . . (Paris: 1653), 321f, 330, 345.

98. Iwanek, *Lilium*, 341–351; Hieronymus Peres Denueros SJ, *Lapidicina Sacra ex qua Eductus Primarius Lapis Ss. Virgo* . . . *Editio Nova* (Lyon: 1679), tr. 1, sect. 12, par. 144f, 58f.

99. Pedro de Morales *In Caput Primum Matthaei* . . . (Lyon: 1614), 812: "Caro enim Christi caro mea est; et sanguis Chrisi sanguis mea est, quia ex eadem Regia tribu ambo procedimus"; 804; 806: "In particulari tamen dux & magister eroum est, qui Eucharistiae mirabile frequentant sacramentum"; 187: "ut propriis contrectaret manibus sacratissimum illud Christi corporis pignus, & ut esset sacratissimae illius carnis nutritius . . . ergo opportuit . . . Iosephi pedes mentis, & affectus esse purissimos, solutos, & separatos ab omni impuritate, corruptione, & macula"; and 187: "Quia si Sacerdotibus, ratione iustissima, inditum est perpetuum castitatis votum, quia sacratissimum Christi corpus consecraturi, manibusque contrectaturi erant: ergo Ioseph, qui ad simile ministerum tangendi Christum, fuit electus, debuit esse simili virginitatis & castitatis consecratus."

100. Arneth, *Das Ringen*, 54; Bergin, *Church, Society and Religious Change*, 208–226.

101. Paul Broutin, *La Réforme Pastorale en France au XVIIe Siècle* (Tournai: Desclee, 1956), vol. 2, 116, citing the manuscript de Courtin, *Vie du v. servieteur de Dieu, messire Adrien Bourdoise*, p. 1003 (Bibliothèque Mazarine/Paris: Ms 2453): "La paroisse est la matrice de la religion, le berceau de chrétiens. C'est là où ils sanctifiés dans la foi par le sacrament."

102. Augustin Zippe, *Von der moralischen Bildung angehender Geistlicher in dem Generalseminario in Prag* (Prague: 1784).

103. Heinrich Braun, *Anleitung zur geistlichen Beredsamkeit* (Munich: 1776), 54.

104. Borromeo, *Acta Ecclesiae Mediolanensis*, vol. 1, 17; Natalis Alexandre, *Commentarius Litteralis et Moralis in omnes Epistulas Sancti Pauli Apostolo et in VII Epistulas Catholicas*, vol. 2 (Paris: 1746), 201.

105. Oktavian Schmucki and Leonhard Lehmann (eds.), *Die ersten Kapuziner-Konstitutionen von 1536* (Münster: Fachstelle Franziskanische Forschung, 2016), 43 (I, 2).

106. F. A. Catalano et al. (eds.), *Le prime costituzioni dei Frati Minori Cappuccini di San Francesco. Roma–S. Eufemia 1536 ; in lingua moderna con note storiche ed edizione critica* (Rome: Italia Francescana, 1982), I (7). Schmucki and Lehmann, *Die ersten Kapuziner-Konstitutionen*, 18, 49ff; Leonhard Lehmann, "Sed sint minores. La minorita nella Regola non bollata," in Luigi Padovese (ed.), *Minores et subditi minores. Tratti caratterizzanti dell'identità Francescana* (Rome: Collegio S. Lorenzo, 2003), 129–147.

107. Schmucki and Lehmann, *Die ersten Kapuziner-Konstitutionen*, 56 (II, 29), 77.

108. Schmucki and Lehmann, *Die ersten Kapuziner-Konstitutionen*, 56 (II, 15), 59f.

109. Schmucki, and Lehmann, *Die ersten Kapuziner-Konstitutionen*, 56 (II, 28), 75; Raymund Linden, *Die Regelobservanz in der Rheinischen Kapuzinerprovinz von der Gründung bis zur Teilung 1611–1668* (Münster: Aschendorff, 1936), 49.

110. Joannes Maria de Noto, *De sacris ritibus iuxta Romanam regulam vsui fratrum minorum s. Francisci vulo Capucini . . .* (Naples: 1626), 7, and see, on the tone of the singing, 135ff: "certum humilis ac flebilis cantus"; on the footwashing, 179. Cf. Linden, *Die Regelobservanz*, 54.

111. Walther Hümmerich, *Anfänge des kapuzinischen Klosterbaues. Untersuchungen zur Kapuzinerarchitektur in den rheinischen Ordensprovinzen* (Mainz: Ges. für Mittelrhein. Kirchengeschichte, 1987); Giuseppina Fortunato, *L'architettura dei frati Cappuccini nella provincia Romana* (Pescara: Carsa Ed. 2012).

112. Schmucki and Lehmann, *Die ersten Kapuziner-Konstitutionen*, 56 (IV, 53ff), 100f; Linden, *Die Regelobservanz*, 19–33.

113. Schmucki and Lehmann, *Die ersten Kapuziner-Konstitutionen*, 56 (V, 63), 111.

114. Schmucki and Lehmann, *Die ersten Kapuziner-Konstitutionen*, 56 (VII, 90), 141; Venantius a Lisle-en-Rigault, *Monumenta ad Constitutiones Ordinis Fratrum Capuccinorum pertinentia* (Rome: Curia Generalia, 1916), 310–335; Linden, *Die Regelobservanz*, 36.

115. Linden, *Die Regelobservanz*, 93; Bonaventura von Mehr, *Das Predigtwesen in der kölnischen und rheinischen Kapuzinerprovinz im 17. Und 18. Jahrhundert*

(Rome: Istituto Storico Dei Fr. Min Cappuccini, 1945), 56–58; Felix Brandimartes, *Sapientiae Tubae Scientia, id est Tractatus scholasticus de Arte concionandi* (Panormi: 1667); Amadeus Bajocensis, *Paulus Ecclesiastes seu Eloquentia Christiana* (Paris: 1662; i.e., 1670). A helpful resource to identify Capuchin writers is still *Bibliotheca scriptorum Ordinis minorum S. Francisci Capuccinorum retexta & extensa a f. Bernardo a Bononia* (Venice: 1747).

116. Schmucki and Lehmann, *Die ersten Kapuziner-Konstitutionen*, 56 (VII, 90ff.), 141f.

117. Schmucki and Lehmann, *Die ersten Kapuziner-Konstitutionen*, 56 (IX, 112f), 165f., cf. Mehr, *Das Predigtwesen*, 30ff.

118. At Mehr, *Das Predigtwesen*, 45.

119. An eighteenth-century manuscript in the Bavarian State Library: Clm 30052. A 1627 manuscript can be found at the Catholic University Leuven Library: KU Leuven Libraries Maurits Sabbe Library GBIB: ACB. III, 7054 (from the former Belgian Archive of the Capuchin Province). Cf. Vittorio Manso, *Praeclara Institutio modi procedendi in causis regularium omnium* (Venice: 1605).

120. Linden, *Die Regelobservanz*; Schmucki and Lehmann, *Die ersten Kapuziner-Konstitutionen*, 56 (VII, 1000), 153. Cf. for the Franciscans, Gaudentius Kerckhove, *Commentarii in Generalia Statuta Ordinis S. Francisi Fratrum Minorum Provinciis Nationis Germano-Belgiciae in Capitulo Toletano anno 1633* (Cologne: 1709), 309ff, and at 310: "Ad Ordinis autem secreta pertinent dissensiones inter Fratres, praelatorum defectus graves, privationis, vel suspensionis, fratrum carcerationes, vel poenitentiae graves, quae gravia arguunt delicta."

121. See, for example, Lukas von Maring, "Ad Rdi. Reginaldi . . . Scriptum conc. statum eiusdem provinciae" (1666), and idem, "Ad R. P. Reginaldi . . . Obiectiones proprias et resolutions responsio" (1666), in Zentralarchiv der deutschen Kapuziner: Acta Provinciae Rhenanae Indivisiae PRC 1 and PRC 1; cited according to Linden, *Die Regelobservanz*, 93. On the apostacy of B. Ochino, see Michele Camaioni, "Capuchin Reform, Religious Dissent and Political Issues in Bernardino Ochino's Preaching in and towards Italy, 1535–1545," in *Religious Orders and Religious Identity Formation, c. 1420–1620* (Leiden and Boston: Brill, 2016), 214–234.

122. Lucian Montifontanus, *Geistliches Kinder-Spill. Das ist. Dreyhundert Sechs und Zwaintzig Neue Predigen Uber den kleinen Catechismum R.P. Petri Canisii Societatis Jesu*, 3 vols. (Augsburg: Reindl und Gastl, 1730), vol. 1, 485, 489ff.

123. Thiessen, *Zeitalter*.

124. Jens Ivo Engels, "Vom vergeblichen Streben nach Eindeutigkeit. Normenkonkurrenz in der europäischen Moderne," in Karsten and von Thiessen (eds.), *Normenkonkurrenz in historischer Perspektive*, 217–237; Zygmunt Bauman, *Modernity and Ambivalence* (Hoboken: Wiley, 2013). Hillard van Thiessen, "Normenkonkurrenz. Handlungsspielräume, Rollen, normativer Wandel und normative Kontinuität vom späten Mittelalter bis zum Übergang zur Moderne," in Karsten and von Thiessen (eds.), *Normenkonkurrenz in historischer Perspektive*, 241–286.

125. Thiessen, *Kapuziner*, 253–258.

# Chapter 3

1. Tobias Lohner, *Instructio Septima de Munere Concionandi, Exhortandi, Catechizandi* . . . (Dillingen: 1682), 4; Carolo Borromeo (ed.), *Acta Ecclesiae Mediolanensis* (Milan: 1582), pars 2, 212–231.

2. *Concilium Tridentinum*, Sessio V, Decretum II (super lectione et praedicatione), in Giuseppe Alberigo et al. (eds.), *Conciliorum Oecumenicorum Decreta* (Freiburg: 2nd ed., Herder, 1962), 643–646. Cf. Joachim Werz, *Predigtmodi im frühneuzeitlichen Katholizismus. Die volkssprachliche Verkündigung von Leonhard Haller und Georg Scherer in Zeiten und Bedrohungen (1500–1605). Reformationsgeschichtliche Studien und Texte 175* (Münster: Aschendorff, 2020), 186ff. For occasions and topics in funeral homilies, see, for example, Franciscus Agricola, *Evangelischer Wegweiser, das ist: Eine Catholische Leich Predigt* (Cologne: 1577); idem, *Von dem christlichen Gebett* . . . (Cologne: 1585), ch. 6, 32–35, and ch. 39, 227–228; Georg Pistorius, *Allgemeines Klaghaus oder Catholische Leichpredigen bey Begräbnissen der Kinder* . . . (Dillingen: 1657), preface; Matthaeus Timpe, *Catholische Leich und Trostpredigen* . . . (Würzburg: 1610); Friedrich Behm O.P., *Tuba D. Vincentii. Das ist Erschallende Posaun . . . von denen 15 erschröcklichen Zeichen . . .* (Kempten: 1691).

3. Barbosa, *Pastoralis*, p. 1, c. 14, 112; Eusebius Amort, *Theologia Moralis Inter Rigorem, et Laxitatem Media*, 2 vols. (Augsburg: 1758), vol. 1, tract. 7, par. 2, 705ff; Josy Birsens, "Katechese, Katechismen und Predigt im Zeitalter der Konfessionalisierung," in Bernhard Schneider (ed.), *Geschichte des Bistums Trier*, vol. 3 (Trier: Paulinus, 2010), 388–403.

4. Thomas Hurtado O.F.M, *Resolutionum Moralium de Residentia Sacra*, vol. 1 (Lyon: 1661), lib. 3, res. 3, 123ff, and, on idleness, subres. 3, 163ff; on the offering of the mass, res. 16, 181f.

5. Immacolata Saulle Hippenmeyer, "Der Pfarrer im Dienste seiner Gemeinde. Ein kommunales Kirchenmodell: Graubünden, 1400–1600," in Norbert Haag et al. (eds.), *Ländliche Frömmigkeit. Konfessionskulturen und Lebenswelten, 1500–1850* (Stuttgart: Thorbecke, 2002), 143–157; Birsens, "Katechese"; Andreas Heinz, *Die sonn- und feiertägliche Pfarrmesse im Landkapitel Bitburg-Kyllburg der alten Erzdiözese Trier von der Mitte des achtzehnten bis zur Mitte des neunzehnten Jahrhunderts* (Trier: Paulinus-Verlag, 1978). John M. Frymire, *The Primacy of the Postils. Catholics, Protestants, and the Dissemination of Ideas in Early Modern Germany* (Leiden and Boston: Brill, 2010), 15ff, the quotation at 17.

6. Benjamin Westervelt, "The Prodigal Son at Santa Justina: the Homily in the Borromean Reform of Pastoral Preaching," *Sixteenth Century Journal* 32 (2001): 109–126; Cf. Borromeo, *Acta Mediolanensis*, pars I, 20f; Anonymous, *Canones Directivi Confraternitatis Sacerdotum Bonae Voluntatis* . . . (Cologne: 1709), 14–20, 169–194, 395.

7. Andreas Heinz, "Das liturgische Leben der Trierischen Kirche zwischen Reformation und Säkularisation," in Bernhard Schneider (ed.), *Geschichte des Bistums Trier*, vol. 3 (Trier: Paulinus, 2010), 267–322, at 277.

8. Urs Herzog, *Geistliche Wohlredenheit. Die katholische Barockpredigt* (Munich: CH. Beck, 1991), 16f.

9. Lohner, *Instructio Septima*, 4, citing Francis de Sales's definition of a homily: "Est publicatio et declamatio divinae voluntatis, facta hominibus, per eum, qui legitime missus est, ad animas docendas et permovendas ad serviendum Deo in hac vita, ut in altera salva fiant."

10. Anonymous, "Predigtstuhl," in *Grosses Universal Lexicon*, ed. J. H. Zedler, vol. 29 (Leipzig and Halle: 1741), 279–290.

11. Jordan Simon, *Jesus der Gekreuzigte, der den Juden eine Aergernis, den Heiden eine Thorheit, den Christen aber die Kraft und Weisheit Gottes ist; in Sittlichen Reden* (Augsburg and Ingolstadt: 1771), 14.

12. On the exegesis of Jonah, see Frank A. Kurzmann, *Die Rede vom Jüngsten Gericht in den Konfessionen der Frühen Neuzeit* (Berlin: DeGruyter, 2019), 50–53; Bernd Roling, *Physica sacra. Wunder, Naturwissenschaft und historischer Schriftsinn zwischen Mittelalter und Früher Neuzeit* (Leiden and Boston: Brill, 2013), 321–402.

13. Annemarie Henle, *Die Typenentwicklung der süddeutschen Kanzel des 18. Jahrhunderts* (Heidelberg: Meister, 1933), 57.

14. Herzog, *Geistliche*, 89–94. For the imitation of St. Peter, see Michael Stainmayr, *Rationale Apostolicum oder Geistliches Brustbild* (Munich: 1684), 77. The placement of the pulpit on either north or south side seems to be highly ambiguous.

15. On the image of being a flame and light, see Ignatius Ertl, *Promontorium Bonae Spei. Himmlisches Vorgebürg der guten Hoffnung . . .* (Augsburg: 1711), 497; Prokop von Templin, *Adventuale ac Natale Jesu Christi sive Deliciae Spiritus Hibernales . . .*, vol. 1 (Munich: 1666), 881, 884; Theophile Raynaud SJ, *Operum Omnium Indices Generales*, vol. 19 (Lyon: 1645), 281; Jose de Barcia y Zambrana, *Espertador christiano quadragessimal de sermones doctrinales*, 4 vols. (Madrid: 1690). On the image of the preacher as physician, see Johannes Pelecyus, *Affectuum Humanorum Morborumque Cura* (Munich: 1617; Strasbourg: 1715), passim, and Franciscus Caccia, *Cura Curiosa oder Heylsame Seelen-Cur* (Vienna: 1708), 128; for very similar French motives, see Thomas Worcester, *Seventeenth-Century Cultural Discourse. France and the Preaching of Bishop Camus* (Berlin: DeGruyter, 1997), 73–75; Herzog, *Geistliche*, 146. On the imagery surrounding the Holy Spirit and a "theology of light," see Prokop von Templin, *Dominicale Paschale et Pentecostale* (Salzburg: 1667), 24–34; Idem, *Patrociniale . . .* (Salzburg: 1674), 10–18; on Epiphany, see Idem, *Adventuale*, 878–885.

16. Frymire, *Primacy*, 126, 130ff, 154ff. Wild's sermons were censored by the Sorbonne and the Spanish Inquisition but continued to be sold in Germany in the sixteenth century (143f).

17. Joachim Werz, "Die Kirche erklären: 'Der Layen Kirchen Spiegel' von Bartholomäus Wagner (ca. 1560–1629) als Beispiel jesuitischer Katechese in der Frühen Neuzeit," in Veit Neumann et al. (eds.), *Glaube und Kirche in Zeiten des Umbruchs. Festschrift für Josef Kreiml* (Regensburg: Pustet, 2018), 529–543, who corrects Frymire, *Primacy*, on Wagner; Joachim Werz, "Predigten des Laien Bartholomäus Wagner (1560–1629," in Christian Bauer and Wilhelm Rees (Eds.), *Laienpredigt—Neue pastorale Chancen* (Freiburg: Herder, 2021), 75–89.

18. Herzog, *Geistliche*, 112.

19. Herzog, *Geistliche*, 19; 351; Werz, *Predigtmodi*, 272f.

20. Constantin Letins, *Theologia Concionatoria Docens et Movens*, vol. 1 (Cologne: 7th ed., 1754), 121.

21. See Thomas Dixon, *From Passions to Emotions. The Creation of a Secular Psychological Category* (Cambridge: Cambridge University Press, 2003), 36.

22. For sacred rhetoric, see, for example, the Capuchin Ange-Joseph de a Bâtie, *Tractatus de rhetorica sacra, ad usum studentium candidatorumque concionatorum Ordinis F.F. Minorum Capucinorum Provinciae Sabaudiae accommodatus* (Chambéry: 1760), 13, 19. For the idea of existential companionship, see Eugen Biser, *Der Helfer. Eine Vergegenwärtigung Jesu* (Munich: Kösel, 1973), 240.

23. A "declaration" on affective theology is printed as prequel to vol. 1 of the German edition of Bail's work. Curiously it is missing in the French original. Louis Bail, *Theologia affectiva . . .* (Cologne: 1712), s.pag.: "Declaratio et usus huius theologiae affectivae pro concionatoribus." Cf. Werz, *Predigtmodi*, 271ff.

24. Gwendolyn Barnes-Karol, "Religious Oratory in a Culture of Control," in Anne Cruz and Mary E. Perry (eds.), *Culture and Control in Counter-Reformation Spain* (Minneapolis: University of Minnesota Press, 1992), 51–77.

25. Johann Laurenz Helbig, *Anatomia Canis Mystica et Moralis. Das ist: Die Eigenschafft eines Hunds, gut und böse*, 2 vols. (Würzburg: 1719/20); idem, *Alveare Catholicum, Per Mysticas Apes Melle et Cera . . . Catholisches Bien-Haus . . .* (Nuremberg: 1714).

26. Herzog, *Geistliche*, 125.

27. Cf. Johannes Prambhofer, *Samsonischer Honig-Fladen für die schleckige Adams Kinder* (Augsburg: 1703).

28. Abraham a St. Clara, *Grammatica Religiosa* (Cologne: 2nd ed., 1705), 547; cf. Herzog, *Geistliche*, 130; cf. on consuming "texts," Franz Eybl, "Vom Verzehr des Textes. Thesen zur Performanz des Erbaulichen," in Andreas Solbach (ed.), *Aedificatio. Edification in the Intercultural Context of the Early Modern Age* (Berlin: DeGruyter, 2005), 95–112.

29. Cajetan Felice Veranus, *De Humanis Affectibus Ciendis et Coercendis*, 3 vols. (Munich: 1710), vol. 1, title page. The Catholic Enlightener Franz Christian Pittroff, *Anleitung zur praktischen Gottesgelehrtheit*, vol. 4 (Prague: 2nd ed., 1784), 112 calls it a verbose but good work. Cf. Edmund Richer, *Obstetrix animorum. Hoc est Brevis et Expedita Ratio Docendi, Studendi, Conversandi, Imitandi, Iudicandi, Componendi* (Paris: 1600).

30. Veranus, *De Humanis*, vol. 1, 181–209; on the topic of spiritual battle and the question of differentiating asceticism and edification, see also Marianne Sammer, "Zur Volksläufigkeit aszetischer Literatur im 17. und 18. Jahrhundert. Lorenzo Scupolis *Geistlicher Kampf* und sein literarischer Nachhall," in Solbach (ed.), *Aedificatio*, 319–332.

31. Veranus, *De Humanis*, vol. 1, 242–246.

32. Dixon, *Passions*, 52.

33. Dixon, *Passions*, 46.

34. Catherine Newmark, *Passion-Affekt-Gefühl. Philosophische Theorien zwischen Aristoteles und Kant* (Hamburg: Meiner, 2008); Richard Hassing, *Cartesian*

*Psychophysics and the Whole Nature of Man. On Descartes' Passions of the Soul* (London: Lexington Books, 2015); on Descartes's love of God, see Peter Losconzi, "Passionate Reason: Science, Theology and the Intellectual Passion of Wonder in Descartes' Meditations," in Willem Lemmens and Walter van Herck (eds.), *Religious Emotions. Some Philosophical Explorations* (Cambridge: Cambridge Scholars Publ., 2008), 131–144. On "holy affections," see Dixon, *Passions*, 26–61; Hannah Newton, "Holy Affections," in Susan Broomhall (ed.), *Early Modern Emotions. An Introduction* (London and New York: Routledge, 2017), 67–71.

35. Dixon, *Passions*, 55.
36. Veranus, *De Humanis*, vol. 1, 8.
37. Veranus, *De Humanis*, vol. 1, 25: "[Musica] quod ad sanctissimam jucunditatem homines promoveat, quorum aures dulcisono demulcet concentu? . . . Ea est vis Musicae, quae casuum acerbitates mellita dulcedine adspergit & abigit . . . Neque ulla est natio, ulla gens, quamvis agrestis rudis, ac efferata, quae artificiosa canendi ratione non mitescat."
38. Veranus, *De Humanis*, vol. 1, 60, 94.
39. Veranus, *De Humanis*, vol. 1, 29; on memorization, see Jeremias Drexel, *Aurifodina Artium & Scientiarum omnium Excerpendi Solertia* (Antwerp: 1641).
40. Lohner, *Instructio Septima*, 2, 5f, 24, 49.
41. Tobias Lohner, *Instructio Practica tertia de Conversatione Apostolica* (Dillingen: 1680), 3f, 14.
42. Maximilian Neumayr, *Die Schriftpredigt im Barock. Auf Grund der Theorie der katholischen Barockhomiletik* (Paderborn: Schöningh, 1937), 26–83; Alphonsus Salmeron, *Commentarii in Evangelicam historiam, et in Acta Apostolorum*, vol. 1 (Cologne: 1612), prolegomenon XIX, 339–357; cf. prolegomenon VII, 68ff. Albertus de Albertis, *In Eloquentiae quum profanae, tum sacrae corruptores* (Milan: 1651), 8–14; cf. Lehner, *On the Road to Vatican II*, 193–238.
43. Adalbert Monacensis, *Thesaurus Absconditus*, vol. 1 (Munich: 1703), 172–185. Johann Andreas Schmeller, *Bayerisches Wörterbuch*, vol. 1 (Munich: Oldenbourg, 2008), 1239; Max Höfler, *Die volksmedizinische Organotherapie und ihr Verhältnis zum Kultopfer* (Stuttgart: UDV, 1908), 85ff; Herzog, *Geistliche*, 130.
44. Frymire, *Primacy*, 255.
45. Herzog, *Geistliche*, 23f; Edmund Mannincor, *Dominicale aus 3jährigen Fastenpredigten*, vol. 2 (Cologne: 1691), 33; Simon, *Jesus*, 12. For Protestant church sleepers, see Ahasverus Fritsch, *Fauler und sündlicher Kirchen-Schläfer. Ehemahlen zur Warnung vorgestellet, anjetzo aber aus eben der guten Absicht mit einer kurtzen Abhandlung vom strafbaren Kirchen-Schwätzer, aufs neue zum Druck befördert* (Frankfurt: 1756).
46. Herzog, *Geistliche*, 25.
47. Cf. Michael Thomas D'Emic, *Justice in the Marketplace in Early Modern Spain. Saravia, Villalon and the Religious Origins of Economic Analysis* (New York et al.: Lexington Books, 2014).
48. Jared Poley, *The Devil's Riches. A Modern History of Greed* (New York: Berghahn, 2017), 13–53, at 18. Cf. also Jean Delumeau, *Sin and Fear. The Emergence of a Western*

*Guilt Culture, 13th–18th Centuries* (New York: St. Martin's Press, 1991), 344ff; cf. Jonathan Patterson, *Representing Avarice in Late Renaissance France* (Oxford: Oxford University Press, 2015), 48f; 63f.

49. Julien Loriot, *Der Irrende auf den Weg zurück geführte Blinde . . .*, vol. 2 (Stadtamhof: 1739), 2–10. Franciscus Partinger, *Ehr-und Tugend-Cron Aller Heiligen* (Augsburg and Graz: 1722), 624: "Weh denen, welche ein Haus an das andere bauen, einen Acker neben den anderen hinweg kauffen, und zwar ohne Noth, als wann sie allein den Erdboden beherrschen und bewohnen. Die gantze Welt wäre dem Geitz oder dem reichen Geitz-Hals nicht zu viel."

50. Prokop von Templin, *Lignum Vitae*, vol. 3 (Munich: 1666), 429.

51. Johann Bodler, *Die Entlarffte Falschheit oder Sonntäglicher Predigen-Curs* (Dillingen: 1697), 171–176.

52. Simeon Manhardt, *Conciones, oder: Christliche Predigen*, vol. 2 (Augsburg: 1628), 154–155.

53. Charles de la Rue SJ, *Christliche Tugend-Schul*, vol. 3 (Augsburg: 1739), 12 homily, 159–171.

54. de la Rue SJ, *Christliche Tugend-Schul*, vol. 3, 161–162.

55. de la Rue SJ, *Christliche Tugend-Schul*, vol. 3, 162, and at 164: "Ach! Es ist denen Armen das Ihrige nicht von denen Armen, sondern von denen Reichen entzogen worden . . . Ihr Reiche, ihr sehet dise Arme mit trockenen Augen an, und was ihr sehet, das ist Euer Laster."

56. Templin, *Lignum*, vol. 1, 125.

57. A good overview is presented by Matthew Levering, *Predestination. Biblical and Theological Paths* (Oxford: Oxford University Press, 2011).

58. Templin, *Lignum*, vol. 1, 131.

59. David Gentilcore, "Adapt Yourselves to the People's Capabilities: Missionary Strategies, methods and Impact in the Kingdom of Naples, 1600–1800," *Journal of Ecclesiastical History* 45 (1994): 269–294.

60. Herzog, *Geistliche*, 37–53; 77–82; Joannes Maior, *Magnum Speculum Exemplorum Ex Plusquam Octoginta Autoribus [1480] . . . Tertia Editio* (Cologne: 1607); Antoine d' Averoult, *Flores Exemplorum sive Catechismus Historialis*, 3 vols. (Cologne: 2nd ed., 1624). Another example for a collection of example stories are the three volumes by Giuseppe Mansi, *Locupletissima bibliotheca moralis praedicabilis*, 3 vols. (Mainz: 1670; Venice: 1737), and Vincent Houdry, *Bibliotheca Concionatoria*, 4 vols. (Augsburg: 1749). Giovanni Rho, *Variae Virtutum Historiae Libri Septem* (Lyon: 1644).

61. Diego Perez de Valdivia, *De sacra ratione concionandi. Opus Iacobi Peresii a Valdiuia Baetici Baëzani . . . Additus est in fine Libellus eiusdem argumenti verè aureus, editus pridiem iussu . . . cardinalis Caroli Borromei archiepiscopi Mediolanensis* (Barcinone: 1588), preface "Ad Sacrae Theologiae studiosos" and lib. III, c. 1, 158. Cf. Robert Bellarmine, *Instructiones Praedicationis Verbi Dei* (s.l., s.a.), 16.

62. Ludwig Pastor, *Geschichte der Päpste*, vol. 14/2 (Freiburg: Herder, 1930), 959; Leonard Goffine, *Seelen-Liechts erster Strahl* (Nürnberg: 1705); Thomas Worcester, "The Classical Sermon," in Joris van Eijnatten (ed.), *Preaching, Sermon and Cultural Change in the Long Eighteenth Century* (Boston and Leiden: Brill, 2009), 133–172.

63. Thomas M. Cohen, *The Fire of Tongues, Antonio Vieira and the Missionary Church in Brazil and Portugal* (Stanford: Stanford University Press, 1998), 67.

64. Cohen, *Fire*, 68.

65. Nicolas Girard, *Sämmtliche Predigten. Zweite Auflage*, vol. 5 (Augsburg: 1772), 332–354.

66. Vernon Hyde Minor, *The Death of the Baroque and the Rhetoric of Good Taste* (Cambridge: Cambridge University Press, 2006), 163; Alberto Vecchi, "I modi della devozione," in Vittore Brance (ed.), *Sensibilità e razionalità nel settecento* (Venice: Sansoi, 1967), 95–124. Eusebius Amort, *Theologia Eclectica*, vol. 4 (Augsburg: 1752), tractatus de praeceptis, 13f.

67. Philipp J. Brunner, *Christliche Reden, welche von katholischen Predigern in Deutschland seit dem Jahr 1770 bei verschiedenen Gelegenheiten vorgetragen worden sind. Als ein merkwürdiger Beitrag zur Aufklärungsgeschichte des katholischen Deutschlands*, vol. 1 (Heidelberg: Pfähler, 1787), preface.

68. Lehner, *Catholic Enlightenment*, passim.

69. Brunner, *Christliche Reden*, vol. 1, 92, 110; vol. 1, 125, 126.

70. Brunner, *Christliche Reden*, vol. 1, 158ff.

71. Brunner, *Christliche Reden*, vol. 2, 2, 114.

72. Brunner, *Christliche Reden*, vol. 2, 134.

73. These fell into the category of passions, see Dixon, *Passions*, 36.

# Chapter 4

1. Cf. a similar assessment in Henry Outram Evennett, *The Spirit of Counter-Reformation* (Notre Dame: University of Notre Dame Press, 1970), 32.

2. August Franzen, "Innerdiözesane Hemmungen und Hindernisse der kirchlichen Reform im 16. und 17. Jahrhundert," in Eduard Hegel (ed.), *Colonia Sacra. Studien und Forschungen zur Geschichte der Kirche im Erzbistum Köln* (Cologne: 1947), 163–201.

3. Bartholomaeus a Martyribus, *Stimulus Pastorum. Zur Spiritualität des Hirtenamts*, ed. Marianne Schlosser (St. Ottilien: Eos, 2018), 33, 61.

4. Martyribus, *Stimulus Pastorum*, 87.

5. See chapter 1.

6. Martyribus, *Stimulus Pastorum*, 142.

7. Martyribus, *Stimulus Pastorum*, 141.

8. This echoed the practice of the *antidoron* in Byzantine churches.

9. On the canonical definition of superstition, see Ferraris, *Bibliotheca Canonica*, vol. 7 (Rome: 1891), 350–362.

10. Joseph Catalano, *Rituale Romanum Benedicti XIV Perpetuis Commentariis Exornatum*, vol. 2 (Patavii: 1760), c. 16–18, 55–64; Marchand, *Hortus*, "Resolutionibus circa Eucharistiam," c. 7 "De missa parochiali audienda," 815: "Quaeri etiam potest cur in quibusdam Provinciis, panis benedictus & in parte

conscissus cunctis praesentibus diebus Dominicis datur? Sic in Gallia Ecclesiis communiter practicatur. Respondeo panem illum esse cuiusdam pacis & unionis Christianae symbolum." Franciscus a S. Augustino Macedo O.Min., *Disquisitio Theologica de Ritu Azymi et Fermentati* (Verona: 1683), 173. Bergin, *Church, Society*, 26, mentions it briefly. Pope Benedict XIV. points to idolatry in his *De Sacrosancto Missae Sacrificio* (Rome: 1748), 381.

11. Cf. *Rubricas Generales de la Missa Gothica-Muzarabe y el Omnium offerentium* (Salamanca: 1772), lxvi; for England, see Michael Alford Griffith SJ, *Fides Regia Britannica sive Annales Ecclesiae Britannicae . . .* vol. 1 (Leodii: 1663), 327.

12. The term "little Christ" for priests is used by Giovanni B. Casali, *De Profanis et Sacris Veteribus Ritibus Opus Tripartitum . . .* (Frankfurt: 1681), 131; cf. Duhamelle, *Grenze.*

13. Louis Châtellier, *The Religion of the Poor. Rural Missions in Europe and the formation of modern Catholicism, c. 1500–c.1800*, trans. Brian Pearce (Cambridge: Cambridge University Press, 1997), 40.

14. Châtellier, *Religion*, 31; 444f; 87. Eudists and Oratorians likewise rejected the theatrical approach, cf. Charles Berthelot DuChesnay, *Les missions de Saint Jean Eudes. Contribution à l'histoire des missions en France au 17. Siècle* (Paris: Procure des Eudistes, 1967); François Thibodeau, *Saint Jean Eudes. Prêtre-missionnaire et l'Eglise en Nouvelle-France* (Quebec: L'Maison des Eudistes, 2014). Since missionaries often traveled with a bookseller, parishioners moved by the event could buy a publication to immerse themselves more fully (Châtellier, "Die Erneuerung," 122).

15. Châtellier, *The Religion of the Poor*, 7f.

16. Châtellier, *The Religion of the Poor*, 15, 47.

17. Nicolaus Cusanus SJ, *Christliche Zucht-Schul Allen Seelsorgern und gemeinem Mann sehr nützlich* (Cologne: 4th ed., 1675). Birsens, "Katechese."

18. At Châtellier, *Religion*, 35.

19. Théodule Rey-Mermet, *Un homme pour les sans-espoir. Alphonse de Liguori, 1696–1787* (Paris: Nouvelle Cité, 1987).

20. Benito Feijoo, *Cartas eruditas, y curiosas . . .*, vol. 5 (Madrid: 1760), Carta 5, 180: "Bueno es introducir en ellas el temor de Dios; pero mejor, y más seguro, hacerlas enamorar de Dios."

21. Reinhard Faust, *Princeps Christano-Politicus. Septem donis Spiritus Sancti Instructus* (Vienna: 1658). Cf. Also Eusebius Nieremberg SJ, *Obras y Días. Manual de Señores y Principes; en que se Propone con su Pureza y Rigor la Especulación y Ejecución Política, Económica y Particular de Todas las Virtudes* (Madrid: 1628); idem, *Theopoliticus sive Brevis Illucidatio et Rationale Divinorum Operum* (Antwerp: 1641).

22. Faust, *Princeps*, 20: "Parce igitur loquere, tege intentionem operis, & caute dissimula, ut sapienter gubernes." Cf. Perez Zagorin, *Ways of Lying. Dissimulation, Persecution, and Conformity in Early Modern Europe* (Cambridge and London: Cambridge University Press, 1990); Nicole Reinhardt, *Voices of Conscience. Royal Confessors and Political Counsel in Seventeenth-Century Spain and France* (Oxford: Oxford University Press, 2016).

23. Faust, *Princeps*, 29–68.

24. Faust, *Princeps*, 86.

25. Faust, *Princeps*, 109–148.

26. Faust, *Princeps*, 150–196.

27. Nicolas Caussin SJ, *The Holy Court*, vol. 1 (London: 4th ed., 1678), "To the Nobility of France," s.pag.: "It remains, Sirs, that you make the court holy, and you shall sanctifie the world."

28. Caussin, *Holy Court*, vol. 1, 2.

29. Caussin, *Holy Court*, vol. 1, 13.

30. Caussin, *Holy Court*, vol. 1, 14: "Vanity would also be more tolerable, were it not that it changeth into cruelty . . . that transform the nature of men into brutishness absolutely savage and tyrannous," and see 14–16 for a criticism of duels.

31. Caussin, *Holy Court*, vol. 1, 21.

32. Caussin, *Holy Court*, vol. 1, 64.

33. Caussin, *Holy Court*, vol. 1, 65.

34. Charles Boileau, *Pensees choises* (Paris: 1709), 75–90, 96.

35. Matthew L. Jones, *The Good Life in the Scientific Revolution. Descartes, Pascal, Leibniz and the Cultivation of Virtue* (Chicago: University of Chicago Press, 2006), 3–5, 50f.

36. Jones, *Good Life*, 9.

37. Jones, *Good Life*, 44f.

38. Jones, *Good Life*, 49f.

39. At Jones, *Good Life*, 50.

40. Franz Xaver Thalhofer, *Entwicklung des katholischen Katechismus in Deutschland von Canisius bis Deharbe* (Freiburg: 1899); Carter, *Creating Catholics*.

41. Vincenzo Lavenia, "Conscience and Catholic Discipline of War: Sins and Crimes," *Journal of Modern History* 18 (2014): 447–471; Thomas Sailly, *Guidon et practique spirituelle du soldat chrestien* (Antwerp: 1590); Jerónimo Gracián, *El soldado catholico, que prueva [ . . . ] que los que no tienen letras, no han de disputar de la fee con los hereges* (Brussels: 1611). For Antonio Tommaso Schiara's influential *Theologia Bellica*, see Vincenzo Lavenia, "The Catholic Theology of War: Law and Religion in an Eighteenth-Century Text," in Wim Decock (ed.), *Law and Religion. The Legal Teachings of the Protestant and Catholic Reformations* (Göttingen: Vandenhoeck & Ruprecht, 2014), 133–148.

42. Reginald M. Schultes, *Fides implicita. Geschichte der Lehre von der fides implicita und explicita in der katholischen Theologie* (Regensburg: F. Pustet, 1920); Philippe d'Outreman, *The True Christian Catholique or Manner How to Live Christianly*, trans. John Heigham (St. Omers: 1622), 298–299.

43. Charles B. Paris, *Marriage in XVIIth Century Catholicism* (Tournai and Montreal: Desclee, 1975), 20–28; Carter, *Creating Catholics*, 37.

44. Shagan, *Belief*, 80. See especially the detailed discussion in Francisco Suarez, *Opus de Virtute Theologia Fide . . .* (Paris: 1621), disp. 2, sect. 6, 34–43, and at 36: "hanc fidem semper fuisse explicitam in Ecclesia," and 37: "Haec fides explicita semper fuit in Ecclesia in capitibus, seu Principius ejus, in communi autem populo fere non fuit, usque ad statum legis gratiae," and on the aspect of unburdening, see disp. 6, sect. 3, 533.

45. Suarez, *Opus de Virtute*, disp. 6, sect. 3, 230.

46. At Robert Ricard, *The Spiritual Conquest of Mexico. An Essay on the Apostolate and the Evangelizing Methods of the Mendicant Orders in New Spain, 1523–1572* (Berkeley: University of California Press, 1966), 86; cf. 106f; Osvaldo F. Pardo, *The Origins of Mexican Catholicism, Nahua Rituals and Christian Sacraments in Sixteenth-Century Mexico* (Ann Arbor: University of Michigan Press, 2004), 20–48.

47. Sabine MacCormack, "The Heart Has Its Reasons: Predicaments of Missionary Christianity in Early Colonial Peru," *Hispanic American Historical Review* 65 (1985): 443–466; R. L. Green, *Tropical Idolatry. A Theological History of Catholic Colonialism in the Pacific World, 1568–1700* (Lanham: Lexington Books, 2018).

48. Lundberg, *Church Life*, 23; cf. Jennifer Ottmann, *Models of Christian Identity in Sixteenth- and Early Seventeenth-Century Nahuatl Catechetical Literature* (PhD Thesis: New Haven, CT, Yale University, 2003).

49. Gianni Criveller, *Preaching Christ in Late Ming China. The Jesuit's Presentation of Christ from Matteo Ricci to Giulio Aleni* (Rome: Ricci Institute, 1997), 130–133.

50. Carter, *Creating Catholics*, 87ff. The same results can be found among English Catholics, see Lucy Underwood, *Childhood, Youth and Religious Dissent in Post-Reformation England* (Basingstoke, UK: Palgrave Macmillan, 2014), 55f. On missionary teachers, see Lehner, *Catholic Enlightenment*, 104–124.

51. Carter, *Creating Catholics*, 130; cf. 225.

52. At Carter, *Creating Catholics*, 75.

53. Franz X. Mayer, *Predigten nach den Bedürfnissen des gemeinen Mannes . . .* (Munich: 1786); Johann Michael Sailer, *Vollständiges Lese-und Gebethbuch für katholischen Christen* (Munich: 3rd ed., 1789).

54. Anonymous, *Catholische Tagzeiten* (Vienna: 1690).

55. Martin von Cochem, *Guldener Himmels-Schlüsel, oder neues Gebett-Buch, zur Erlösung der lieben Seelen deß Fegfeurs. Zum sonderlichen Gebrauch deß andächtigen Weiber-Geschlechts* (Augsburg: 1696).

56. See, for example, Anonymous, *Zwölf Geistliche Kirchengesäng* (Ingolstadt: 1586); Christopher Flurhaim, *Alte Kirchengesäng und Gebett des ganzen Jars* (s.l.: 1581); Anonymous, *Alte Catholische Geistliche Kirchengesäng* (Paderborn: 1609); Anonymous, *Christlich Catholisch Gesangbuch* (Paderborn: 1628). For Hungary, see Gabriella Gilanyi, "Der einstimmige lateinische liturgische Gesang in Ungarn nach dem Tridentinischen Konzil," in Marta Fata and Andras Forgo (eds.), *Das Trienter Konzil und seine Rezeption im Ungarn des 16. und 17. Jahrhunderts* (Münster: Aschendorff, 2019), 261–290.

57. Francesco Sacchini, *De Ratione libros cum profectu legend libellus* (Flexiae: 1617), ch. 14; Lorenz Forer SJ, *Disputir-Kunst für die Einfältigen Catholischen . . .* (Ingolstadt: 1656).

# Chapter 5

1. Constance Jordan, *Renaissance Feminism* (Ithaca: Cornell University Press, 1990). See the excellent overview by Rüdiger Schnell, "Geschlechterbeziehungen und Textfunktionen. Probleme und Perspektiven eines Forschungsansatzes," in idem

(ed.), *Geschlechterbeziehungen und Textfunktionen. Studien zu Eheschriften der Frühen Neuzeit* (Tübingen: Niemeyer, 1998), 1–58.

2. Cf. Rüdiger Schnell, *Histories of Emotion. Premodern—Modern* (Berlin: DeGruyter, 2020).

3. Schnell, "Geschlechterbeziehungen"; Katrin Graf, "Der Dialog *Conjugium* des Erasmus von Rotterdam in deutschen Übersetzungen des 16. Jahrhunderts," in Schnell (ed.), *Geschlechterbeziehungen*, 259–274; Katrin Graf, "ut suam quisque vult esse, ita est. Die Gelehrtenehe als Frauenerziehung. Drei Eheschriften des Erasmus von Rotterdam," in Schnell (ed.), *Geschlechterbeziehungen*, 233–257. See also Rüdiger Schnell, *Sexualität und Emotionalität in der vormodernen Ehe* (Cologne: Böhlau, 2002).

4. Henkel and Saranyana, *Die Konzilien in Lateinamerika, vol. 2. Lima* (Paderborn: Schöningh, 2010), 32ff.

5. Rouven Wirbser, "A Law Too Strict? The Cultural Translation of Catholic Marriage in the Jesuit Mission to Japan," in Antje Flüchter and Rouven Wirbser (eds.), *Translating Catechisms, Translating Cultures. The Expansion of Catholicism in the Early Modern World* (Leiden and Boston: Brill, 2014), 252–283; Hélène Vu Thanh, *Devenir japonais. La mission jésuite au Japon. 1549–1614* (Paris: Pups, 2016), 258–277.

6. Johannes B. Gonet, *Clypeus Theologicae Thomisticae*, vol. 5 (Antwerp: 8th ed., 1725), 468: "ad animos conjugum sanctificandos." Giovanni Bellarino, *Doctrina Catholica ex Sacro Concilio Tridentino . . .* (Venice: 1620), 629, with reference to the Old Testament book of Tobit.

7. On the baroque revival of the cult, see the excellent study of Jennifer Welsh, *The Cult of St. Anne in Medieval and Early Modern Europe* (New York; Routledge, 2017), 184–210, on the decline of kinship, 187–192; and 166–169 on the decline of the cult and the controversy over her *Trinubium* in the early sixteenth century. For a classic post-Tridentine treatment of St. Anne, see the works of Jacobus Polio O.F.M., *Exegeticon Historicon Sanctae Annae* (Cologne: 1640); idem, *Historia Sanctorum Joachim et Annae. Geneseos, Vitae, Transitus et Connexorum* (Würzburg: 1652); Joannes Thomas a S. Cyrillo O.C.D., *S. Anna sive de laudibus . . . Divae Annae* (Cologne: 1657). On the role of St. Anne, see also Angelika Dörfler-Dierken, *Die Verehrung der heiligen Anna in Spätmittelalter und früher Neuzeit* (Göttingen: Vandenhoeck & Ruprecht, 1992), 45–74.

8. Cf. Briggs, *Communities of Belief*, 236; John Bossy, "The Counter-Reformation and the People of Catholic Europe," *Past and Present* 47 (1970): 51–70.

9. Cf. Christian E. Brugger, *The Indissolubility of Marriage and the Council of Trent* (Washington, DC: Catholic University of America Press, 2017).

10. Against Briggs, *Communities of Belief*, 246.

11. On the importance of local legal traditions, see Simon Teuscher, *Lords' Rights and Peasant Stories. Writing and the Formation of Tradition in the Later Middle Ages* (Philadelphia: University of Pennsylvania Press, 2012).

12. Duhamelle, *Grenze*, passim.

13. Christopher J. Lane, *Callings and Consequences. The Making of Catholic Vocational Culture in Early Modern France* (Montreal: McGill University Press, 2021).

14. Rüdiger Schnell, *Frauendiskurs, Männerdiskurs, Ehediskurs. Textsorten und Geschlechterkonzepte in Mittelalter und Früher Neuzeit* (Frankfurt/Main: Campus Verlag, 1998), 77, 89, 135–139.

15. Templin, *Lignum*, vol. 2, 269; Johann Wild, *Gemeine, Christliche und Catholische Busspredigen* . . . (Mainz: 1564), clvii. A preacher could even address superstitious customs and beliefs about nuptials: Only because the marriage candle of the husband burnt a bit brighter, this would not mean that he would necessarily survive his wife (Templin, *Lignum*, vol. 2, 275–278, see 276: "Weisst du aber was . . . für ein Weib du nemmen sollest . . . Quamsi ducturus, teneat p. quinque Puella: Sit pia, sit prudens, pulchra, pudica, potens"). See also Benedict Fidelis a S. Philippo, *Paradisus Voluptatis Verbi Incarnato. Hoc est Sermones in Evangelia Dominicalia. Ed. Jakob Emans . . .* (Cologne: 1659), 276–288.

16. Pilar Latasa, "Tridentine Marriage Ritual in Sixteenth- to Eighteenth-Century Peru. From Global Procedures to American Idiosyncrasies," *Legal History* 27 (2019): 105–121; Paris, *Marriage*, 69ff; Allyson M. Poska, "When Love Goes Wrong. Getting Out of Marriage in Seventeenth-Century Spain," *Journal of Social History* 29 (1996): 871–882. On discernment before marriage, see Anonymous, *Deliberir-Büchlein, oder Berathschlagung von Erwählung eines Stands für das weibliche Geschlecht . . .* (Munich: 1734). Cf. also the guidebooks for discernment over marriage, e.g., Franciscus Agricola, *Biblischer-Ehespiegel . . .* (Cologne: 1599); Aegidius Albertinus, *Hausspolicey . . .* (Munich: 1602); Anonymus, *Kleiner Ehe-Spiegel darinnen sich alle christliche Ehe-Leuth zu ersehen . . .* (Munich: 1741); Anonymous, *Engel-Schuel und zugleich heller Ehe-spiegel. Das ist das gold-werthe Canonische . . . Büchlein Tobias* (Munich: 1723).

17. Rüdiger Schnell, "Concordia im Haus—Vielfalt der Diskurse (1300–1700)," in Christina Schaefer and Simon Zeisberg (eds.), *Das Haus schreiben. Bewegungen ökonomischen Wissens in der Literatur der Frühen Neuzeit* (Wiesbaden: Harrassowitz, 2018), 29–65; Schnell, *Sexualität*, 102–105; Schnell, *Frauendiskurs*, passim.

18. Schnell, "Concordia."

19. Schnell, *Frauendiskurs*, 77, 89, 135–139.

20. Martin Eisengrein, *Anderer Theil, Der Postillen, oder Christlicher Catholischer Auslegung der Sontaeglichen auch etlich anderer Fest Evangelien* (Ingolstadt: 1583), 88ff.

21. Montifontanus, *Geistliches Kinder-Spill*, 185.

22. Paris, *Marriage*, 40; Philippe d'Outreman, *Paedagogus Christianus seu Recta Hominis Christiani Institutio*, vol. 2 (Augustae Trevirorum: 1656), 531. Outreman also gives the advice to celebrate the wedding anniversary. See also Lane, *The Diversity*, 160, who mentions the identical advice of Claude La Colombière (1641–1682).

23. Paris, *Marriage*, 60.

24. Andreas Holzem, "Kinder nicht um Gott betrügen–historisch, Andachtsbuch und religiöser Erziehungsrat in der frühen Neuzeit," in Reinhold Boschki et al. (eds.), *Religionspädagogische Grundoptionen. Elemente einer gelingenden Glaubenskommunikation. Feschrift Albert Biesinger* (Freiburg: Herder, 2008), 255–274, at 265. See Vincent Houdry, *Bibliotheca Concionatoria Ethices Christianae . . . Argumenta . . . Editio Novissma*, vol. 3 (Augsburg: 1775), 45–63, for a typical overview;

for a typical Catholic housebook for the family and its treatment of marriage, see Georg Wittweiler SJ, *Catholisch Hausbuch* (Munich: 1631), 897–921, and, in comparison on ordination, see 873–896. See also Delumeau, *Sin and Fear*, 434, 440.

25. Shaji George Kochuthara, *The Concept of Sexual Pleasure in the Catholic Moral Tradition* (Rome: Pontificia Università Gregoriana, 2007), 226.

26. Cited at Kochuthara, *Concept*, 236.

27. Cited at Kochuthara, *Concept*, 236. See also Fernanda Alfieri, "Urge without Desire? Confession Manuals, Moral Casuistry and the Features of *Concupiscentia* between the Fifteenth and Eighteenth Centuries," in Kate Fisher and Sarah Toullalan (eds.), *Bodies, Sex and Desire from the Renaissance to the Present* (London: Palgrave Macmillan, 2014), 151–167; idem, *Nella camera degli sposi. Tomás Sánchez, il matrimonio, la sessualità, Secoli XVI–XVII* (Bologna: Il Mulino, 2010). For an overview of accepted and rejected sexual practices, see Sanchez, *Disputationum*.

28. Such sermons also gave generic advice on how to virtuously celebrate nuptials. Those who had a good conscience and remained chaste could dance during the wedding feast like King Salomon himself, an eighteenth-century priest exclaimed (Franciscus Hoeger, *Die Siben Brodt in der Wuesten von Christo gesegnet* (Ingolstadt: 1726), 98). Cf. Johann Hesselbach, *Epithalamia. Das ist: Hochzeit-Predigen* (Salzburg: 1663), 435–443; on the need for the public proclamation, see the reform decree of the Council of Trent, session 24.

29. Gregor Rippel, *Die wahre Schönheit der Religion . . . Gründliche Erklärung der Ceremonien . . .* (Mainz: 1777), 641f. The kiss of peace after exchanging the vows was already in the eighteenth century no longer used.

30. *Rituale Romanum seu Manuale Romanum . . .* (Antwerp: 1673), 451ff; cf. *Rituale Romanum Benedicti XIV*, vol. 1 (Patavii: 1760), 441–453.

31. Balthasar Antonio Ziegler, *Kurtze Ermahnungen so denen neuen Eheleuthen bey der Copulation können gegeben werden* (Prague: 1698), 34.

32. Hesselbach, *Epithalamia*, 387, mentions that a man would also have to fulfill his sexual duty toward a morbidly obese wife. Often, Islam was cited as a negative example for the treatment of women, see Johann Gualbert Seger, *Concha Margaritifera Spiritualis . . .* (Nuremberg: 1705), 58. On the decline of sexual modesty and the problems it created in Spain, see Carmen Gaite, *Love Customs in Eighteenth-Century Spain. Trans. Maria Tomsich* (Berkeley: University of California Press, 1991), 111; Anonymous, *Consideraciones politicas sobe la conducta qu debe observarse entre marido y mujer* (Madrid: 1792), 4. On the housefather's duty to protect his children from immodest behavior, see Paul De Barry, *Le Mort de Paulin et d'Alexis* (Lyon: 1658), 86f; Briggs, *Communities of Belief*, 250.

33. Christopher Puchner, *Fragmenta Nuptialia. Id est: Exhortationes Nuptiales LXXII* (New Prague: 1704), 36; Hesselbach, *Epithalamia*, 366. For an overview of Protestant nuptial sermons, see Ephraim Praetorio, *Des homiletischen Bücher-Vorraths Erster Theil* (Leipzig: 3rd ed., 1713), 1087–1116 and Erik Margraf, *Die Hochzeitspredigt der frühen Neuzeit* (Munich: Utz, 2007), who only deals with five Catholic authors. Gaite, *Love Customs*, 96. On the wife as *socia*, see Rüdiger Schnell, "Die Frau als Gefährtin des Mannes. Eine Studie zur Interdependenz von Textsorte, Adressat und Aussage,"

in idem (ed.), *Geschlechterbeziehungen*, 119–170. For the very similar Jesuit preaching on marriage in seventeenth-century China, see Amsler, *Jesuits and Matriarchs*, 67–86.

34. Goffine, *Seelen-Liechts*, 72–75.

35. Hoeger, *Die Siben Brodt*, 99.

36. Gaite, *Love Customs*, 109; Paris, *Marriage*, 117. On the theological dimension of restoring the purity of somebody's good intentions, see Diego Alvarez de Paz SJ, *De Exterminatione Mali et Promotione boni. Opera Omnia*, vol. 2 (Lyon: 1613), 1030–103.

37. Henri Boudon, *La science et la pratique du Chrestien* (Paris: 1681), ch. 2, 9; and ch. 3 on the immense love of God and vocation (13–27).

38. Paris, *Marriage*, 79; Charles Gobinet, *The Instruction of Youth in Christian Piety* (London: 8th ed., 1824), vol. 1, part 5, 169; Goffine, *Seelen-Liechts*, 72–75.

39. Henri Boudon, *Dieu Seul* (Brussels: 6th ed., 1700), ch. 6, 49–70. Translated into Latin (1691), Dutch (1688), Spanish (1731), Italian (1673), German (1686).

40. Boudon, *Dieu Seul*, rule 4, 20.

41. Matthäus Johannes Felner, *Adiutum pro Clero in Silesia. Sive Materia pro Copulandis utilis* (Erfurt: 1718), 210, 212.

42. Puchner, *Fragmenta*, 39ff; Hesselbach, *Epithalamia*, 366f.

43. Beda Mayr, *Predigten ueber den Catechismus fur gemeine Leute* (Augsburg: 1781), vol. 1, 577.

44. Mayr, *Predigten*, vol. 1, 580–581.

45. Mayr, *Predigten*, vol. 1, 603, 610; Cf. Eisengrein, *Anderer Theil*, 79 ff.

46. Templin, *Lignum*, vol. 2, 358; cf. Mayr, *Predigten*, vol. 1, 571–583, 619–632; Mayr, *Predigten*, vol. 2, 242.

47. Templin, *Lignum*, vol. 2, 367: "Moralischer oder sittlicher Weiss aber gibts die Experienz und Erfahrnis dass leyder die Mannen nur gar zu oft zu Weibern und die Weiber zu Mannen werden."

48. Templin, *Lignum*, vol. 2, 320; cf. Hesselbach, *Epithalamia*, 384.

49. Templin, *Lignum*, vol. 2, 342.

50. Jacob Feucht, *Postilla Catholica Evangeliorum de Tempore totius Anni, Theil Eins* (Cologne: 1597), 325; on Feucht, see Frymire, *Primacy*, 304–313.

51. Feucht, *Postilla*, 165.

52. Montifontanus, *Geistliches Kinder-Spill*, vol. 1, 494.

53. Montifontanus, *Geistliches Kinder-Spill*, vol. 1, 495; 515. Cf. Hieronymus Fordenbach, *Hertz-Bewegende Catholische Predigen* (Augsburg: 1712), 23.

54. Montifontanus, *Geistliches Kinder-Spill*, vol. 2, 5. idem, *Geistliches Kinder-Spill*, vol. 1, 251, on godparents; Adrien Gambart, *Landpfarrer und Gay-Prediger*, vol. 1 (Vienna: 1730), 159.

55. Montifontanus, *Geistliches Kinder-Spill*, vol. 1, 451.

56. Montifontanus, *Geistliches Kinder-Spill*, vol. 1, 452.

57. Montifontanus, *Geistliches Kinder-Spill*, vol. 1, 517.

58. Montifontanus, *Geistliches Kinder-Spill*, vol. 1, 525. Cf. Franciscus Settelin, *Agricultura Spiritualis . . .*, vol. 6 (Salzburg: 1680), 56ff. Cf. Gabriel Erich, *Sitten-und Kirchen-Lehren*, vol. 1 (Augsburg and Wurzburg: 1747), 188–205.

59. Montifontanus, *Geistliches Kinder-Spill*, vol. 1, 529f.

60. Templin, *Lignum*, vol. 2, 424; cf. Georg Pistorius, *Allgemeines Klaghauß Oder Catholische Leichpredigen. Bey Begräbnussen der Kinder, Jüngling, Jungfrawen . . . zugebrauchen* (Dillingen: Mayer, 1663),

61. Pistorius, *Allgemeines Klaghauß*, 1–9; Thomas de Vio Cajetan, *De purgatori quaestiones duae, in Opusculum Opera*, vol. 1 (Lyon: 1587), tract. 23, 117.

62. Francesco Emanuele Cangiamila, *Embryologia sacra, sive, De officio sacerdotum, medicorum, et aliorum circa aeternam parvulorum in utero existentium salutem, libri quatuor* (Panormi: 1758), lib. I, c. 1, 1–4. Cangiamila cites Scipione Mercurio O.P. (1540/50–1615) on midwifery, idem, *La comare, o ricoglitrice* (Venice: 1596).

63. Cangiamila, *Embryologia sacra*, lib. I, c. 2, 5.

64. Cangiamila, *Embryologia sacra*, lib. I, c. 3, 8.

65. Cangiamila, *Embryologia sacra*, lib. I, c. 12, 46.

66. Cangiamila, *Embryologia sacra*, lib. I, c. 12, 47–51.

67. Cangiamila, *Embryologia sacra*, lib. III, c. 10, 158–163.

68. Cf. Lehner, *Catholic Enlightenment*.

69. Carter, *Creating Catholics*, 57; Marc R. Forster, *Catholic Revival in the Age of the Baroque. Religious Identity in Southwest Germany, 1550–1750* (Cambridge: Cambridge University Press, 2007); Keith P. Luria, *Sacred Boundaries. Religious Coexistence and Conflict in Early-Modern France* (Washington: Catholic University of America Press, 2005).

70. At Carter, *Creating Catholics*, 3. On direct admonition of parents not to hit their children, see Templin, *Lignum*, vol. 2, 430–466, and cf. 467–478 for a series of fourteen spiritual hymns.

71. Matthaeus Tympe, *Kinderzucht oder kurtzer Bericht von der Eltern Sorg und Fürsichtigkeit in Aufferziehung ihrer lieben Kinder zu Gottes Ehr und dem Vatterlandt und Gemeinem Wesen zum besten* (Münster: 1610), dedication s.pag., 1, 68–95.

72. Tympe, *Kinderzucht*, 14, 32.

73. Tympe, *Kinderzucht*, 18.

74. Worcester, "The Classical Sermon," 158f; Lawrence Wolff, "Parents and Children in the Sermons of P. Bourdaloue: A Jesuit Perspective on the Early Modern Family," in Christopher Chapple (ed.), *The Jesuit Tradition in Education and Missions* (Scranton: Scranton University Press, 1993), 81–94.

75. In Lima, pressure to oblige with parental wishes seems to have been stronger than in other regions of the world, see María Emma Mannarelli, *Private Passions and Public Sins. Men and Women in Seventeenth-Century Lima, Diálogos* (Albuquerque: University of New Mexico Press, 2007), 99; Jennifer de la Coromoto González, *"To Better Serve God and to Save My Soul." Marriage, Gender and Honor in Spanish New Mexico, 1681–1730* (PhD Thesis: Michigan State, 2016). On forcing children into a monastery, see Letins, *Concionatoria*, vol. 1, 225, 230–234 ("De obedientia parentibus debita quoad electionem status"). On physical abuse by parents, see Letins, *Concionatoria*, vol. 1, 239–241; 253: "Dico 1. Parentes, qui proles graviter vulnerant . . . peccant mortaliter. Ratio est: quia similis in punitione paterna excessus semper est gravis, adeoque prolibus injuriosus, praesertim cum numquam liceat ob qualecumque delictum . . . privato alium graviter vulnerare, sed hoc spectat ad potestatem publicam."

76. Christoph Ott SJ, *Hohe Schuel der lieben Eltern . . .* (Ingolstadt: 1671), 134–182; cf. Bartholomäus Wagner, *Catechesis oder Catholische Kinderlehr . . .* (Freiburg: 1609). Wagner was a layman but became a priest in 1621, see Werz, "Die Kirche erklären."

77. Tympe, *Kinderzucht*, 31: "Wann dir Gott Kinder gibt, uberantwortet er dir eine ungestalte massam."

78. Philippe Berlaymont, *Paradisus Puerorum* (Cologne: 1619), 2; at 773 he also treats postmortem apparitions of deceased boys. For the author, see also Theodor Brüggemann (ed.), *Handbuch zur Kinder- und Jugendliteratur von 1570 bis 1750* (Stuttgart: Metzler, 1991), 1093.

79. Bernardino Rosignoli, *Stimuli Virtutum Adolescentiae Christianae* (Cologne: 1594), 17ff, at 19: "Atque hoc initium est velitationis, seu potius belli spiritualis."

80. Rosignoli, *Stimuli Virtutum*, 39, 291–309, 310, cf. 54, 84–94.

81. Rosignoli, *Stimuli Virtutum*, 71; ibid., 172. Cf. Ulrich Probst SJ, *Heylsame Gedancken von der Tugend der Keuschheit . . .* (Augsburg: 1754); Hecht, *Bildtheologie*, 82; Johannes David, *Veridicus Christianus. Editio Altera* (Antwerp: 1606), 351.

82. Rosignoli, *Stimuli Virtutum*, 134–140, see 134 on the congregations in the Americas.

83. Rosignoli, *Stimuli Virtutum*, 142; see 145: "Quartum sit, ut ne quis animum despondeat, si comitibus destituatur in via ad salutem"; cf. 408.

84. Rosignoli, *Stimuli Virtutum*, 228–234, 248f.

85. Rosignoli, *Stimuli Virtutum*, 198; cf. 264–270; at 273: "Errant qui virginitatis commendationem ad foeminas solum pertinere putant."

86. Gobinet, *The Instruction of Youth*, vol. 1, part 2, ch. 15, 59; on bad parenting, see 74f. Henri Boudon, *Das Reich Gottes im innern Gebethe . . .*, trans. Fulgentius a S. Maria (Cologne: 1711), ch.7, 62ff; cf. idem, *La Regne de Dieu . . . Nouvelle Edition* (Paris: 1702), ch. 7, 60ff: "ferveurs sensibles."

87. Pelecyus, *Affectuum Humanorum*; idem, *Seelen-Cur, das ist: Auserlesener und heilsamer, und nothwendiger Tractat von unordentlichen und schaedlichen Anmuetungen oder Begirden des Menschen . . .* (Munich: 1618).

88. Pelecyus, *Seelen-Cur*, preface to the reader, s.p. His German translation for passion is "Anmuttung," "Neiglichkeit," and "Begirde."

89. Catherine Newmark, *Passion-Affekt-Gefühl. Philosophische Theorien zwschen Aristoteles und Kant* (Hamburg: Meiner, 2008); Richard Hassing, *Cartesian Psychophysics and the Whole Nature of Man. On Descartes' Passions of the Soul* (London: Lexington Books, 2015); on Descartes's love of God, see Peter Losconzi, "Passionate Reason: Science, Theology and the Intellectual Passion of Wonder in Descartes' Meditations," in Willem Lemmens and Walter van Herck (eds.), *Religious Emotions. Some Philosophical Explorations* (Cambridge: Cambridge Scholars Publ., 2008), 131–144. On "holy affections," see Dixon, *Passions*, 26–61; Hannah Newton, "Holy Affections," in Susan Broomhall (ed.), *Early Modern Emotions. An Introduction* (London and New York: Routledge, 2017), 67–71.

90. Pelecyus, *Seelen Cur*, 187.

91. Pelecyus, *Seelen Cur*, 206.

92. Pelecyus, *Seelen Cur*, 215.

93. Pelecyus, *Seelen Cur*, 284.

94. At Minor, *Death of the Baroque*, 40; cf. Muratori, *Opere*, vol. 8 (Arezzo: 1768), 67.
95. Minor, *Death of the Baroque*, 43; Muratori, *Opere*, vol. 8, 88; on passions and affections in the Enlightenment, see Dixon, *Passions*, 62–97, yet without covering any Catholic thinker.
96. Cf. Augustin Schelle, *Versuch über den Einfluß der Arbeitsamkeit auf Menschenglück* (Salzburg: 1790); Jakob Danzer, *Anleitung zur christlichen Moral* (Salzburg: 1791); Joseph Lauber, *Anleitung zur christlichen Sittenlehre*, vol. 3 (Vienna: 1786), 102ff; cf. Ulrich L. Lehner, *Enlightened Monks. The German Benedictines, 1740–1803* (Oxford: Oxford University Press, 2010).

# Chapter 6

1. An excellent introduction to the phenomenon of confraternities is Christopher F. Black, *Italian Confraternities in the Sixteenth Century* (Cambridge: Cambridge University Press, 1989). I am grateful to Dr. Michael Maher, SJ, for his comments on this chapter.
2. Anonymous, *Jesus Christus der verborgenen Gott im hochheiligen Altarsgeheimnisse zur öffentlichen Anbethung . . .* (Munich: 1778).
3. Colleen Gray, *The Congrégation de Notre-Dame. Superiors, and the Paradox of Power: 1693-1796* (Montreal: McGill-Queen's University Press, 2007), 33–34. Murdo J. MacLeod, "Confraternities in Colonial New Spain. Mexico and Central America," in Konrad Eisenbichler (ed.), *A Companion to Medieval and Early Modern Confraternities* (Leiden and Boston: Brill, 2019), 280–306.
4. Anonymous, *Vera Confraternitas S. Trinitatis Redemptionis Captivorum Christianorum. Editio Secunda* (Vienna: 1715).
5. Cyriano a S. Maria, *Thesaurus Carmelitarum sive Confraternitatis Scapularis excellentia* (Cologne: 1627), 348.
6. Adam Walasser, *Von der Gnadreichen . . . Bruderschaft des Psalters oder Rosenkrantz Marie . . .* (Dillingen: 1572), preface; Sebastian Schletstätter, *Triumph des heiligen Rosenkrantz* (Augsburg: 1667).
7. Confraternity books allowed a member even to calculate how many indulgences of purgatory time one could receive per day and month, see, for example, Schletstätter, *Triumph*.
8. See especially Council of Trent, 14th session on the sacrament of penance, DH 1667–1693; on indulgences, DH 1835.
9. See especially Council of Trent, 25th session on Purgatory, DH 1820.
10. James Banker, *Death in the Community. Memorialization and Confraternities in an Italian Commune in the Late Middle Ages* (Athens-London: University of Georgia Press, 1988).
11. Martin Rosshirdt, *Franciscaner Bruderschafft Büchlein* (Salzburg: 1653), 55–56; Anonymous, *Vinculum Charitatis oder Seraphisches Liebs-Band . . .* (Vienna: 1716); cf. Rupert Klieber, *Bruderschaften und Liebesbünde nach Trient, Ihr Totendienst,*

*Zuspruch und Stellenwert im kirchlichen und gesellschaftlichen Leben am Beispiel Salzburgs, 1600–1950* (Frankfurt: Peter Lang, 1999), 245–248. For the transformative power of confession, see Michael Maher, "Confession and Consolation: The Society of Jesus and Its Promotion of the General Confession," in Katharine J. Lualdi and Anne T. Thayer (eds.), *Penitence in the Age of Reformations* (Aldershot: Ashgate, 2017), 184–200.

12. On the value of almsgiving as a meritorious act, see Cajetan Felix Verani, *Theologia Universa Speculativa . . .*, vol. 6 (Munich: 1700), disp. 13, 220–227; disp. 14, 227–247; and at 229: "Eleemosyna est opus quo datur aliquid indigenti ex compassione propter Deum" (Thomas Aquinas, STh II/II, q. 32, art. 1). Verani, *Theologia*, vol. 6, 241–245. The Jesuit Gilles de Coninck argued that justice would oblige one to give to the poor, see idem, *De Moralitate Natura et Effectibus Actuum Supernaturalium* (Lyon: 1623), disp. 27, dub. 6, 444f; dub. 11, 457ff.

13. Anonymous, *Bruderschafft des heiligen Ertz-Engel und Himmelsfürsten Michael . . .* (Munich: 1696), 1–3; Anonymous, *Apostolica institutio et regulae confraternitatis . . . erectae in ecclesia P.P. Cappucinorum Coloniae* (Cologne: 1613), 10: "Confratres vocati sunt, ante omnia salus propria sit: ideo charitatis flamma, veraque pietate in eum accensi." Klieber, *Bruderschaften*, 26–30, 571–573.

14. Anonymous, *Constitutiones Archiconfraternitatis Charitatis de Urbe* (Rome: 1603), chs. 7–12, ch. 14; Anonymous, *Constitutiones Archiconfraternitatis S. Hieronymi Charitatis de Urbe* (Rome: 1694). That this confraternity actually engaged in charity is buttressed by Giovanni Battista Scanaroli, *De Visitatione Carceratorum* (Rome: 1655), 67ff. On the various services of confraternities, see Elisabeth Lobenwein et al. (eds.), *Bruderschaften als multifunktionale Dienstleister der Frühen Neuzeit in Zentraleuropa* (Vienna: Böhlau, 2018).

15. Lance Gabriel Lazar, *Working in the Vineyard of the Lord. Jesuit Confraternities in Early Modern Italy* (Toronto: University of Toronto Press, 2005), 60; Elizabeth Rapley, *The Dévotes. Women and Church in Seventeenth-Century France* (Montreal: McGill University Press, 1990); Samuel Kline Cohn, *Death and Property in Siena, 1205–1800. Strategies for the Afterlife* (Baltimore: Johns Hopkins University Press, 1988), 198–201; Hoffman, *Church and Community*, 144–145; Stephanie Fink de Backer, *Widowhood in Early Modern Spain. Protectors, Proprietors, and Patrons* (Leiden and Boston: Brill, 2010); cf. Sandra Cavallo, *Charity and Power in Early Modern Italy. Benefactors and Their Motives in Turin, 1541–1789* (Cambridge: Cambridge University Press, 1995); Black, *Italian Confraternities*, 35–38, 103f. On the violent culture of confraternities, see Jacques Rossiaud, "Fraternités de jeunesse et niveaux de culture dans les villes du Sud-Est à la fin du Moyen-Age," *Cahier d'histoire* 21 (1976): 67–102. On eighteenth-century Spanish reform, see David Carbajal López, "Mujeres y reforma de cofradías en Nueva España y Sevilla, ca. 1750–1830," *Estudios de Historia Novohispana* 55 (2016): 64–79.

16. On superabundance, see Charles-Rene Billuart, *Summa S. Thomae sive cursus Theologiae Hodiernis Academicarum Moribus Accomodata, Secunda Secundae* (Venice: 1778), 144–149; Anonymous, *Cursus Theologiae Moralis Salmanticensis*, vol. 5 (Venice: 1750), ch. 7, pt. 1, 148. On the effects of the works of mercy, see Cajetan

Felix Verani, *Theologia Universa Speculativa* . . . vol. 6 (Munich: 1700), disp. 14, 240: "Divitiae non damnatur, sed earumdem culpatur abusus." On different membership expectation, see Anonymous, *Sacrosanctae Sodalitas Sacerdotum Secularium Urbis Constitutiones* (Rome: 1644), ch. 10–12, 17–19.

17. Cf. Black, *Italian Confraternities*; Klieber, *Bruderschaften*, 585, 601; cf. Maureen Flynn, *Sacred Charity. Confraternities and Social Welfare in Spain, 1400–1700* (Ithaca/New York: 1989); Benedict Poiger, *Versuch zur Errichtung einer pfärrlichen Armeleute-Bruderschaft* (Reichenhall: 1786), preface; Black, *Church, Religion and Society*, 131–141.

18. For the understanding of alms for the poor souls, see, for example, the copperplate for Joseph Joannneser SJ, *Lieb-volle Seelen-Huelff zu Nutz der Abgeleibten und Lehr der Lebenden* (Stadtamhof: 1745), with a list of one hundred Bavarian confraternities dedicated to the Poor Souls, 564–565; Ludovico Muratori, *Gründliche Auslegung des grossen Geboths von der Liebe des Nächsten. Trans. Peter Obladen* (Augsburg: 2nd ed., 1768), par. 13, 257–276; Pierre Nicole, *Unterricht ueber das erste Gebot des Dekalogs*, vol. 2 (Bamberg and Würburg: 1783), Neunter Unterricht, 414f; Pierre Nicole, *Instructions Theologiques et Morales sur le Premier Commandment du Decalogue, Nouvelle Edition*, vol. 2 (Paris: 1742), sect. 9, 417; Poiger, *Versuch*.

19. Brian Larkin, *The Very Nature of God. Baroque Catholicism and Religious Reform in Bourbon Mexico City* (Albuquerque: University of New Mexico Press, 2010), 99f, quotation at 144.

20. Erin Rowe, *Black Saints in Early Modern Catholicism* (Cambridge: Cambridge University Press, 2019); Lehner, *Catholic Enlightenment*, 181–205.

21. William B. Hart, "The Kindness of the Blessed Virgin. Faith, Succour, and the Cult of Mary among Christian Hurons and Iroquois in Seventeenth-Century New France," in Nicholas Griffiths and Fernando Cervantes (eds.), *Spiritual Encounters. Interactions between Christianity and Native Religions in Colonial America* (Lincoln: University of Nebraska Press, 1999), 80; Nancy Shoemaker, *Negotiators of Change. Historical Perspectives on Native American Women* (New York and London: Routledge, 1995), 49–71.

22. Nancy M. Farriss, *Maya Society under Colonial Rule. The Collective Enterprise of Survival* (Princeton: Princeton University Press, 1984), 286–319.

23. Farriss, *Maya*, 321–326. See especially Barry D. Sell, Larissa Taylor, and Asunción Lavrin (eds.), *Nahua Confraternities in Early Colonial Mexico. The 1552 Nahuatl Ordinances of Fray Alonso de Molina, OFM* (Berkeley: Academy of American Franciscan History, 2002); Albert Meyers and Diane E. Hopkins (eds.), *Manipulating the Saints. Religious Brotherhoods and Social Integration in Postconquest Latin America* (Hamburg: Wayasbah, 1988); Laura Dierksmeier, *Charity for and by the Poor. Franciscan-Indigenous Confraternities in Mexico, 1527–1700* (Norman: University of Oklahoma Press, 2020).

24. Michael Maher, "Financing Reform: The Society of Jesus, the Congregation of the Assumption, and the Funding of the Exposition of the Sacrament in Early Modern Rome," *Archiv für Reformationsgeschichte—Archive for Reformation History* 93 (2002): 126–144.

25. Lazar, *Working in the Vineyard*, 11.

26. Louis Châtellier, *The Europe of the Devout. The Catholic Reformation and the Formation of a New Society* (Cambridge: Cambridge University Press, 1991), 51.

27. Châtellier, *The Europe of the Devout*, 55.

28. Placidus Angermayr, *Militia Sacra, das ist. Marianischer Werb- und Waffenplatz*, vol. 2 (Kempten: 1722), 13.

29. Angermayer, *Militia Sacra*, vol. 2, 14.

30. Châtellier, *The Europe of the Devout*, 65; cf. 108f.

31. Châtellier, *The Europe of the Devout*, 208f.

32. Châtellier, *The Europe of the Devout*, 116, 118f.

33. Châtellier, *The Europe of the Devout*, 183, 197. Cf. François Coster SJ, *Enchiridion Controversiarium Praecipuarum Nostri Temporis De Religione in Gratiam Sodalitatis* (Cologne: 1596).

34. Cf. Katherine A. Lynch, *Individuals, Families, and Communities in Europe, 1200–1800. The Urban Foundations of Western Society* (Cambridge: Cambridge University Press, 2003), 87–88.

35. Châtellier, *The Europe of the Devout*, 6; 9; 21.

36. Châtellier, *The Europe of the Devout*, 13; 255.

37. Châtellier, *The Europe of the Devout*, 20.

38. Châtellier, *The Europe of the Devout*, 36; 40.

39. Haruko Ward, *Women Religious Leaders in Japan's Christian Century, 1549–1650* (Aldershot: Ashgate, 2009), 335, 337.

40. Lazar, *Working in the Vineyard*, 28.

41. Lazar, *Working in the Vineyard*, 52–54; cf. on the practice of "recogimiento," Nancy van Deusen, *Between the Sacred and the Worldly. The Institutional and Cultural Practice of recogimiento in Colonial Lima* (Stanford: Stanford University Press, 2001).

42. At Lazar, *Working in the Vineyard*, 91.

43. Egid Boerner, *Dritter Orden und Bruderschaften der Franziskaner in Kurbayern* (Werl: 1988), provides exciting statistical material for Bavaria.

44. Benedict XIII, *Constitutio pro Tertiariis Sancti Francisci* . . . (Rome: 1726), 5: "sed etiam sanctitatis egregiae fructus uberrimos protulisse." Thomas Francisco Rotario, *Theologia Moralis Regularium*, vol. 3 (Venice: 1735), c. 5, pt. 1, 413f lists as first those living in "claustro," second those who live like "saeculares," and the third group with some kind of vow and community life, who are not regulars.

45. Cf. "Tertiarii," in F. Lucii Ferraris, *Bibliotheca Canonica Juridica Moralis Theologica*, vol. 7 (Rome: 1891), 405–415; Engelbert Pauck, *Tertia Seraphica Vinea sive Tertius Ordo de Poenitentia* (Cologne: 1720); Anna Elisabeth Rifeser, *Die Frömmigkeitskultur der Maria Hueber (1653–1705) und der Tiroler Tertiarinnen. Institutionelle Prozesse, kommunikative Verflechtungen und spirituelle Praktiken* (Munster: Aschendorff, 2019), 48–75, at 52.

46. Ferraris, *Bibliotheca*, vol. 9, 409; cf. Didacus Tafuri, *Franciscus Ter Legislator Evangelicus Fratrum Minorum Strictior* . . ., vol. 1 (Rome: 1667), tract. 6, lib. 12, 474. Therefore, Third Order Seculars, who would not follow the rule were also *not*

considered apostates (Francesco Bordoni, *Operum Tomus Secundus. Pars Prima* [Lyon: 1655], 414, pt. 12).

47. Angelo Auda da Lantosca, *Regola del terz'ordine de penitenti del serafico P.S. Francesco . . . nuovamente corretta* (Rome and Milan: 1665), 174. On membership as a vocation, see Anonymous, *Der in den Ohren Gottes lieblich klingende Harpfen-Klang der Büßenden* . . . (Salzburg: 1762), 5; Adam Bürvenich, *Vierfacher Seelen-Spiegel* (Cologne: [orig. 1684] 1713), 13.

48. Anonymous, *Dreyfacher Tugend-Spiegel* . . . (Munich: 1755), "In Jesu, Maria und Francisco," s.pag.

49. Anonymous, *Unterrichtungen der heylsamen Buss des Dritten Ordens . . . von einem Franciscaner Oesterreichischer Provinz* (Vienna: 1736), 27–28.

50. Juan B. de Murcia OFMCap, *Regl-Büchlein Deß dritten Ordens Sancti Francisci von der Buß genannt* (Burghausen: Samm, 1733), 23.

51. Murcia, *Regl-Büchlein*, 24.

52. Cf. Kerkhove, *Commentarii*, 580: "Alii sunt Tertiarii cum Fratribus claustralibus habitantes." One of the few studies on the Third Order in modernity is Boerner, *Dritter Orden*, 81–266. On the medieval roots of the Third Order, see Gilles-Gèrard Meersseman, *Ordo fraternitatis confraternite e pieta dei Laici*, 3 vols. (Rome: Herder, 1977).

53. Murcia, *Regl-Büchlein*, 254; cf. the profession formula, 246. Cf. Rotario, *Theologia Moralis*, vol. 3, 414: "Modus liber vivendi, & serviendi Deo magis perfectus sub quadam regula a S. Sede approbata, & sub directione Religiosorum proprii Ordinis."Ascanio Tamburinio de Marradio, *De iure Abbatissarum et Monialium sive Praxis Gubernandi Moniales* (Rome: 1638), XXIV: "Et quamvis istorum coetus non sit Religio, est tamen Ordo, & quidam modus bene vivendi." Such cannot be said of most confraternities; see Ellen Decraene, "Sisters of Early Modern Confraternities in a Small Town in the Southern Netherlands (Aalst)," *Urban History* 40 (2013): 247–270.

54. Brianna Leavitt-Alcantara, *Single Women and Devotion in Guatemala, 1670–1870* (Stanford: Stanford University Press, 2018)is unaware of this important distinction and therefore arrives at false conclusions about the clothing of Third Order members.

55. Against Leavitt-Alcantara, *Alone*, 81ff. Cf. Anonymous, *Regelbüchlein des Dritten Ordens S. Francisci* (Munich: 1728), 109f; Kerckhove, *Commentarii*, 147ff; Lucio Ferrarri, *Prompta Bibliotheca Canonica* . . ., vol. 7 (Bologna: 1746), 444, nr. 35: "Habitum seu Scapulare parvum."

56. Anonymous, *Unterrichtungen der heylsamen Buss*, 23. Cf. Anonymous, *Regl-Buechlein des Dritten Ordens S. Francisci . . . in der chur-Bayrischen Provinz* (Cologne: 1732). Kerckhove, *Commentarii*, and idem, *Gründliche kurtze Erklärung über die Regel der Minder-Brüder. Auss underschiedlichen päpstlichen Erklärungen und vieler fürnehmer Lehrer Ausslegungen zusamen getragen* (Fulda: 1692; reprinted Regensburg: 1732). Cf. also Petrus Marchant, *Constitutions des religieuses réformées pénitentes du tierce ordre de S. François* (Ghent: 1635).

57. Anonymous, *Dreyfacher Tugend-Spiegel*, 219.

58. Murcia, *Regl-Büchlein*, 2544; cf. the profession formula, 246.

59. Leavitt-Alcantara, *Single Women*, 19–40; quotation at 59. Cf. Antonio Rubial García, *Profetisas y solitarios. Espacios y mensajes de una religión dirigida por ermitaños y beatas laicos en las ciudades de Nueva España* (México: Universidad Nacional Autónoma de México, 2006).

60. Leavitt-Alcantara, *Alone*, 79.

61. Amsler, *Jesuits and Matriarchs*, 139–151.

62. Nancy E. van Deusen, *Embodying the Sacred. Women Mystics in Seventeenth-Century Lima* (Durham: Duke University Press, 2018), 26ff.

63. At Alison Weber, *Teresa of Avila and the Rhetoric of Femininity* (Princeton, NJ: Princeton University Press, 1990), 34.

64. Cf. Weber, *Teresa of Avila*, 97.

65. John Bossy, *The English Catholic Community, 1570–1870* (London: Darnton, Longman and Todd: 1975), 150–158; on Dorothy Lawson as a major example of such matriarchy, see Underwood, *Childhood*. For the relationship between religious men and women, see the insightful article by Patrick Collison, "Not Sexual in the Ordinary Sense. Women, Men and Religious Transactions," in idem, *Elizabethan Essays* (London: Hambledon Press, 1994), 119–150.

66. Cf. Susannah Monta, "Uncommon Prayer? Robert Southwell's Short Rule for a Good Life and Catholic Domestic Devotion in Post-Reformation England," in Lowell Gallagher (ed.), *Redrawing the Map of Early Modern English Catholicism* (Toronto: University of Toronto Press, 2012), 245–271, at 254.

67. Amsler, *Jesuits and Matriarchs*, 113–137.

68. *Real-Zeitung*, ed. Johann H. Gross, Nr. 89 (1786), 779; Andreas Rutz, *Bildung–Konfession–Geschlecht. Religiöse Frauengemeinschaften und die katholische Mädchenbildung im Rheinland* (Mainz: Zabern, 2006), 385–420.

69. Kilian Kazenberger, *Der Tertiarien Glory, das ist, Ein Begriff vieler anderer die Tertiaren Betreffender Büchern . . .* (Augsburg: 1724).

70. E.g., Hermann Born, *Seraphisches Firmament oder Stern-Himmel . . .* , 12 vols. (Cologne: 1715); Anonymous, *Trost-Lehr-und Ehren-Predig für den dritten Orden deren Büssenden des H. Seraphischen Vatters* (Linz: 1740); Anonymous, *Der in dem Weingarten Christi, oder in der Heil. Cathol. Kirch, durch Göttliche Gnad von dem Seel-eyferend und unermüdthen Weingartnern Francisco Seraphico nutzlich gepflantzte . . . Seraphische Weinstock. das ist Schuldigiste Ehr- und Lob-Red des Heil. dritten Seraphischen Ordens der Büssenden* (Augsburg: 1752).

71. Anonymous, *Abbildung und Wahrer Begriff des Uralten Heil. Dritten Ordens des Heiligen Norberti* (Passau: 1751); Anonymous, *Der in den Ohren Gottes*, 114.

72. Anonymous, *Dreyfacher Tugend-Spiegel*, 40–41.

73. Anonymous, *Dreyfacher Tugend-Spiegel*, 219.

74. William Stanney, *A Treatise of Penance* (Douay: 1617), dedication, s.pag; Anonymous, *Dreyfacher Tugend-Spiegel*, 238; on normative conflicts, see Thiessen, *Kapuziner*, 253–262, 319–364.

75. Stanney, *A Treatise*, s.pag.

76. Stanney, *A Treatise*, 1–34.

77. Stanney, *A Treatise*, 36–38.

78. Stanney, *A Treatise*, 102.

79. Anonymous, *Weis und Manier, wie man mit guter Meynung die von der Regel des Dritten Ordens des Heiligen Francisci vorgeschriebene Tag-Zeiten . . . betten koenne* (Vienna: 1746), 46.

80. Anonymous, *Unterrichtungen von der Heylsamen Buss.*

81. Louis Châtellier, "Die Erneuerung der Seelsorge und die Gesellschaft nach dem Konzil von Trient," in Prodi and Reinhard (eds.), *Das Konzil von Trient und die Moderne*, 106–123.

82. Rapley, *The Dévotes*, 75; on Ségolène de Dainville-Barbiche, "Les communautés paroissiales de Paris au XVIIIe siècle. Sociétés de prêtres ou auberges ecclésiastiques," *Revue d'Histoire de l'Eglise de France* 93 (2007): 267–280; on Olier, see Maurice Vidal, *Jean-Jacques Olier homme de talent, serviteur de l'Évangile, 1608–1657* (Paris: Desclée de Brouwer, 2009).

83. At Barbara Diefendorf, *From Penitence to Charity. Pious Women and the Catholic Reformation on Paris* (Oxford: Oxford University Press, 2004), 67.

84. Jeanne de la Nativite, *Le triomphe de l'amour divin dans la vie d'une grande servante de Dieu, nommèe Armelle Nicolas, dècèdèe l'an de Nôtre Seigneur 1671. Fidellement ecrite par une religieuse du monastère de sainte Ursule . . . Première [-seconde] partie* (s.l.: 1676), part 2, ch. 2, 31f. Most library catalogs name Jeanne Le Royer as author, although she was born in 1732!

85. Jeanne de la Nativite, *Le triomphe*, part 2, ch. 3, 38.

86. Diefendorf, *From Penitence to Charity*, 74.

87. "It is better, wives, you break your own heads with willing obedience than that your husbands break them with their fists" (Templin, *Lignum*, vol. 2, 352; cf. Mayr, *Predigten*, vol. 1, 615).

88. Michaele Bill-Mrziglod, *Luisa de Carvajal y Mendoza (1566–1614) und ihre Gesellschaft Mariens* (Hamburg: Kovač, 2014), 181f, 203, 205–212. On other Spanish *beatas* and their visions, see Andrew W. Keitt, *Inventing the Sacred. Imposture, Inquisition, and the Boundaries of the Supernatural in Golden Age Spain* (Leiden and Boston: Brill, 2005).

89. Diefendorf, *From Penitence to Charity*, 83–84; Optat de Veghel, "Aux sources d'une spiritualité des laïcs. Le P. Benoit de Canfield et L'Exercice de la volonté de Dieu," *Etudes Franciscaines* 15 (1965): 33–44; see also the excellent introduction in Kent Emery, *Renaissance Dialectic and Renaissance Piety. Benet of Canfield's Rule of Perfection. A Translation and Study* (Binghamton, NY: Medieval & Renaissance Texts & Studies, 1987); Daniel Vidal, *Critique de la raison mystique—Benoît de Canfield. Possession et dépossession au XVIIe siècle* (Grenoble: Millon, 1990), and concentrating on Canfield's concept of love of God, see Camille Bérubé, *L'amour de Dieu. Selon Jean Duns Scot, Porète, Eckhart, Benoît de Canfield et les Capucins* (Rome: Istituto storico dei Cappuccini, 1997); Anthony D. Wright, *The Division of French Catholicism, 1629–1645* (Aldershot: Ashgate, 2011), 15ff; Joseph Bergin, *Cardinal de la Rochefoucauld. Leadership and Reform in the French Church* (New Haven: Yale University Press, 1987), 43–52; P. Renee Baernstein, *A Convent Tale. A Century of Sisterhood in Spanish Milan* (New York and London: Routledge, 2002), 32; cf. Federico Chabod, *Lo Stato e la vita religiosa a Milano nell'epoca di Carlo V* (Turin: Einaudi, 1971), 270–271.

90. Stanney, *A Treatise*, 228–229; McClain, *Divided Loyalties*, 133f.

91. Juan de Salinas O.P. at Ahlgren, *Teresa of Avila*, 155. Ellen A. Macek, "Devout Recusant Women, Advice Manuals, and the Creation of Holy Households 'Under Siege,'" in Alison Weber (ed.), *Devout Laywomen in the Early Modern World* (New York: Routledge, 2016), 235–252; McClain, *Divided Loyalties*, 79–116, 157–194; Lisa McClain, *Lest We Be Damned. Practical Innovation and Lived Experience among Catholics in Protestant England, 1559-1642* (New York: Routledge, 2004). In the eighteenth century disobedient priests were characterized as "effeminate" (see McClain, *Divided Loyalties*, 183).

92. Rutz, *Bildung*, 191, 193. Michaela Bill-Mrziglod, "Spiritualität im Semireligiosentum—Frömmigkeitsformen, literarische Zeugnisse und Lektürepraxis," in Yvonne Bergerfurth and Anne Conrad (eds.), *Welt-geistliche Frauen in der Frühen Neuzeit Studien zum weiblichen Semireligiosentum* (Münster: Aschendorff, 2013), 60–92, at 65; cf. Eadem, *Luisa de Carvajal y Mendoza (1566-1614) und ihre "Gesellschaft Mariens." Spiritualität, Theologie und Konfessionspolitik in einer semireligiosen Frauengemeinschaft des 17. Jahrhunderts* (Hamburg: Kovač, 2014).

93. Bill-Mrziglod, "Spiritualität im Semireligiosentum," 72; Cf. Rady Roldan-Figueroa, *The Ascetic Spirituality of Juan de Avila, 1499-1569* (Leiden and Boston: Brill, 2010).

94. Moshe Sluhovsky, *Believe Not Every Spirit. Possession, Mysticism, & Discernment in Early Modern Catholicism* (Chicago: University of Chicago Press, 2007), 186; Diego Perez de Valdivia, *Aviso de gente recogida y especialmente de la dedicada al servicio de Dios [1585]*(Universidad Pontificia de Salamanca: 1977); Stephen Halliczer, *Sexuality in the Confessional. A Sacrament Profaned* (Oxford: Oxford University Press, 1996), 110ff; 157 analyzes what the author deems Valdivia's "sexual fantasies."

95. Van Deusen, *Between the Sacred and the Worldly.*

96. Alison Weber, "Devout Laywomen in the Early Modern World: The Historiographic Challenge," in idem (ed.), *Devout Laywomen in the Early Modern World*, 1–28, at 5.

97. Weber, "Devout Laywomen," 6; cf. Diego Pèrez de Valdivia, *Aviso de gente recogida* (Salamanca: Universidad Pontificia de Salamanca, 1977).

98. Hermann Busenbaum SJ, *Lilien under den Dörneren, das ist Gott verlobter Jungfrawen und Witwen Welt-geistlicher Standt* (Cologne: 1660), 228–230.

99. Anne Conrad, *Zwischen Kloster und Welt. Ursulinen und Jesuitinnen in der katholischen Reformbewegung des 16./17.Jahrhunderts* (Mainz: 1991), 79–83; Rapley, *The Dévotes*, 61–73. Eusebius Amort, *Kurtzer Lebens-Begriff Des Seeligen Petri Forerij, Regulierten Chorherren und Pfarrern zu Mataincur* (Munich: 1730); Helene Derréal, *Un missionaire de la Contre-Réforme. Saint Pierre Fourier et l'Institution de la Congrégation de Notre-Dame* (Paris: Librairie Lon., 1965); Gray, *Congrégation.*

100. Elizabeth A. Lehfeldt, *Religious Women in Golden Age Spain. The Permeable Cloister* (Aldershot: Ashgate, 2005); idem, "Discipline, Vocation and Patronage. Spanish Religious Women in a Tridentine Microclimate," *Sixteenth Century Journal* 30 (1999): 1009–1030.

101. Susanne Schulz, "Der Diskurs über den welt-geistlichen Stand. Überlegungen zur rechtlichen Lage semireligioser Gemeinschaften," in in Bergerfurt and Conrad (eds.), *Welt-geistliche Frauen*, 25–60; Conrad, *Zwischen Kloster und Welt*, 250–251; Nicolaus Onstenk, "De constitutione S. Pii C. '*Circa Pastoralis*' super clausura

monialium et tertiarium," *Periodica de re morali, canonica, liturgica* 39 (1950): 213–230; 317–363; 40 (1951): 210–255.

102. Relinde Meiwes, *Von Ostpreussen in die Welt. Die Geschichte der ermländischen Katharinenschwestern (1772–1914)* (Paderborn: Ferdinand Schöningh, 2011), 20–66. Barbara Gerarda Śliwińska, *Geschichte der Kongregation der Schwestern der heiligen Jungfrau und Martyrin Katharina 1571–1772* (Münster: Historischer Verein des Ermlands, 1999). Anne Conrad, "Ein mittlerer Weg. Welt-geistliche Frauen im konfessionalisierten Katholizismus," in Bergerfurt and Conrad (eds.), *Welt-geistliche Frauen*, 7–24.

103. Hansgeorg Molitor, "Mehr mit den Augen als mit den Ohren glauben. Frühneuzeitliche Volksfrömmigkeit in Köln und Jülich-Berg," in *Volksfrömmigkeit in der frühen Neuzeit* (Münster: Aschendorff, 1994), 89–106; Gray, *Congrégation*, 34. For a colonial confraternity, see Susan V. Webster, "Native Brotherhoods and Visual Culture in Colonial Quito (Ecuador): The Confraternity of the Rosary," in Nicholas Terpstra et al. (eds.), *Faith's Boundaries. Laity and Clergy in Early Modern Confraternities* (Turnhout: Brepols, 2012), 277–302; for the confraternities that practiced public flagellation, see Galvin Hammel, "Revolutionary Flagellants? Clerical Perceptions of Flagellant Brotherhoods in Late Medieval Flanders and Italy," in ibid., 303–330, and for a variety of late medieval and early modern confraternities the other essays of that collection.

104. Querciolo Mazzonis, "The Company of St. Ursula in Counter-Reformation Italy," in Weber (ed.), *Devout Laywomen in the Early Modern World*, 48–68.

105. Conrad, *Zwischen Kloster und Welt*, 23–28.

106. Laurence Lux-Sterritt, *Redefining Female Religious Life. French Ursulines and English Ladies in Seventeenth-Century Catholicism* (Aldershot: Ashgate, 2005), 20; 130–153; Mazzonis, "The Company," 57.

107. Châtellier, *The Europe of the Devout*, 17.

108. Rapley, *The Dévotes*, 16.

109. Baernstein, *A Convent Tale*, 27–45.

110. Baernstein, *A Convent Tale*, 47–49.

111. Baernstein, *A Convent Tale*, 59.

112. Baernstein, *A Convent Tale*, 65–73; Carlo Borromeo (ed.), *Acta Mediolanensis*, vol. 1 (Lyon: 1683), 38ff.

113. Diefendorf, *From Penitence to Charity*, 19: "The penitential asceticism these women practiced was intensely permeated with the desire to emulate the caritas, or self-sacrificial love, displayed by Christ.... And if the intensity of the ascetic impulse waned by the 1630s, the transition from penitence to charity was neither thoroughgoing nor complete."

114. Linda Lierheimer, *Female Eloquence and Maternal Ministry. The Apostolate of Ursuline Nuns in Seventeenth-Century France* (PhD Thesis: Princeton University, 1994), 15; Lux-Sterritt, *Redefining*, 62; Matthieu Brejon de Lavergnée, *Histoire des Filles de la charité* (Paris: Fayard, 2011); Elizabeth Rapley, "A New Approach: The filles séculières (1630–1660)," *Vincentian Heritage Journal* 16 (1995): 111–136; Susan E. Dinan, *Women and Poor-Relief in Seventeenth-Century France* (Aldershot: Ashgate, 2006).

115. Rapley, *The Dévotes*, 86.

116. Rapley, *The Dévotes*, 86.

117. Rapley, *The Dévotes*, 93.

118. Frances Ryan and John E. Rybolt (eds.), *Vincent de Paul and Louise de Marillac. Rules, Conferences, and Writings* (New York: Paulist Press, 1995), 169.

119. Rapley, *The Dévotes*, 99; cf. Marguerite Vacher, *Des "règulières" dans le siècle. Les Soeurs de Saint-Joseph du Père Mèdaille aux XVIIe et XVIIIe siècles* (Clermont-Ferrand: Adosa, 1992); idem, *Nuns without Cloister. Sisters of St. Joseph* (Lanham, MD: Rowman & Littlefield, 2010).

120. Georg Dusseldorpiensis OFMCap, *Hortus Irriguus . . .* (Cologne: 1696), 118: "Dies ist das Ambt der Devoten/dass sie allzeit vor Gott stehen in seiner Gegenwart/dass sie sich allzeit in denen dingen finden lassen/die ihres Vatters seynd."

121. Lehner, *Turtur Sacer*, 247.

122. Lehner, *Turtur Sacer*, 248–254.

123. Dusseldorpiensis, *Hortus Irriguus*, 49–50: "Zum anderen wie die haaren zwaren in dem Fleisch stehen/ Aber kein Fleisch seynd ? und nichts fleischliches an sich haben/ also sollen die Devoten als Weltgeistliche in der Welt und in dem Fleisch durch ihren ehrbahren Wandel also stehen/dass in ihnen nichts weltliches/nichts fleischliches gefunden werde."

124. Dusseldorpiensis, *Hortus Irriguus*, 50.

125. Dusseldorpiensis, *Hortus Irriguus*, 50.

126. Haruko Nawata Ward, "Women Apostles in Early Modern Japan, 1549–1650," in Weber (ed.), *Devout Laywomen in the Early Modern World*, 312–330; Ward, *Women*.

127. Ward, *Women*, 75–88; Eduard Hagemann, "The Persecution of the Christians in Japan in the Middle of the Seventeenth Century," *Pacific Historical Review* 11 (1942): 151–160; Takao Abé, *The Jesuit Mission to New France. A New Interpretation in the Light of the Earlier Jesuit Experience in Japan* (Leiden and Boston: Brill, 2011), 17–43, 223–225.

128. Nancy E. van Deusen, *The Souls of Purgatory. The Spiritual Diary of a Seventeenth-Century Afro-Peruvian Mystic, Ursula de Jesus* (Albuquerque: University of New Mexico Press, 2004), 1–10, 27–32. Cf. in general, idem, *Embodying the Sacred*, 95–116; Jacqueline Holler, *Escogidas Plantas. Nuns and Beatas in Mexico City, 1531–1601* (New York: Columbia University Press, 2005).

129. Jennifer Hillman, *Female Piety and the Catholic Reformation in France* (London: Pickering and Chatto, 2014), 6ff, 128.

130. Hillman, *Female Piety*, 37.

131. Hillman, *Female Piety*, 53, 131. Dena Goodman, *Becoming a Woman in the Age of Letters* (Ithaca, NY: Cornell University Press, 2009), 306–307.

132. Hillman, *Female Piety*, 73, 77.

# Chapter 7

1. Jean B. Thiers, *De la plus solide, la plus necessaire, et souvent la plus negligée de toutes les devotions*, vol. 2 (Paris: 1703), ch. 22, 473–500; idem, *Von der gründlichsten und*

*nothwendigsten aus allen Andachten . . ., trans. Kaspar Marberger* (Vienna: 1782), ch. 22, 268–286; idem,; Maher, "How the Jesuits Used Their Congregations to Promote Frequent Communion," in Patrick Donelly (ed.), *Confraternities and Catholic Reform in Italy, France and Spain* (Kirsville: Thomas Jefferson University Press, 1999), 75–95.

2. Bonsignore Cacciaguerra, *Trattato della communione* (Vercelli: 1561); idem, *De Frequenti Communione. Ausfürlicher Bericht und erklärung von der Communion . . .*, trans. Philipp Dobereiner (Dillingen: 1571). Louis de Granada, *Trattato della confessione & communione* (Venice: 1580); idem, *De Frequenti Communione Libellus cum Dialogu* (Cologne: 1586). On the practice, see also José de Barcia y Zambrana, *Despertador christiano de sermones doctrinales* (Lisbon: 1679), vol. 4, 62 homily, num. 5, 470.

3. Louis de Granada, *A Memoriall of a Christian Life* (Rouen: 1586), 379.

4. Granada, *A Memoriall*, 382.

5. Cf. Piero Camporesi, *The Fear of Hell. Images of Damnation and Salvation in Early Modern Europe.* Trans. Lucinda Byatt (University Park: Pennsylvania State University Press, 1991), 158. *The Catechism of the Council of Trent*, 249–251.

6. Michael a S. Catharina, *Trinum Perfectum*, vol. 3, par. 1029, 369.

7. On a changed heart as indicator for reception in a state of grace, see Francesco Marchese, *Pane Quotidianao dell'Anima . . .* (Venice: 1693; orig., Rome: 1681), vol. 2, 443–444. Giovanni Battista Novati, *Eucharistici Amores ex Canticis Canticorum Enucleati* (s.l.: 1645); Franciotti, *Himmlische Tischreden*, vol. 5, 47: "weil du deinen Geliebten hast wie ein Büschel Myrrhen zwischen deinen Brüsten, kannst Du Ihn mit höchster Inbrunst deiner Liebe in dein Herz schliessen." Lucian Montifontanus, *Geistliches Kinder-Spiel*, vol. 2 (Constance: 1709), 822.

8. Ulrich Probst, *Zur Erweckung Zartister Andacht und Inbrünstigen Anmuthungen . . . für alle Persohnen jedes Stands . . . Dritte Auflage*, 2 vols. (Augsburg: 1756); Franciotti, *Himmlische Tischreden*, vol. 5, preface.

9. Charly Coleman, *The Spirit of French Capitalism. Economic Theology in the Age of Enlightenment* (Stanford: Stanford University Press, 2021).

10. At Pete Sigal, *From Moon Goddesses to Virgins. The Colonization of Maya Sexual Desire* (Austin: University of Texas Press, 2000), 64ff.

11. Frederick J. McGinness, "Roma Sancta and the Saint: Eucharist, Chastity and the Logic of Catholic Reform," *Historical Reflections* 15 (1988): 99–116. *Probabilis* meant (1) a rationally defensible opinion for a certain action, or (2) an authoritatively approved opinion. On probabilism, see especially Stefania Tutino, *Uncertainty in Post-Reformation Catholicism. A History of Probabilism* (New York: Oxford University Press, 2018); Rudolf Schüssler, *The Debate on Probable Opinions in the Scholastic Tradition* (Leiden and Boston: Brill, 2019).

12. Ted Campbell, *The Religion of the Heart. A Study of European Religious Life in the Seventeenth and Eighteenth Centuries* (Columbia: University of South Carolina Press, 1991), 1–18, 27–30. Cf. also C. P. Voorwelt, *De Amor Poenitens van Johannes van Neercassel, 1626–1686* (Zeist: Kerckebosch, 1984); Johannes Neercassel, *Amor Poenitens sive de Divini Amoris ad Poenitentiam Necessitate* (Ebricae: 1683).

13. Marchese, *Pane Quotidianao*, vol. 1, 330–345; Dionysios Petavius SJ, *Opus de Theologicis Dogmatibus*, vol. 3 (Antwerp: 1700), lib. 4, 275– 284; Joseph Richter, *Von der öfteren Kommunion* ... (Vienna: 1783), 15ff. Cf. Bertrand de Margerie, "Theological and Pastoral Reflections on the History of Frequent Communion," in CIEL UK (ed.), *The Veneration and Administration of the Eucharist* (Southhampton: The Saint Austin Press, 1997), 146–157.

14. Benedict Fidelis a S. Philippo OFM, *Paradisus Eucharisticus. Hoc est Theoremata Moralia ex Psalmo XXII* (Cologne: 1659), 152–163, 242–279. Cf. Simon Gourdan, *Elévations à Dieu sur les psaumes, disposées pour tous les jours du mois, dont on peut se servir très-utilement avant et après la Sainte Communion* (Paris: 1766), 120–126; Michele Ayguani O. Carm, *Commentaria in psalmos Davidicos auctoris incogniti. Ed. F. Gregorii Canalii. Editio octava* (Lyon: 1652), 200ff; Pietro Ansalone, *David al cenacolo ciove il Salmo ventesimo secondo* ... (Naples: 1715).

15. Francisco Falck, *Der betrachtende Thomas von Kempen als ein Spiegel ... des vierten Buchs Spiegel der inniglichen Vereinigung mit Christo Jesu im h. Sakrament des Altars*, vol. 4.2 (Mainz: 1756), 582f., 603.

16. Louis Richemone, *Tableaux sacrez des figures mystiques du tres-auguste Sacrifice et Sacrement de l'Eucharistie* ... (Paris: 1601); idem, *Heilige Taflen der geheimreichen Figuren des allerheiligsten Sacrifitz und Sacraments der Eucharistie* (Augsburg: 1621), 37. An English translation appeared in 1619.

17. Richemone, *Heilige Taffeln*, 50.

18. Richemone, *Heilige Taffeln*, 91–92.

19. Richemone, *Heilige Taffeln*, 142.

20. Richemone, *Heilige Taflen*, 201.

21. Richemone, *Heilige Taflen*, 260ff.

22. Richemone, *Heilige Taflen*, 270ff.

23. Richemone, *Heilige Taflen*, 295ff.

24. Richemone, *Heilige Taflen*, 320; on spiritual communion, 344.

25. Richemone, *Heilige Taflen*, 366f.

26. Cf. Jacob Feucht, *Drey Catholische Communion Predigen am Palmsonntag* ... (Bamberg: 1572), 4f; cf. Petrus Canisius, *Catechismi Latini et Germanici*, ed. Friedrich Streicher, 2 vols. (Rome: Pont. Universitas Gregoriana, 1933ff), vols. 1 and 2.

27. Pierre Pennequin, *Isagoge ad Amorem Divinum* (Antwerp: 1641), 138, 415–430, 550; cf. for an explanation for children, Anonymous, *Das brochne Brod der Kleinen*, vol. 1 (Augsburg: 1736), 61. Cf. Fulvio Androzzi, *Considerationes de frequentanda communione* (Mainz: 1598); Joseph Waldner, *Das Catholische Strassburger Bett-Buch* (Augsburg: 1757), 281–310; *Catechism of the Council of Trent for Parish Priests* (Rockford: Tan Publ., 1982), 249; Paul G. Monson, "Sub signis visibilibus. Visual Theology in Trent's Decrees on the Eucharist," *Logos. A Journal of Catholic Thought and Culture* 15 (2012): 145–158; Michael a S. Catharina, *Trinum Perfectum*, vol. 3, par. 1042–1047, 375ff.

28. Angelus Silesius, *Ecclesiologia oder Kirche-Beschreibung*, vol. 1 (Kempten: 1735), 585; cf. Nicolas de Tourneyx, *De la meilleure maniere d'entendre la Sainte Messe* (Paris: 1680), 161, whose work was also translated into German and Dutch; see idem,

*Die beste Weise die heilige Messe zu hören* (Vienna: 1734), and idem, *De beste Maniere om Misse te hooren* (Ghent: 1713).

29. Marchese, *Pane Quotidianao*, vol. 1, preface: "affinche in essa possa non solo abitare, ma ancora passeggiare"; cf. idem, *Das tägliche Brod, oder zur täglichen Verehrung vorgestellte . . . Sacrament des Altars*, 2 vols. (Augsburg: 1700).

30. Alphonsus of Liguori, *Visits to the Most Blessed Sacrament and the Blessed Virgin Mary* (orig. 1745) (Liguori: Liguori Publ., 1990).

31. The most thorough treatment, outlining the theological problems of conceding the laity offering the sacrifice without qualification, gives Francisco Suarez, *Commentariorum ac Disputationum in tertiam Partem Divi Thomae Tomus Tertius* (Mainz: 1619), Disp. 72, sect. III, 934f. Moreover, I refer to Bona, *Opera Omnia*, 106: "Alter offerens est ipsa Catholica Ecclesia, cujus Sacerdos Minister est, & in ea omnes fideles non excommunicati, qui etiam aliqua ratione sunt offerentes per Sacerdotum." Franciscus Sylvius, *Commentarius in Tertiam Partem S. Thomae Aquinatis*. Editio Sexta (Antwerp: 1695), q. 83, art. 1, quaer. VI, concl. 3, 378: "Laici fideles recte etiam dicuntur offerentes, non quasi per se sacrificent: sed partim, qui operunt per ministerium sacerdotum, partim quia suam intentionem conjungunt cum intentione sacerdotis sacrificantis." Benedict XIV, *De Sacrosancto Missae Sacrificio Libri Tres* (Rome: 1748), lib. 2, cap. 13, 143: "denique Laicos etiam offerentes, vel quod per ministerium sacerdotum offerunt, vel quod suam cum sacerdotum intentione conjungunt." See especially the decision of Trent, session 22, ch. 6, in which it endorses private masses because in each of them the whole church "communicates spiritually" and because they are celebrated for all the faithful (DH 1747). Cap. 1 reminds that the whole Church offers the sacrifice (*se ipsum ab Ecclesia per sacerdotes*). Dominicus de Marinis, *Commentariorum in Tertiam Partem Sancti Thomae, pars altera, quae est de Sacramentis* (Lyon: 1668), 383.

32. Jacob Merlo Horstius, *Gottliebender Seelen Paradeys* . . . (Bamberg: 1697), 484; Marcellino de Pise, *Moralis Encyclopdaeia, id est, Scientiarum Omnium Chorus* . . . *De festis Christo Domino*, vol. 1 ( Lyon: 1656), 218, writes of the faithful as "participes corporis sacri."

33. The faithful could (and still can) offer a stipend to the priest for celebrating a mass. See Adalbert Mayer, *Triebkräfte und Grundlinien der Entstehung des Meßstipendiums* (St. Ottilien: EOS, 1976); Robert J. Daly, "The Council of Trent," in Lee Palmer Wandel (ed.), *A Companion to the Eucharist in the Reformation* (Leiden and Boston: Brill, 2014), 159–184 and Isabelle Brian, "Catholic Liturgies of the Eucharist in the Time of Reform," in ibid., 185–204.

34. Frymire, *Primacy*, 359.

35. Petrus Canisius, *Catechismi Latini et Germanici*, vol. 1/2 , 60f. Pierre Badoire, *Prônes sur le Sacrifice de la Messe* (Paris: 1757), 107f: "le fidèles sont associés au sacerdoce de Jesus-Christ." Jean Richard, *Pratique de Piete pour honorer Le S. Sacrament . . .* (Cologne: 1683), 363; cf. Jacob Janson, *In Sacrum Missae Canonem* (Lyon: 1586), quoting St. Augustine: "Ab omnibus namque offeri recte intelligitur, quibus placet qod offertur." A Spanish example is Juan Elías Gómez de Terán, *Assistencia de los fieles a los Divinos oficios, y Missas* (Madrid: 1736), 37f.

36. Jacques B. Bossuet, *Catechisme du Diocese de Meaux* (Paris: 1687), 207–209.

37. Jean Vigeuer, *Institutiones ad Naturalem et Christianam Philosophia . . .* (Lyon: 1671), 377.

38. Louis Bourdalou, *Exhortations et Instructions Chretiennes. Nouvelle Edition,* vol. 2 (Lyon: 1758), 236: "Car tout fidéle peut & doit s'unir ainsi au pêtre, en assistant à la Messe, pour offrir lui le sacrifice"; cf. idem, *Pensées du pere Bourdaloue de la Compagnie de Jesus sur divers sujets de religion et de morale,* vol. 3 (Paris: 1736), 231. Cf. Francois A. Pouget, *Instructions generales en firme de Catechisme. Nouvelle Edition,* vol. 3 (Paris: 1739), partie II, sect. II, ch 7, par. 22, nu. 13, 187: "Que le peuple doit s'unir au Prêtre, & offrir le Sacrifice avec lui, puisque c'est son sacrifice aussie-bien que celui du Prêtre." See also the mandate of the bishop of Auxerre of 1751, Charles-Daniel-Gabriel de Thubières de Caylus, *Mandement de Monseigneur l'évêque d'Auxerre, portant permission de manger des oeufs pendant le Carême de la présente année 1751* (s.l.: 1751), 7ff.

39. Bourdalou, *Exhortations,* vol. 2, 236: "puisque nous en sommes tous le misistres, quoique d'une manière differente."

40. Bartholomeo Gavanto, *Thesaurus Sacrorum Rituum,* ed. Gaetano-Maria Merati (Augsburg: 1763), vol. 1, part 2, tit. 3, n. 7, 173; *Sacrae Caeremoniae . . . Fratrum Eremitarum S. Augustini* (Rome: 1714); Valentin Thalhofer, *Handbuch der katholischen Liturgik,* vol. 2 (Freiburg: 1890), 62f; *Decreta Authentica Congregationis Sacrorum Rituum,* vol. 1 (Rome: 1898), nr. 1332, February 13, 1666: "In Missa dicendum est *Confiteor* pure et simpliciter prout habetur in *Missali Romano* absque additione alicuius Sancti etiam Patroni." Cf. ibid., nr. 2142 of July 12, 1704, forbidding the church in Valentia to add St. Andrew. Also see vol. 2, nr. 2297.

41. Georg Vogler, *Catechismus in auserlesenen Exempeln . . .* (Würzburg: 1652), 429; Simon Verepe, *Recueil, ou Manuel Catholique d'oraisons Devotes* (Anvers: 1593), 41; Pierre du Moulin, *Anatomie de la Messe. Troisieme Edition,* vol. 1 (Geneva: 1640), 144–155.

42. Amort, *Theologia moralis,* vol. 1, 20: "Scrupulus . . . est imprudens apprehensio peccati ordinarie cum quaedam passione vani metus conjuncta"; and see also at 21: "Causae autem possunt esse sequentes: 1. Temperamentum melancholicum . . . 2. Superbia . . . 3. Ignorantia . . . 4. Pusillanimitas . . . 5. Conversatio cum scrupulosis . . . 6. Fraus daemonis." Cf. Ilkka Kantola, *Probability and Moral Uncertainty in Late Medieval and Early Modern Times* (Helsinki: Luther-Agricola-Society, 1994); Sven Grosse, *Heilsungewissheit und Scrupulositas im späten Mittelalter. Studien zu Johannes Gerson und Gattungen der Frömmigkeitstheologie seiner Zeit* (Tübingen: JCB Mohr, 1994).

43. Michael a S. Catharina, *Trinum Perfectum,* vol. 2, par. 131–137, 45–47; at par. 135, 4; Delumeau, *Sin and Fear,* 314ff.

44. Jean-Louis Quantin, "Catholic Moral Theology, 1550–1800," in Ulrich L. Lehner et al. (eds.), *Oxford Handbook of Early Modern Theology, 1600–1800* (Oxford: Oxford University Press, 2016), 119–134.

45. Anonymous, *De confessionibus scrupulosorum brevis tractatus . . .* (Mexico City: 1723), 13ff. This book was incorrectly ascribed to Francis de Sales. It relies heavily on the moral theology of Claude Lacroix SJ (1652–1714).

46. Anonymous, *De confessionibus scrupulosorum,* 19.

47. Neudecker, *Schola*, vol. 1, 326–334, 38, 383–399; Thomas a Jesu, *Aerumnae Jesu. Das ist: Betrangnussen Unsers Erlösers Christi deß Herrn, Welche er von seiner Empfängnus an, biß in seinen Todt erlidten. Mit vierfachen zu End gesetzten Register*, translated from the French by Wolfgang Eder (Munich: 1678), nu. 27.

48. Neudecker, *Schola*, vol. 1, 207f–214; vol. 2, 100–118.

49. Bernard McGinn, *The Persistence of Mysticism in Catholic Europe. France, Italy and Germany, 1500–1675* (New York: Herder, 2020), 304–308.

50. Jean-Baptiste Saint-Jure, *Erkandtnuß und Liebe deß Sohns Gottes unsers Herrn Jesu Christi. Zu vollkommener Erleuchtung und hertzlicher Anflammung aller Christliebenden Seelen* (Ingolstadt: 1676), 596; Noel Courbon, *Pratiques pour se conserver en la présence de Dieu* (s.l.: 1699; reprinted until the end of the eighteenth century); Jérôme de Gonnelieu, *De la presence de Dieu, qui renferme tous les principes de la view interieure* (Paris: 1703), preface; Hueber, *Marianischer*, vol. 1, 84.

51. Jean-Joseph Languet de Gergy, *Traité de la confiance en la miséricorde de Dieu, augmenté d'un Traité du faux bonheur des gens du monde et du vrai bonheur de la vie chrétienne* (Paris: [1st ed. 1718] 1720), 1–5. I identified these translations: Spanish (1725), Slovak (1732), Italian (1733), Flemish (1734), German (1738), Polish (1772), Czech (1737), English (1739).

52. Languet de Gergy, *Traité*, 6–27; on "abba," see 28.

53. Languet de Gergy, *Traité*, 39.

54. Languet de Gergy, *Traité*, 41–69.

55. Languet de Gergy, *Traité*, 74.

56. Languet de Gergy, *Traité*, 88–91; at 88: "Plus je suis pécheur, plus il déploie toute la magnificence de ses miséricordes. C'est ainsi qu'il triomphe dans ses Saints."

57. Cf. Louis Antoine, *Deux spirituels au siècle des Lumières, Ambroise de Lombez, Philippe de Madiran* (Paris: 1975); P. Leonard d'Auch, *Historie de la vie du R. P. Ambroise de Lombez* (Toulouse: 1782).

58. Cf. Antoine, *Deux spirituels*; d'Auch, *Historie*.

59. Ambroise de Lombez, *Traité de la Paix Intérieure en quatre parties* (Paris: 2nd ed., 1758), part 2, ch. 7, 62–67.

60. Lombez, *Traité*, part 3, ch. 6, 123.

61. Lombez, *Traité*, part 3, ch. 6, 126.

62. Lombez, *Traité*, part 3, ch. 9, 150–154; ch. 10, 154–158.

63. Louis de Granada, *The Sinner's Guide* (New York: 1890), 265.

64. See especially the canons of the Council of Trent on justification in 1547 (DH 1520ff) and the censoring of Michael Bajus in 1567 (DH 1901–1980).

65. Michael a S. Catharina, *Trinum Perfectum*, vol. 1, par. 135, 48f.

66. Michael a S. Catharina, *Trinum Perfectum*, vol. 1, par. 158, 55; cf. ibid., par. 159ff, 56f.

67. Michael a S. Catharina, *Trinum Perfectum*, vol. 1, par. 215, 75.

68. Michael a S. Catharina, *Trinum Perfectum*, vol. 1, par. 225f, 79f.

69. Michael a S. Catharina, *Trinum Perfectum*, vol. 1, par. 270–281, 95–99; 276, 97.

70. Michael a S. Catharina, *Trinum Perfectum*, vol. 1, par. 797–803, 299–301.

71. Michael a S. Catharina, *Trinum Perfectum*, vol. 1, par. 764ff, 286ff. On the laity being especially tempted to follow the road to perdition because of trusting in one's

natural powers, see par. 1113–1127, 417–421; par. 1128 on religious; par. 1138ff on cloistered nuns.

72. Michael a S. Catharina, *Trinum Perfectum*, vol. 2, par. 802, 319: "Mulierium contactum vitandum"; par. 808f, 321ff.

73. Michael a S. Catharina, *Trinum Perfectum*, vol. 2, par. 815, 323; par. 837, 331.

74. Bette Talvacchia, "The Word Made Flesh. Spiritual Subjects and Carnal Depictions in Renaissance Art," in Marcia B. Hall and Tracy E. Cooper (eds.), *The Sensuous in the Counter-Reformation Church* (Cambridge: Cambridge University Press, 2013), 49–73, at 53; Maria H. Loh, "La Custodia Degli Occhi: Disciplining Desire in Post-Tridentine Italian Art," in ibid., 91–112.

75. See Lehner, *Enlightened Monks*; idem, *On the Road to Vatican II*.

76. Louis de Granada O.P., *De Doctrina Sive Disciplina Vitae Spiritualis, Libellus* . . . (Cologne: 1607), pars XI, 315 and 322; cf. idem, *A spiritval doctrine, conteining a rvle to liue wel, with diuers praiers and meditations. Abridged and devided into sixe treatises* . . . (Leuven: 1599).

77. Granada, *De Doctrina*.

78. Granada, *A Memoriall*, 101.

79. Granada, *A Memoriall*, 102.

80. Granada, *A Memoriall*, 114. On the hatred of self, see Granada, *The Sinner's Guide*, 394–412; cf. Granada, *Opuscula*, 126.

81. Teresa of Avila, *Moradas del castilio interior/Obras completas*, 1M1; 3M1; 4M3.

82. Brochhagen, *Kirchliche Kontrolle*; Josef Wicki, "Die unmittelbaren Auswirkungen des Konzils von Trient auf Indien," *Archivum Historiae Pontificae* 1 (1963): 241–263.

83. Michael a S. Catharina, *Trinum Perfectum*, vol. 2, par. 408, 162; cf. Andreas Heinz, "Die Feier der Firmung nach römischer Tradition. Etappen in der Geschichte eines abendländischen Sonderwegs," *Liturgisches Jahrbuch* 39 (1989): 67–88; Burkhard Neunheuser, *Taufe und Firmung. Handbuch der Dogmengeschichte 4/2* (Freiburg: Herder, 2nd ed., 1983).

84. Patrick O'Banion, *The Sacrament of Penance and Religious Life in Golden Age Spain* (University Park: Pennsylvania State Press, 2012), 1–18, 70–90; Prosperi, "Die Beichte"; Vincenzo Lavenia, *L'infamia e il perdono. Tributi, pene e confessione nella teologia morale della prima eta moderna* (Bologna: Il Mulino, 2004).

85. Prosperi, *Tribunali*.

86. Maria Pia Lorenz-Filograno, "Das Inquisitionsverfahren beim Heiligen Offizium. Juristische Aspekte und Analyseperspektiven," *Zeitschrift der Savigny-Stiftung f. Rechtsgeschichte. Kanonistische Abteilung* 101 (2015): 317–372; Elena Brambilla, *La giustizia intollerante. Inquisizione e tribunali confessionali in Europa (secoli IV–XVIII)* (Roma: Carocci, 2006). On the reserved case of absolving heretics, see Jessica M. Dalton, *Between Popes, Inquisitors and Princes. How the First Jesuits Negotiated Religious Crisis in Early Modern Italy* (Leiden and Boston: Brill, 2020).

87. O'Banion, *The Sacrament*, 51ff; Antonio Mostaza, "Forum internum–forum externum, En torno a la naturaleza juridica del fuero interno," *Revista Española de derecho canonico* 23 (1967): 274–284; 24 (1968): 339–364; 24 (1968), S. 339–364. The groundbreaking scholarship of Wim Decock has put the spotlight on early

modern legal thought, see Wim Decock, "From Law to Paradise: Confessional Catholicism and Legal Scholarship," *Rechtsgeschichte–Legal History* 18 (2011): 12–34; idem, *Theologians and Contract Law. The moral transformation of the ius commune, ca. 1500–1650* (Leiden and Boston: Brill, 2013), 69–85. An unfortunate example for a tendentious historiography of the confessional is Anton Grabner-Haider et al. (eds.), *Kulturgeschichte der Frühen Neuzeit* (Göttingen: Vandenhoeck and Ruprecht, 2014), 58.

88. *Cursus Theologiae Moralis Salmanticensis*, vol. 5 (Venice: 1737), tract. 20, c. 3, 7.

89. Council of Trent, session 14, ch. 3, DH 1673.

90. Council of Trent, session 14, ch. 5 and 6, DH 1679–1685.

91. Underwood, *Childhood*, 24, 40.

92. Hans-Peter Arendt, *Bussakrament und Einzelbeichte, Die tridentinischen Lehraussagen über das Sündenbekennntis und ihre Verbindlichkeit für die Reform des Bussakramentes* (Freiburg: Herder, 1981), 232–259; John Schwaller, "Introduction," in Stafford Poole (ed.), *The Directory for Confessors, 1585. Implementing the Catholic Reformation in New Spain* (Norman: University of Oklahoma Press, 2015), 3–28; Delumeau, *Sin and Fear*, 428–431; O'Banion, *The Sacrament*, 19–42.

93. See Council of Trent, session 14, ch. 7, DH 1686.

94. Franciscus Herzog, *Manuale Confessarii, seu Methodus compendiosa munus confessarii rite obeundi . . . Editio Quarta*, vol. 2 (Augsburg: 1727), ch. 1, 4.

95. Herzog, *Manuale*, vol. 2, 11; 19: "Pro Regula proinde Confessarii hic est: ut prudenter dijudicet, an admonitio since scandalo, & gravi incommodo poenitentis fieri possit."

96. Herzog, *Manuale*, vol. 2, 51ff. See also Delumeau, *Sin and Fear*, passim.

97. Poole (ed.), *The Directory*, 292.

98. See Council of Trent, session 14, ch. 4, DH 1678.

99. Cf. P. De Letter, "Two Concepts of Attrition and Contrition," *Theological Studies* 11 (1950): 3–33; Trent Pomplun, "Catholic Sacramental Theology in the Baroque Age," in Lehner et al. (eds.), *Oxford Handbook of Early Modern Theology*, 135–149, at 143; Jean-Pascal Gay, *Morales en conflit. Théologie et polémique au Grand Siècle, 1640–1700* (Paris: Cerf, 2011), 35ff. Anthony D. Wright, *The Divisions of French Catholicism, 1629–1645* (Farnham et al.: Ashgate, 2011), 33f.

100. Neercassel, *Amor Poenitens*, lib. 1, ch. 1, 15–23; ch. 2, 24–34; on the necessity of contrition for absolution, ch. 17, 187–197; on the negation or delay of absolution, lib. 2, ch. 5f, 346–377 (most of book 2 is dedicated to this topic). Cf. Jean Delumeau, *Catholicism between Luther and Voltaire. A New View of the Counter-Revolution* (Philadelphia: Westminster Pr., 1977), 108.

101. Johannes a S. Maria, *Opera Omnia*, vol. 2, 228–229.

102. Guillermo Lohmann Villena, *La restitución por conquistadores y encomenderos. Un aspecto de la incidencia lascasiana en el Perú* (Sevilla: Escuela de Estudios Hispanoamericanos, 1966); Mariano Delgado and Lucio Gutierrez, *Die Konzilien auf den Philippinen* (Paderborn: Schöningh, 2008), 27–66; Bergin, *Church, Society*, 399–413.

103. Henkel, *Die Konzilien in Lateinamerika, vol. 1. Mexiko*, 70.

104. Ricard, *The Spiritual Conquest*, 116f; 123ff.; Pardo, *Origins*, 102f, 131–158.

105. Cf. Worcester, *Seventeenth-Century*, 66–72; Marcel Bernos, "Confession et conversion," in *La conversion au XVII siecle* (Marseille: Actes du XII Colloque de Marseille, 1982), 283–296.

106. Joannes a Jesu Maria, *Opera Omnia*, vol. 2, 228.

107. Joannes a Jesu Maria, *Opera Omnia*, vol. 2, 186–246, here: 186–193.

108. Joannes a Jesu Maria, *Opera Omnia*, vol. 2, 196–198.

109. Joannes a Jesu Maria, *Opera Omnia*, vol. 2, 198.

110. Joannes a Jesu Maria, *Opera Omnia*, vol. 2, 216–218. Joannes spends considerable time on the reform of the sense of smell and the temptation of "exquisite smells"; see also Joannes a Jesu Maria, *De Schola Jesu Christi Liber* (Cologne: 1612), 260–262; on the taming of one's curiosity, see 277.

111. Joannes a Jesu Maria, *Opera Omnia*, vol. 2, 219.

112. Joannes a S. Maria, *Opera Omnia*, vol. 2, 231–238.

113. One of the most cogently argued Jansenist works on this is Jan van Opstraet, *Dissertatio Theologica de Conversione Peccatoris* (Leuven: 2nd ed., 1688).

114. Bergin, *Church, Society*, 264; Antonio de San Roman OSA, *Consuelo de Penitentes o Mesa Franca de spirituales manjares* (Sevilla: 1585); Ignacio de la Erbada, *Puerta Franca del Cielo* (Madrid: 1783).

115. Robert Birely, "Two Works by Jean Delumeau," *Catholic Historical Review* 77 (1991): 78–88, has fairly pointed out the one-sidedness of Delumeau's, eclipsing evidence that would have nuanced his emphasis on fear. See also Jean Delumeau, "The Journey of a Historian," *Catholic Historical Review* 96 (201): 434–448.

116. Thomas Tentler, *Sin and Confession on the Eve of the Reformation* (Princeton: Princeton University Press, 1977), 348; Stephen Haliczer, *Sexuality in the Confessional. A Sacrament Profaned* (Oxford: Oxford University Press, 1996), 34–41.

117. Herzog, *Manuale*, vol. 1, 22ff; Worcester, *Seventeenth-Century*, 73.

118. Joannes a Jesu Maria, *Opera Omnia*, vol. 2, ch. 5, 176. Cf. Bertin Bertaut, *Le Directeur des confesseurs en forme de catéchisme* (Paris: 5th ed., 1638); idem, *Directorium confessariorum* (Venice: 1654); idem, *Il Direttorio de confessori...* (Milan: 1666); idem, *Director (!) Confessariorum . . .* pars 1, trans. Adalrich Schwarz (Dillingen: 1709), 119–145; cf. Herzog, *Manuale*, vol. 1, 132f.

119. Duhamelle, *Grenze*, 108–116, 73; Andrea Molfesio, *Promputuarii Triplicis Iuris Divini, Canonici et Civilis, seu Summae Moralis Theologiae, & Casuum Conscientiae. Pars Prima* (Naples: 1619), tract. 7, cap. 22, 478–479.

120. *Allgemeine deutsche Bibliothek* 71, pt. 1 (1787), 253; Pons-Augustin Alletz, *Die Kunst Seelen im Beichtstuhle zu rühren*, 2 vols. (Bamberg and Würzburg: 1785).

121. *Cursus Theologiae Moralis Salmanticensis*, vol. 5, tract. 21, cap. 4, pt. 3, num. 43, 214: "Ratio est: quia cum lex sit poenalis extendenda non est ad alios casus, quos ipsa non exprimit: cum ergo solum lata sit denuntiationis lex contra solicitantes ad turpia in confessione, seu Poenitentiae Sacramento, ad alia sacramenta non est extendenda." Amort, *Theologia Eclectica*, vol. 3, tractatus de poenitentiae, disp. 10, 435–450; cf. Gregory XV's constitution *Contra Solicitantes in Confessionibus* (1622) and Benedict XVI's constitution *Sacramentum Poenitentiae* (1740). Cf. Martin Bonacina, *Opera Omnia*, vol. 1 (Antwerp: 1632), tractationes variae, disp. 6, punctum III, 641f. On the

question of getting drugged, see ibid., q. 9, num. 10, 72f. See also Antonio Santarelli, *Tractatus de Haeresi, Schismate, Apostasia, Sollicitatione* (Rome: 1625); Antonio de Sousa, *Aphorismi Inquisitorum in Quatur Libros Distributi* (s.l.: 1630), 131; Amort, *Theologia Eclectica*, vol. 4, de praeceptis, disp. 7, 206. On fornication of priests, see Johann L. Hennebel, *Thesis Theologica de Sacerdote Lapsi* . . . (Leuven: 1690), 10; idem, *Opuscula a eximii Viri J.L. Hennebel accedunt Martini Steyaert . . . objectiones* (Leuven: 1703). A good introduction to the field is Haliczer, *Sexuality*. In detail on solicitation in Spain, see Adelina Sarrión Mora, *Sexualidad y confesión. La solicitación ante el Tribunal del Santo Oficio* (Cuenca: Ediciones de la Universidad de Castilla-La Mancha, 2010); Juan Antonio Alejandre, *El veneno de Dios. La Inquisición de Sevilla ante el Delito de solicitación en confesión* (Madrid: Siglo XXI de España, 1994). On Portugal, see Jaime Ricardo Gouveia, *O sagrado e o profano em choque no confessionário. O delito de solicitação no Tribunal da Inquisição, Portugal 1551-1700* (Coimbra: Palimage Editores, 2011).

122. John F. Chuchiak, "The Sins of the Fathers. Franciscan Friars, Parish Priests, and the Sexual Conquest of the Yucatec Maya, 1545-1808," *Ethnohistory* 54 (2007): 69-126; Sigal, *From Moon Goddesses to Virgins*, 73, calls this "strategic inversion."

123. *Cursus Theologiae Moralis Salmanticensis*, vol. 5 (Madrid: 1714), tract. 21, cap. 4, pt. 2, num. 10, 204; num. 12, 205. "Sodomy" was at the time an umbrella term for both anal intercourse of all sorts and homosexual acts.

124. Gérard Dufour, *Clero y Sexto Mandamiento. La confesión en la España del siglo XVIII* (Valladolid: Ámbito, 1996); Luis René Guerrero Galván, *Procesos inquisitoriales por el pecado de solicitación en Zacatecas (siglo XVIII)* (Zacatecas, Mexico: Tribunal Superior de Justicia del Estado de Zacatecas, 2003); Hersche, *Muße*, vol. 1, 303-308.

125. Beda Mayr, *Festpredigten nebst einem Anhang*, vol. 5 (Augsburg: 1782), 526-527; 530: "Aus eurer Schuld wird ein Unschuldiger ein Sünder, dieser Sünder aber wieder ein Verführer, er richtet andre zu Grunde . . . Diese andere wieder andere. Welch eine fürchterliche Kette von Lasterthaten."

126. Cf. Thomas Betteridge (ed.), *Sodomy in Early Modern Europe* (Manchester: Manchester University Press, 2007).

127. Juan de Azevedo, *Tribunal Theologicum & Juridicum Contra Subdolos Confessarios* (Ulyssipone Occidentali: 1726), conf. 3, delib. 22, 127: "praetextu illi tradendi chirographum de obligatione annuae confessionis." The phrase "ducit puerum in cubiculum" is a standard phrase of the time.

128. Antonio Sanctarelli, *De Haeresi, Schismate, Apostasia, Sollicitatione in sacramento Poenitentiae* (Rome: 1625), tract. 1, cap. 45, 462-465; Cunha, *Tractatus de Confessariis Solicitantibus*, q. 6, 52ff; on the question of evidence, see Joao Scobar a Corro, *Tractatus Tres Selectissimi et Absolutissimi*, vol. 2 (Cordoba: 1642), pars II, q. 4, 195ff; on punishment, see pars II, q. 5, num. 11, 220ff; on solicitation of boys, see de Sousa, *Aphorismi*, 86, 89. See also Hersche, *Muße*, vol. 1, 305-306.

129. de Sousa, *Aphorismi*, 89; Ludovico a Paramo, *De Origine et Progressu Officii Sanctae Inquisitionis eiusque dignitate & utilitate* (Madrid: 1598), q. 10, num. 11-12, 844; Haliczer, *Sexuality*, 86; Manuel González Rincón, "La crítica sexual anticlerical en el Apókopos de Bergadís. La sollicitatio durante la confesión," *Byzantion Nea Hellas*

29 (2010): 113–133; Jorge René González Marmolejo, *Sexo y confesion. La iglesia y la penitencia en los siglos XVIII y XIX en la Nueva España* (Mexico City: Editores Plaza y Valdés, 2002).

130. Ulrich L. Lehner, *Im Klosterkerker der Mönche und Nonnen* (Kevaler: ToposPlus, 2015).

131. On the rite of degradation, see the *Pontificale Romanum* (Antwerp: 1765), pars 3, 453. Cf. on its practice, see de Cortiada, *Decisiones*, vol. 1, dec. XXXIV, nu. 120, 424; Petrus Caballus, *Resolutionum Crimnialium . . . pro serenissima magno duce Hetrurie . . .* (Frankfurt: 1613), casus 87, 131f.

132. Zeb Tortorici, "Masturbation, Salvation and Desire. Connecting Sexuality and Religiosity in Colonial Mexico," *Journal of the History of Sexuality* 16 (2007): 355–372.

# Chapter 8

1. See Louis Dupre and Don E. Saliers (eds.), *Christian Spirituality. Post-Reformation and Modern* (New York: Crossroad, 1989).

2. See Anne Jacobson Schutte, *Aspiring Saints. Pretense of Holiness, Inquisition, and Gender in the Republic of Venice, 1618–1750* (Baltimore: Johns Hopkins University Press, 2003); Nora Jaffary, *False Mystics. Deviant Orthodoxy in Colonial Mexico* (Lincoln: University of Nebraska Press, 2008); Álvaro Castro Sánchez, *Franciscanos, místicos, herejes y alumbrados* (Córdoba: Servicio de Publicaciones, Universidad de Córdoba, 2010).

3. John E. Longhurst, "Saint Ignatius at Alcala, 1526–1527," *Archivum Historicum Societatis Iesu* 26 (1957): 252–256.

4. Evennett, *The Spirit*, 28–41; on normative centering, see Hamm, "Normative." On the Catholic understanding of justification and sanctification, see the decree on justification by the Council of Trent, session VI (1547), especially ch. 3–7 and 10–11, DH 1523–1531 and DH 1535–1539.

5. Council of Trent, session 6, ch.14–16, DH 1542–1550.

6. Council of Trent, session 6, ch.12–13, DH 1539–1540.

7. Johann Auer, *Die Entwicklung der Gnadenlehre in der Hochscholastik. Teil 1. Das Wesen der Gnade* (Freiburg: Herder, 1942), and idem, *Die Entwicklung der Gnadenlehre in der Hochscholastik. Teil 2. Das Wirken der Gnade* (Freiburg: Herder, 1951); Robert Fastiggi, "Francisco Suarez and the Non-Believers," *Pensamiento 74* (2018): 263–270; Eric Demeuse, "The World Is Content with Words. Jansenism between Thomism and Calvinism," in Jordan Ballor et al. (eds.), *Beyond Dordt and de Auxiliis. The Dynamics of Protestant and Catholic Soteriology in the Sixteenth and Seventeenth Century* (Leiden and Boston: Brill, 2019), 245–276.; Thomas Marschler, "Providence, Predestination and Grace," in Lehner et al. (eds.), *Oxford Handbook of Early Modern Theology*, 89–103.

8. François-Marc Gagnon, *La conversion par l'image. Un aspect de la mission des jésuites auprès des indiens du Canada au XVII siècle* (Montreal: Les Editions Bellarmin, 1975), 23; Shoemaker, *Negotiators of Change*, 58ff. On Nobletz, see also Franz Reitinger, "The Persuasiveness of Cartography. Michel le Nobletz and the

School of Le Conquet," *Cartographica* 40 (2005): 79–103; François Trémolières, "L'enseignement par l'image de Michel Le Nobletz L'enseignement par l'image de Michel Le Nobletz," in Ralph Dekoninck and Agnès Guiderdoni-Bruslé (eds.), *Emblemata sacra. Rhétorique et herméneutique du discours sacré dans la littérature en images* (Turnhout: Brepols, 2007), 553–568. An important critique of the view that European literacy was considered by natives with "awe" is Peter Wogan, "Perceptions of European Literacy in Early Contact Situations," *Ethnohistory* 3 (1994): 407–429.

9. Michael a S. Catharina, *Trinum Perfectum*, vol. 3, par. 776, 281.

10. Cf. Susan C. Karant-Nunn, *The Reformation of Feeling. Shaping the Religious Emotions in Early Modern Germany* (Oxford: Oxford University Press, 2010), 12, 32, 37.

11. Against Bernhard Groethuysen, *Die Entstehung der bürgerlichen Welt-und Lebensanschauung in Frankreich*, vol. 1 (Frankfurt: Suhrkamp, 1978), 85, 118–121.

12. Carlos Eire, "The Good Side of Hell: Infernal Meditations in Early Modern Spain," *Historical Reflections* 26 (2000): 285–310.

13. Cf. Karant-Nunn, *The Reformation of Feeling*, 60.

14. Roldan-Figueroa, *The Ascetic Spirituality*, 12f; cf. Jodi Bilinkoff, *The Avila of Saint Teresa* (Ithaca: Cornell University Press, 1989), 53–77. San Juan de Avila, *Obras completas, nueva edición crítica*, ed. Luis Sala Balust and Francisco Martín Hernández, vol. 3 (Madrid: Biblioteca de Autores Cristianos, 2003), 369; translation at Roldan-Figueroa, *The Ascetic Spirituality*, 197. Cf. Avila, *Obras completas*, vol. 3, 374; translation at Roldan-Figueroa, *The Ascetic Spirituality*, 205.

15. On the motive of the ascension of the mind in general, see Robert Bellarmine, *De Ascensione Mentis in Deum* (Cologne: 1615);Joannes Crombecius, *Ascensus Moysis in montem seu de Oratione tractatus . . .* (Audomari: 1618), 22–35.

16. Bona, *Opera Omnia*, 620. See also Reinhard Körner, "Was ist 'inneres Beten'? Ein kurzer Gang durch die Begriffsgeschichte," *Communio* 26 (1997): 338–355.

17. Francis Nephew SJ, *The Method of Mental Prayer* (London: 1694), preface: "The name mental prayer makes most people afraid . . . that this kind of prayer is only proper for Souls that are already perfect."

18. Jose Pereira and Robert Fastiggi, *The Mystical Theology of the Catholic Reformation* (Washington, DC: Catholic University of America Press, 2006), 80; Cf. Francisco Suarez, *De Religione*, vol. 2 (Lyon: 1630), lib. 2, c. 1, 79–81.

19. Keitt, *Inventing the Sacred*, 72; Laura Calvert, *Francisco de Osuna and the Spirit of the Letter* (Chapel Hill, NC: University of North Carolina Press, 1973); Hans-Jürgen Prien, *Francisco de Osuna—Mystik und Rechtfertigung ein Beitrag zur Erforschung der spanischen Theologie und Frömmigkeit in der ersten Hälfte des sechzehnten Jahrhunderts* (Hamburg: Kovač, 2014).

20. Elena Carrera, "The Emotions in Sixteenth-Century Spanish Spirituality," *Journal of Religious History* 31 (2007): 235–252, at 242; cf. Turley, *Franciscan Spirituality*, 5ff. Cf. Francisco Osuna, *The Third Spiritual Alphabet*, ed. and trans. Mary E. Giles (New York: Paulist Press, 1981), 154–155; Sluhovsky, *Believe Not Every Spirit*, 181.

21. Sluhovsky, *Believe Not Every Spirit*, 104–107.

22. Keitt, *Inventing the Sacred*, 71; Sluhovsky, *Believe Not Every Spirit*, 181.

23. For the text of Cano's critique, see Thomas O'Reilly, *From Ignatius of Loyola to John of the Cross. Spirituality and Literature in Sixteenth-Century Spain* (Aldershot: Variorum, 1995), part V: 1–22; see also "Melchor Cano and the Spirituality of St. Ignatius of Loyola," part V: 369–380.

24. Sluhovsky, *Believe Not Every Spirit*, 3; Janice Boddy, "Spirit Possession Revisited: Beyond Instrumentality," *Annual Review of Anthropology* 23 (1994): 407–434.

25. Carrera, "Emotions," 249; Karl Rahner, "The Logic of Concrete Existential Knowledge in Ignatius Loyola," in idem, *The Dynamic Element in the Church* (London: Burns and Oates, 1964), 84–170.

26. Silvia Mostaccio, "Shaping the Spiritual Exercises. The *Maisons de retraites* in Brittany during the Seventeenth Century as a Gendered Pastoral Tool," *Journal of Jesuit Studies* 2 (2015): 659–684.

27. See Silvia Mostaccio, *Early Modern Jesuits between Obedience and Conscience during the Generalate of Claudio Acquaviva (1581–1615)* (Farnham: Ashgate, 2014), ch. 4.

28. See, for example, the early English translation Luis de la Puente, *Meditations Vpon the Mysteries of Our Holie Faith. With the Practise of Mental Prayer Touching the Same* (S. Omers: 1619); cf. Rady Roldan-Figueroa, "The Mystical Theology of Luis de la Puente," in Robert Maryks (ed.), *Brill's Companion to Jesuit Mysticism* (Leiden and Boston: Brill, 2017), 54–81.

29. Heinrich Braun, *Katholisches Gebeth-und Erbauungsbuch* (Augsburg: 1783), preface.

30. Thomas a Jesu, "Via Brevis et Plana Orationis Mentalis," in *Opera Omnia*, vol. 2 (Cologne: 1634), c. 1, 46; c. 2 and c. 3 on acquired and infused mental prayer.

31. Boileau, *Pensees choises*, 107–119; Pierre Nicole, *Instructions Theologiques et Morales sur l'Oraison Dominicale* (Paris: 1718), ch. 4, 11 (*oraison mentale*).

32. Miguel de San Agustin, *Introductio in terram Carmeli, et gustatio fructuum illius, seu introductio ad vitam vere Carmelitanum seu mysticam* (Brussels: 1659), "ad omnes vitae internae amatores."

33. Thomas a Jesu, *Compendio de los grados de oracion por donde se sube a la perfeta contemplacion. Sacado de las obras de la santa Madre Teresa de Iesus, fundadora de la reformacion de Carmelitas Descalços* (Madrid: 1615); idem, *Summarium undt Kurtzer Inhalt der Staffeln des Innerlichen Gebetts* (Munich: 1634); idem, *Compendio dell' oratione mentale* (Milan: 1657).

34. San Agustin, *Introductio*, 230.

35. San Agustin, *Introductio*, 315f, 318.

36. San Agustin, *Introductio*, 323.

37. *Archiconfraternitas B. V. Mariae de Consolatione* (Munich: 1674), 63f. Joseph Ximenez Samaniego, *Statuorum generalium compilatio pro familia cismontana Regularis Observantiae Seraphici . . .* (Madrid: 1704), 77.

38. Pedro de Alcantara, *Instruction oder Underweisung wol zu meditiren . . .* (Cologne: 1605), 4, 137–150; Karl Heinrich Seibt, *Katholisches Lehr-und Gebethbuch. 4 edition* (Prague: 1794), 76 on appropriation.

39. Franciscus Agricola, *Von dem christlichen Gebett . . .* (Cologne: 1585), 134.

40. *Piarum et Christ. Institutionum Libri Tres in Usum Sodalitatis B. Mariae Virginis* ... (Cologne: 1581), 97: "Ex ipsa meditatione occasio sumi debet dulcissimae, atque ex intimo corde ductae gratiarum actionis." Cf. Johann Altenstaig, *Lexicon Theologicum* ... (Antwerp: 1576), 223f. Cf. Lucien Febvre, "Aspects méconnus d'un renouveau religieux en France entre 1590 et 1620," *Annales ESC* (1958): 639–650.

41. Teresa of Avila, *Moradas del castilio interior/Obras completas*, 1M1.

42. François Coster, *Libellus Sodalitatis hoc est Christianarum institutionum libri quinque* (Antwerp: 1586), 79–80.

43. Joannes a Jesu Maria, *Opera Omnia*, vol. 2, "Theologia Mystica," ch. 3, 429: "Meditatio est discursus intellectus sategentis voluntatem vel a malo arcere, vel ad bonum impellere"; 430 citing St. Bonaventure "Contemplatio est actus intellectus non impediti, gratia sanati, in aeterna spectacula directi, & admiratione suspensi."

44. Sluhovsky, *Believe Not Every Spirit*, 101–105; Antonio a Spiritu Sancto, *Directorium*, tract. III, disp. 3, sect. , 117.

45. Cf. Sluhovsky, *Believe Not Every Spirit*, 101f, 138.

46. Joannes a Jesu Maria, *Opera Omnia*, vol. 2, 143–184.

47. Joannes a Jesu Maria, *Opera Omnia*, vol. 2, ch. 5, 152.

48. Joannes a Jesu Maria, *Opera Omnia*, vol. 2, ch. 5, 156.

49. Joannes a Jesu Maria, *Opera Omnia*, vol. 2, ch. 5, 183, on the discernment of goods in the sexual act among married spouses.

50. Ronald de Sousa, *The Rationality of Emotion* (Cambridge: Cambridge University Press, 1987), 6, 297.

51. Carrera, "The Emotions," 236.

52. Carrera, "The Emotions," 236.

53. Veranus, *De Humanis*, vol. 1, 343f.; at 345: "Oratio enim non solum orantem sejungit ab humo, sed etiam Deo jungit."

54. Veranus, *De Humanis*, vol. 1, 347, 349.

55. For this practice in early modern Marian devotional books, see Christine Getz, *Mary, Music, and Meditation. Sacred Conversations in Post-Tridentine Milan* (Indianapolis, IN: Indiana University Press, 2013), 1–17. Cf. Ian Christopher Levy, *Introducing Medieval Biblical Interpretation* (Grand Rapids: Baker Academic, 2018); Henri de Lubac, *Medieval Exegesis*, 3 vols. (Grand Rapids: Eerdmans, 1998ff).

56. Veranus, *De Humanis*, vol. 1, 336f; on tears, see vol. 1, 315–332.

57. Louis Bail, *La théologie affective ou Saint Thomas d'Aquin en méditation* (Paris: 1671), vol. 1, preface. Cf. on passions, Bail, *La théologie affective*, vol. 2, 121ff.

58. Bail, *La théologie affective*, vol. 2, 93ff.

59. Bail, *La théologie affective*, vol. 2, 133, with reference to Alvarez.

60. Bail, *La théologie affective*, vol. 2, 136: "Cette méthode est plus douce & humaine, & plus générale, réussit plus aisément."

61. Bail, *La théologie affective*, vol. 3, 431; vol. 1, preface.

62. Vincent Contenson, *Theologia Mentis et Cordis* (Venice: 1727), vol. 1, lib. I, praeloquium, 1.

63. Cf. Laun, *Der Salesianische Liebesbegriff*, 328f; David Gentilcore, *Food and Health in Early Modern Europe* (London et al.: Bloombury, 2016), 95–114; Eunan McDonnell,

*The Concept of Freedom in the Writings of St. Francis de Sales* (Oxford et al.: Peter Lang, 2009), 128.

64. McDonnell, *The Concept of Freedom*, 176–181; Jacques Leclercq, *Saint François de Sales, docteur de la perfection* (Paris: Casterman, 1948), 37. Cf. Manfred Tietz, *Saint François de Sales' Traité de l'amour de Dieu (1616) und seine spanischen Vorläufer. Cristóbal de Fonseca, Diego de Estella, Luis de Granada, Santa Teresa de Jesús und Juan de Jesús Maria* (Wiesbaden: F. Steiner, 1973); Etienne Lajeunie, *Saint Francis De Sales, the Man, the Thinker, His Influence* (Bangalore: S.F.S. Publications, 1986). De Sales follows in his interpretation of the Song of Songs Gilbert Genebrard, *Canticum Canticorum Salomonis Versibus et Commentariis illustratum* (Paris: 1585).

65. Laun, *Der Salesianische Liebesbegriff*, 43.

66. William C. Marceau, *Stoicism and St. Francis de Sales* (Lewiston: Edwin Mellen Press, 1989), 62–64.

67. Francis de Sales, *Treatise on the Love of God* (Douai: 1630), bk. 10, ch. 5.

68. On the question of disinterestedness in de Sales, Bossuet, and Fenelon, see Michael Moriarty, *Fallen Nature, Fallen Selves. Early Modern French Thought*, vol. 2 (Oxford: Oxford University Press, 2006), 207–217.

69. Johannes Kraus, "Fenelons Moraltheologisches Leitbild der Seelenführung nach den Lettres Spirituelles," in idem (ed.), *Fenelon. Persönlichkeit und Werk* (Baden-Baden: Verlag f. Kunst, 1953), 155–233; Chad Helms, "Introduction," in idem (ed.), *Fenelon. Selected Writings. The Classics of Western Spirituality* (New York: Paulist Press, 2006), 1–113.

70. A Protestant example for pious "sighs" for university students is Joachim Fellern, *Der andächtige Student. Das ist. Andächtige Seuffzer und Gebethe…* (Leipzig: 1718). Henricus Jonghen, *Vera Fraternitas Declamanda Confratribus . . .* (Antwerp: 1662), 692: "Nos autem & aliam possumus superaddere moralizationem, utilem & consolatoriam illis, quorum cor inter orandum distractionibus multiplicibus inquietatur." Antoine Balinghem, *De Orationibus Iaculatoriis Libri IV* (Antwerp: 1618).

71. Ludovicus Blosius, *Opera Omnia* (Antwerp: 1632), "Institutio Spiritualis," ch. 4–5, 306–308; Johann Landsperger, *Pharetra Divini Amoris* (Cologne: 1533).

72. Neudecker, *Schola*, 347: "Ad Lotionem: Da Domine virtutem manibus meis ad abstergendam omnem maculam, ut sine pollutione mentis et corporis valeam tibi servire. Eccl."

73. Bona, *Opera Omnia*, 65f. Cf. also the Discalced Carmelite Joannes a S. Maria, *Opera Omnia*, vol. 2, 161, 336, 392; on Jesus's teaching of jaculatory prayer, see also Neudecker, *Schola*, 342. Cf. Balinghem, *De Orationibus*, 320.

74. Neudecker, *Schola*, 342–345. On Spee's use of this method, see Josef Sudbrack, "Mystik und Methode. Ganzheitliches Beten bei Friedrich Spee von Langenfeld," in Michael Sievernich (ed.), *Friedrich von Spee. Priester-Poet-Prophet* (Frankfurt: Knecht, 1986), 107–118.

75. Petrus Canisius, *Bettbuch und Catechismus* (Dillingen: 1590), 65–68: "Herr Gott verleyhe uns ein selige Stund zuleben und zusterben durch Jesus Christum unsern Herrn. Amen. . . . Der Nam des Herrn sey gebendeyet, und sein will geschehe. . . . Gott geb seiner Kirchen frid und einigkeit"; see also 368ff; cf. Joannes a Jesu Maria, *Opera Omnia*, vol. 2, 634.

76. For St Teresa, see Alphonsus de Andrade SJ, *Avisos Espirituales de Santa Theresa de Jesus comentados* (Madrid: 1647), later also translated into German and Italian. Cf. Antoine Balinghem, *Thesaurus Orationum Iaculatoriarum ex Sacris Bibliis addita explicatione* (Cologne: 1626). For arrow prayers in confraternities, see *Aspirationes Sacrae Sodalis Mariana ad Deiparam Virginem . . .* (Vienna: 1676); *Schnell-Abfliegende Hertzen-Pfeil* (Munich: 1730). For preparation before communion and the sacraments in general, see Diego Alvarez, *Mensis Eucharisticus, hoc est praeparationes, aspirationes et gratiarum actiones . . .* (Madrid: 1789); Giovanni Bona, *Divinum profluvium orationum et aspirationum . . .* (Leuven: 1735).

77. Balinghem, *De Orationibus*, 65; cf. Antonio de Molina O.Cart., *Exercicios Espirituales . . . y necessidad de la Oracion Mental* (Buros: 1630), tract. 1, ch. 17, 116–122.

78. Balinghem, *De Orationibus*, 193; on how to evoke contrition from a dying person, see John Polanco SJ, *Methodus ad eos adiuvandos qui moriuntur* (Rome: 1577), ch. 5, 19–22.

79. Michael a S. Catharina, *Trinum Perfectum*, vol. 3, par. 745ff, 270ff. Elizabeth C. Tingle, *Purgatory and Piety in Brittany, 1480–1720 (Catholic Christendom, 1300–1700)* (Aldershot: Ashgate, 2012), 79. For an overview, see Tomas Maly, "Early Modern Purgatory: Reformation Debates and Post-Tridentine Change," *Archiv für Reformationsgeschichte* 106 (2015): 242–272; see 269ff on the parallels between the passion of Christ and purgatory; Christine Göttler, *Last Things. Art and the Religious Imagination in the Age of Reform* (Turnhout: Brepols, 2010).

80. On the Catholic concept of purgatory, see Heinrich Ott, *Eschatologie in der Scholastik. Handbuch der Dogmengeschichte*, vol. IV/7b (Freiburg: Herder, 1990), and Philipp Schäfer, *Eschatologie. Trient und Gegenreformation. Handbuch der Dogmengeschichte*, vol. IV/7c (Freiburg: Herder, 1984).

81. Michael a S. Catharina, *Trinum Perfectum*, vol. 3, par. 745ff, 270ff; Saussay, *Panoplia Sacerdotalis*, 420–426; Luca Pinelli, *De Virtute Seu Energia & admirandis Sacrosanctae Missae effectibus* (Cologne: 1608), lib. 2, c. 7, 325–352; James Monford SJ, *Tractatus de Misericordia Fidelibus Defunctis exhibenda* (Cologne: 1649). On the fruits of the Mass, see Johannes Brinktrine, "Zur Lehre von den sogenannten Messopferfrüchten," *Theologie und Glaube* 41 (1951): 260–265; Helmut Hoping, *Für Euch hingegeben. Geschichte und Theologie der Eucharistie* (Freiburg: Herder, 2nd ed., 2015), 235–295.

82. Joseph de Galliffet, *De Cultu sacrosancti Cordis Dei ac Domini Jesu Christi . . .* (Rome: 1726), 108f, 125. van Deusen (ed.), *The Souls of Purgatory*; Haliczer, *Sexuality*, 33f.; on women patrons, see Tingle, *Purgatory*, 97ff. Against Ellen Gunnarsdóttir, *Mexican Karismata. The Baroque Vocation of Francisca De Los Ángeles, 1674–1744* (Lincoln: University of Nebraska Press, 2004), 83. See also María de San José, *A Wild Country Out in the Garden. The Spiritual Journals of a Colonial Mexican Nun*, ed. Kathleen Ann Myers and Amanda Powell (Bloomington: Indiana University Press, 1999), 265; Ann W. Ramsey, *Liturgy, Politics and Salvation. The Catholic League in Paris and the Nature of Catholic Reform, 1540–1630* (Rochester, NY: University of Rochester Press, 1999), 3.

83. Jane Owen, *An Anti-Dote against Purgatory . . .* (St. Omer: 1634), 239f.

84. Owen, *An Anti-Dote*, 261; 276. Cf. Caspar Druzbicki SJ, *Opera Omnia Ascetica*, vol. 1 (Ingolstadt: 1732), 295f.

85. Martin de Roa, *Estado de las almas de Purgatorio. Correspondencia que hazen a sus Bienchores* . . . (Sevilla: 1619), ch. 24, 146–152; Alfonso de Mendoza OESA, *Quaestiones Quodlibeticae et Relectio de Christi regno ac dominio* (Salamanca: 1596), 350ff. On the vain exercise of necromancy, however, see Benito Pereira SJ, *Opera Theologica* (Cologne: 1620), 254–256, 374–376; Petrus Thuraeus SJ, *De Apparitionibus Spirituum tractatus Duo* (Cologne: 1600), 88–122; Franciscus Torreblanca, *Epitome Delictorum sive de Magia* (Lyon: 1678), lib. 1, c. 16, 88–93; Thomas White, *Devotion and Reason. Wherein Modern Devotion for the Dead Is Brought to Solid Principles and Made Rational* (Paris: 1661), 66.

86. Elias a S. Teresia, *Legatio Ecclesiae Triumphantis*, 2 vols. (Antwerp: 1638), vol. 1, 138; cf. 137–143.

87. Cf. Anonymous, *Seelen-Peyn in dem Fegfeuer* . . . (Munich: 1732); Georg Raw, *Abgeferrtigter Herold aus der andern Welt, von denen im Fegfewer leydenden Seelen in dise Welt gesandt* (Munich: 1658); de Roa, *Estado de las almas*; Tobias Lohner, *Geistliche Haus-Bibliothec. Das ist allerley heilsame Tractätlein zu sonderbarem Trost der Lebendigen und Abgestorbenen* . . . , vol. 3 (Munich: 1684).

88. Cf. Alessio Segala de Salo OFMCap, *Trionfo delle anime del purgatorio. Opera del R.P.F. Alessio Segala. Di nouo posto in luce, e di vaghe figure ornato* (Brescia: 1620); French edition: *Le triomphe des âmes du purgatoire, divisé en deux parties* (Lyon: 1621); cf. Kirstin Noreen, "Ecclesiae militantis triumphi: Jesuit Iconography and the Counter-Reformation," *Sixteenth Century Journal* 29 (1998): 689–715.

89. Cf. Louis of Blois, *Spiritual Works*, ed. John Edward Bowden (London: Washbourne, 1903), 251.

90. For the general thesis of purgatory as expression of individualized judgment, see Philippe Aries, *The Hour of Our Death* (Harmondsworth: Penguin, 2013). Cf. Tingle, *Purgatory*, 58–86, for a careful overview of research on this topic.

91. Tingle, *Purgatory*, 84.

92. Girolamo Baruffaldo, *Ad Rituale Romanum Commentaria* (Augsburg and Dillingen: 1735), 331–332.

93. Baruffaldo, *Ad Rituale*, 335.

94. Baruffaldo, *Ad Rituale*, 352.

95. Anonymous, *Erklärung der Prose Dies Irae, oder Affekte eines Sünders* (Mainz: 1786), preface.

96. Annette Albert-Zerlik, *Liturgie als Sterbebegleitung und Trauerhilfe. Spätmittlelaterliches Erbe und pastorale Gegenwart unter besonderer Berücksichtigung der Ordines von Castelani (1523) und Sanctorius (1602)* (Tübingen: Francke, 2003); Cf. Joseph Catalano, *Rituale Romanum Benedicti XIV. Perpetuis Commentariis Exornatum*, vol. 1 (Patavii: 1760), 370; *Rituale Romanum* (Rome: 1614), 87.

97. Procopius von Templin, *Funerale* (Salzburg: 1670), 27–44.

98. Procopius, *Funerale*, 93.

99. Procopius, *Funerale*, 94. See also Martin Prugger, *Lehr-und Exempelbuch fuer die Krancke und Sterbende* . . . (Augsburg: 6th ed., 1762). See also Anonymus, *Heylsamer Spring-Brunn zum Ewigen Leben* . . . (Würzburg: 1662).

100. de Roa, *Estado de las Almas*, ch. 5, 20–26; Franziskus Suter, *Underirdische Goldgrub. Das ist trewherziger Bericht von dem Zustand der armen Seelen im Fegfewr* (Lucerne: 1692), 25–74.

101. Fasso, *Juramentum*, 22.

102. Fasso, *Juramentum*, 582–594.

103. Johann Lorenz Helbig, *Traurige Gedancken zur Nutzlichen Zeit-Vertreibung oder Hundert Discursen* (Nürnberg: 1704), 681–707; Pistorius, *Allgemeines Klaghauß*, 277; Tingle, *Purgatory*, 175–219.

104. Cf. Marc de Bonnyers SJ, *L'advocat des ames de purgatoire ou moyens faciles pour les aider* (Lille: 1640), with many later editions and translations in many languages. For "compassion" toward the poor souls, see as an example Lorenzo de S. Francisco, *Tesoro Celestial y Divino* . . . (Sevilla: 1650), pars 3, ch. 4, 504–515; Juan Francisco Bullon, *Consuelo de las Almas del Purgatorio* . . . (Zaragoca: 1683). On the practice of personal meditation on purgatory and its pains, see, for example, Felice Fossa, *Juravium Animarium in Purgatorio* . . . *Das ist: Helffenburg* (Salzburg: 1718), 14–29.

105. Suter, *Underirdische Goldgrub*, 81–87; Johann Hofer SJ, *Nützliche Geschichte und Annehmliche Exempel der Thieren zur Unterrichtung der Menschen* (Ingolstadt: 1739); idem, *Magisterium Divinae Sapientiae per bruta hominem erudientis ad justitiam* (Trent: 1735). See also Procopius, *Funerale*, 44–52.

106. On the change of perception of the afterlife, see Diethard Sawicki, *Leben mit den Toten. Geisterglauben und die Entstehung des Spiritismus in Deutschland 1770-1900* (Paderborn: Schöningh, 2nd ed., 2016), 42; Bernhard Lang and Colleen McDannell, *Der Himmel. Eine Kulturgeschichte des ewigen Lebens* (Frankfurt: Insel, 1990), 242–245. In theology handbooks of the time one will find a discussion of this in treatises "de beatitudine," e.g., Wilhelm Herincx, *Summa Theologicae Scholasticae et Moralis, Pars Secunda* (Antwerp: 1640), tractatus 1 "De ultimo fine seu beatitudine hominis et miseriis," 3–61, here at 21: "Sic indubie Beati de iisdem etiam bonis habebunt gadium multiplex ex amore Dei proveniens, sed velut accidentale, prout ipsa bona, ex quibus hauritur, sund beatitudini accidentialia." Pelbarto de Themesvar OFM, *Stellarium Coronae Gloriosissimae Virginis* (Venice: 1686), lib. 10 (de assumptione beatae Mariae), 185: "Unde immensa dilectio beatorum & multiplex, quam inter se habent mutuo multiplicat inter eos, quasi in infinitu numerum gaudiorum," and "diligi se cognoscunt." On the joys of sight in Heaven, see Robert Bellarmine, *De Aeterna Felicitate Sanctorum* (Antwerp: 1616), lib. 4, ch. 5, 195: "Quid igitur erit videre sanctum Stephanum."

107. On the cognitive powers of the *anima*, see, for example, Domingo Bañez, *Scholastica commentaria in primam partem Angelici Doctoris S. Thomae, vol. 2* (Douai: 1614), q. 89, 419–436.

108. Prokop von Templin, *Sanctorale* . . . *Discurs oder Predigen*, vol. 2 (Salzburg: 1668), vol. 2, 573 ("De Beatitudine Corporum & Quinque Sensuum in coelo").

109. Templin, *Lignum*, vol. 2, 465. On the fate of dead children, see Pistorius, *Allgemeines Klaghauß*, 2–10.

110. Veranus, *De Humanis*, vol. 1, 355. Council of Trent, Session 6, ch. 10, DH 1535.

111. Veranus, *De Humanis*, vol. 1, 434f.

112. Michael a S. Catharina, *Trinum Perfectum*, vol. 2, par. 933, 366; par. 941, 369; par. 960, 376f. Veranus, *De Humanis*, vol. 1, 389–403, 441f, 444. On the beauty of the human body, see Andre du Laurens, *Historia Anatomica* (Paris: 1600), ch. 2, 2.

113. Michael a S. Catharina, *Trinum Perfectum*, vol. 2, par. 966, 378: "Monent tamen auctores vitandum esse scandalum; ideoque indecens esse Clericos, & Religiosos his uti, tum erga foeminas etiam sanguine conjunctas, tum erga pueros valde formosos. Osculari infantium carnes ex amore infantiis aetatis non est peccatum. Coeterum si haec fiant carnalis delectationis causa, erunt communiter mortale peccatum; quia jam sunt venerea, & ad luxuriam immediate, & per se notabiliter provocantia. Nu. 28. Tangere etiam foeminarum pudenda ex causa honesta, & necessaria non est illicitum, ut patet in Chirurgo medente; recta enim ratio permittit, quod omnes corporis partes, si infirmae sint curari possint." See also Paulus Hieronymus a S. Helena OCD, *Sacrae Theologiae Moralis Medulla Recens ad Mentem Salmanticensium* (Bologna: 2nd ed., 1753), cap. 1, 10; cf. *Cursus Theologiae Moralis Salmanticensis*, vol. 5 (Venice: 1778), cap. III, pt. 3, 109, which points out how easily kisses and embraces can cause scandal: "Tum erga pueros, maxime decoros, quia ex similibus osculis [kiss of peace] frequenter scandalum orit." Lessius asks whether kisses, hugs, etc., could be mortal sins, but insists: "non enim decet viros Ecclesiasticos, maxime Religiosos, hoc modo testari amicitiam erga foeminas; etiamsi aliqo modo sanguine iunctae essent; vel pueros, ex quibus aliquid periculi vel scandali nasci posset." Leonhard Lessius, *De Iustitia Aliisque Virtutibus* (Lyon: 1630), dub. 8, num. 56, 628. On the "male virtue," see Veranus, *De Humanis*, vol. 1, 500: "Castitas est virtus mascula, quae in arena fortiter pugnat, & sibi insultantes heroice expugnat." Cf. also ibid., 530f.

114. Neudecker, *Schola*, vol. 2, 164ff.

115. McKnight, *The Mystic of Tunja*, 162; cf. Brian Larkin, *The Very Nature of God. Baroque Catholicism and Religious Reform in Bourbon Mexico City* (Albuquerque: University of New Mexico Press, 2010), 28–51.

116. Michael a S. Catharina, *Trinum Perfectum*, vol. 2, par. 964, 377: "Hinc unguentis & suavibus odoribus respiratione attractis redit quasi anima, id est, halitus vitalis antea laguidus, prostratus & emoriens." Cf. Steven E. Turley, *Franciscan Spirituality and Mission in New Spain, 1524–1599* (Aldershot: Ashgate, 2014), 299.

117. Jodi Campbell, *At the First Table. Food and Social Identity in Early Modern Spain* (Lincoln, NE: 2017), 71–78, 95.

118. Andrew Drenas, *The Standard Bearer of the Roman Church. Lawrence of Brindisi & Capuchin Missions in the Holy Roman Empire, 1599–1613* (Washington: Catholic University of America Press, 2018), 119–120, wording of the quotation changed by me. Cf. also for example, Franciscus Agricola, *Biblischer Fastenspiegel. Das ist grundtlicher unnd dieser Zeit nötiger bericht was das recht . . . fasten sey . . .* (Cologne: 1589).

119. Francesco Cardinal Brancraccio, *De chocolatis potu diatribe* (Rome: 1664); Beth Marie Forrest and April L. Najjaj, "Is Sipping Sin Breaking Fast? The Catholic Chocolate Controversy and the Changing World of Early Modern Spain," *Food and Foodways* 15 (2007): 31–52.

120. Asuncion Lavrin, "The Role of Nunneries in the Economy of New Spain in the Eighteenth Century," *American Historical Review* 46 (1966): 371–393, at 382; cf. Nicephorus Sebastus, *De Chocolatis potione* (Naples: 1665; 1671).

121. Neudecker, *Schola*, vol. 2, 136; 140: "Mortificatio . . . rationabilis est"; see 147–168 on external mortification. On the duty to preserve one's body, see John da Sylveira O.Carm., *Opuscula Varia* (Lyon: 1687), "Vita conservanda," 413ff; Blois, *Spiritual Works*, 255–260. Cf. Tessa Storey, "English and Italian Health Advice: Protestant and Catholic Bodies," in Sandra Cavallo et al. (eds.), *Conserving Health in Early Modern Culture* (Manchester: Manchester University Press, 2017), 210–234, at 220. On the rejection of mortification by enlightened Benedictines, see Lehner, *Enlightened Monks*.

122. See Anne Jacobson Schutte, *Aspiring Saints. Pretense of Holiness, Inquisition, and Gender in the Republic of Venice, 1618–1750* (Baltimore: Johns Hopkins University Press, 2003); Nora Jaffary, *False Mystics. Deviant Orthodoxy in Colonial Mexico* (Lincoln: University of Nebraska Press, 2008); Álvaro Castro Sánchez, *Franciscanos, místicos, herejes y alumbrados* (Córdoba: Servicio de Publicaciones, Universidad de Córdoba, 2010); Lehner, Enlightened Monks; idem, On the Road to Vatican II.

# Chapter 9

1. Adalbert Deckert, *Karmel in Straubing. 1368–1968* (Rome: Institutum Carmelitanum, 1968). For oval churches as innovation, see Sylvie Duvernoy, "Baroque Oval Churches: Innovative Geometrical Patters in Early Modern Sacred Architecture," *Nexus Network Journal* 17 (2015): 425–456, and especially Bruno Adorni, *Jacopo Barozzi da Vignola* (Milan: Skira, 2008). For the imagery of drapery, although not always agreeing with my interpretation, see Andrea Sigel, *Der Vorhang der Sixtinischen Madonna. Herkunft und Motiv eines Motivs der Marienikonographie* (Zurich: Juris, 1977); Johann Konrad Eberlein, *Apparitio regis—revelatio veritatis. Studien zur Darstellung des Vorhangs in der bildenden Kunst von der Spätantike bis zum Ende des Mittelalters* (Frankfurt: Gerbrun, 1992).

2. At Mario Praz, *Studies in Seventeenth Century Imagery*, vol. 1 (London: Arburg Institute, 1939), 16; cf. Peter Daly, *The Emblem in Early Modern Europe. Contributions to the Theory of the Emblem* (Aldershot: Ashgate, 2014).

3. Praz, *Studies*, 17f. Anja Hoffmann, *Sakrale Emblematik in St. Michael in Bamberg. Lavabo hortum meum . . .* (Wiesbaden: Harrassowitz, 2001).

4. Michael a S. Catharina, *Trinum Perfectum*, vol. 3, par. 994–1022, 357–367; cf. *Acta Ecclesiae Mediolanensis*, vol. 1 (Lyon: 1682), Pars IV, 404: "Ut signo campanae dato, quo ad Missae Sacrum vocatur, paulisper se colligens, mortalis peccati conscius, dolore ex eo affectus, propositio illius confitendi suscepto supplex a Deo veniam petat." Cf. "De Campanarum Ministro," in Andrea Piscara Castaldo, *Praxis Caeremoniarum seu Sacrorum Romanae Ecclesiae Rituum Accurata Tractatio* (Sulzbach: 1715), 31–35. On the use and practice of bells in a monastery, see the rules of the Discalced Trinitarians, but this could be easily found also in ritual or

ceremony books of other religious orders, see *Reformatorium Fratrum Ordinis Sanctissimae ac Individuae Trinitatis Redemptionis Captivorum Aragonica Provinciae* (Barcelona: 1563), 109–110, or the Discalced Augustinians, *Liber Caeremoniarum Fratrum Discalceatorum Ordinis Eremitarum S. Patris Augustini Galliarum* (Lyon: 1642), cap. 26: "De diversis campanae signis," 77–83.

5. Nicolas Remy, *Daemonolatreia Libri Tres* (Cologne: 1596), lib. 1, c. 26.

6. At Alexander J. Fisher, *Music, Piety, and Propaganda. The Soundscapes of Counter-Reformation Bavaria* (Oxford: Oxford University Press, 2014), 160.

7. Henry Kamen, *The Phoenix and the Flame. Catalonia and the Counter-Reformation* (New Haven: Yale University Press, 1993), 29; Allyson M. Poska, *Regulating the People. The Catholic Reformation in Seventeenth-Century Spain* (Leiden and Boston: Brill, 1998), 32f; Antonio Peñafiel Ramón, *Mentalidad y religiosidad popular murciana en la primera mitad del siglo XVIII* (Murcia: Universidad de Murcia, 1988), 128–129; cf. John H. Arnold and Caroline Goodson, "Resounding Community: The History and Meaning of Medieval Church Bells," *Viator* 43 (2012): 99–130; Duhamelle, *Grenze,*130–133.

8. See Remi Chiu, "Singing on the Street and in the Home in Times of Pestilence. Lessons from the 1576–78 Plague of Milan," in Maya Corry et al. (eds.), *Domestic Devotion in Early Modern Italy* (Leiden and Boston: Brill, 2019), 27–44; cf. David Freedberg, *The Power of Images. Studies in the History and Theory of Response* (Chicago: University of Chicago Press, 1989), 161–191; Kathryn Rudy, "A Guide to Mental Pilgrimage: Paris, Bibliothèque de L'Arsenal Ms. 212," *Zeitschrift für Kunstgeschichte* 63 (2000): 494–515. Carlo Borromeo, "De Cura Pestilentiae," in *Constitutiones et Decreta on provincialia Synodo Mediolanensi Quinta* (Milan: 1580), 159: "libros in singulas familias introducendos." Chiu, "Singing," misses this important instruction completely.

9. *Geistlicher Paradeis-Vogel der Catholischen Deutschen* (Neuss: 1687; 1st ed.,1663).

10. *Geistlicher Paradeis-Vogel,* 420ff, prints a song that gives a moral lesson for each hour of the day, and at 428 a song against the Turks. Cf. Fisher, *Music,* 18. On the concepts of soundscape and sensory profiles, see Ari Kelman, "Rethinking the Soundscape: A Critical Genealogy of a Key Term in Sound Studies," *Senses and Society* 5 (2010): 212–224; cf. Bruce R. Smith, *The Acoustic World of Early Modern England. Attending to the O-Factor* (Chicago: University of Chicago Press, 1999); Fisher, *Music,* 141–146. Dietz-Rüdiger Moser, *Verkündigung durch Volksgesang. Studien zur Liedpropaganda und -katechese der Gegenreformation* (Berlin: E. Schmidt, 1981).

11. Anonymous, *Geistlicher Paradeis-Vogel,* 385–415. Songs that focused entirely on sin and how to avoid it, made up only a small part of these song books; see Anonymous, *Catholisches Gesang-Buch zum Gebrauch des Bisthums Strasburg,* 299–306, 316–327; also, on death, see 369–388; on hell 403f; and on Heaven 413f. A similar distribution in Anonymous, *Lob-Klingende Harffe des Neuen Testaments* (Königgrätz: 1730); Anonymous, *Catholische Kirchengesänge* (Mainz: 1631).

12. Anonymous, *Heil-und Hülfsmittel,* 21; Nicolaus Beuttner, *Catholisches Gesangs-Buch* (Graz: 1718), 77, 217f; Anonymous, *Catholisches Gesang-Buch zum Gebrauch des Bisthums Strasburg,* 192–209 (on love).

—

13. Georg Kauffmann SJ, *Catholisch ist gut sterben. Aus der merkürdigen Bekehrung etlicher Gefangenen zu Neustadt an der Haard . . .* (Cologne: 1739), 9. Archiv der Evangelischen Landeskirche Rheinland-Pfalz: Taufbuch Haardt, Abschrift, 616.

14. Kauffmann, *Catholisch ist gut sterben*, 55. Cf. the new edition by Nicolaus Weislinger, *Catholisch ist gut sterben* (Strassburg: 1744).

15. Kauffmann SJ, *Catholisch ist gut sterben*, 70; 72. Archiv des Bistums Speyer: Pfarrarchiv Neustadt, Begräbnisbuch 1732; Weislinger, *Catholisch ist gut sterben*, 112f.

16. For the text, see, for example, *Alte und newe christlich-katholische Gesäng auf Sonn- u. Festtäg des Jahrs* (Würzburg: 1649), 93ff, or *Catholisches Gesang-Buch zum Gebrauch des Bistums Strasburg* (Strasburg: 1752), 71f.

17. Anonymous, *Heil-und Hülfsmittel zum thätigen Christentum* (Brix/Dresden: 1767), 404.

18. Zwyssig, *Täler voller Wunder. Eine katholische Verflechtungsgeschichte der Drei Bünde und des Veltlins (17. und 18. Jahrhundert)* (Affalterbach: Didymos, 2018), 324; Kim Siebenhüner, "Things That Matter. Zur Geschichte der materiellen Kultur in der Frühneuzeitforschung," *Zeitschrift für Historische Forschung* 42 (2015): 373–409; cf. Caroline Bynum, *Christian Materiality. An Essay on Religion in Late Medieval Europe* (New York: Zone, 2011); Philippa Woodcock, "The French Counter-Reformation: Patrons, Regional Styles, and Rural Art," *Church History and Religious Culture* 94 (2014): 22–49.

19. As an example for such a catechism class, see Sebastian Heinrich Penzinger, *Gute Ordnung darauf Kinder-Lehr . . .* (Vienna: 1696), 30–35. For the use of the *Agnus Dei* in Mexico, see, for example, Luys de Cisneros, *Historia de el Principio, y Origen, Progressos, Venidas á México, y Milagros de la Santa Ymagen de Nuestra Señor de los Remedios, Extramuros de México* (Blanco de Alcaçar: México, 1621), 66, 115. For the use in the African Congo, see Michelangelo Guattini, *Viaggio nel regno del Congo* (Venice: 1679), 40ff.

20. Thiessen, *Kapuziner*, 438–445; Caroline B. Brettell, "The Priest and His People. The Contractual Basis for Religious Basis in Rural Portugal," in Ellen Badone (ed.), *Religious Orthodoxy and Popular Faith in European Society* (Princeton: Princeton University Press, 1990), 55–75; Marc R. Forster, *The Counter-Reformation in the Villages. Religion and Reform in the Bishopric of Speyer, 1560–1720* (Ithaca: Cornell University Press, 1992), 55f.

21. Amsler, *Jesuits and Matriarchs*, 87–98; Aislinn Muller, "The *agnus dei*, Catholic Devotion, and Confessional Politics in Early Modern England," *British Catholic History* 34 (2018): 1–28; Suzanna Ivanič, *Cosmos and Materiality in Early Modern Prague* (Oxford: Oxford University Press, 2021), 47–73.

22. Francesco Caccia, *Innocentia Apostolica. Die Apostolische Unschuld* (Neuss: 1696), xc, xci, 176; many more examples in Antoine d'Averoult, *Flores exemplorum sive Catechismus historialis*, 3 vols. (Douai: 1616).

23. Augustinus Castani, *De Maxima Supernaturali Agnus Dei Virtute Theologica Dissertatio* (Verona: 1669), 4; Vincenco Bonardo, *Discorso intorno all' origine Antichita, et Virtu de gli Agnus Dei di cera Benedetti* (Rome: 1586).

24. Ubald Stoiber, *Armamentarium Ecclesiasticum complectens Arma spiritualia, fortissima ad insultus diabolicos elidendo . . .*, vol. 1 (Augsburg: 1736), 256: "Sicut ergo diabolus horret & fugit Agnum illum immaculatum, ceu victorem & triumphatorem suum." In 1753 Stoiber's book came onto the Index of Forbidden Books. Cf. Pedro Pinamonti, *Exorcista rite Edoctus. Omne Maleficorum genus probe, ac prudenter curandi* (Venice: 1712), 72.

25. Castani, *De Maxima*, 24ff. Andreas Strobl, *Aufgemachter Schlüssel zu dem Geistlichen Karten-Spiehl . . .* (Augsburg: 1708), 62ff.

26. Irena Galandra Cooper, "Investigating the 'Case' of the Agnus Dei in Sixteenth-Century Italian Homes," in Corry et al. (eds.), *Domestic Devotions in Early Modern Italy*, 220–243, at 227.

27. Cf. Cooper, "Investigating," 337; Castani, *De Maxima*, 28; Wolff, *Rugitus*, 408; Frederick J. McGinness, *Right Thinking and Sacred Oratory in Counter-Reformation Rome* (Princeton: Princeton University Press, 1995), 87–107.

28. On various uses of material objects in Christianity during the early modern era, see the excellent volume Suzanna Ivanič, and Mary Laven (eds.), *Religious Materiality in the Early Modern World* (Amsterdam: Amsterdam University Press, 2020).

29. See, for example, Ivanič, *Cosmos*, 58–60, 200–202.

30. Christoph Ulrich Neuburger, *Conciones Rurales. Oder: Gantze doch kurtze Predigen*, vol. 1 (Salzburg: 1661), 76.

31. Anonymous, *Religionsklagen gegen Herrn Peter Trunk* (s.l.: 1779). On the question of magic and popular belief, see Kaspar von Greyerz, *Religion and Culture in Early Modern Europe, 1500–1800* (Oxford: Oxford University Press, 2008); Rainer Decker, *Witchcraft and the Papacy. Trans. Erik Midelfort* (Charlottesville: University of Virginia Press, 2010); Lehner, *Catholic Enlightenment*.

32. *Kleines Magazin für Katholische Religionslehrer* 3 (1803): 125; Marchese, *Pane quotidiano*, vol. 4, 160–165.

33. Freedberg, *The Power of Images*, xii, 7–9, 48.

34. Freedberg, *The Power of Images*, 160–164.

35. Denis Amelote, *La vie de soeur Marguerite du S. Sacrement, religieuse Carmelite du monastere de Beaune. Composee par un prestre de la Congregation de l'Oratoire de Nostre Seigneur Iesus-Christ, docteur en theologie* (Paris: 1654), 251–256. Jesus supposedly told her in 1632: "I want to reveal through you the miracles of my childhood"(Amelote, *La vie de soeur Marguerite*, 257).

36. Amelote, *La vie de soeur Marguerite*, 263–270.

37. F. Hartmann, *Wissenschaft der Heiligen. Das ist Betrachtungen von der Kindheit . . . Jesu Christi*, vol. 1 (Kempten: 1787), 654–690; cf. *La Devotion a la Sainte Enfance de Jesus* (Paris: 1733); Denis Amelote, *Le Petit Office du S. Enfant Jesus . . .* (Paris: 1668).

38. Anonymous, *Die Kindheit Christi Jesu in dem innerlichen Gebet verehret . . . nach Regel des H. Patriarchen Benedicti* (Augsburg and Innsbruck: 1764), 32f, 400. Cf. also Anonymous, *Haus-Genossenschaft des Heiligen Kind Jesu, seiner h. Mutter und des Heiligen Joseph . . .* (Vienna: 1723); Anonymous, *Die Kindheit Christi Jesu in dem innerlichen Gebet verehret* (Augsburg and Innsbruck: 1764); Rupert a St. Bennone, *Sprach der Kinder Gottes. Das ist Grund-Regeln des beschaulich und würkenden Lebens . . .* (Munich: 1744).

39. Anonymous, *Verehrung des göttlichen Kindlein Jesu oder besondere Andacht zu Nutz und Trost denen in das Pragerische Kindlein verliebten Seelen* (Bamberg: 1761). Bail, *La théologie affective*, vol. 4 (Paris: 1671), tract. 2, med. VII, 609f: "Leur cinquième ressemblance est en une tendre dévotion pour l'enfance sacrée de Jésus-Christ: cette dévotion es toit mêlée de crainte & d'amour, d'adoration & d'affection très sincère & très cordiale; tantôts ils l'adoraient par respect après une très haute contemplation, dans la vue de sa Divinité." Ibid., 612: "Combien plus se pourra t'il dire, que dans le ciel le cœur de Marie & de Joseph, & je l'ose encore dire, de Jésus, trois cœurs très purs & très sincères, ne sont, qu'un seul cœur, si bien que quiconque a gagne le cœur de Marie, ou de Joseph, ou de Jésus, possède trois cœurs tout a la fois, qui conspirent d'une semblable ardeur a son bien & a son avantage."

40. Galliffet, *De Cultu*, 1–48; at 103: "Christus Jesus immensam Patris in homines charitatem exprimere volens . . . Nihil majus, nihil divinius dici potuit." Anton Ginther, *Speculum Amoris & Doloris in Sacratissimo ac divinissimo Corde Jesu . . .* (Augsburg: 1706), 1–8, 122.

41. Francesco Pona, *Cardiomorpheoseos sive ex corde desumpta emblemata sacra* (Verona: 1645), 4: "Creavit igitur, ut amaret, utque amaretur; fons enim, & origo amoris, imo amor est." Cf. also Praz, *Studies*, vol. 1, 139ff.

42. Benedict Haeften, *Schola Cordis sive Aversi a Deo Cordis ad eumdem Reductio, et Instructio* (Antwerp: 1635), 1: "Gymnasium cordis aperimus"; 67: "Quae enim est haec mulier pulchra, nisi quaelibet anima ad pulcherrimam Dei imaginem & similitudinem"; 151: "Solam Sanctissimam Trinitatem triangulare Cor replere, & inhabitare."

43. Haeften, *Schola Cordis*, 369ff, 477–488.

44. See also Mostaccio, "Shaping."

45. Friedrich Polleross, "Architektur und Panegyrik. Eine Allegorie der Jesuiten zur Geburt von Erzherzog Leopold Joseph 1682," in Martin Engel (ed.), *Barock in Mitteleuropa. Werke, Phänomene, Analysen* (Vienna: Böhlau, 2007), 375–391. On the theology of emblems, see Henri Engelgrave, *Lux Evangelica sub Velum Emblematum*, 2 vols. (Antwerp: 1648).

46. Hermann Hugo, *Pia Desideria* (Antwerp: 1624), many editions and translations, including idem, *Pia Desideria or Divine Addresses* (London: 3rd ed., 1702); cf. Praz, *Studies*, 131; Gabriel Rödter, *Via piae animae. Grundlagenuntersuchung zur emblematischen Verknüpfung von Bild und Wort in den Pia desideria des Hermman Hugo SJ* (Frankfurt et al.: Peter Lang, 1992).

47. Jan David, *Veridicus Christianus. Editio Altera* (Antwerp: 1606); Walter S. Melion, "Coemeterium Schola. The Emblematic Imagery of Death in Jan David's Veridicus Christianus," in idem et al. (eds.), *Quid est Sacramentum? Visual Representation of Sacred Mysteries in Early Modern Europe, 1400–1700* (Leiden and Boston: Brill, 2020), 533–579. For an excellent in-depth analysis of emblematic meditation books, in particular of Jan David's, see Anne-Katrin Sors, *Allegorische Andachtsbücher in Antwerpen. Jan Davids Texte und Theodor Galles Illustrationen in den jesuitischen Buchprojekten der Plantiniana* (Göttingen: Universitätsverlag Göttingen, 2015).

48. Alexandra Walsham, *Catholic Reformation in Protestant Britain* (London: Routledge, 2016), 216; Trevor Johnson, "Guardian Angels and the Society of Jesus," in Peter Marshall and Alexandra Walsham (eds.), *Angels in the Early Modern World*

(Cambridge: Cambridge University Press, 2006), 191–213. See especially *Acta Sanctorum*, ed. Johannes Stiltingh et al., vol. 8 (Antwerp: 1762), 4–123 on St. Michael and "all the angels"; and for the feast of the guardian angel, see Giovanni Cavalieri, *Opera omnia Liturgica seu Commentaria in . . . Sacra Rituum Congregationis Decreta . . .*, vol. 1 (Venice: 1758), ch. 29, 119–123. The mistake of not distinguishing between the hierarchy of liturgical feasts is made by Josephine von Henneberg, "Saint Francesca Romana and Guardian Angels in Baroque Art," *Religion and the Arts* 2 (1998): 467–487.

49. Francisco Suarez, *De Angelis. Opera Omnia*, vol. 2 (Paris: 1856), lib. 7, ch. 4, par. 7–12, 810b–812b; cf. Bernd Roling, "Ein Anfang ohne Umkehr. Der Sündenfall und die Unmöglichkeit der Reue zwischen Mittelalter und Neuzeit," *Frühmittelalterliche Studien* 48 (2014): 389–412.

50. Francesco Albertini, *Trattato dell'Angelo Custode* (Rome and Naples: 1612); cf. Johnson, "Guardian Angels."

51. Walsham, *Catholic Reformation*, 225–231; Tricoire, *Mit Gott rechnen*, 54ff.

52. Maria Tausiet, "Patronage of Angels and Combat of Demons: Good versus Evil in Seventeenth-Century Spain," in Marshall and Walsham (eds.), *Angels*, 233–256, at 234. Francisco Blasco Lanuza, *Patrocinio de angeles y combate de demonios* (San Juan de la Pena, 1652).

53. Wilhelm Ganspeckh OESA, *Englischer Magnet-Stein, Das ist: Englisches Leß- und Bett-Buch*, vol. 1 (Munich: 1738), vol. 1, passim.

54. Jeremias Drexel, *Gymnasium Patientiae* (Munich: 1631); idem, *Palaestra Christiana* (Munich: 1648).

55. Tausiet, "Patronage," 244; see also Bellarmine, *De Ascensione*, gradus IX ("ex consideratione angelorum"), 186–208.

56. Jeremias Drexel, *Opera Omnia . . . In das Hochdeutsche versetzt*, vol. 1 (Würzburg: 1662), 334–455; idem, *Heliotropium seu conformatio humanae voluntatis cum divina* (Douai: 1621), title copperlate. Cf. Henneberg, "Saint Francesca Romana"; Johnson, "Guardian Angels." Cf.

57. Ganspeckh, *Englischer*, vol. 1, 26. Cf. also Henri Boudon, *Devotion to the Nine Choirs of Holy Angels . . . trans. Edward H. Thompson* (London: 1869), 20f.

58. Most theologians at the time agreed that the belief in a guardian angel could not be rejected without temerity, but that it was no dogma, see Cresoli, *Mystagogus*, 660–672. The Franciscan Clemens Brancasius, *De Angelis* (Naples: 1656), 463–474, gives a good overview of early modern Catholic opinions on guardian angels. On angels as protectors of the unbaptized, see Burchard a S. Matthaeo OCD, *Fida Angelorum Custodia sive Tractatus brevis & curiosus de Angelis Sanctis Homonum Custodibus . . .* (Munich: 1690), 5f, and 46–49 on purgatory.

59. Emmanuel Navarro OSB, *Prolegomena de Angelis in quibus Disseritur de Cognitione Spirituum, quam habuerunt Philosophis Ethnicis* (Salamanca: 1708).

60. Malte Goga, *Engel-Bilder. Die Sichtbarkeit von Engelfiguren in Italienischer Malerei um 1600* (Munich: Fink, 2015), 11f; Sally A. Struthers, *Donatelli's Putti. Their Genesis, Importance, and Influence on Quattrocento Sculpture and Painting* (PhD Thesis: Columbus, Ohio State University, 1992); Charles Dempsey, *Inventing the Renaissance Putto* (Chapel Hill: University of North Carolina Press, 2001).

61. Fernando Cervantes, "Angels Conquering and Conquered: Changing Perceptions in Spanish America," in Marshall and Walsham (eds.), *Angels*, 104–133; cf. Bernardino de Sahagún, *Psalmodia Christiana*, trans. from the original Nahuatl by A. Anderson (Salt Lake City: University of Utah Press, 1993).

62. Erika Langmuir, *Imagining Childhood* (New Haven and London: Yale University Press, 2006); cf. Jeannie Labno, *Commemorating the Polish Renaissance Child. Funeral Monuments and Their European Context* (London: Routledge, 2016), 170.

63. Sauerländer, *Der katholische Rubens*, 35–43.

64. George Tavard, *Die Engel. Handbuch der Dogmengeschichte*, vol. 2/2b (Freiburg: Herder, 1968), 76.

65. Brancasio de Caravinea, *De Angelis* (Naples: 1646), 566–576; Hieronymus Columbi, *De Angelica et Humana Hierarchia* (Lyon: 1647), lib 2, ch. 54, 145.

66. Tausiet, "Patronage, 249f.

67. Cf. Delumeau, *Catholicism*, 170–175.

68. For the belief that saints curse or are demigods, see the sixteenth-century work of Remy, *Daemonolatreia*, lib. 3, c. 1, 295: "Eodem mentis error nos nunc Divos morborum authores facere"; and 297: ". . . quod est etiam non minori impietate coniunctum, quasi cordi ijs esset humana sic incendiis, caedibus, ac ruinis dum odia sua explent permiscere, ac labefactere."

69. Anonymous, *S. Michael der höchste Seraphin über die himmlische Geister* (Munich: 1699); Andres Serrano, *Feliz Memoria de los Siete Principes de los Angeles Assistentes . . .* (Mexico: 1699); Carlos Sommervogel, *Bibliotheque de Compagnie de Jesus*, vol. 7 (Brussels and Paris: 1896), 1150; Benedict XIV, *Dissertationes de Canonizatione Sanctorum*, vol. 1 (Venice: 1751), dissertatio 35: "De cultu Sanctorum veteris Testamenti & Angelorum," 501–511, at 507.

70. Ramón Mujica Pinilla, *Ángeles apócrifos en la América virreinal* (México: Fondo de Cultura Económica, 1996); idem, "Angels and Demons in the Conquest of Peru," in Fernando Cervantes and Andrew Redden (eds.), *Angels, Demons and the New World* (Cambridge: Cambridge University Press, 2013), 171–211.

71. Templin, *Sanctorale*, vol. 2, 1026; for Suarez, see Bernd Roling, *Locutio Angelica. Die Diskussion der Engelsprache als Antizipation einer Sprechakttheorie in Mittelalter und Früher Neuzeit* (Leiden and Boston: Brill, 2008), 347–388; on Scotus's angelology, see Tobias Hoffmann, "Duns Scotus's Action Theory in the Context of His Angelology," *Archa Verbi. Subsidia* 5 (2010): 403–420.

72. Bergin, *Church, Society*, 334; Sommervogel, *Bibliotheque*, vol. 2 (Brussels and Paris: 1891), 1447–1465. Jacques Coret, *L'Ange Gardien Protecteur . . .* (Caen: 1662), completely revised under the title *L'Ange Conducteur, Contenant Les Prières Du Matin & Du Soir; Prières Pendant La Sainte Messe* (Paris: 1681); Dutch translation (1711), German translation (1740).

73. Ganspeckh, *Englischer*, vol. 1, 308; Henri Boudon, *Andacht zu den Neun Chören der Englen* (Augsburg: 1687), 313.

74. Benedikt Maria Werkmeister, *Ueber den neuen katholischen Katechismus* (Frankfurt: 1789), 89f; Heinrich Braun, *Deutsches Brevier für Stiftsdamen*, vol. 4 (Augsburg: 1792), 11f; Ferdinand Sterzinger, *Geister-und Zauberkatechismus* (Munich: 1783), 8f, 61.

# Chapter 10

1. Michael a S. Catharina, *Christlicher Seelenspiegel*, 2 vols. (Augsburg: 1731), vol. 2, 459f; idem, *Trinum Perfectum*, vol. 3, par. 922, 332: "nullum servorum Deiparae Virginis degere apud inferos!"; see also 926f., 333; cf. Adrian van Lyere, *Trisagion Marianum* (Antwerp: 1648); on the veneration of Mary as a sign of predilection, see Julius Caesar Recupito SJ, *De signis Praedestinationis et Reprobationis et de Numero Praedestinatorum ac Reproborum* (Lyon: 1643), ch. 13, 420–516.

2. Damien Tricoire, "What Was the Catholic Reformation? Marian Piety and the Universalization of Divine Love," *Catholic Historical Review* 103 (2017): 20–49.

3. An excellent overview of Marian piety is provided by Bernhard Jahn and Claudia Schindler (eds.), *Maria in den Konfessionen und Medien der Frühen Neuzeit* (Berlin: DeGruyter, 2020). Unsurpassed as a research tool for Marian piety is Remigius Bäumer and Leo Scheffczyk (eds.), *Marienlexikon*, 6 vols. (St. Ottilien: EOS Verlag, 1989–1994).

4. An early Spanish example where the full text is already present is Antonio de Nebrija, *Aurea hymnorum expositorum* (Granada: 1534). Cf. also Bona, *Opera Omnia*, 483.

5. Petrus Canisius, *Commentariorum de Verbi Dei Corruptelis* . . . (Paris: 1584), lib. 3, ch. 3, 349ff. On the conversion of Lutherans through the Ave Maria, see Tommaso Auriemma, *Affetti scambievoli tra la Vergine santissima, e i suoi divoti. Dimostrati da questi con ossequij, da Maria con gratie, e favori singolari, in particolare nelle sue sette feste*, vol. 1 (Venice: 1747), 44f. On England, see Lisa McClain, "Using What's at Hand. English Catholic Reinterpretations of the Rosary, 1559–1642," *Journal of Religious History* 27 (2003): 161–176; for an overview, see Nathan Mitchell, *The Mystery of the Rosary. Marian Devotion and the Reinvention of Catholicism* (New York: New York University Press, 2009); on medieval roots of the rosary, see Anne Winston-Allen, *Stories of the Rose. The Making of the Rosary in the Middle Ages* (University Park: University of Pennsylvania Press, 1997), 13–30; at 145 Winston-Allen notes widespread use of the petitionary part by the seventeenth century but does not provide any other information. An example for the use in France is Pierre Boulenger, *Institutionum Christianorum Libri Octo* (Paris: 1560), 78v–79v.

6. Qu Yi & 藝 曲, "Song Nianzhu Guicheng (Die Anweisung zur Rezitation des Rosenkranzes). Ein illustriertes christliches Buch aus China vom Anfang des 17. Jahrhunderts," *Monumenta Serica* 60 (2012): 195–290, at 211.

7. Criveller, *Preaching Christ*, 133.

8. *Magnum Bullarium Romanum*, ed. Angelo Cherubini, vol. 2 (Luxemburg: 1727), 305f.

9. Auriemma, *Affetti scambievoli*, vol. 1, 38: "Imaginiamoci ancor noi Maria Vergine presente, quando recitiamo la Salve."

10. Auriemma, *Affetti scambievoli*, vol. 1, 317: "imaginandi"; also 318f.

11. Auriemma, *Affetti scambievoli*, vol. 1, 262.

12. Auriemma, *Affetti scambievoli*, vol. 1, 115–139, 198–209.

13. Tommaso Auriemma, *Affetti scambievoli tra la Vergine santissima, e i suoi divoti. Dimostrati da questi con ossequij, da Maria con gratie, e favori singolari, in particolare*

*nelle sue sette feste*, 2 vols. (Bologna: 1657). Cited according to the edition idem, *Affetti Scambievoli tra la Vergine Santissima*, 2 vols. (Venice: 1747). Cf. Carlos Sommervogel, *Bibliotheque de la Compagnie de Jesus*, vol. 1 (Brussels and Paris: 1890), 662–665.

14. Auriemma, *Affetti scambievoli*, vol. 1, 69.

15. Auriemma, *Affetti scambievoli*, vol. 1, 78: "Ave desperantium spes opportuna, & auxilio destitutorum adjutrix potentissima Maria." Cf. Louis Blois, *Opera Quae Quidem Conscripsit Omnia* (Cologne: 1572), 672 ("Endologia ad Mariam IV").

16. Michael a S. Catharina, *Christlicher*, vol. 2, 459f; idem, *Trinum Perfectum*, vol. 3, par. 922, 332: "nullum servorum Deiparae Virginis degere apud inferos!"; also 926f., 333; cf. Adrian van Lyere, *Trisagion Marianum* (Antwerp: 1648); on the veneration of Mary as a sign of predilection, see Julius Caesar Recupito SJ, *De signis Praedestinationis et Reprobationis et de Numero Praedestinatorum ac Reproborum* (Lyon: 1643), ch. 13, 420–516; Francisco Mendoca, *Viridarium sacrae ac profanae eruditionis* (Lyon: 1632), passim, 40. Cf. François Poiré, *La triple couronne de la Bien-heureuse Vierge Mere de Dieu*, 2 vols. (Paris: 1630).

17. Michael a S. Catharina, *Trinum Perfectum*, vol. 3, par. 964, 346.

18. Alfonso Maria de'Liguori, *Le glorie di Maria. Opere Ascetiche*, vol. 6 (Rome: Redemptoristi, 1936).

19. Cf. Tricoire, "What was the Catholic Reformation?"; Karl A. E. Enenkel, "Energeia Fireworks: Jesuit Image Theory in Franciscus Neumayr's Rhetorical Manual (Idea Rhetoricae, 1748) and His Tragedies," in Wietse de Boer et al. (eds.), *Jesuit Image Theory* (Leiden and Boston: Brill, 2016), 146–188, at 170f. Sauerländer, *Der katholische Rubens*, 36. On trends toward more individualized veneration of saints, see Pamela Voekel, *Alone before God. The Religious Origins of Modernity in Mexico* (Durham: Duke University Press, 2002); Brian Larkin, "Confraternities and Community : The Decline of the Communal Quest for Salvation in Eighteenth-Century Mexico City," in Martin Nesvig (ed.), *Local Religion in Colonial Mexico* (Albuquerque : University of New Mexico, 2006), 189–213; Klieber, *Bruderschaften*.

20. Hart, "Kindness," 72.

21. Hart, "Kindness," 65–90, at 65f.

22. Auriemma, *Affetti scambievoli*, vol. 2, 69–77.

23. Auriemma, *Affetti scambievoli*, vol. 2, 78: "fossere penne."

24. Auriemma, *Affetti scambievoli*, vol. 2, 78: "mutazione de' costumi."

25. Cf. Jean J. Baiole, *Annales Congregationum Beatissimiae Virginis Mariae collecti ex annalibus Societatis Jesu* (Burdigalae: 1624); Joannes Nadasi, *Annales Mariani Societatis Jesu* (Rome: 1657); Kaspar Lechner, *Sodalis Parthenius* (Ingolstadt: 1621).

26. Petrus Paul Rosenberger, *Zodiacus Marianus. Marianische Lob-Reden . . . denen ernannten Bruderschaften eyfrigen Vorstehern . . .* (Augsburg: 1698); Joseph a Virgine, *Alphabethum Marianum oder Marianische Lob-und Ehren Predigen . . . auch denen Herren Vorstehern der Marianischen Bruderschafften zum Besten . . .* (Frankfurt and Nürnberg: 1716).

27. Templin, *Sanctorale*, 331.

28. Ferdinand Hueber, *Marianischer Himmel oder Astronomische Observation . . .* (Ingolstadt: 1746), 101; cf. 133.

29. Matthäus Vogel SJ, *Catholischer Catechismus oder gründliche Unterweisung*, vol. 2 (Strassburg: 1750), 22–34; Otto Casmann, *Trost und Fried und Frewde. Oder Innerliche und sehr trostreiche Ansprachung und Ermahnung . . . an alle Schwermütige/ Traurige/Bussfertige Christenhertzen* (s.l.: 1607), 17: "Du musst zwischen der Hoffnung und Furcht mitten hindurch gehen: aber allzeit mehr unnd starcker hoffen/ denn fürchten."

30. For standard discussions I refer here to two textbooks, namely Angelo Petricca a Sonnino, *Turris David . . . De Militante ac triumphante Ecclesia* (Rome: 1647), lib. 6, disp. 5, 229ff., and the widely popular polemical theology Vitus Pichler SJ, *Theologia polemica* (Venice: 1749), pars 2, art. 4, par. 3, 369: "spuriam hanc & stultum certitudinem, ac fraudulentiam praesumptionem."

31. Blois, *Spiritual Works*, 112.

32. Thomas a Virgine Maria, *Typus Mariae seu Discursus Morales, Praedicabiles ad Fidelium Animos in Deiparae Devotionem Instimulandos* (Cologne: 1687), 339: "hoc est, Maria ex parte sua per suam apud Filium intercessionem tam multum conabitur, & precabitur, ut omnibus illis qui illius Scapularis habitum pie gestaverint, sufficientem ad salutem consequendam procurabit gratiam, sic tamen ut ex parte nostra gravioribus peccatis salutem non impediamus. At nondum argumenti finis est: nam urgebat forte quis: Si ex parte nostra a peccatis mortalibus nos cavere debeamus, ut per S. Scapularis gestatiomem salvemur, quid nobis proderit Scapulare." Cf. Joachim a S. Maria OCD, *Mystica Anatomia A. Nomnis Deiparae Virginis Mariae* (Venice: 1690), 198.

33. Adrianus a S. Francisco, *S. Scapularis Partheno-Carmelitici . . . Excrusus Paraenetici . . .* (Frankfurt: 1685); Thomas a Virgine Maria, *Typus Mariae*, 341–364; Theophil Raynaud, *Opera Omnia. Marialia*, vol. 7 (Lyon: 1665), 249–300; David a Mauden, *Discursus Morales in Decem Decalogi Praecepta* (Bruxelles: 1627), in I. praec., disc. 76, 429ff; Heribert von Salurn OFMCap, *Concionum Pastoralium Pars Secunda* (Salzburg: 1699), 339–340.

34. Daniele a Virgine Maria, *S. Scapularis Beatissimae Virginis Mariae de Monte Carmeli. Origo, privilegia, & vera ac solida devotio* (Antwerp: 1673), 18; idem, *Speculum Carmelitanum sive historia Eliani ordinis . . .* (Antwerp: 1680), lib. 5, p. 3, 515–1585; lib. 6, p. 3, 588–652. Cf. Macarius Wengel, "Zur Frage der historischen Forschung über das Skapulier," *Münchener Theologische Zeitschrift* 2 (1951): 124; idem, "Zur Frage der Zeugnisse der Tradition des hl. Skapuliers," *Münchener Theologische Zeitschrift* 2 (1951): 251–262.

35. On the scapular use in Brazil, see Hugh Cagle, *Assembling the Tropics. Science and Medicine in Portugal's Empire, 1450–1700* (Cambridge: Cambridge University Press, 2018), 284ff. See also Cypriano a. S. Maria, *Thesaurus Carmelitarum sive Confraternitatis Sacri Scapularis excellentia* (Cologne: 1627); Paulus ab Omnibus Sanctis, *Clavis aurea Thesauri Partheno-Carmelitici . . .* (Vienna: 1669), 17–23; on the ancient roots of the scapular, see Andrew Jotischky, *The Carmelites and Antiquity. Mendicants and Their Past in the Middle Ages* (Oxford: Oxford University Press, 2002). On the theology of the image, see Christian Hecht, *Katholische Bildertheologie der frühen Neuzeit* (Berlin: Gebr. Mann, 2012), 58; Hugo, *Pia Desideria*, many editions

and translations, including idem, *Pia Desideria or Divine Addresses*; cf. Praz, *Studies*, vol. 1, 131.

36. Angelicus Maria Myller, *Peregrinus in Jerusalem. Fremdling zu Jerusalem* (Vienna and Nürnberg: 1735), 663f.

37. Cf. Johannes B. Lerchenfeldt, *Marianische Versamblung under einem himmelblauen Scapulier . . .* (Munich: 1696). Accursio Passaviensi, *Neuer Krieg von der unbefleckten Empfängnis Mariae, welche unter dem Kriegs-Fahn oder himmel-blauen Scapulier . . . verfochten wird* (Vienna: 1728); Anonymous, *Himmlische Liberey der andächtigen zur unbefleckten Empfägnus Mariae bestehend in dem himmelblauen Scapulier . . .* (Salzburg: 1720).

38. Francisco, *Scapularis Partheno-Carmelitici*, 20f; Fulgentio Petrello a Sigillo, *De Intercessione B. Deip. Mariae Virg, Qua salvari gravissimos Peccatores eidem devotos probatur . . .* (Rome: 1647), passim; Thomas a Virgine Maria, *Typus Mariae* 329ff; 336: "Ex his omnibus hanc iubet facere conclusionem: cum iuxta sacratissimae Virginis testimonium sacrum Scapulare sit salutis signum in quo quis moriens aeternum non patietur incendium: ergo sapienter atq. prudenter omnes S. Scapularis faciunt Sodales, qui eodem tamquam certo quodam adipiscendae salutis utuntur medio." See also Joachim a S. Maria OCD, *Mystica Anatomia*, 115, 116; Paulus ab Omnibus Sanctis, *Marianischer Gnaden-Schatz des Bergs Carmeli . . .* (Vienna: 1664)gives a chronological list of miracles.

39. Thomas a Virgine Maria, *Typus Mariae*, 43, 50, 52.

40. Joannes a S. Felice, *Triumphus Misericordiae, id est Sacrum SSS. Trinitatis Institutum Redemptio Captivorum* (Vienna: 1704), 95. The comparison with an ocean can be also found in Jacob Lobbetius Leodiensis SJ, *Conciones in Evangelia Feriarum Totius Quadragesimale* (Leodii: 1672), 151; Anonymous, *Entretiens Spirituels en Forme de Prieres . . .* (Paris: 1721), 451; Louise de la Valliere, *Reflexions sur la Misericorde de Dieu* (La Haye: 1681), 69, speaks of the "ocean of love." Bellarmine, *De Ascensione*, gradus XIV, 312–335.

41. Christian P. Ceroke, "The Scapular Devotion," in Juniper Carol (ed.), *Mariology*, vol. 3 (Post Falls: Mediatrix Press, 2nd ed., 2019), 131–146.

42. Archangelus a S. Georgio, *Heilige Wunder-Sprüch. Das ist: Ausser-Ordentliche Feyrtags-Predigten* (Augsburg: 1619), 153; Anonymous, *Leben des gottseeligen . . . Diener Gottes Dominici von Jesu-Maria, des Barfüsser Carmeliten-Ordens General . . .* (Munich: 1685).

43. Jean Iennyn, *Vera Confraternitas S. Trinitatis de Redemptione Captivorum . . .* (Bruge: 1649), 9–19; Joannes a S. Felice, *Triumphus Misericordiae*, 43–57; Bernardo de Vargas, *Chronica sacri et Militaris Ordinis B. Mariae de Mercede Redemptionis Captivorum* (Panormi: 1619), 9; Bartolomej Georgijević, *De Afflictione tam Captivorum quam etiam sub Turcae tributo viventium Christianorum* (Antwerp: 1544). Cf. Nancy Johnson Black, *The Frontier Mission and Social Transformation in Western Honduras. The Order of Our Lady of Mercy, 1525–1773* (Leiden: Brill, 1995).

44. On the spiritual idea of Jesus as a captive, see Johannes a S. Felice, *Triumphus Misericordiae*; Andrzej Witko, "The Trinitarian Iconography," *Folia Historica Cracoviensia* 13 (2007): 145–152; cf. idem, *Jesús Nazareno Rescatado sobre la*

*iconografía de la Orden de la Santísima Trinidad en los siglos XVII–XX* (Roma: Curia Generalizia dei Trinitari, 2004).

45. Cf. Ansgar Wucherpfenning, *Josef der Gerechte. Eine exegetische Untersuchung zu Mt 1–12. Herders Biblische Studien* (Freiburg: Herder, 2008); Joseph Seitz, *Das Josephsfest in der lateinischen Kirche in seiner Entwicklung bis zum Konzil von Trient* (Freiburg: 1908), 4; *Decreta Authentica Congregationis Sacorum Rituum . . .*, ed. Aloys Gardellini. Editio tertia, vol. 1 (Rome: 1856), nu. 598; "Cult de Saint Joseph," in: *Analecta Juris Pontifici* (Rome: 1881), 824–843.

46. Paul de Barry, *Speißkammer der Andacht gegen dem H. Joseph, Jesu Christi Zucht-Vattern, nach Jesu und Maria dem allerholdseeligisten Heyligen*, trans. Christoph Schachner (Munich: 1650), 44ff. On leadership, see Iwanek, *Lilium*, 511–514; on Joseph as a model for the paterfamilias, see ibid., 492ff. The silence of scripture about St. Joseph was a frequent theme in scholastic theology, see, for example, Johannes Seidel SJ, *Templum Honoris Gloriae Virginae* (Prague: 1716), thesis 1 (s.pag.).

47. *Analecta Juris Pontifici* (Rome: 1881), 835f. Isidor Isolani, *Summa de Donis de S. Joseph* (Rome: 1887); Joseph Seitz, *Die Verehrung des Hl. Joseph in seiner geschichtlichen Entwicklung bis zum Konzil von Trient* (Freiburg: 1908); Otto Pfülf, "Die Verehrung des hl. Joseph," *Stimmen aus Maria Laach* 38 (1890): 137–161, 282–302; Joseph Müller, *Der Heilige Joseph. Die dogmatischen Grundlagen seiner besonderen Verehrung* (Münster: Rauch, 1937).

48. Michael a S. Catharina, *Trinum Perfectum*, vol. 2, par. 272, 103.

49. Sauerländer, *Der katholische Rubens*, 84; 179ff; cf. Wilhelm Damus Lindanus, "Candido Lectori Christiano," in Caesare Baronio Sorano, *Martyrologium Romanum . . . accesserunt Notationesque . . .* (Antwerp: 2nd ed., 1589), s.pag.: "vanas, apocryphas, & aniles, ne dicam superstitiosas execrati fabellas, quae . . . sacras contaminaverunt SS. Martyrum historias."

50. For Rubens, see Sauerländer, *Der katholische Rubens*, 52–55; Baronio, *Martyrologium Romanum*, 326, frankly confesses about St. Christopher: "Huius quidem acta depravatae ac inter se diversa admodum reperiuntur." The decree on images of December 3, 1563, is found in Heinrich Denzinger and Peter Hünermann (eds.), *Compendium of Creeds, Definitions, and Declarations on Matters of Faith and Morals*, trans. Robert Fastiggi and Anne Englund Nash (San Francisco: Ignatius Press, 2012), DH 1821–1825. See also Jesse M. Locker, "Rethinking Art after the Council of Trent," in idem (ed.), *Art and Reform in the late Renaissance. After Trent* (London and New York: Routledge, 2019), 1–19.

51. Francisco Antonio a Lorenzana, *Concilium Mexicanum Provinciale III* (Mexico: 1770), 113; Josef Metzler, *Die Synoden in China, Japan und Korea, 1570–1931* (Paderborn: Schöningh, 1980), 28.

52. On Joseph's freedom from mortal sin, see Isolani, *Summa*, 92–96, 192–197; on his nonexisting fear of death, ibid., 288f; on his integrity, see Isolani, *Summa*, 172ff, and Karl Stengel OSB, *Iosephus. Hoc est Sanctissimi Educatoris Christi . . .* (Munich: 1616), 39ff; on Joseph giving Jesus his name, see Stengel, *Iosephus*, 135–145, and Isolani, *Summa*, 116–118; on the imitation of St. Joseph, see Georg Iwanek SJ, *Lilium Paradisi Coelestis S. Josephus . . .* (New Prague: 1688), 329–505; see ibid. on domestic

tyranny, 496: "Nam, quia paterfamilias se esse dominium, materfamilias dominam circumspicit, putat sibi in familiam omnia licere, nec tam ut familiam, quam ut mancipia tractat.... Cujusvis, etiam servilis hominis, pretium est Sanguis Christi ... confer cum hoc pretio totius mundi opes thesauros, gazas; quid erunt hae omnia ad Christi Sanguinem comparata? Nihil. . . . Et tamen hunc hominem, hunc servum, hanc ancillam, saepe tam indigne tractamus, ut si hic vel illa nauci, flocci, titivilliti, ac nihil foret." For Teresa of Avila's and Francis de Sales's veneration of St. Joseph, see Joseph Chorpenning, "St. Joseph in the Spirituality of Teresa of Avila and of Francis de Sales: Convergences and Divergences," in Christopher Wilson (ed.), *The Heirs of St. Teresa of Avila* (Washington, DC: ICS Publ., 2006), 123–140. For Rubens, see Sauerländer, *Der katholische Rubens*, 52–55. Since it was assumed that Joseph had named Jesus, the increase of the "Holy Name of Jesus"–devotion in early modernity is intrinsically connected to the cult of St. Joseph, cf. see Peter Biasiotto, *History of the Development of Devotion to the Holy Name* (St. Bonaventure, NY: St. Bonaventure College and Seminary, 1943).

53. Elizabeth Lehfeldt, "Ideal Men. Masculinity and Decline in Seventeenth-Century Spain," *Renaissance Quarterly* 61 (2008): 463–494, at 474.

54. Lehfeldt, "Ideal Men"; cf. Iwanek, *Lilium*, 501ff.

55. Pedro de Morales SJ, *In Caput Primum Matthaei . . .* (Lyon: 1614), lib. 1, tr. 1, n. 22, 14: "Ex praedictis, unca principalis colligitur conclusio Jesum, Mariam & Iosephum fuisse terrestrem Trinitatem, ad similitudinem caelestis."

56. Charlene Villasenor Black, "Love and Marriage in the Spanish Empire. Depictions of Holy Matrimony and Gender Discourses in the Seventeenth Century," *Sixteenth Century Journal* 32 (2001): 637–667; see idem, *Saints and Social Welfare in Golden Age Spain: The Imagery of the Cult of St. Joseph* (PhD Thesis: University of Michigan, 1995).

57. Andres de Soto, *Libro de la vida y excellencias de el glorioso S. Ioseph, esposo de la Virgen N. Señora* (Brussels: 1600); Jerónimo Gracián, *Sumario de las Excelencias del Glorioso S. Ioseph, Esposo de la Virgen Maria* (Rome: 1597).

58. Gracián, *Sumario*, 112 at Sophia Boffa, *Joseph of Nazareth as Man and Father in Jerónimo Gracián's Summary of the Excellencies of St. Joseph (1597)* (PhD Thesis: University of Notre Dame Australia, 2016), 108. See also Ignatius a Sancto Francisco, *Synopsis*, pars 1, tract. 2, 126–129, on the beauty of Joseph's body being proportionate to Mary's beauty.

59. Boffa, *Joseph*, 135–140.

60. Ignatius a Sancto Francisco, *Synopsis magnalium Divi Josephi in tres partes* (Leodii: 1684), pars 1, tract. 1, sect. 2 and 3, 19ff. Cf. James L. Kugel, *In Potiphar's House* (Cambridge: Harvard University Press, 1994).

61. Ignatius a Sancto Francisco, *Synopsis*, pars 1, tract. 2, ch. 13, 102f.; Joseph Chorpenning, "The Enigma of St. Joseph in Poussin's Holy Family on the Steps," *Journal of the Warburg and Courtauld Institutes* 60 (1997): 276–281; Iwanek, *Lilium*, 329–505; on economic success ibid., 498. Cf. Hildegard Erlemann, *Die Heilige Familie. Ein Tugendvorbild der Gegenreformation im Wandel der Zeit. Kult und Ideologie* (Münster: Ardey-Verl, 1993).

62. Cf. Groethuysen, *Die Entstehung*. See Ignatius a Sancto Francisco, *Synopsis*, pars 1, tract. 2, sect. 2, 106f; Iwanek, *Lilium*, 504.

63. Cf. Anonymous, *Josephische Liebesflammen*, 13f. On Mary's virginity, see Gerhard Ludwig Müller, *Maria—Die Frau im Heilsplan Gottes. Mariologische Studien XV* (Würzburg: Echter, 2002); Juniper Carol (ed.), *Mariology*, 3 vols. (s.l.: Mediatrix Press, 2018).

64. McGinness, "Roma Sancta," 110; Robert Bellarmine, *Opera oratoria postuma*, ed. Sebastian Tromp, vol. 9 (Rome: Gregorian University, 1948), 391–395.

65. On St. Joseph's assistance for priestly chastity, see Johann Reuter SJ, *Confessarius Practice Instructus . . . Editio tertia* (Cologne: 1752), 358, 82ff; Iwanek, *Lilium Paradisi*, 334–362. On the sinlessness of St. Joseph, see Ignatius a Sancto Francisco, *Synopsis*, pars 2, tract. 1, ch. 4, 186–199; Anonymous, *Josephische Liebesflammen oder Lebens-Beschreibung des . . . Heiligen Joseph* (Vienna: 1692), ch. 3, 12–16; Isolani, *Summa*, 31–35, on the sanctification in utero; Morales, *In Caput*, 188 (on his virginity; at 601, that Joseph was only once married) and 331 (on his never sinning: "Joseph in toto vitae suae curriculo nullum peccatum mortale commissit"); on the view that Joseph was sanctified *outside* the uterus, see Claude Dausque, *Sancti Josephi sanctificatio extra uterum . . . adversus F. Marchantii Minoritae Exprovincialis* (Lyon: 1631), and idem, *Sancti Pauli sanctificatio extra uterum* (Paris: 1627).

66. Heinrich Kellerhaus SJ, *Saamen des Göttlichen Worts*, vol. 3 (Augsburg and Graz: 1735), 188, 194–199; Morales, *In Caput*, 304; 482f.

67. Virgil Kleinmayer, *Josephinisches Priesterthum . . .* (Steyer: 1718), 3f; Augustin Fischer, *Sacerdotium Infiniti Pretii Muneris . . . Deificum . . .* (Krems: 1729); Zeger Bernhard van Espen, *Opuscula Varia*, vol. 3 (Madrid: 1778), 133.

68. *Rituale Romanum*, 363ff. Moshe Sluhovsky, "Introduction," in idem (ed.), *Into the Dark Night and Back. The Mystical Writings of Jean-Joseph Surin* (Leiden and Boston: Brill, 2018), 1–18, at: 8f; Jean-Joseph Surin, "The Triumph of Divine Love over the Powers of Hell," in ibid., 33, 45, 51f. On the explicit invocation of St. Joseph, see Surin, "The Triumph," 42, 45f; 113; idem, "The Experimental Science of the Things of the Other life," ibid., 343ff.

69. de Barry, *Speißkammer*, 182.

70. Paul de Barry, *Pious Remarks upon the Life of St. Joseph. Second edition* (Dublin: 1700), 102; on the conversations of St. Joseph, see also Morales, *In Caput*, 138.

71. Gabriel Reeb, *Newe Bruederschafft des glorwürdigsten . . . Manns Mariae Joseph* (Ingolstadt: 1649). The confraternity in Feylaw only required to hear the mass weekly, monthly a rosary, and reception of H. Communion three times a year, besides having a veneration for St. Joseph and to pray for the dead (Bayerische Staatsbibliothek München: Einbl. VII,60—*Andachtszettel der Bruderschaft St Joseph zu Feylaw* (Augsburg: 1669).

72. Morales, *In Caput*, 970: "Christus Dominus propria manu clausit occulos eius, & vultum composuit, et benedixit corpori eius." He is following the pious tradition begun by Jean Gerson.

73. De Barry, *Pious*, 112–116.

74. Antonio de Peralta, *Dissertationes scholasticae de S. Joseph* (Mexico City: 1729); Morales, *In Caput*, 229: "Quia noster Joseph fuit coniunctissimus alter, et primario

principio scilicet Christo Domino." On the concept of heroic virtue for canonizations, see Massimo Leone, *Saints and Signs. A Semiotic Reading of Conversion in Early Modern Catholicism* (Berlin: De Gruyter, 2010); Jacyln Duffin, *Medical Miracles. Doctors, Saints, and Healing in the Modern World* (Oxford: Oxford University Press, 2009); Romeo de Maio, "L'ideale eroico nei processi di canonizzazione della Controriforma," in idem (ed.), *Riforme emiti nella Chiesa del cinquecento* (Naples: Guida, 1973), 257–278; Lehner, *Catholic Enlightenment*, 127ff. Cf. the three-volume excerpts from the work of Pope Benedict XIV, *Heroic Virtue. A Portion of the Treatise of Benedict XIV on the Beatification and Canonization of the Servants of God*, 3 vols. (London: 1850/52).

75. Morales, *In Caput*, 981ff.

76. Prokop Schaffgottsch, *Rede auf das Fest des heiligen Joseph* (Prague: 1772); cf. Rudolf Svoboda, *Johann Prokop Schaffgotsch. Das Leben eines böhmischen Prälaten in der Zeit des Josephinismus* (Frankfurt: Peter Lang, 2015).

77. Anonymous, *Grüssauer Josephbuch . . .* (Schweidnitz: 1777).

# Conclusion

1. Nicholas of Cusa, "General Reform of the Church," in idem, *Writings on Church and Reform. Trans. By Thomas M. Izbicki. The I Tatti Renaissance Library* (Cambridge: Harvard University Press, 2008), 550–593, at 559.

2. On representation, see Carlo Ginzburg, *Wooden Eyes. Nine Reflections on Distance* (London: Verso, 2002), passim.

3. See also the helpful anthologies by John C. Olin, *The Catholic Reformation. Savonarola to Ignatius Loyola. Reform in the Church, 1495–1540* (New York: Fordham University Press, 1992), and idem, *Catholic Reform. From Cardinal Ximenes to the Council of Trent 1495–1563* (New York: Fordham University Press, 1991).

4. Ethan H. Shagan, *The Birth of Modern Belief. Faith and Judgment from the Middle Ages to the Enlightenment* (Princeton: Princeton University Press, 2018), 86.

5. For the relationship of unity in faith and devotional diversity, see the brilliant study by Eric Demeuse, *Unity and Catholicity. The Ecclesiology of Francisco Suarez* (Oxford: Oxford University Press, 2022).

6. Shagan, *Birth*, 83.

7. Paolo Giustiniani and Pietro Querini, *Libellus. Addressed to Leo X, Supreme Pontiff. Translated by Stephen M. Beall* (Milwaukee: Marquette University Press, 2016), 117: "It is certain, then, that one who is less concerned with his sheep than with earthly riches is not playing the role of a good shepherd, but rather that of a wicked hireling."

8. I borrow the term from Günther Wassilowsky, " 'Wo die Messe fellet, so liegt das Bapstum.' Zur Kultur päpstlicher Repräsentation in der Frühen Neuzeit," in Birgit Emich et al. (eds.), *Kulturgeschichte des frühneuzeitlichen Papsttums. Zeitschrift für historische Forschung. Beiheft 48* (Berlin: Duncker & Humblot, 2013), 219–247, but do not use it exclusively for priestly actions.

9. On the history of the concept of grace in scholasticism is still indispensable Auer, *Die Entwicklung*, 2 vols. On early modern Catholic discourse on grace, see Marschler, "Providence," 89–103.

10. See also David Salomoni, *Educating the Catholic People. Religious Orders and Their Schools in Early Modern Italy (1500–1800)* (Leiden and Boston: Brill, 2021).

11. Wassilowksy, "Wo die Messe fellet," 233.

12. Teresa, *La Vida*, V, 9, n. 5, in *Obras completas*; McGinn, *Mysticism in the Golden Age of Spain*, 158–160.

13. St. Teresa of Avila uses the image of chicken steps (*paso de gallina*), see *Vida*, 13, n. 5 in idem, *Obras*.

14. See, for example, Robert Bellarmine, *On Purgatory*, trans. Ryan Grant (Post Falls, ID: Mediatrix Press, 2017), and Catherine of Genoa, *Purgation and Purgatory. The Spiritual Dialogue* (New York: Paulist Press, 1979).

# Bibliography of Primary Sources

## Collections of Ecclesiastical Sources and Liturgical Books

*Acta Sanctorum*, ed. Johannes Stiltingh et al., vol. 8 (Antwerp: 1762).

Alberigo, Giuseppe, et al. (eds.). *Conciliorum Oecumenicorum Decreta* (Freiburg: 2nd ed., Herder, 1962).

*Bibliotheca scriptorum Ordinis minorum S. Francisci Capuccinorum*, ed. Bernardo a Bononia (Venice: 1747).

*Bullarium Carmelitanum*, ed. Eliseo Monsignano, 2 vols. (Rome: 1715).

*Catechism of the Council of Trent for Parish Priests*. Trans. John A. McHugh and Charles J. Callan (Rockford: TAN Publ., 1982).

*Collectio omnium conclusionum et resolutionum quae in causis propositis apud sacram Congregationem Cardinalium S. Concilii Tridentini interpretum*, ed. Salvatore Pallotini, 17 vols. (Rome: 1867ff).

Denzinger, Heinrich, and Hünermann, Peter (eds.). *Compendium of Creeds, Definitions, and Declarations on Matters of Faith and Morals*. Trans. Robert Fastiggi and Anne Englund Nash (San Francisco: Ignatius Press, 2012) [abbreviated as DH].

*Decreta Authentica Congregationis Sacorum Rituum . . .* (Rome: 1898).

Ehses, Stephan (ed.). *Concilium Tridentinum. Diariorum, Actorum, Epistularum, Tractatuum*, vol. 9 (Freiburg: Herder, 1965).

*Liber Caeremoniarum Fratrum Discalceatorum Ordinis Eremitarum S. Patris Augustini Galliarum* (Lyon: 1642).

*Magnum Bullarium Romanum*, ed. Angelo Cherubini (Luxembourg: 1727ff).

*Pontificale Romanum* (Antwerp: 1765).

*Rituale Romanum* (Rome: 1614).

*Rituale Romanum seu Manuale Romanum . . .* (Antwerp: 1673).

Schmucki, Oktavian, and Lehmann, Leonhard (eds.). *Die ersten Kapuziner-Konstitutionen von 1536* (Münster: Fachstelle Franziskanische Forschung, 2016).

## Other Primary Sources

Since early modern texts tended to appear in varying editions, they are cited in the footnotes with book (lib. or bk.) and chapter numbers (ch. or c.), "punctum" (pt.), etc., to make it easier to find the cited text in a different edition.

Abraham a St. Clara. *Grammatica Religiosa* (Cologne: 2nd ed., 1705).

Accursio von Passau. *Neuer Krieg von der unbefleckten Empfängnis Mariae, welche unter dem Kriegs-Fahn oder himmel-blauen Scapulier . . . verfochten wird* (Vienna: 1728).

Adrianus a S. Francisco. *S. Scapularis Partheno-Carmelitici . . . Excursus Paraenetici . . .* (Frankfurt: 1685).

Agricola, Franciscus. *Biblischer-Ehespiegel*... (Cologne: 1599).

Agricola, Franciscus. *Evangelischer Wegweiser, das ist: Eine Catholische Leich Predigt* (Cologne: 1577).

Agricola, Franciscus. *Von dem christlichen Gebett*... (Cologne: 1585).

Albertini, Francesco. *Trattato dell'Angelo Custode* (Rome and Naples: 1612).

Albertinus, Aegidius. *Hausspolicey*... (Munich: 1602).

Albertis, Albertus de. *In Eloquentiae quum profanae, tum sacrae corruptores* (Milan: 1651).

Alcantara, Pedro de. *Instruction oder Underweisung wol zu meditiren*... (Cologne: 1605).

Alexandre, Natalis. *Commentarius Litteralis et Moralis in omnes Epistulas Sancti Pauli Apostolo et in VII Epistulas Catholicas*, vol. 2 (Paris: 1746).

Alfonso de Mendoza. *Quaestiones Quodlibeticae et Relectio de Christi regno ac dominio* (Salamanca: 1596).

Alletz, Pons-Augustin. *Die Kunst Seelen im Beichtstuhle zu rühren*, 2 vols. (Bamberg and Würzburg: 1785).

Altenstaig, Johann. *Lexicon Theologicum*... (Antwerp: 1576).

Alvarez de Paz, Diego. *De Exterminatione Mali et Promotione boni. Opera Omnia*, vol. 2 (Lyon: 1613).

Alvarez de Paz, Diego. *Mensis Eucharisticus, hoc est praeparationes, aspirationes et gratiarum actiones*... (Madrid: 1789).

Amelote, Denis. *La vie de soeur Marguerite du S. Sacrement, religieuse Carmelite du monastere de Beaune. Composee par un prestre de la Congregation de l'Oratoire de Nostre Seigneur Iesus-Christ, docteur en theologie* (Paris: 1654).

Amelote, Denis. *La vie du Père Charles de Condren* (Paris: 1643).

Amelote, Denis. *Le petit office du S. Enfant Jesus*... (Paris: 1668).

Amort, Eusebius. *Kurtzer Lebens-Begriff Desz Seeligen Petri Forerij, Regulierten Chorherren und Pfarrern zu Mataincur* (Munich: 1730).

Amort, Eusebius. *Theologia Moralis Inter Rigorem, et Laxitatem Media*, 2 vols. (Augsburg: 1758).

Amort, Eusebius. *Theologia Eclectica*, 4 vols. (Augsburg: 1752f).

Andrade, Alphonsus, de. *Avisos Espirituales de Santa Theresa de Jesus comentados* (Madrid: 1647).

Androzzi, Fulvio. *Considerationes de frequentanda communione* (Mainz: 1598).

Ange-Joseph de a Bâtie. *Tractatus de rhetorica sacra, ad usum studentium candidatorumque concionatorum Ordinis F.F. Minorum Capucinorum Provinciae Sabaudiae accommodatus* (Chambéry: 1760).

Angermayr, Placidus. *Militia Sacra, das ist: Marianischer Werb- und Waffenplatz*, vol. 2 (Kempten: 1722).

Anonymous. *Abbildung und Wahrer Begriff des Uralten Heil. Dritten Ordens des Heiligen Norberti* (Passau: 1751).

Anonymous. *Alte Catholische Geistliche Kirchengesäng* (Paderborn: 1609).

Anonymous. *Alte und newe christlich-katholische Gesäng auf Sonn- u. Festtäg des Jahrs* (Würzburg: 1649).

Anonymous. *Apostolica institutio et regulae confraternitatis . . . erectae in ecclesia P.P. Cappucinorum Coloniae* (Cologne: 1613).

Anonymous. *Archiconfraternitas B.V. Mariae de Consolatione* (Munich: 1674).

Anonymous. *Aspirationes Sacrae Sodalis Mariana ad Deiparam Virginem . . .* (Vienna: 1676).

Anonymous. *Bruderschafft des heiligen Ertz-Engel und Himmelsfürsten Michael . . .* (Munich: 1696).

Anonymous. *Canones Directivi Confraternitatis Sacerdotum Bonae Voluntatis . . .* (Cologne: 1709).

Anonymous. *Cathalogus aller verstorbenen Brüder und Schwestern aus der Seraphinisch-Chur-Cöllnischen Erzbruderschfat des heiligen und grossen Himmelsfürsten St. Michael zu Josephsburg nächst München* (Munich: 1765).

Anonymous. *Catholische Kirchengesänge* (Mainz: 1631).

Anonymous. *Catholisches Gesang-Buch zum Gebrauch des Bistums Strasburg* (Strasburg: 1752).

Anonymous. *Christlich Catholisch Gesangbuch* (Paderborn: 1628).

Anonymous. *Constitutiones Archiconfraternitatis S. Hieronymi Charitatis de Urbe* (Rome: 1694).

Anonymous. *Constitutiones Archiconfraternitatis Charitatis de Urbe* (Rome: 1603).

Anonymous. *Cursus Theologiae Moralis Salmanticensis*, vol. 5 (Venice: 1750).

Anonymous. *Das brochne Brod der Kleinen*, vol. 1 (Augsburg: 1736).

Anonymous. *La dévotion à la sainte enfance de Jesus* (Paris: 1733).

Anonymous. *De confessionibus scrupulosorum brevis tractatus . . .* (Mexico City: 1723).

Anonymous. *Deliberir-Büchlein, oder Berathschlagung von Erwählung eines Stands für das weibliche Geschlecht . . .* (Munich: 1734).

Anonymous. *Der in dem Weingarten Christi, oder in der Heil. Cathol. Kirch, durch Göttliche Gnad von dem Seel-eyferend und unermüdthen Weingartnern Francisco Seraphico nutzlich gepflantzte . . . Seraphische Weinstock: Das ist Schuldigiste Ehr- und Lob-Red des Heil. dritten Seraphischen Ordens der Büssenden* (Augsburg: 1752).

Anonymous. *Der in den Ohren Gottes lieblich klingende Harpfen-Klang der Büßenden . . .* (Salzburg: 1762).

Anonymous. *Die Kindheit Christi Jesu in dem innerlichen Gebett verehret* (Augsburg and Innsbruck: 1764).

Anonymous. *Die Kindheit Christi Jesu in dem innerlichen Gebett verehret . . . nach Regel des H. Patriarchen Benedicti* (Augsburg and Innsbruck: 1764).

Anonymous. *Doctrina Pastoralis. Cum Idea Reformationis Cleri et Populi ad Mentem Concilii Tridentini . . .* (Augsburg: 1802).

Anonymous. *Dreyfacher Tugend-Spiegel . . .* (Munich: 1755).

Anonymous. *Engel-Schuel und zugleich heller Ehe-spiegel: Das ist das gold-werthe Canonische . . . Büchlein Tobias* (Munich: 1723).

Anonymous. *Entretiens spirituels en forme de prières . . .* (Paris: 1721).

Anonymous. *Erklärung der Prosa des* Dies Irae, *oder Affekte eines Sünders* (Mainz: 1786).

Anonymous. *Geistlicher Paradeis-Vogel der Catholischen Deutschen* (Neuss: 1687; 1st ed.: 1663).

Anonymous. *Grüssauer Josephbuch . . .* (Schweidnitz: 1777).

Anonymous. *Haus-Genossenschaft des Heiligen Kind Jesu, seiner h. Mutter und des Heiligen Joseph . . .* (Vienna: 1723).

Anonymous. *Heil-und Hülfsmittel zum thätigen Christentum* (Brix/Dresden: 1767).

Anonymus. *Heylsamer Spring-Brunn zum Ewigen Leben . . .* (Würzburg: 1662).

Anonymous. *Himmlische Liberey der andächtigen zur unbefleckten Empfägnus Mariae bestehend in dem himmelblauen Scapulier . . .* (Salzburg: 1720).

Anonymous. *Jesus Christus der verborgene Gott im hochheiligen Altarsgeheimnisse zur öffentlichen Anbethung . . .* (Munich: 1778).

Anonymous. *Josephische Liebesflammen oder Lebens-Beschreibung des . . . Heiligen Joseph* (Vienna: 1692).

Anonymous. *Kleiner Ehe-Spiegel darinnen sich alle christliche Ehe-Leuth zu ersehen* . . . (Munich: 1741).

Anonymous. *Lamindi Pritanii redivivi Epistola Paraenetica ad patrem Benedictum Plazza SJ* (Venice: 1755).

Anonymous. *Leben des gottseeligen* . . . *Diener Gottes Dominici von Jesu-Maria, des Barfüsser Carmeliten-Ordens General* . . . (Munich: 1685).

Anonymous. *Lob-Klingende Harffe des Neuen Testaments* (Königgrätz: 1730).

Anonymous. "Predigtstuhl," in J. H. Zedler (ed.), *Grosses Universal Lexicon*, vol. 29 (Leipzig and Halle: 1741), 279–290.

Anonymous. *Regelbüchlein des Dritten Ordens S. Francisci* (Munich: 1728).

Anonymous. *Regl-Buechlein des Dritten Ordens S. Francisci* . . . *in der chur-Bayrischen Provinz* (Cologne: 1732).

Anonymous. *Religionsklagen gegen Herrn Peter Trunk* (s.l.: 1779).

Anonymous. *S. Michael der höchste Seraphin über die himmlische Geister* (Munich: 1699).

Anonymous. *Sacrae Caeremoniae* . . . *Fratrum Eremitarum S. Augustini* (Rome: 1714).

Anonymous. *Sacrosanctae Sodalitas Sacerdotum Secularium Urbis Constitutiones* (Rome: 1644).

Anonymous. *Schnell-Abfliegende Hertzen-Pfeil* (Munich: 1730).

Anonymous. *Seelen-Peyn in dem Fegfeuer* . . . (Munich: 1732).

Anonymous. *Trost-Lehr-und Ehren-Predig für den dritten Orden deren Büssenden des H. Seraphischen Vatters* (Linz: 1740).

Anonymous. *Unterrichtungen der heylsamen Buss des Dritten Ordens* . . . *von einem Franciscaner Oesterreichischer Provinz* (Vienna: 1736).

Anonymous. *Vera Confraternitas S. Trinitatis Redemptionis Captivorum Christianorum. Editio Secunda* (Vienna: 1715).

Anonymous. *Verehrung des göttlichen Kindlein Jesu oder besondere Andacht zu Nutz und Trost denen in das Pragerische Kindlein verliebten Seelen* (Bamberg: 1761).

Anonymous. *Vinculum Charitatis oder Seraphisches Liebs-Band* . . . (Vienna: 1716).

Anonymous. *Weis und Manier, wie man mit guter Meynung die von der Regel des Dritten Ordens des Heiligen Francisci vorgeschriebene Tag-Zeiten* . . . *betten koenne* (Vienna: 1746).

Anonymous. *Zwölf Geistliche Kirchengesäng* (Ingolstadt: 1586).

Ansalone, Pietro. *David al cenacolo ciove il Salmo ventesimo secondo* . . . (Naples: 1715).

Antonio de San Roman. *Consuelo de Penitentes o Mesa Franca de spirituales manjares* (Seville: 1585).

Antonio a Spiritu Sancto. *Directorium Mysticum* . . . (Lyon: 1677).

Archangelus a S. Georgio. *Heilige Wunder-Sprüch. Das ist: Ausser-Ordentliche Feyrtags-Predigten* (Augsburg: 1619).

Auriemma, Tommaso. *Affetti scambievoli tra la Vergine santissima, e i suoi divoti. Dimostrati da questi con ossequij, da Maria con gratie, e favori singolari, in particolare nelle sue sette feste*, 2 vols. (Venice: 1747).

Ayguani, Michele. *Commentaria in psalmos Davidicos auctoris incogniti. Ed. F. Gregorii Canalii. Editio octava* (Lyon: 1652).

Azevedo, Juan de. *Tribunal Theologicum & Juridicum Contra Subdolos Confessarios* (Ulyssipone Occidentali: 1726).

Badoire, Pierre. *Prônes sur le Sacrifice de la Messe* (Paris: 1757).

Bail, Louis. *La théologie affective ou Saint Thomas d'Aquin en méditation*, 3 vols. (Paris: 1671).

Bail, Louis. *Theologia affectiva . . .* 3 vols. (Cologne: 1712).

Baiole, Jean J. *Annales Congregationum Beatissimiae Virginis Mariae collecti ex annalibus Societatis Jesu* (Burdigalae: 1624).

Bajocensis, Amadeus. *Paulus Ecclesiastes seu Eloquentia Christiana* (Paris: 1662, i.e. 1670).

Balinghem, Antoine. *De Orationibus Iaculatoriis Libri IV* (Antwerp: 1618).

Balinghem, Antoine. *Thesaurus Orationum Iaculatoriarum ex Sacris Bibliis addita explicatione* (Cologne: 1626).

Báñez, Domingo. *Scholastica commentaria in primam partem Angelici Doctoris S. Thomae*, vol. 2 (Douai: 1614).

Barbosa, Aghostino. *Pastoralis solicitudinis sive de officio et potestate parochi* (Lyon: 1640; 4th ed., 1655).

Barcia y Zambrana, José de. *Christ-eyffriger Seelen-Wecker* (Augsburg and Dillingen: 1715).

Barcia y Zambrana, José de. *Despertador christiano de sermones doctrinales*, 4 vols. (Lisbon: 1679; Madrid: 1690).

Baronio, Caesare Sorano. *Martyrologium Romanum . . . accesserunt Notationesque . . .* (Antwerp: 2nd ed., 1589).

Barry, Paul de. *Le mort de Paulin et d'Alexis* (Lyon: 1658).

Barry, Paul de. *Pious Remarks upon the Life of St. Joseph. Second edition* (Dublin: 1700).

Barry, Paul de. *Speißkammer der Andacht gegen dem H. Joseph, Jesu Christi Zucht-Vattern, nach Jesu und Maria dem allerholdseeligisten Heyligen*, trans. Christoph Schachner (Munich: 1650).

Bartholomaeus a Martyribus. *Stimulus Pastorum. Zur Spiritualität des Hirtenamts*, ed. Marianne Schlosser (St. Ottilien: Eos, 2018).

Baruffaldo, Girolamo. *Ad Rituale Romanum Commentaria* (Augsburg and Dillingen: 1735).

Behm, Friedrich. *Tuba D. Vincentii: das ist Erschallende Posaun . . . von denen 15 erschröcklichen Zeichen . . .* (Kempten: 1691).

Bellarino, Giovanni. *Doctrina Catholica ex Sacro Concilio Tridentino . . .* (Venice: 1620).

Bellarmine, Robert. *Auctuarium Bellarminianum*, ed. Xavier Le Bachelet (Paris: 1913).

Bellarmine, Robert. *De Aeterna Felicitate Sanctorum* (Antwerp: 1616).

Bellarmine, Robert. *De Ascensione Mentis in Deum* (Cologne: 1615).

Bellarmine, Robert. *Instructiones Praedicationis Verbi Dei* (s.l., s.a.).

Bellarmine, Robert. *Opera oratoria postuma*, ed. Sebastian Tromp, vol. 9 (Rome: Gregorian University, 1948).

Benedict Fidelis a S. Philippo OFM. *Paradisus Eucharisticus. Hoc est Theoremata Moralia ex Psalmo XXII* (Cologne: 1659).

Benedict Fidelis a S. Philippo OFM. *Paradisus Voluptatis Verbi Incarnato. Hoc est Sermones in Evangelia Dominicalia. Ed. Jakob Emans . . .* (Cologne: 1659).

Benedict XIII. *Constitutio pro Tertiariis Sancti Francisci . . .* (Rome: 1726).

Benedict XIV. *De Sacrosancto Missae Sacrificio* (Rome: 1748).

Benedict XIV. *Dissertationes de Canonizatione Sanctorum*, vol. 1 (Venice: 1751).

Benedict XIV. *Heroic Virtue. A Portion of the Treatise of Benedict XIV on the Beatification and Canonization of the Servants of God*, 3 vols. (London: 1850/52).

Benedict XIV. *Institutiones Ecclesiasticae*, 3 vols. (Leuven: 1762).

Benedict XIV. *Rituale Romanum Benedicti XIV*. (Patavii: 1760).

Bernières de Louvigny, Jean de. *Pensées ou Sentimens du chrestien intérieur sur les principaux mystères de la Foi* (Paris: 1676).

Bertaut, Bertin. *Director Confessariorum* . . . , trans. Adalrich Schwarz (Dillingen: 1709).

Bertaut, Bertin. *Directorium confessariorum* (Venice: 1654).

Bertaut, Bertin. *Il direttorio de confessori* . . . (Milan: 1666).

Bertaut, Bertin. *Le directeur des confesseurs en forme de catéchisme* (Paris: 5th ed., 1638).

Berulle, Pierre. *Oeuvres completes de Berulle*, ed. Francois Bourgoing and Jacques-Paul Migne (Paris: 1856).

Billuart, Charles-Rene. *Summa S. Thomae sive cursus Theologiae Hodiernis Academicarum Moribus Accomodata, Secunda Secundae* (Venice: 1778).

Blasco Lanuza, Francisco. *Patrocinio de angeles y combate de demonios* (San Juan de la Pena: 1652).

Blosius [Blois], Ludovicus. *Opera Omnia* (Antwerp: 1632).

Blosius [Blois], Ludovicus. *Opera Quae Quidem Conscripsit Omnia* (Cologne: 1572).

Blosius [Blois], Ludovicus. *Spiritual Works*, ed. John Edward Bowden (London: Washbourne, 1903).

Bodler, Johann. *Die Entlarffte Falschheit oder Sonntäglicher Predigen-Curs* (Dillingen: 1697).

Boileau, Charles. *Pensées choisies* (Paris: 1709).

Bona, Giovanni. *Divinum profluvium orationum et aspirationum* . . . (Leuven: 1735).

Bona, Giovanni. *Opera Omnia* (Venice: 1752).

Bonacina, Martin. *Opera Omnia* (Antwerp: 1632).

Bonardo, Vincenco. *Discorso intorno all' origine Antichita, et Virtu de gli Agnus Dei di cera Benedetti* (Rome: 1586).

Bonnyers, Marc de. *L'advocat des ames de purgatoire ou moyens faciles pour les aider* (Lille: 1640).

Bordoni, Francesco. *Operum Tomus Secundus. Pars Prima* (Lyon: 1655).

Born, Hermann. *Seraphisches Firmament oder Stern-Himmel* . . ., 12 vols. (Cologne: 1715).

Borromeo, Carlo (ed.), *Acta Ecclesiae Mediolanensis* (Milan: 1582; Lyon: 1682f).

Borromeo, Carlo. "De Cura Pestilentiae," in: idem (ed.), *Constitutiones et Decreta in provincialia Synodo Mediolanensi Quinta* (Milan: 1580).

Bossuet, Jacques B. *Catechisme du Diocese de Meaux* (Paris: 1687).

Boudon, Henri. *Andacht zu den Neun Chören der Englen* (Augsburg: 1687).

Boudon, Henri. *Das Reich Gottes im innern Gebethe* . . . trans. Fulgentius a S. Maria (Cologne: 1711).

Boudon, Henri. *Dieu seul.* (Brussels: 6th ed., 1700).

Boudon, Henri. *La regne de Dieu* . . . *Nouvelle Edition* (Paris: 1702).

Boudon, Henri. *La science et la pratique du Chrestien* (Paris: 1681).

Boudon, Henri. *La science sacrée du Catéchisme* (Paris: 1678).

Boulenger, Pierre. *Institutionum Christianorum Libri Octo* (Paris: 1560).

Bourdalou, Louis. *Exhortations et instructions Chretiennes. Nouvelle Edition*, vol. 2 (Lyon: 1758).

Bourdalou, Louis. *Pensées du père Bourdaloue de la Compagnie de Jesus sur divers sujets de religion et de morale*, vol. 3 (Paris: 1736).

Brancasio de Caravinea, Clemens. *De Angelis* (Naples: 1646).

Brancraccio, Francesco. *De chocolatis potu diatribe* (Rome: 1664).

Brandimartes, Felix. *Sapientiae Tubae Scientia, id est Tractatus scholasticus de Arte concionandi* (Panormi: 1667).

Brandmeyer, Johann Adam. *Schema Introductionis in Universam Theologiam Catholicam* (Mannheim: 1780).

Braun, Heinrich. *Anleitung zur geistlichen Beredsamkeit* (Munich: 1776).

Braun, Heinrich. *Deutsches Brevier für Stiftsdamen*, 4 vols. (Augsburg: 1792).

Braun, Heinrich. *Katholisches Gebeth-und Erbauungsbuch* (Augsburg: 1783).

Brocardus a S. Nicolao, *Professio Fidei Catholicae secundum veras verae fidei regulas*, 3 vols. (Frankfurt: 1758).

Brunner, Philipp J. *Christliche Reden, welche von katholischen Predigern in Deutschland seit dem Jahr 1770 bei verschiedenen Gelegenheiten vorgetragen worden sind: Als ein merkwürdiger Beitrag zur Aufklärungsgeschichte des katholischen Deutschlands*, 4 vols. (Heidelberg: 1787ff).

Bullon, Juan Francisco. *Consuelo de las Almas del Purgatorio* ... (Zaragoca: 1683).

Burchard a S. Matthaeo, *Fida Angelorum Custodia sive Tractatus brevis & curiosus de Angelis Sanctis Homonum Custodibus* ... (Munich: 1690).

Bürvenich Adam. *Vierfacher Seelen-Spiegel* (Cologne: 1713).

Busaeus, Johannes. *De Statibus Hominum* (Mainz: 1613).

Busaeus, Johannes. *Summa Rerum seu Antidotorum contra animi morbus* (Venice: 1615).

Busenbaum, Hermann. *Lilien under den Dörneren, das ist Gott verlobter Jungfrawen und Witwen Welt-geistlicher Standt* (Cologne: 1660).

Caballus, Petrus. *Resolutionum Crimnialium* ... *pro serenissima magno duce Hetrurie* ... (Frankfurt: 1613).

Caccia, Francesco. *Cura Curiosa oder Heylsame Seelen-Cur* (Vienna: 1708).

Caccia, Francesco. *Innocentia Apostolica. Die Apostolische Unschuld* (Neuss: 1696).

Cacciaguerra, Bonsignore. *De Frequenti Communione. Ausfürlicher Bericht und Erklärung von der Communion* ... trans. Philipp Dobereiner (Dillingen: 1571).

Cacciaguerra, Bonsignore. *Trattato della communione* (Vercelli: 1561).

Cajetan, Thomas de Vio. *De purgatorio quaestiones duae*. In *Opusculum Opera*, vol. 1 (Lyons: 1587), tract. 23.

Canfield, Benet of. *Renaissance Dialectic and Renaissance Piety: Benet of Canfield's Rule of Perfection. A Translation and Study*, ed. Kent Emery (Binghamton, NY: Medieval & Renaissance Texts & Studies, 1987).

Cangiamila, Francesco Emmanuele. *Embryologia sacra, sive, De officio sacerdotum, medicorum, et aliorum circa aeternam parvulorum in utero existentium salutem, libri quatuor* (Panormi: 1758).

Canisius, Petrus. *Bettbuch und Catechismus* (Dillingen: 1590).

Canisius, Petrus. *Catechismi Latini et Germanici*, ed. Friedrich Streicher, 2 vols. (Rome: Pont. Universitas Gregoriana, 1933ff).

Canisius, Petrus. *Commentariorum de Verbi Dei Corruptelis* ... (Paris: 1584).

Casmann, Otto. *Trost und Fried und Frewde: Oder Innerliche und sehr trostreiche Ansprachung und Ermahnung* . . . *an alle Schwermütige/Traurige/Bussfertige Christenhertzen* (s.l.: 1607).

Castaldo, Andrea Piscara. *Praxis Caeremoniarum seu Sacroum Romanae Ecclesiae Rituum Accurata Tractatio* (Sulzbach: 1715).

Castani, Augustinus. *De Maxima Supernaturali Agnus Dei Virtute Theologica Dissertatio* (Verona: 1669).

Catalano, F. A., et al. (eds.). *Le prime costituzioni dei Frati Minori Cappuccini di San Francesco: Rom—S. Eufemia 1536. In lingua moderna con note storiche ed edizione critica* (Rome: Italia Francescana, 1982).

Catalano, Joseph. *Rituale Romanum Benedicti XIV Perpetuis Commentariis Exornatum*, vol. 2 (Patavii: 1760).

Caussin, Nicolas. *The Holy Court*, 3 vols. (London: 4th ed., 1678).

Cavalieri, Giovanni. *Opera omnia Liturgica seu Commentaria in . . . Sacra Rituum Congregationis Decreta . . .*, vol. 1 (Venice: 1758).

Cisneros, Luys de. *Historia de el Principio, y Origen, progressos, venidas á México, y milagros de la Santa Ymagen de Nuestra Señor de los Remedios, Extramuros de México* (Blanco de Alcaçar: México, 1621).

Cochem, Martin von. *Guldener Himmels-Schlüsel, oder neues Gebett-Buch, zur Erlösung der lieben Seelen deß Fegfeurs: Zum sonderlichen Gebrauch deß andächtigen Weiber-Geschlechts* (Augsburg: 1696).

Columbi, Hieronymus. *De Angelica et Humana Hierarchia* (Lyon: 1647).

Coninck, Gilles de. *De Moralitate Natura et Effectibus Actuum Supernaturalium* (Lyon: 1623).

Contenson, Vincent. *Theologia Mentis et Cordis*, 2 vols. (Venice: 1727).

Contarini, Gasparo. *The Office of a Bishop—De Officio Viri Boni Et Probi Episcopi*. Trans. John Patrick Donnelly (Milwaukee: Marquette University Press, 2002).

Coret, Jacques. *L'Ange Conducteur, contenant Les Prières Du Matin & Du Soir; Prières Pendant La Sainte Messe, Etc.* (Paris: 1681).

Coret, Jacques. *L'Ange Gardien Protecteur . . .* (Caen: 1662).

Cortiada, Don Michaelis de. *Decisiones Cancellarii et Sacri Regii Senatus Cathaloniae . . . Editio Correctior*, vol. 2 (Lyon: 1699).

Coster, François. *Enchiridion Controversiarium Praecipuarum Nostri Temporis De Religione in Gratiam Sodalitatis* (Cologne: 1596).

Courbon, Noel. *Pratiques pour se conserver en la présence de Dieu* (s.l.: 1699).

Cresoli, Ludovicus. *Mystagogus de Sacrorum Hominum Disciplina* (Paris: 1629).

Cunha, Rodrigo de. *Tractatus de Confessariis Solicitantibus* (Valladolid: 1620).

Cusa, Nicholas. *Writings on Church and Reform*. Trans. Thomas M. Izbicki. The I Tatti Renaissance Library (Cambridge: Harvard University Press, 2008).

Cusanus, Nicolaus. *Christliche Zucht-Schul allen Seelsorgern und gemeinem Mann sehr nützlich* (Cologne: 4th ed., 1675).

Cypriano a. S. Maria, *Thesaurus Carmelitarum sive Confraternitatis Sacri Scapularis excellentia* (Cologne: 1627).

d'Auch, P. Leonard. *Histoire de la vie du R. P. Ambroise de Lombez* (Toulouse: 1782).

d'Averoult, Antoine. *Flores Exemplorum sive Catechismus Historialis*, 3 vols. (Douai: 1616; Cologne: 3rd ed., 1624).

d'Outreman, Philippe. *Paedagogus Christianus seu Recta Hominis Christiani Institutio*, 2 vols. (Augustae Trevirorum: 1656).

d'Outreman, Philippe. *The True Christian Catholique or the Manner How to Live Christianly*. Trans. John Heigham (St. Omers: 1622).

Daniele a Virgine Maria. *S. Scapularis Beatissimae Virginis Mariae de Monte Carmeli. Origo, privilegia, & vera ac solida devotio* (Antwerp: 1673).

Daniele a Virgine Maria. *Speculum Carmelitanum sive historia Eliani ordinis . . .* (Antwerp: 1680).

Danzer, Jakob. *Anleitung zur christlichen Moral* (Salzburg: 1791).

Dausque, Claude. *Sancti Josephi sanctificatio extra uterum . . . adversus F. Marchantii Minoritae Exprovincialis* (Lyon: 1631)

Dausque, Claude. *Sancti Pauli sanctificatio extra uterum* (Paris: 1627).

David, Jan. *Veridicus Christianus. Editio Altera* (Antwerp: 1606).

Drexel, Jeremias. *Aurifodina Artium & Scientiarum omnium Excerpendi Solertia* (Antwerp: 1641).

Drexel, Jeremias. *Gymnasium Patientiae* (Munich: 1631).

Drexel, Jeremias. *Heliotropium seu conformation humanae voluntatis cum divina* (Douai: 1621).

Drexel, Jeremias. *Opera Omnia . . . In das Hochdeutsche versetzt*, 5 vols. (Würzburg: 1662).

Drexel, Jeremias. *Palaestra Christiana* (Munich: 1648).

Druzbicki, Caspar. *Opera Omnia Ascetica* (Ingolstadt: 1732).

Eisengrein, Martin. *Anderer Theil, Der Postillen, oder Christlicher Catholischer Auslegung der Sontaeglichen auch etlich anderer Fest Evangelien* (Ingolstadt: 1583).

Elias a S. Teresia. *Legatio Ecclesiae Triumphantis*, 2 vols. (Antwerp: 1638).

Engelgrave, Henri. *Lux Evangelica sub Velum Emblematum*, 2 vols. (Antwerp: 1648).

Erasmus of Rotterdam. *Ausgewählte Schriften*, ed. Werner Welzig (Darmstadt: WBG, 1968).

Erbada, Ignacio de la. *Puerta Franca del Cielo* (Madrid: 1783).

Erich, Gabriel. *Sitten-und Kirchen-Lehren*, vol. 1 (Augsburg and Würzburg: 1747).

Ertl, Ignatius *Promontorium Bonae Spei: Himmlisches Vorgebürg der guten Hoffnung . . .* (Augsburg: 1711).

Espen, Zeger Bernhard van. *Dissertatio canonica de veterum canonum et in eis contentae canonicae disciplinae stabilitate . . .* (Vienna: 1776).

Espen, Zeger Bernhard van. *Jus Ecclesiasticum Universum Hodiernae Disciplinae Accomodatum*, 5 vols. (Madrid: 1778).

Espen, Zeger Bernhard van. *Opuscula Varia* (Madrid: 1778).

Fabri, Basilius. *Thesaurus Eruditionis Scholasticae. Recensitus ac emendates a Augustum Buchnerum* (Wittenberg and Leipzig: 1655).

Faciuta, Sebastianus. *De Vita & Honestate Clericorum* (Florence: 1576).

Faillon, Etienne-Michel. *Vie de M. Olier*, vol. 1 (Le Mans: 1841).

Falck, Francisco. *Der betrachtende Thomas von Kempen als ein Spiegel . . . des vierten Buchs Spiegel der inniglichen Vereinigung mit Christo Jesu im h. Sakrament des Altars*, vol. 4/2 (Mainz: 1756).

Faust, Reinhard. *Princeps Christiano-Politicus: Septem donis Spiritus Sancti Instructus* (Vienna: 1658).

Feijoo, Benito. *Cartas eruditas, y curiosas . . .*, vol. 5 (Madrid: 1760).

Fellern, Joachim. *Der andächtige Student: Das ist: Andächtige Seuffzer und Gebethe . . .* (Leipzig: 1718).

Felner, Matthäus Johannes. *Adiutum pro Clero in Silesia: Sive Materia pro Copulandis utilis* (Erfurt: 1718).

Ferrarris, F. Lucio. *Prompta Bibliotheca Canonica . . .*, 9 vols. (Bologna: 1746).

Ferraris, F. Lucio. *Prompta Bibliotheca Canonica Juridica Moralis Theologica*, ed. Ianuarius Bucceroni, 9 vols. (Rome: 1885ff).

Feucht, Jacob. *Drey Catholische Communion Predigen am Palmsonntag . . .* (Bamberg: 1572).

Feucht, Jacob. *Postilla Catholica Evangeliorum de Tempore totius Anni. Theil Eins* (Cologne: 1597).

Fischer, Anselm, and Mosmiller, Meinrad. *Das äusserliche Leben mit dem Nächsten oder Geistreiche Unterweisung wie ein Ordens-Geistlicher fromm und gottselig mit seinem Nächsten wanderen könne*, 2 vols. (Augsburg: 1763).

Fischer, Anselm, and Mosmiller, Meinrad. *Conversatio externa religiosa, modus pie, & religiose vivendi in communitate, & societate hominum* (Constance: 1711).

Fischer, Augustin. *Sacerdotium Infiniti Pretii, Muneris Reverentiae et Dignitatis Deificum* (Krems: 1729).

Flurhaim, Christopher. Alte *Kirchengesäng und Gebett des ganzen Jars* (s.l.: 1581).

Fordenbach, Hieronymus. *Hertz-Bewegende Catholische Predigen* (Augsburg: 1712).

Forer, Lorenz. *Disputir-Kunst für die Einfältigen Catholischen* . . . (Ingolstadt: 1656).

Fossa, Felice. *Juravium Animarium in Purgatorio* . . . *Das ist: Helffenburg* (Salzburg: 1718).

Franciotti, Cesare. *Himmlische Tischreden, oder das grosse Communion-Buch*, vol. 5 (Vienna: 1650).

Francisco Antonio a Lorenzana, *Concilium Mexicanum Provinciale III* (Mexico: 1770).

Franciscus a S. Augustino Macedo. *Disquisitio Theologica de Ritu Azymi et Fermentati* (Verona: 1683).

Fritsch, Ahasverus. *Fauler und sündlicher Kirchen-Schläfer: Ehemahlen zur Warnung vorgestellet, anjetzo aber aus eben der guten Absicht mit einer kurtzen Abhandlung vom strafbaren Kirchen-Schwätzer, aufs neue zum Druck befördert* (Frankfurt: 1756).

Fulgentio Petrello a Sigillo. *De Intercessione B. Deip. Mariae Virg. Qua salvari gravissimos Peccatores eidem devotos probatur* . . . (Rome: 1647).

Galliffet, Joseph de. *De Cultu sacrosancti Cordis Dei ac Domini Jesu Christi* . . . (Rome: 1726).

Gambart, Adrien. *Landpfarrer und Gay-Prediger*, 2 vols. (Vienna: 1730).

Ganspeckh, Wilhelm. *Englischer Magnet-Stein, Das ist: Englisches Leß- und Bett-Buch*, 3 vols. (Munich: 1738).

Gavanto, Bartholomeo. *Thesaurus Sacrorum Rituum*, ed. Gaetano-Maria Merati (Augsburg: 1763).

Genebrard, Gilbert. *Canticum Canticorum Salomonis Versibus et Commentariis illustratum* (Paris: 1585).

Georg Dusseldorpiensis, *Hortus Irriguus* . . . (Cologne: 1696).

Georgijević, Bartolomej. *De Afflictione tam Captivorum quam etiam sub Turcae tributo viventium Christianorum* (Antwerp: 1544).

Gerbert, Martin. *Principia Theologiae Mysticae ad Renovationem Interiorem et Sanctificationem Christiani Hominis* (St. Blasien: 1758).

Ginther, Anton. *Speculum Amoris & Doloris in Sacratissimo ac divinissimo Corde Jesu* . . . (Augsburg: 1706).

Girard, N. *Sämmtliche Predigten*. 5 vols. (Augsburg: 2nd ed., 1772).

Giustiniani, Paolo, and Querini, Pietro. *Libellus. Addressed to Leo X, Supreme Pontiff*. Trans. Stephen M. Beall (Milwaukee: Marquette University Press, 2016).

Gobinet, Charles. *The Instruction of Youth in Christian Piety* (London: 8th ed., 1824).

Goffine, Leonard. *Seelen-Liechts erster Strahl* (Nürnberg: 1705).

Gómez de Terán, Juan Elías. *Assistencia de los fieles a los Divinos oficios, y Missas* (Madrid: 1736).

Gonet, Johannes B. *Clypeus Theologicae Thomisticae*, vol. 5 (Antwerp: 8th ed., 1725).

Gonnelieu, Jérôme de. *De la présence de Dieu, qui renferme tous les principes de la vie intérieure* (Paris: 1703).

Gourdan, Simon. *Elévations à Dieu sur les psaumes, disposées pour tous les jours du mois, dont on peut se servir très-utilement avant et après la Sainte Communion* (Paris: 1766).

Gracián, Jerónimo. *El soldado catholico, que prueva [ . . . ] que los que no tienen letras, no han de disputar de la fee con los hereges* (Brussels: 1611).

Gracián, Jerónimo. *Sumario de las Excelencias del Glorioso S. Ioseph, Esposo de la Virgen Maria* (Rome: 1597).

Granada, Louis de. *De Doctrina Sive Disciplina Vitae Spiritualis, Libellus* . . . (Cologne: 1607).

Granada, Louis de. *De Frequenti Communione Libellus cum Dialogu* (Cologne: 1586).

Granada, Louis de. *A Memoriall of a Christian Life* (Rouen: 1586).

Granada, Louis de. *Trattato della confessione & communione* (Venice: 1580).

Granada, Louis de. *The Sinner's Guide* (New York: 1890).

Granada, Louis de. *A Spiritval Doctrine, Conteining a Rvle to Liue Wel, with Diuers Praiers and Meditations. Abridged and Devided into Sixe Treatises* . . . (Leuven: 1599).

Griffith, Alford. *Fides Regia Britannica sive Annales Ecclesiae Britannicae* . . . vol. 1 (Leodii, 1663).

Guattini, Michelangelo. *Viaggio nel regno del Congo* (Venice: 1679).

Haeften, Benedict. *Schola Cordis sive Aversi a Deo Cordis ad eumdem Reductio, et Instructio* (Antwerp: 1635).

Hartmann, Franz. *Wissenschaft der Heiligen: das ist Betrachtungen von der Kindheit* . . . *Jesu Christi*, 3 vols. (Kempten: 1787).

Helbig, Johann Laurenz. *Alveare Catholicum, Per Mysticas Apes Melle et Cera* . . . *Catholisches Bien-Haus* . . . (Nuremberg: 1714).

Helbig, Johann Laurenz. *Anatomia Canis Mystica et Moralis: Das ist: Die Eigenschafft eines Hunds, gut und böse* . . ., 2 vols. (Würzburg: 1719/20).

Helbig, Johann Laurenz. *Traurige Gedancken zur Nutzlichen Zeit-Vertreibung oder Hundert Discursen* (Nürnberg: 1704).

Hennebel, Johann L. *Opuscula a exmimii Viri J. L. Hennebel accedunt Martini Steyaert* . . . *objectiones* (Leuven: 1703).

Hennebel, Johann L. *Thesis Theologica de Sacerdote Lapsi* . . . (Leuven: 1690).

Heribert von Salurn. *Concionum Pastoralium Pars Secunda* (Salzburg: 1699).

Herincx, Wilhelm. *Summa Theologicae Scholasticae et Moralis, Pars Secunda* (Antwerp: 1640).

Herzog, Franciscus. *Manuale Confessarii, seu Methodus compendiosa munus confessarii rite obeundi* . . . *Editio Quarta*, 2 vols. (Augsburg: 1727).

Hesselbach, Johann. *Epithalamia: das ist: Hochzeit-Predigen* (Salzburg: 1663).

Hoeger, Franciscus. *Die Siben Brodt in der Wuesten von Christo gesegnet* (Ingolstadt: 1726).

Hofer, Johann. *Magisterium Divinae Sapientiae per bruta hominem erudientis ad justitiam* (Trent: 1735).

Hofer, Johann. *Nützliche Geschichte und Annehmliche Exempel der Thieren zur Unterrichtung der Menschen* (Ingolstadt: 1739).

Horstius, Jacob Merlo. *Gottliebender Seelen Paradeys* . . . (Bamberg: 1697).

Houdry, Vincent. *Bibliotheca Concionatoria* . . . (Augsburg: 1749; 1775).

Hueber, Ferdinand. *Marianischer Himmel oder Astronomische Observation* . . . (Ingolstadt: 1746).

Hugo, Hermann. *Pia Desideria* (Antwerp: 1624).

Hugo, Hermann. *Pia Desideria or Divine Addresses*.(London: 3rd ed., 1702).

Hurtado, Thomas. *Resolutionum Moralium de Residentia Sacra*, vol. 1 (Lyon: 1661).

Iennyn, Jean. *Vera Confraternitas S. Trinitatis de Redemptione Captivorum* . . . (Bruge: 1649).

Ignatius a Sancto Francisco. *Synopsis magnalium Divi Josephi in tres partes* (Leodii: 1684).

Isolani, Isidor. *Summa de Donis de S. Joseph* (Rome: 1887).

Iwanek, Georg. *Lilium Paradisi Coelestis S. Josephus* . . . (New Prague: 1688).

Jansen, Cornelius. *De interioris hominis Reformatione* (Antwerp: 1628).

Janson, Jacob. *In Sacrum Missae Canonem* (Lyon: 1586).

Jeanne de la Nativité, *Le triomphe de l'amour divin dans la vie d'une grande servante de Dieu, nommée Armelle Nicolas, décédée l'an de Nôtre Seigneur 1671. Fidellement écrite par une religieuse du monastère de sainte Ursule* . . . *Première [-seconde] partie* (s.l.: 1676).

Joachim a S. Maria OCD. *Mystica Anatomia A. Nominis Deiparae Virginis Mariae* (Venice: 1690).

Joachim Rapperswilanus, *Reformatio Difformis & Deformis*..., 2 vols. (Argentati: 1726).

Joannes a Jesu Maria. *De Schola Jesu Christi Liber* (Cologne: 1612).

Joannes a Jesu Maria. *Opera Omnia*, 3 vols., ed. Ildephons a S. Aloysio (Florence: 1772f).

Joannes a S. Felice. *Triumphus Misericordiae, id est Sacrum SSS. Trinitatis Institutum Redemptio Captivorum* (Vienna: 1704).

Joannes Thomas a S. Cyrillo, *S. Anna sive de laudibus... Divae Annae* (Cologne: 1657).

Johanneser, Joseph. *Lieb-volle Seelen-Huelff zu Nutz der Abgeleibten und Lehr der Lebenden* (Stadtamhof: 1745).

Jonghen, Henricus. *Vera Fraternitas Declamanda Confratribus...* (Antwerp: 1662).

Joseph a Virgine. *Alphabethum Marianum oder Marianische Lob-und Ehren Predigen ... auch denen Herren Vorstehern der Marianischen Bruderschafften zum Besten...* (Frankfurt and Nürnberg: 1716).

Kauffmann, Georg. *Catholisch ist gut sterben. Aus der merkürdigen Bekehrung etlicher Gefangenen zu Neustadt an der Haard...* (Cologne: 1739).

Kazenberger, Kilian. *Der Tertiarien Glory, das ist, Ein Begriff vieler anderer die Tertiaren Betreffender Büchern...* (Augsburg: 1724).

Kellerhaus, Heinrich. *Saamen des Göttlichen Worts*, 3 vols. (Augsburg and Graz: 1733ff).

Kendlmayr, Johannes Eusebius. *Canonica Reformatio Hominis Veteris per Decem Dies...* (Vienna: 1691).

Kerckhove, Gaudentius van der. *Commentarii in Generalia Statuta Ordinis S. Francisci...* (Cologne: 1709).

Kerckhove, Gaudentius van der. *Gründliche kurtze Erklärung über die Regel der Minder-Brüder: auss underschiedlichen päpstlichen Erklärungen und vieler fürnehmer Lehrer Ausslegungen zusamen getragen* (Fulda: 1692; reprinted Regensburg: 1732).

Kleienmayer, Virgil. *Josephinisches Priesterthum...* (Steyer: 1718).

Lamy, Bernard. *Entretiens sur les sciences* (Paris: 1752).

Landsperger, Johann. *Pharetra Divini Amoris* (Cologne: 1533).

Languet Gergy, Jean-Joseph de. *Traité de la confiance en la miséricorde de Dieu, augmenté d'un Traité du faux bonheur des gens du monde et du vrai bonheur de la vie chrétienne* (Paris: 1720).

Lantosca, Angelo Auda da. *Regola del terz'ordine de penitenti del serafico P.S. Francesco... nuovamente corretta* (Rome and Milan: 1665).

Lauber, Joseph. *Anleitung zur christlichen Sittenlehre*, vol. 3 (Vienna: 1786).

Lechner, Kaspar. *Sodalis Parthenius* (Ingolstadt: 1621).

Lehner, Karl Joseph. *Turtur Sacer oder geistliche Turteltaub* (Cologne: 1720).

Lerchenfeldt, Johannes B. *Marianische Versamblung under einem himmelblauen Scapulier...* (Munich: 1696).

Lessius, Leonhard. *De Iustitia Aliisque Virtutibus* (Lyon: 1630).

Letins, Constantin. *Theologia Concionatoria Docens et Movens*, 2 vols. (Cologne: 7th ed., 1754).

Liguori, Alphonsus. *Le glorie di Maria. Opere Ascetiche*, vol. 6 (Rome: Redemptoristi, 1936).

Liguori, Alphonsus. *Visits to the Most Blessed Sacrament and the Blessed Virgin Mary* (orig. 1745) (Liguori: Liguori Publ., 1990).

Lobbetius Leodiensis, Jacob. *Conciones in Evangelia Feriarum Totius Quadragesimale* (Leodii: 1672).

Lohner, Tobias. *Geistliche Haus-Bibliothec: Das ist allerley heilsame Tractätlein zu sonderbarem Trost der Lebendigen und Abgestorbenen...* (Munich: 1684f).

Lohner, Tobias. *Instructio Practica tertia de Conversatione Apostolica* (Dillingen: 1680).

Lohner, Tobias. *Instructio Septima de Munere Concionandi, Exhortandi, Catechizandi . . .* (Dillingen: 1682).

Lombez, Ambroise de. *Traité de la Paix Intérieure en quatre parties* (Paris: 2nd ed., 1758).

Lorenzo de S. Francisco, *Tesoro Celestial y Divino . . .* (Seville: 1650).

Loriot, Julien. *Der Irrende auf den Weg zurück geführte Blinde . . .*, 2 vols. (Stadtamhof: 1739).

Lyere, Adrian van. *Trisagion Marianum* (Antwerp: 1648).

Maior, Joannes. *Magnum Speculum Exemplorum ex Plusquam Octoginta Autoribus [1480] . . ., Tertia Editio* (Cologne: 1607).

Manhardt, Simeon. *Conciones, oder: Christliche Predigen*, 2 vols. (Augsburg: 1628).

Man(n)incor, Edmund. *Dominicale aus dreijährigen Fastenpredigten*, 3 vols. (Cologne: 1691).

Mansi, Giuseppe. *Il Vero Ecclesiastico Studioso di Conoscere e di corrispondere alla sua Vocazione* (Rome: 1673; Venice: 10th ed., 1712; last Italian edition, Venice: 1755).

Mansi, Giuseppe. *Locupletissima bibliotheca moralis praedicabilis*, 3 vols. (Mainz: 1670; Venice: 1737).

Mansi, Giuseppe. *Verus Ecclesiasticus* (Frankfurt: 1693).

Manso, Vittorio. *Praeclara Institutio modi procedendi in causis regularium omnium* (Venice: 1605).

Marchand, Jacques. *Candelabrum Mysticum* (Montibus: 1630).

Marchand, Jacques. *Hortus pastorum sacræ doctrinæ floribus polymitus: Exemplis selectis adornatus, in lectionum areolas partitus* (Montibus: 1626; Lyon: 1682).

Marchant, Petrus. *Constitutions des religieuses réformées pénitentes du tierce ordre de S. François* (Ghent: 1635).

Marchese, Francesco. *Das tägliche Brod, oder zur täglichen Verehrung vorgestellte . . . Sacrament des Altars*, 2 vols. (Augsburg: 1700).

Marchese, Francesco. *Pane Quotidianao dell'Anima . . .*, vol. 1 (Venice: 1693; orig., Rome: 1681).

María de San José. *A Wild Country Out in the Garden: The Spiritual Journals of a Colonial Mexican Nun*, ed. Kathleen Ann Myers and Amanda Powell (Bloomington: Indiana University Press, 1999).

Marinis, Dominicus de. *Commentariorum in Tertiam Partem Sancti Thomae, pars altera, quae est de Sacramentis* (Lyon: 1668).

Mauden, David a. *Discursus Morales in Decem Decalogi Praecepta* (Bruxelles: 1627).

Mayer, Franz X. *Predigten nach den Bedürfnissen des gemeinen Mannes, Pedigern zum gemeinnützigen Kanzelvortrag und christlichen Familien zur Selbstbelehrung und Erbauung dienlich* (Munich: 1786).

Mayr, Beda. *Festpredigten nebst einem Anhang*, 5 vols. (Augsburg: 1782).

Mayr, Beda. *Predigten ueber den Catechismus fur gemeine Leute*, 2 vols. (Augsburg: 1781).

Mendoca, Francisco. *Viridarium sacrae ac profanae eruditionis* (Lyon: 1632).

Mercuri, Scipione. *La Commare . . . Kindmutter- oder Hebammen-Buch* (Leipzig: 1652).

Michael a S. Catharina. *Trinum Perfectum. Via, Veritas Vita*, 3 vols. (Augsburg: 1st ed., 1710; 4th ed., 1739).

Michael a S. Catharina. *Christlicher Seelenspiegel*, 2 vols. (Augsburg: 1731).

Miguel de San Agustin. *Introductio in terram Carmeli, et gustatio fructuum illius, seu introductio ad vitam vere Carmelitanum seu mysticam* (Brussels: 1659).

Molfesio, Andrea. *Promputuarii Triplicis Iuris Divini, Canonici et Civilis, seu Summae Moralis Theologiae, & Casuum Conscientiae. Pars Prima* (Naples: 1619).

Molina, Antonio de. *Exercicios Espirituales . . . y necessidad de la Oracion Mental* (Buros: 1630).

Molina, Antonio de. *Instruccion de sacerdotes* (Burgos: 1608).

Molina, Antonio de. *Instructio Sacerdotum ex SS. Patribus . . .* (Antwerp: 1618).

Monacensis, Adalbert. *Thesaurus Absconditus*, vol. 1 (Munich: 1703).

Monford, James. *Tractatus de Misericordia Fidelibus Defunctis exhibenda* (Cologne: 1649).

Montifontanus, Lucian. *Geistliches Kinder-Spiel*, 2 vols. (Constance: 1709).

Montifontanus, Lucian. *Geistliches Kinder-Spill. Das ist: Dreyhundert Sechs und Zwaintzig Neue Predigen Uber den kleinen Catechismum R.P. Petri Canisii Societatis Jesu*, 3 vols. (Augsburg: Reindl und Gastl, 1730).

Morales, Pedro de. *In Caput Primum Matthaei . . .* (Lyon: 1614).

Moulin, Pierre du. *Anatomie de la Messe. Troisieme Edition*, vol. 1 (Geneva: 1640).

Muratori, Ludovico. *De Ingeniorum Moderatione in Religionis negotio* (Augsburg: 1779).

Muratori, Ludovico. *Epistola Paraenetica ad Superiores Religiosorum* (Augsburg: 1765).

Muratori, Ludovico. *Gründliche Auslegung des grossen Geboths von der Liebe des Nächsten. Trans. Peter Obladen* (Augsburg: 2nd ed., 1768).

Muratori, Ludovico. *Opere*, vol. 8 (Arezzo: 1768).

Murcia, Juan B. de. *Luz seráfica de la venerable Tercera Orden de Penitencia de Nuestro Seráfico Padre San Francisco* (Valencia: 1718).

Murcia, Juan B. de. *Regl-Büchlein Deß dritten Ordens Sancti Francisci von der Buß genannt* (Burghausen: Samm, 1733).

Myller, Angelicus Maria. *Peregrinus in Jerusalem. Fremdling zu Jerusalem* (Vienna and Nürnberg: 1735).

Nadasi, Joannes. *Annales Mariani Societatis Jesu* (Rome: 1657).

Navarro, Emmanuel. *Prolegomena de Angelis in quibus Disseritur de Cognitione Spirituum, quam habuerunt Philosophis Ethnicis* (Salamanca: 1708).

Nazari, Giovanni Paolo. *Aureus de reformatione Religiosorum Libellus* (Brussels: 1637).

Nebrija, Antonio de. *Aurea hymnorum expositorum* (Granada: 1534).

Neercassel, Johannes. *Amor Poenitens sive de Divini Amoris ad Poenitentiam Necessitate* (Ebricae: 1683).

Nephew, Francis. *The Method of Mental Prayer* (London: 1694).

Neuburger, Christoph Ulrich. *Conciones Rurales, oder: Gantze doch kurtze Predigen*, vol. 1 (Salzburg: 1661).

Neudecker, Sigismud. *Schola Religiosa seu Tractatus Asceticus Universalis. Pars Prior, Editio Secunda* (Munich and Ingolstadt: 1757).

Nicole, Pierre. *Instructions theologiques et morales sur l'oraison dominicale* (Paris: 1718).

Nicole, Pierre. *Instructions theologiques et morales sur le premier commandment du Decalogue. Nouvelle Edition*, 2 vols. (Paris: 1742).

Nicole, Pierre. *Unterricht über das erste Gebot des Dekalogs*, 2 vols. (Bamberg and Würburg: 1783).

Nider, Johannes. *De reformatione religiosorum libri tres*, ed. Johannes Boucquet (Antwerp: 1611).

Nieremberg, Eusebius. *Obras y Días. Manual de Señores y Principes; en que se Propone con su Pureza y Rigor la Especulación y Ejecución Política, Económica y Particular de Todas las Virtudes* (Madrid: 1628).

Nieremberg, Eusebius. *Theopolicitus sice Brevis Illucidatio et Rationale Divinorum Operum* (Antwerp: 1641).

Noto, Joannes Maria de. *De sacris ritibus iuxta Romanam regulam vsui fratrum minorum s. Francisci vulgo Capucini . . .* (Naples: 1626).

Novati, Giovanni Battista. *Eucharistici Amores ex Canticis Canticorum Enucleati* (s.l.: 1645).

Olier, Jean-Jacques. *Catechisme chrestien pour la vie interieure* (Paris: 1657).

Olier, Jean-Jacques. *Vie intérieure de la très-sainte Vierge*, ed. Etienne-M. Faillon (s.l.: 1866).

Opstraet, Jan van. *Dissertatio Theologica de Conversione Peccatoris* (Leuven: 2nd ed., 1688).

Opstraet, Jan van. *Quid est theologus?* (Vienna: 1788).

Osuna, Francisco. *The Third Spiritual Alphabet*, ed. and trans. Mary E. Giles (New York: Paulist Press, 1981).

Otrokocsi Foris, Ferenc. *Restitutio Israel futura seu Tractatus quo ex tetxtu Hoseae* (Vienna: 1712).

Ott, Christoph. *Hohe Schuel der lieben Eltern . . .* (Ingolstadt: 1671).

Owen, Jane. *An Anti-Dote against Purgatory . . .* (St. Omer: 1634).

Paramo, Ludovico a. *De Origine et Progressu Officii Sanctae Inquisitionis eiusque dignitate & utilitate* (Madrid: 1598).

Partinger, Franciscus. *Ehr-und Tugend-Cron Aller Heiligen* (Augsburg and Graz: 1722), 624.

Pauck, Engelbert. *Tertia Seraphica Vinea sive Tertius Ordo de Poenitentia* (Cologne: 1720).

Paulus ab Omnibus Sanctis. *Clavis aurea Thesauri Partheno-Carmelitici . . .* (Vienna: 1669).

Paulus ab Omnibus Sanctis. *Marianischer Gnaden-Schatz des Bergs Carmeli . . .* (Vienna: 1664).

Paulus Hieronymus a S. Helena. *Sacrae Theologiae Moralis Medulla Recens ad Mentem Salmanticensium* (Bologna: 2nd ed., 1753).

Pelecyus, Johannes. *Affectuum Humanorum Morborumque Cura* (Munich: 1617; Strasbourg: 1715).

Pelecyus, Johannes. *Seelen-Cur, das ist: Auserlesener und heilsamer, und nothwendiger Tractat von unordentlichen und schaedlichen Anmuetungen oder Begirden des Menschen . . .* (Munich: 1618).

Pelbarto de Themesvar. *Stellarium Coronae Gloriosissimae Virginis* (Venice: 1686).

Pennequin, Pierre. *Isagoge ad Amorem Divinum* (Antwerp: 1641).

Penzinger, Heinrich. *Gute Ordnung darauf Kinder-Lehr . . .* (Vienna: 1696).

Peralta, Antonio de. *Dissertationes scholasticae de S. Joseph* (Mexico City: 1729).

Pereira, Benito. *Opera Theologica* (Cologne: 1620).

Peres Denueros, Hieronymus. *Lapidicina Sacra ex qua Eductus Primarius Lapis Ss. Virgo . . . Editio Nova* (Lyon: 1679).

Perez de Valdivia, Diego. *Aviso de gente recogida y especialmente de la dedicada al servicio de Dios* [1585] (Universidad Pontificia de Salamanca: 1977).

Perez de Valdivia, Diego. *De sacra ratione concionandi. Opus Iacobi Peresii a Valdiuia Baetici Baëzani . . . Additus est in fine Libellus eiusdem argumenti verè aureus, editus pridiem iussu . . . cardinalis Caroli Borromei archiepiscopi Mediolanensis* (Barcinone: 1588).

Petavius, Dionysios. *Opus de Theologicis Dogmatibus*, vol. 3 (Antwerp: 1700).

Petricca a Sonnino, Angelo. *Turris David . . . De Militante ac triumphante Ecclesia* (Rome: 1647).

Pfaff, Christoph Matthäus. *Dissertatio de Praejudicatis Opinionibus . . .* (Hagen: 1719).

Pichler, Vitus. *Theologia polemica* (Venice: 1749).

Pinamonti, Pedro. *Exorcista rite Edoctus. Omne Maleficorum genus probe, ac prudenter curandi* (Venice: 1712).

Pinelli, Luca. *De Virtute Seu Energia & admirandis Sacrosanctae Missae effectibus* (Cologne: 1608).

Pise, Marcellino de. *Moralis Encyclopdaeia, id est, Scientiarum Omnium Chorus . . . De festis Christo Domino*, vol. 1 (Lyon: 1656).

Pistorius, Georg. *Allgemeines Klaghaus oder Catholische Leichpredigen bey Begräbnissen der Kinder . . .* (Dillingen: 1657).

Pittroff, Christian Franz. *Anleitung zur praktischen Gottesgelehrtheit*, 4 vols. (Prague: 2nd ed., 1784).

Poiger, Benedict. *Versuch zur Errichtung einer pfärrlichen Armeleute-Bruderschaft* (Reichenhall: 1786).

Poiré, François. *La triple couronne de la Bien-heureuse Vierge Mère de Dieu*, 2 vols. (Paris: 1630).

Polanco, John. *Methodus ad eos adiuvandos qui moriuntur* (Rome: 1577).

Polio, Jacobus. *Exegeticon Historicon Sanctae* Annae (Cologne: 1640).

Polio, Jacobus. *Historia Sanctorum Joachim et Annae: Geneseos, Vitae, Transitus et Connexorum* (Würzburg: 1652).

Pona, Francesco. *Cardiomorpheoseos sive ex corde desumpta emblemata sacra* (Verona: 1645).

Porter, Franciscus. *Palinodia Religionis Praetensae Reformatae . . .* (Rome: 1679).

Pouget, Francois A. *Instructions generales en firme de Catechisme. Nouvelle Edition.* vol. 3 (Paris: 1739).

Praetorio, Ephraim. *Des homiletischen Bücher-Vorraths Erster Theil. Dritte Auflage* (Leipzig: 1713).

Prambhofer, Johannes. *Samsonischer Honig-Fladen für die schleckige Adams Kinder* (Augsburg: 1703).

Presinger, Rupert. *Neu-angehendes Ordens-Kind des heiligen Ertz-Vatters Benedicti, da es noch in der Welt lebet . . .* (Salzburg: 1737).

Probst, Ulrich. *Heylsame Gedancken von der Tugend der Keuschheit . . .* (Augsburg: 1754).

Probst, Ulrich. *Zur Erweckung Zartister Andacht und Inbrünstigen Anmuthungen . . . für alle Persohnen jedes Stands . . . Dritte Auflage.* 2 vols. (Augsburg: 1756).

Prokop von Templin. *Adventuale ac Natale Jesu Christi sive Deliciae Spiritus Hibernales . . .* (Munich: 1666).

Prokop von Templin. *Dominicale Paschale et Pentecostale* (Salzburg: 1667).

Prokop von Templin. *Funerale . . .* (Salzburg: 1670).

Prokop von Templin. *Lignum Vitae*, 3 vols. (Munich: 1666).

Prokop von Templin. *Patrociniale . . .* (Salzburg: 1674).

Prokop von Templin. *Sanctorale . . . Discurs oder Predigen*, 2 vols. (Salzburg: 1668).

Prugger, Martin. *Lehr-und Exempelbuch fuer die Krancke und Sterbende . . .* (Augsburg: 6th ed., 1762).

Puchner, Christopher. *Fragmenta Nuptialia: id est: Exhortationes Nuptiales LXXII* (New Prague: 1704).

Puente, Luis de la. *Meditations Vpon the Mysteries of Our Holie Faith: With the Practise of Mental Prayer Touching the Same* (S. Omers: 1619).

Raw, Georg. *Abgeferrtigter Herold aus der anderen Welt, von denen im Fegfewer leydenden Seelen in dise Welt gesandt* (Munich: 1658).

Raynaud, Theophil. *Confiteor Reformatum dissertatio de Paternitate Spirituali* (Lyon: 1654).

Raynaud, Theophil. *Opera Omnia*, vol. 7: *Marialia* (Lyon: 1665).

Raynaud, Theophil. *Opera Omnia*, vol. 16: *Heteroclita Spiritualia et Anomalia Pietatis Terrestrium Spectantium Morales* (Lyon: 1665).

Raynaud, Theophil. *Operum Omnium Indices Generales*. vol. 19 (Lyon: 1665).

Recupito Julius Caesar. *De signis Praedestinationis et Reprobationis et de Numero Praedestinatorum ac Reproborum* (Lyon: 1643).

Reding, August. *Oecumenici Tridentini Concilii Veritas Inextincta*, 5 vols. (Einsiedeln: 1684).

Reeb, Gabriel. *Newe Bruederschafft des glorwürdigsten . . . Manns Mariae Joseph* (Ingolstadt: 1649).

Remy, Nicolas. *Daemonolatreia Libri Tres* (Cologne: 1596).

Reuter, Johann. *Confessarius Practice Instructus . . . Editio tertia* (Cologne: 1752).

Rho, Giovanni. *Variae Virtutum Historiae Libri Septem* (Lyon: 1644).

Richemone, Louis. *Heilige Taflen der geheimreichen Figuren des allerheiligsten Sacrifitz und Sacraments der Eucharistie* (Augsburg: 1621).

Richemone, Louis. *Tableaux sacrez des figures mystique du Tres-Auguste Sacrifice et Sacrement de l'Eucharistie . . .* (Paris: 1601).

Richer, Edmund. *Obstetrix animorum. Hoc est Brevis et Expedita Ratio Docendi, Studendi, Conversandi, Imitandi, Iudicandi, Componendi* (Paris: 1600).

Richter, Joseph. *Von der öfteren Kommunion . . .* (Vienna: 1783).

Rippel, Gregor *Die wahre Schönheit der Religion . . . Gründliche Erklärung der Ceremonien . . .* (Mainz: 1777).

Roa, Martin de. *Estado de las almas de Purgatorio. Correspondencia que hazen a sus Bienchores . . .* (Seville: 1619).

Rojas, Antonio de. *Vida del espiritu para saber tener oracion y union con Dios . . .* (Madrid: 1630).

Rosenberger, Petrus Paul. *Zodiacus Marianus: Marianische Lob-Reden . . . denen ernannten Bruderschaften eyfrigen Vorstehern . . .* (Augsburg: 1698).

Rosignoli, Bernardino. *Stimuli Virtutum Adolescentiae Christianae* (Cologne: 1594).

Rosshirdt, Martin. *Franciscaner Bruderschafft Büchlein* (Salzburg: 1653).

Rotario, Thomas Francisco. *Theologia Moralis Regularium*, vol. 3 (Venice: 1735).

Rue, Charles de la. *Christliche Tugend-Schul*, 4 vols. (Augsburg: 1739).

Rupert a St. Bennone. *Sprach der Kinder Gottes. Das ist Grund-Regeln des beschaulich und würkenden Lebens . . .* (Munich: 1744).

Sacchini, Francesco. *De Ratione libros cum profectu legend libellus* (Flexiae: 1617).

Sahagún, Bernardino de. *Psalmodia Christiana*. Trans. from the original Nahuatl by A. Anderson (Salt Lake City: University of Utah Press, 1993).

Sailer, Johann Michael. *Vollständiges Lese-und Gebethbuch für katholischen Christen. Dritte Auflage* (Munich: 1789).

Sailly, Thomas. *Guidon et practique spirituelle du soldat chrestien* (Antwerp: 1590).

Saint-Jure, Jean-Baptiste. *Erkandtnuß und Liebe deß Sohns Gottes unsers Herrn Jesu Christi: zu vollkommener Erleuchtung und hertzlicher Anflammung aller Christliebenden Seelen* (Ingolstadt: 1676).

Salamancans, *Cursus Theologiae Moralis Salmanticensis*, vol. 5 (Venice: 1737).

Sales, Francis de. *Treatise on the Love of God* (Douai: 1630).

Sales, Francis de. *Werke des Hl. Franz von Sales*, 6 vols. (Eichstätt and Vienna: Franz Sales Verlag, 1960ff).

Salmeron, Alphonsus. *Commentarii in Evangelicam historiam, et in Acta Apostolorum*, vol. 1 (Cologne: 1612).

Samaniego, Joseph Ximenez. *Statuorum generalium compilatio pro familia cismontana Regularis Observantiae Seraphici*... (Madrid: 1704).

Sanches, Thomas. *Disputationum de Sancto Matrimonio Sacramento* (Antwerp: 1614).

Sanctarelli, Antonio. *De Haeresi, Schismate, Apostasia, Sollicitatione in sacramento Poenitentiae* (Rome: 1625).

Sardagna, Carolus. *Theologia Dogmatico-Polemica*..., 6 vols. (Regensburg: 1771).

Saussay, Andre. *Panoplia Sacerdotalis seu de Venerando Sacerdotum habitu* . . . (Paris: 1653).

Scanaroli, Giovanni Battista. *De Visitatione Carceratorum* (Rome: 1655).

Schaffgottsch, Prokop. *Rede auf das Fest des heiligen Joseph* (Prague: 1772).

Schelle, Augustin. *Versuch über den Einfluß der Arbeitsamkeit auf Menschenglück* (Salzburg: 1790).

Schletstätter, Sebastian. *Triumph des heiligen Rosenkrantz* (Augsburg: 1667).

Scobar a Corro, Joao. *Tractatus Tres Selectissimi et Absolutissimi*, vol. 2 (Cordoba: 1642).

Sebastus, Nicephorus. *De Chocolatis potione* (Naples: 1665; 1671).

Sebastiani, Giuseppe Maria. *De consolatione ad episcopos sub analogia episcopatus, et martyrij* (Rome: 1685).

Segala de Salo, Alessio. *Le triomphe des âmes du purgatoire. Divisé en deux parties* (Lyon: 1621).

Segala de Salo, Alessio. *Trionfo delle anime del purgatorio. Opera del R.P.F. Alessio Segala. Di nouo posto in luce, e di vaghe figure ornato* (Brescia: 1620).

Seger, Johann Gualbert. *Concha Margaritifera Spiritualis*... (Nuremberg: 1705).

Seibt, Karl Heinrich. *Katholisches Lehr-und Gebethbuch.* (Prague: 4th ed., 1794).

Seidel, Johannes. *Templum Honoris Gloriae Virginae* (Prague: 1716).

Senault, Jean-François. *De l'usage des passions* (Paris: 1641).

Senault, Jean-François. *The Use of Passions* (London: 1671).

Serrano, Andres. *Feliz Memoria de los Siete Principes de los Angeles Assistentes* . . . (Mexico: 1699).

Settelin, Franciscus. *Agricultura Spiritualis*..., vol. 6 (Salzburg: 1680).

Silesius, Angelus. *Ecclesiologia oder Kirche-Beschreibung* (Kempten: 1735).

Simon, Jordan. *Jesus der Gekreuzigte, der den Juden eine Aergernis, den Heiden eine Thorheit, den Christen aber die Kraft und Weisheit Gottes ist* (Augsburg and Ingolstadt: 1771).

Soto, Andres de. *Libro de la vida y excellencias de el glorioso S. Ioseph, esposo de la Virgen N. Señora* (Brussels: 1600).

Soto, Pedro de. *Tractatus de institutione sacerdotum* (Antwerp: 1560; 1566).

Sousa, Antonio de. *Aphorismi Inquisitorum in Quatur Libros Distributi* (s.l.: 1630).

Stanney, William. *A Treatise of Penance* (Douay: 1617).

Stainmayr, Michael. *Rationale Apostolicum oder Geistliches Brustbild* (Munich: 1684).

Stengel, Karl. *Iosephus. Hoc est Sanctissimi Educatoris Christi*... (Munich: 1616).

Sterzinger, Ferdinand. *Geister-und Zauberkatechismus* (Munich: 1783).

Stoiber, Ubald. *Armamentarium Ecclesiasticum complectens Arma spiritualia, fortissima ad insultus diabolicos elidendos*..., vol. 1 (Augsburg: 1736).

Strobl, Andreas. *Aufgemachter Schlüssel zu dem Geistlichen Karten-Spiehl* . . . (Augsburg: 1708).

Suarez, Francisco. *Commentariorum ac Disputationum in tertiam Partem Divi Thomae Tomus Tertius* (Mainz: 1619).

Suarez, Francisco. *De Angelis. Opera Omnia*, vol. 2 (Paris: 1856).

Suarez, Francisco. *De Religione*, vol. 2 (Lyon: 1630).

Suarez, Francisco. *Opus de Virtute Theologia Fide . . .* (Paris: 1621).

Surin, Jean-Joseph. *Into the Dark Night and Back. The Mystical Writings of Jean-Joseph Surin*. Ed. Moshe Sluhovsky (Leiden and Boston: Brill, 2018).

Suter, Franziskus. *Underirdische Goldgrub. Das ist trewherziger Bericht von dem Zustand der armen Seelen im Fegfewr* (Lucerne: 1692).

Sylveira, John da. *Opuscula Varia* (Lyon: 1687).

Sylvius, Franciscus. *Commentarius in Tertiam Partem S. Thomae Aquinatis*. Editio Sexta (Antwerp: 1695).

Tafuri, Didacus. *Franciscus Ter Legislator Evangelicus Fratrum Minorum Strictior . . .*, vol. 1 (Rome: 1667).

Tamburinio de Marradio, Ascanio. *De iure Abbatissarum et Monialium sive Praxis Gubernandi Moniales* (Rome: 1638).

Teresa a Ávila. *Obras completas*, Ed. Alberto Barrientos (Madrid: Editorial de Esp., 6th ed., 2016).

Teresa a Ávila. *Werke und Briefe Gesamtausgabe*, ed. Ulrich Dobhan and Elisabeth Peeters, 2 vols. (Freiburg: Herder, 2015).

Thiers, Jean B. *De la plus solide, la plus necessaire, et souvent la plus negligée de toutes les devotions*, vol. 2 (Paris: 1703).

Thiers, Jean B. *Von der gründlichsten und nothwendigsten aus allen Andachten . . . trans. Kaspar Marberger* (Vienna: 1782).

Thomas a Jesu. *Aerumnae Jesu, Das ist: Betrangnussen Unsers Erlösers Christi deß Herrn, Welche er von seiner Empfängnus an, biß in seinen Todt erlidten: Mit vierfachen zu End gesetzten Register*, trans. from the French by Wolfgang Eder (Munich: 1678).

Thomas a Jesu. *Compendio dell' oratione mentale* (Milan: 1657).

Thomas a Jesu. *Compendio de los grados de oracion por donde se sube a la perfeta contemplacion: Sacado de las obras de la santa Madre Teresa de Iesus, fundadora de la reformacion de Carmelitas Descalços* (Madrid: 1615).

Thomas a Jesu. *Opera Omnia*, 2 vols. (Cologne: 1634).

Thomas a Jesu. *Summarium undt Kurtzer Inhalt der Staffeln des Innerlichen Gebetts* (Munich: 1634).

Thomas a Virgine Maria. *Typus Mariae seu Discursus Morales, Praedicabiles ad Fidelium Animos in Deiparae Devotionem Instimulandos* (Cologne: 1687).

Thomassin, Louis. *Vetus et nova ecclesiae disciplina*, 3 vols. (Luca: 1728).

Thubières de Caylus, Charles-Daniel-Gabriel de. *Mandement de Monseigneur l'evêque d'Auxerre, portant permission de manger des oeufs pendant le Carême de la présente année 1751* (s.l.: s.n, 1751).

Thuraeus, Petrus. *De Apparitionibus Spirituum tractatus duo* (Cologne: 1600).

Torreblanca, Franciscus. *Epitome Delictorum sive de Magia* (Lyon: 1678).

Tourneyx, Nicolas de. *De la meilleure maniere d'entendre la Sainte Messe* (Paris: 1680).

Tourneyx, Nicolas de. *Die beste Weise die heilige Messe zu hören* (Vienna: 1734).

Tourneyx, Nicolas de. *De beste Maniere om Misse te hooren* (Gent: 1713).

Trinitarians. *Reformatorium Fratrum Ordinis Sanctissimae ac Individuae Trinitatis Redemptionis Captivorum Aragonica Provinciae* (Barcelona: 1563).

Tympe, Matthaeus. *Kinderzucht oder kurtzer Bericht von der Eltern Sorg und Fürsichtigkeit in Aufferziehung ihrer lieben Kinder zu Gottes Ehr und dem Vatterlandt und Gemeinem Wesen zum besten* (Münster: 1610).

Tympe, Matthaeus. *Catholische Leich und Trostpredigen . . .* (Würzburg: 1610).

Ursula de Jesus. *The Souls of Purgatory. The Spiritual Diary of a Seventeenth-Century Afro-Peruvian Mystics*, ed. Nancy E. Van Deusen (Albuquerque: University of New Mexico Press, 2004).

Valliere, Louise de la. *Reflexions sur la Misericorde de Dieu* (La Haye: 1681).

Vargas, Bernardo de. *Chronica sacri et Militaris Ordinis B. Mariae de Mercede Redemptionis Captivorum* (Panormi: 1619).

Veranus, Cajetan Felix. *De Humanis Affectibus Ciendis et Coercendis*, 3 vols. (Munich: 1710).

Veranus, Cajetan Felix. *Theologia Universa Speculativa . . .*, 8 vols. (Munich: 1700).

Verepe, Simon. *Recueil, ou Manuel Catholique d'Oraisons Devotes* (Anvers: 1593).

Vigeuer, Jean. *Institutiones ad Naturalem et Christianam Philosophia . . .* (Lyon: 1671).

Vincentius Ilger, *Observationes in Secula Christiana de disciplina et moribus*, 4 vols. (St. Blasien: 1791).

Vogel, Matthäus. *Catholicher Catechismus oder gründliche Unterweisung*, 2 vols. (Strasbourg: 1750).

Vogler, Georg. *Catechismus in auserlesenen Exempeln . . .* (Würzburg: 1652).

Wagner, Bartholomäus. *Catechesis oder Catholische Kinderlehr . . .* (Freiburg: 1609).

Wagner, Franz. *Universae Phraseologiae Latinae Corpus* (Trinava: 1775).

Walasser, Adam. *Von der Gnadreichen . . . Bruderschaft des Psalters oder Rosenkrantz Marie . . .* (Dillingen: 1572).

Waldner, Joseph. *Das Catholische Strassburger Bett-Buch* (Augsburg: 1757).

Weislinger, Nicolaus. *Catholisch ist gut sterben* (Strassburg: 1744).

Werkmeister, Benedikt Maria. *Ueber den neuen katholischen Katechismus* (Frankfurt: 1789).

White, Thomas. *Devotion and Reason. Wherein Modern Devotion for the Dead Is Brought to Solid Principles and Made Rational* (Paris: 1661).

Wild, Johann. *Gemeine, Christliche und Catholische Busspredigen . . .* (Mainz: 1564).

Wittweile, Georg. *Catholisch Hausbuch* (Munich: 1631).

Ziegler, Balthasar Antonio. *Kurtze Ermahnungen so denen neuen Eheleuthen bey der Copulation können gegeben werden* (Prague: 1698).

Zippe, Augustin. *Von der moralischen Bildung angehender Geistlicher in dem Generalseminario in Prag* (Prague: 1784).

# Bibliography of Secondary Sources

Abé, Takao. *The Jesuit Mission to New France. A New Interpretation in the Light of the Earlier Jesuit Experience in Japan* (Leiden and Boston: Brill, 2011).

Adorni, Bruno. *Jacopo Barozzi da Vignola* (Milan: Skira, 2008).

Ahlgren, Gillian. *Teresa of Avila and the Politics of Sanctity* (Ithaca: Cornell University Press, 2019).

Alberigo, Giuseppe. "Carlo Borromeo come modello di vescovo nella chiesa post-tridentina," *Rivista storica Italiana* 79 (1967): 1031–1052.

Alberigo, Giuseppe. "Die Ekklesiologie des Konzils von Trient [1964]," in Remigius Bäumer (ed.), *Concilium Tridentinum. Wege der Forschung* (Darmstadt: WBG, 1976), 278–300.

Alberigo, Giuseppe. "From the Council of Trent to Tridentinism," in Raymond F. Bulman et al. (eds.), *From Trent to Vatican II. Historical and Theological Investigations* (Aldershot: Ashgate, 2006), 19–37.

Alberigo, Giuseppe. "La réception du Concile de Trente par l'Église catholique romaine," *Irenikon* 58 (1985): 311–337.

Albert-Zerlik, Annette. *Liturgie als Sterbebegleitung und Trauerhilfe. Spätmittlelaterliches Erbe und pastorale Gegenwart unter besonderer Berücksichtigung der Ordines von Castelani (1523) und Sanctorius (1602)* (Tübingen: Francke, 2003).

Alejandre, Juan Antonio. *El veneno de Dios. La Inquisición de Sevilla ante el Delito de solicitación en confesión* (Madrid: Siglo XXI de España, 1994).

Alfieri, Fernanda. *Nella camera degli sposi. Tomás Sánchez, il matrimonio, la sessualità, Secoli XVI–XVII* (Bologna: Il Mulino, 2010).

Alfieri, Fernanda. "Urge without Desire? Confession Manuals, Moral Casuistry and the Features of *Concupiscentia* between the Fifteenth and Eighteenth Centuries," in Kate Fisher and Sarah Toullalan (eds.), *Bodies, Sex and Desire from the Renaissance to the Present* (London: Palgrave Macmillan, 2014), 151–167.

Antoine, Louis. *Deux spirituels au siècle des Lumières. Ambroise de Lombez, Philippe de Madiran* (Paris: P. Lethielleux, 1975).

Arendt, Hans-Peter. *Bussakrament und Einzelbeichte, Die tridentinischen Lehraussagen über das Sündenbekennntis und ihre Verbindlichkeit für die Reform des Bussakramentes* (Freiburg: Herder, 1981).

Aries, Philippe. *The Hour of Our Death* (Harmondsworth: Penguin, 2013).

Arneth, Michael. *Das Ringen um Geist und Form der Priesterbildung im Säkularklerus des 17. Jahrhundert* (Würzburg: Echter, 1970).

Arnold, John H., and Goodson, Caroline. "Resounding Community. The History and Meaning of Medieval Church Bells," *Viator* 43 (2012): 99–130.

Auer, Johann. *Die Entwicklung der Gnadenlehre in der Hochscholastik. Teil 1: Das Wesen der Gnade* (Freiburg: Herder, 1942).

Auer, Johann. *Die Entwicklung der Gnadenlehre in der Hochscholastik. Teil 2: Das Wirken der Gnade* (Freiburg: Herder, 1951).

Backer, Stephanie Fink de. *Widowhood in Early Modern Spain. Protectors, Proprietors, and Patrons* (Leiden and Boston: Brill, 2010).

Baernstein, P. Renee. *A Convent Tale. A Century of Sisterhood in Spanish Milan* (New York and London: Routledge, 2002).

Banker, James. *Death in the Community. Memorialization and Confraternities in an Italian Commune in the Late Middle Ages* (Athens-London: University of Georgia Press, 1988).

Barnes, Andrew. *The Social Dimension of Piety* (New York: Paulist Press, 1993).

Barnes-Karol, Gwendolyn. "Religious Oratory in a Culture of Control," in Anne Cruz and Mary E. Perry (eds.), *Culture and Control in Counter-Reformation Spain* (Minneapolis: University of Minnesota Press, 1992), 51–77.

Baufine, André. *L'union à Jésus-Christ dans les mystères de sa vie. D'après le cardinal de Bérulle* (Paris: Saint-Paul, 1970).

Bauman, Zygmunt. *Modernity and Ambivalence* (Hoboken: Wiley, 2013).

Bäumer, Remigius, and Scheffczyk, Leo (eds.), *Marienlexikon*, 6 vols. (St. Ottilien: EOS Verlag, 1989–1994).

Bergerfurth, Yvonne, and Conrad, Anne (eds.), *Welt-geistliche Frauen in der Frühen Neuzeit Studien zum weiblichen Semireligiosentum* (Münster: Aschendorff, 2013).

Bergin, Joseph. *Cardinal de la Rochefoucauld. Leadership and Reform in the French Church* (New Haven: Yale University Press, 1987).

Bergin, Joseph. *Church, Society and Religious Change in France, 1580–1730* (New Haven, CT: Yale University Press, 2009).

Bernos, Marcel. "Confession et conversion," in *La conversion au XVII siecle* (Marseille: Actes du XII Colloque de Marseille, 1982), 283–296.

Bérubé, Camille. *L'amour de Dieu. Selon Jean Duns Scot, Porète, Eckhart, Benoît de Canfield et les Capucins* (Rome: Istituto storico dei Cappuccini, 1997).

Betteridge, Thomas (ed.). *Sodomy in Early Modern Europe* (Manchester: Manchester University Press, 2007).

Biasiotto, Peter. *History of the Development of Devotion to the Holy Name* (St. Bonaventure, NY: St. Bonaventure College and Seminary, 1943).

Bilinkoff, Jodi. *The Avila of Saint Teresa* (Ithaca: Cornell University Press, 1989).

Bill-Mrziglod, Michaela. *Luisa de Carvajal y Mendoza (1566–1614) und ihre "Gesellschaft Mariens." Spiritualität, Theologie und Konfessionspolitik in einer semireligiosen Frauengemeinschaft des 17. Jahrhunderts* (Hamburg: Kovač, 2014).

Bill-Mrziglod, Michaela. "Spiritualität im Semireligiosentum—Frömmigkeitsformen, literarische Zeugnisse und Lektürepraxis," in Bergerfurth and Conrad (eds.), *Welt-geistliche Frauen*, 60–92.

Birely, Robert. "Two Works by Jean Delumeau," *Catholic Historical Review* 77 (1991): 78–88.

Birsens, Josy. "Katechese, Katechismen und Predigt im Zeitalter der Konfessionalisierung," in Bernhard Schneider (ed.), *Geschichte des Bistums Trier*, vol. 3 (Trier: Paulinus, 2010), 388–403.

Biser, Eugen. *Der Helfer. eine Vergegenwärtigung Jesu* (Munich: Kösel, 1973).

Black, Charlene Villasenor. "Love and Marriage in the Spanish Empire. Depictions of Holy Matrimony and Gender Discourses in the Seventeenth Century," *Sixteenth Century Journal* 32 (2001): 637–667.

Black, Charlene Villasenor. *Saints and Social Welfare in Golden Age Spain. The Imagery of the Cult of St. Joseph* (PhD Thesis: University of Michigan, 1995).

Black, Christopher F. *Italian Confraternities in the Sixteenth Century* (Cambridge: Cambridge University Press, 1989).

Black, Christopher F. *Society in Early Modern Italy* (New York: Palgrave Macmillan, 2004).

Black, Nancy Johnson. *The Frontier Mission and Social Transformation in Western Honduras. The Order of Our Lady of Mercy, 1525–1773* (Leiden: Brill, 1995).

Boddy, Janice. "Spirit Possession Revisited. Beyond Instrumentality," *Annual Review of Anthropology* 23 (1994): 407–434.

Boer, Wietse de. "Boundaries in Early Modern Europe," in Abigail Firey (ed.), *A New History of Penance* (Leiden and Boston: Brill, 2008), 343–346.

Boer, Wietse de. *The Conquest of the Soul. Confession, Discipline, and Public Order in Counter-Reformation Milan* (Leiden and Boston: Brill, 2001).

Boerner, Egid. *Dritter Orden und Bruderschaften der Franziskaner in Kurbayern* (Werl: Dietrich Coelde Verlag, 1988).

Boffa, Sophia. *Joseph of Nazareth as Man and Father in Jerónimo Gracián's Summary of the Excellencies of St. Joseph (1597)* (PhD Thesis, University of Notre Dame Australia, 2016).

Boon, Jessica A. *The Mystical Science of the Soul. Medieval Cognition in Bernardino de Laredo's Recollection Method* (Toronto: University of Toronto Press, 2012).

Bossy, John. "The Counter-Reformation and the People of Catholic Europe," *Past and Present* 47 (1970): 51–70.

Bossy, John. *The English Catholic Community, 1570–1870* (London: Darnton, Longman and Todd, 1975).

Brambilla, Elena. *La giustizia intollerante. Inquisizione e tribunali confessionali in Europa (secoli IV–XVIII)* (Roma: Carocci, 2006).

Brejon de Lavergnée, Matthieu. *Histoire des Filles de la charité* (Paris: Fayard, 2011).

Bremond, Henri. *A Literary History of Religious Thought in France*, vol. 3 (London: SPCK, 1936).

Brettell, Caroline B. "The Priest and His People. The Contractual Basis for Religious Basis in Rural Portugal," in Ellen Badone (ed.), *Religious Orthodoxy and Popular Faith in European Society* (Princeton, NY: Princeton University Press, 1990), 55–75.

Brian, Isabelle. "Catholic Liturgies of the Eucharist in the Time of Reform," in Lee Palmer Wandel (ed.), *A Companion to the Eucharist in the Reformation* (Leiden and Boston: Brill, 2014), 185–204.

Brinktrine, Johannes. "Zur Lehre von den sogenannten Messopferfrüchten," *Theologie und Glaube* 41 (1951): 260–265.

Briggs, Robin. *Communities of Belief. Cultural and Social Tension in Early Modern France* (Oxford: Clarendon Press, 1989).

Brochhagen, Johannes N. *Kirchliche Kontrolle und religiöse Kommunikation im kolonialzeitlichen Andenraum. Die bischöfliche Visitation ländlicher Pfarreien der Diözese La Paz (17.–18. Jahrhundert)* (PhD Thesis: University of Hamburg/ Germany, 2017).

Broutin, Paul. *La réforme pastorale en France au XVIIe siècle*, 2 vols. (Tournai: Desclee, 1956).

Brugger, Christian E. *The Indissolubility of Marriage and the Council of Trent* (Washington, DC: Catholic University of America Press, 2017).

Burzer, Katja. *San Carlo Borromeo. Konstruktion und Inszenierung eines Heiligenbildes im Spannungsfeld zwischen Mailand und Rom* (Munich: Deutscher Kunstverlag, 2011).

Bynum, Caroline. *Christian Materiality. An Essay on Religion in Late Medieval Europe* (New York: Zone, 2011).

Cagle, Hugh. *Assembling the Tropics. Science and Medicine in Portugal's Empire, 1450–1700* (Cambridge: Cambridge University Press, 2018).

Calvert, Laura. *Francisco de Osuna and the Spirit of the Letter* (Chapel Hill: University of North Carolina Press, 1973).

Camaioni, Michele. "Capuchin Reform, Religious Dissent and Political Issues in Bernardino Ochino's Preaching in and towards Italy, 1535–1545," in Bert Roest et al. (eds.), *Religious Orders and Religious Identity Formation, c. 1420–1620* (Leiden and Boston: Brill, 2016), 214–234.

Campbell, Jodi. *At the First Table. Food and Social identity in Early Modern Spain* (Lincoln, NE: University of Nebraska Press, 2017).

Campbell, Ted. *The Religion of the Heart. A Study of European Religious Life in the Seventeenth and Eighteenth Centuries* (Columbia: University of South Carolina Press, 1991).

Camporesi, Piero. *The Fear of Hell. Images of Damnation and Salvation in Early Modern Europe.* Trans. Lucinda Byatt (University Park: Pennsylvania State University Press, 1991).

Carbajal López, David. "Mujeres y reforma de cofradías en Nueva España y Sevilla, ca. 1750–1830," *Estudios de Historia Novohispana* 55 (2016): 64–79.

Carol, Juniper (ed.). *Mariology*, 3 vols. (Post Falls: Mediatrix Press, 2018/2019).

Carrera, Elena. "The Emotions in Sixteenth-Century Spanish Spirituality," *Journal of Religious History* 31 (2007): 235–252.

Carter, Karen. *Creating Catholics. Catechism and Primary Education in Early Modern France* (Notre Dame, IN: University of Notre Dame Press, 2011).

Carter, Karen. *Scandal in the Parish. Priests and Parishioners Behaving Badly in Eighteenth-Century France* (Montreal: McGill University Press, 2019).

Cashner, Andrew A. *Hearing Faith. Music as Theology in the Spanish Empire* (Leiden and Boston: Brill, 2020).

Cattaneo, Enrico. "La singolare fortuna degli *Acta ecclesiae Mediolanensis*," *Scuola cattolica* 111 (1983): 191–217.

Cavallo, Sandra. *Charity and Power in Early Modern Italy. Benefactors and Their Motives in Turin, 1541–1789* (Cambridge: Cambridge University Press, 1995).

Ceroke, Christian P. "The Scapular Devotion," in Carol (ed.), *Mariology*, vol. 3, 131–146.

Cervantes, Fernando. "Angels Conquering and Conquered. Changing Perceptions in Spanish America," in Marshall and Walsham (eds.), *Angels*, 104–133.

Chabod, Federico. *Lo Stato e la vita religiosa a Milano nell'epoca di Carlo V* (Turin: Einaudi, 1971).

Châtellier, Louis. "Die Erneuerung der Seelsorge und die Gesellschaft nach dem Konzil von Trient," in Prodi and Reinhard (eds.), *Das Konzil von Trient und die Moderne*, 106–123.

Châtellier, Louis. *The Europe of the Devout. The Catholic Reformation and the Formation of a New Society* (Cambridge: Cambridge Univ. Press, 1991).

Châtellier, Louis. *The Religion of the Poor. Rural Missions in Europe and the Formation of Modern Catholicism, c.1500–c.1800* (Cambridge, UK: Cambridge University Press, 1997).

Chiu, Remi. "Singing on the Street and in the Home in Times of Pestilence. Lessons from the 1576–78 Plague of Milan," in Corry et al. (eds.), *Domestic Devotion in Early Modern Italy*, 27–44.

Chorpenning, Joseph. "St. Joseph in the Spirituality of Teresa of Avila and of Francis de Sales. Convergences and Divergences," in Christopher C. Wilson (ed.), *The Heirs of St. Teresa of Avila* (Washington, DC: ICS Publ., 2006), 123–140.

Chuchiak, John F. "The Sins of the Fathers. Franciscan Friars, Parish Priests, and the Sexual Conquest of the Yucatec Maya, 1545–1808," *Ethnohistory* 54 (2007): 69–126.

Cohen, Thomas M. *The Fire of Tongues, Antonio Vieira and the Missionary Church in Brazil and Portugal* (Stanford: Stanford University Press, 1998).

Cohn, Samuel Kline. *Death and Property in Siena, 1205–1800. Strategies for the Afterlife* (Baltimore: Johns Hopkins University Press, 1988).

Coleman, Charly. *The Spirit of French Capitalism. Economic Theology in the Age of Enlightenment* (Stanford: Stanford University Press, 2021).

Collison, Patrick. "Not Sexual in the Ordinary Sense. Women, Men and Religious Transactions," in idem, *Elizabethan Essays* (London: Hambledon Press, 1994), 119–150.

Comerford, Cathleen. *Reforming Priests and Parishes. Tuscan Dioceses in the First Century of Seminary Education* (Leiden and Boston: Brill, 2006).

Conrad, Anne. "Ein mittlerer Weg. Welt-geistliche Frauen im konfessionalisierten Katholizismus," in Bergerfurt and Conrad (eds.), *Welt-geistliche Frauen*, 7–24.

Conrad, Anne. *Zwischen Kloster und Welt. Ursulinen und Jesuitinnen in der katholischen Reformbewegung des 16./17.Jahrhunderts* (Mainz: Zabern, 1991).

Cooper, Irena Galandra. "Investigating the 'Case' of the Agnus Dei in Sixteenth-Century Italian Homes," in Corry et al. (eds.), *Domestic Devotions in Early Modern Italy*, 220–243.

Coromoto González, Jennifer de la. *"To Better Serve God and to Save My Soul." Marriage, Gender and Honor in Spanish New Mexico, 1681–1730* (PhD Thesis: Michigan State, 2016).

Corry, Maya, et al. (eds.), *Domestic Devotion in Early Modern Italy* (Leiden and Boston: Brill, 2019).

Criveller, Gianni. *Preaching Christ in Late Ming China. The Jesuit's Presentation of Christ from Matteo Ricci to Giulio Aleni* (Rome: Ricci Institute, 1997).

Curatulo, Emilio. *Die Kunst der Juno Lucina in Rom. Geschichte der Geburtshilfe von ihren ersten Anfängen bis zum 20. Jahrhundert* (Berlin: Hirschwald, 1902).

D'Emic, Michael Thomas. *Justice in the Marketplace in Early Modern Spain. Saravia, Villalon and the Religious Origins of Economic Analysis* (New York et al.: Lexington Books, 2014).

Dainville-Barbiche, Ségolène de. "Les communautés paroissiales de Paris au XVIIIe siècle. sociétés de prêtres ou auberges ecclésiastiques," *Revue d'Histoire de l'Eglise de France* 93 (2007): 267–280.

Dalton, Jessica M. *Between Popes, Inquisitors and Princes. How the First Jesuits Negotiated Religious Crisis in Early Modern Italy* (Leiden and Boston: Brill, 2020).

Daly, Peter. *The Emblem in Early Modern Europe. Contributions to the Theory of the Emblem* (Aldershot: Ashgate, 2014).

Daly, Robert J. "The Council of Trent," in Lee Palmer Wandel (ed.), *A Companion to the Eucharist in the Reformation* (Leiden and Boston: Brill, 2014), 159–184.

Decker, Rainer. *Witchcraft and the Papacy.* Trans. Erik Midelfort (Charlottesville: University of Virginia Press, 2010).

Deckert, Adalbert. *Karmel in Straubing. 1368–1968* (Rome: Institutum Carmelitanum, 1968).

Decock, Wim. "From Law to Paradise. Confessional Catholicism and Legal Scholarship," *Rechtsgeschichte–Legal History* 18 (2011): 12–34.

Decock, Wim. *Theologians and Contract Law. The Moral Transformation of the ius commune, ca. 1500–1650* (Leiden and Boston: Brill, 2013).

Decraene, Ellen. "Sisters of Early Modern Confraternities in a Small Town in the Southern Netherlands (Aalst)," *Urban History* 40 (2013): 247–270.

Delgado, Mariano, and Gutierrez, Lucio. *Die Konzilien auf den Philippinen* (Paderborn: Schöningh, 2008).

Delgado, Mariano, Gutierrez, Lucio, and Ries, Markus (eds.). *Karl Borromaeus und die katholische Reform* (Stuttgart: Kohlhammer, 2010).

Delumeau, Jean. *Catholicism between Luther and Voltaire. A New View of the Counter-Revolution* (Philadelphia: Westminster Pr., 1977).

Delumeau, Jean. *Sin and Fear. The Emergence of a Western Guilt Culture, 13th–18th Centuries* (New York: St. Martin's Press, 1991).

Demeuse, Eric. *Unity and Catholicity. The Ecclesiology of Francisco Suarez* (Oxford: Oxford University Press, 2022).

Demeuse, Eric. "The World Is Content with Words. Jansenism between Thomism and Calvinism," in Jordan Ballor et al. (eds.), *Beyond Dordt and de Auxiliis. The Dynamics of Protestant and Catholic Soteriology in the Sixteenth and Seventeenth Century* (Leiden and Boston: Brill, 2019), 245–276.

Dempsey, Charles. *Inventing the Renaissance Putto* (Chapel Hill: University of North Carolina Press, 2001).

Derréal, Helene. *Un missionaire de la Contre-Réforme. Saint Pierre Fourier et l'Institution de la Congrégation de Notre-Dame* (Paris: Librairie Lon., 1965).

Deusen, Nancy van. *Between the Sacred and the Worldly. The Institutional and Cultural Practice of recogimiento in Colonial Lima* (Stanford: Stanford University Press, 2001).

Deusen, Nancy van. *Embodying the Sacred. Women Mystics in Seventeenth-Century Lima* (Durham: Duke University Press, 2018).

Deusen, Nancy van (ed.). *The Souls of Purgatory. The Spiritual Diary of a Seventeenth-Century Afro-Peruvian Mystic, Ursula de Jesus* (Albuquerque: University of New Mexico Press, 2004).

Dierksmeier, Laura. *Charity for and by the Poor. Franciscan-Indigenous Confraternities in Mexico, 1527–1700* (Norman: University of Oklahoma Press, 2020).

Dinan, Susan E. *Women and Poor-Relief in Seventeenth-Century France* (Aldershot: Ashgate, 2006).

Ditchfield, Simon. "Catholic Reformation and Renewal," in Peter Marshall (ed.), *The Oxford Illustrated History of Christianity. The Reformation* (Oxford: Oxford University Press, 2015), 152–185.

Ditchfield, Simon. "Decentering the Catholic Reformation. Papacy and Peoples in the Early Modern World," *Archiv für Reformationsgeschichte* 101 (2010): 186–208.

Ditchfield, Simon. "Tridentine Catholicism," in Alexandra Bamji et al. (eds.), *The Ashgate Research Companion to the Counter-Reformation* (Farnham: Ashgate, 2013), 15–32.

Dixon, Thomas. *From Passions to Emotions. The Creation of a Secular Psychological Category* (Cambridge: Cambridge University Press, 2003).

Dörfler-Dierken, Angelika. *Die Verehrung der heiligen Anna in Spätmittelalter und früher Neuzeit* (Göttingen: Vandenhoeck & Ruprecht, 1992).

Drenas, Andrew. *The Standard Bearer of the Roman Church. Lawrence of Brindisi & Capuchin Missions in the Holy Roman Empire, 1599–1613* (Washington: Catholic University of America Press, 2018).

DuChesnay, Charles Berthelot. *Les missions de Saint Jean Eudes. Contribution à l'histoire des missions en France au 17. Siècle* (Paris: Procure des Eudistes, 1967).

Duffin, Jacyln. *Medical Miracles. Doctors, Saints, and Healing in the Modern World* (Oxford: Oxford University Press, 2009).

Dufour, Gérard. *Clero y Sexto Mandamiento La confesión en la España del siglo XVIII* (Valladolid: Ámbito, 1996).

Duhamelle, Christophe. *Die Grenze im Dorf. Katholische Identität im Zeitalter der Aufklärung* (Baden-Baden: Ergon Verlag, 2018).

Duhamelle, Christophe. *La frontière au village Une identité catholique allemande au temps des Lumières* (Paris: École des hautes études en sciences sociales, 2010).

Duvernoy, Sylvie. "Baroque Oval Churches. Innovative Geometrical Patters in Early Modern Sacred Architecture," *Nexus Network Journal* 17 (2015): 425–456.

Eberlein, Johann Konrad. *Apparitio regis—revelatio veritatis. Studien zur Darstellung des Vorhangs in der bildenden Kunst von der Spätantike bis zum Ende des Mittelalters* (Frankfurt: Gerbrun, 1992).

Eire, Carlos. "The Good Side of Hell. Infernal Meditations in Early Modern Spain," *Historical Reflections* 26 (2000): 285–310.

Eire, Carlos. *Reformations. The Early Modern World, 1450-1650* (New Haven: Yale University Press, 2016).

Emery, Kent. *Renaissance Dialectic and Renaissance Piety. Benet of Canfield's Rule of Perfection. A Translation and Study* (Binghamton, NY: Medieval & Renaissance Texts & Studies, 1987).

Enenkel, Karl A. E. "Energeia Fireworks. Jesuit Image Theory in Franciscus Neumayr's Rhetorical Manual (Idea Rhetoricae, 1748) and His Tragedies," in Wietse de Boer et al. (eds.), *Jesuit Image Theory* (Leiden and Boston: Brill, 2016), 146–188.

Engels, Jens Ivo. "Vom vergeblichen Streben nach Eindeutigkeit. Normenkonkurrenz in der europäischen Moderne," in Karsten and von Thiessen (eds.), *Normenkonkurrenz in historischer Perspektive*, 217–237.

Erlemann, Hildegard. *Die Heilige Familie Ein Tugendvorbild der Gegenreformation im Wandel der Zeit Kult und Ideologie* (Münster: Ardey-Verl, 1993).

Evennett, Henry Outram. *The Cardinal of Lorraine and the Council of Trent. A Study in the Counter-Reformation* (Cambridge: Cambridge University Press, 1930).

Evennett, Henry Outram. *The Spirit of Counter-Reformation* (Notre Dame: University of Notre Dame Press, 1970).

Eybl, Franz. "Vom Verzehr des Textes. Thesen zur Performanz des Erbaulichen," in Andreas Solbach (ed.), *Aedificatio. Edification in the Intercultural Context of the Early Modern Age* (Berlin: DeGruyter, 2005), 95–112.

Farriss, Nancy M. *Maya Society under Colonial Rule The Collective Enterprise of Survival* (Princeton: Princeton University Press, 1984).

Farriss, Nancy M. *Tongues of Fire. Language and Evangelization Colonial Mexico* (Oxford: Oxford University Press, 2018).

Fastiggi, Robert. "Francisco Suarez and the Non-Believers," *Pensamiento* 74 (2018): 263–270.

Febvre, Lucien. "Aspects méconnus d'un renouveau religieux en France entre 1590 et 1620," *Annales ESC* (1958): 639–650.

Fenlon, Dermot. *Heresy and Obedience in Tridentine Italy Cardinal Pole and the Counter Reformation* (Cambridge: Cambridge University Press, 1972).

Finger, Heinz. "Das Konzil von Trient und die Ausbilung der Säkularkleriker in Priesterseminaren während der Frühen Neuzeit," in Wim Francois and Violet Soen (eds.), *The Council of Trent. Reform and Controversy in Europe and Beyond (1545–1700)*, vol. 2 (Göttingen: Vandenhoeck & Rupprecht, 2018), 33–60.

Flüchter, Antje. *Der Zölibat zwischen Devianz und Norm. Kirchenpolitik und Gemeindealltag in den Herzogtümern Jülich und Berg im 16. und 17. Jahrhundert* (Cologne et al.: Böhlau, 2006).

Flynn, Maureen. *Sacred Charity. Confraternities and Social Welfare in Spain, 1400–1700* (Ithaca/New York: Macmillan, 1989).

Forrest, Beth Marie, and Najjaj, April L. "Is Sipping Sin Breaking Fast? The Catholic Chocolate Controversy and the Changing World of Early Modern Spain," *Food and Foodways* 15 (2007): 31–52.

Forrestal, Alison. *Fathers, Pastors and Kings. Visions of Episcopacy in Seventeenth-Century France* (Manchester: Manchester University Press, 2004).

Forrestal, Alison. *Vincent de Paul, the Lazarist Mission and French Catholic Reform* (Oxford: Oxford University Press, 2017).

Forster, Marc R. *Catholic Revival in the Age of the Baroque. Religious Identity in Southwest Germany, 1550–1750* (Cambridge: Cambridge University Press, 2007).

Forster, Marc R. *The Counter-Reformation in the Villages. Religion and Reform in the Bishopric of Speyer, 1560–1720* (Ithaca: Cornell University Press, 1992).

Fortunato, Giuseppina. *L' architettura dei frati Cappuccini nella provincia Romana* (Pescara: Carsa Ed. 2012).

Franzen, August. "Innerdiözesane Hemmungen und Hindernisse der kirchlichen Reform im 16. und 17. Jahrhundert," in Eduard Hegel (ed.), *Colonia Sacra. Studien und Forschungen zur Geschichte der Kirche im Erzbistum Köln* (Cologne: Pick, 1947), 163–201.

Freedberg, David. *The Power of Images. Studies in the History and Theory of Response* (Chicago: University of Chicago Press, 1989).

Freitag, Werner. *Pfarrer, Kirche und ländliche Gemeinschaft. Das Dekanat Vechta 1400–1803* (Bielefeld: Verlag für Regionalgeschichte, 1998).

Frymire, John M. *The Primacy of the Postils. Catholics, Protestants, and the Dissemination of Ideas in Early Modern Germany* (Leiden and Boston: Brill, 2010).

Gagnon, François-Marc. *La conversion par l'image. Un aspect de la mission des jésuites auprès des indiens du Canada au XVIIe siècle* (Montreal: Les Editions Bellarmin, 1975).

Gaite, Carmen. *Love Customs in Eighteenth-Century Spain*. Trans. Maria Tomsich (Berkeley: University of California Press, 1991).

Galván, Luis René Guerrero. *Procesos inquisitoriales por el pecado de solicitación en Zacatecas (siglo XVIII)* (Zacatecas, Mexico: Tribunal Superior de Justicia del Estado de Zacatecas, 2003).

Ganter, Bernard J. *Clerical Attire. A Historical Synopsis and a Commentary* (Washington, DC: Catholic University of America Press, 1955).

Gay, Jean-Pascal. *Morales en conflit. Théologie et polémique au Grand Siècle, 1640–1700* (Paris: Cerf, 2011).

Gentilcore, David. "Adapt Yourselves to the People's Capabilities. Missionary Strategies, Methods and Impact in the Kingdom of Naples, 1600–1800," *Journal of Ecclesiastical History* 45 (1994): 269–294.

Gentilcore, David. *Food and Health in Early Modern Europe* (London et al.: Bloomsbury, 2016).

Gerarda Śliwińska, Barbara. *Geschichte der Kongregation der Schwestern der heiligen Jungfrau und Martyrin Katharina 1571–1772* (Münster: Historischer Verein des Ermlands, 1999).

Getz, Christine. *Mary, Music, and Meditation. Sacred Conversations in Post-Tridentine Milan* (Indianapolis: Indiana University Press, 2013).

Gilanyi, Gabriella. "Der einstimmige lateinische liturgische Gesand in Ungarn nach dem Tridentinischen Konzil," in Marta Fata and Andras Forgo (eds.), *Das Trienter Konzil und seine Rezeption im Ungarn des 16. und 17. Jahrhunderts* (Münster: Aschendorfff, 2019), 261–290.

Goga, Malte. *Engel-Bilder. Die Sichtbarkeit von Engelfiguren in Italienischer Malerei um 1600* (Munich: Fink, 2015).

González García, José Antonio. *Fray Martín de Valencia y Santo Toribio de Mayorga vidas paralelas de dos leoneses preclaros del siglo XVI. Valencia de Don Juan, Mayorga de Campos* (Madrid: Pliega, 2010).

González Marmolejo, Jorge René. *Sexo y confesion. La iglesia y la penitencia en los siglos XVIII y XIX en la Nueva España* (Mexico City: Editores Plaza y Valdés, 2002).

Goodman, Dena. *Becoming a Woman in the Age of Letters* (Ithaca, NY: Cornell University Press, 2009).

Gose, Peter. *Invaders as Ancestors. On the Intercultural Making and Unmaking of Spanish Colonialism in the Andes* (Toronto: University of Toronto Press, 2008).

Göttler, Christine. *Last Things. Art and the Religious Imagination in the Age of Reform* (Turnhout: Brepols, 2010).

Gouveia, Jaime Ricardo. *O sagrado e o profano em choque no confessionário. O delito de solicitação no Tribunal da Inquisição, Portugal 1551-1700* (Coimbra: Palimage Editores, 2011).

Grabner-Haider, Anton, et al. (eds.). *Kulturgeschichte der Frühen Neuzeit* (Göttingen: Vandenhoeck and Ruprecht, 2014).

Graf, Katrin. "Der Dialog *Conjugium* des Erasmus von Rotterdam in deutschen Übersetzungen des 16. Jahrhunderts," in Schnell (ed.), *Geschlechterbeziehungen*, 259–274.

Graf, Katrin. "ut suam quisque vult esse, ita est. Die Gelehrtenehe als Frauenerziehung. Drei Eheschriften des Erasmus von Rotterdam," in Schnell (ed.), *Geschlechterbeziehungen*, 233–257.

Gray, Colleen. *The Congrégation De Notre-Dame, Superiors, and the Paradox of Power. 1693-1796* (Montreal: McGill-Queen's University Press, 2007).

Green, R. L. *Tropical Idolatry. A Theological History of Catholic Colonialism in the Pacific World, 1568-1700* (Lanham: Lexington Books, 2018).

Greer, Allan, and Bilinkoff, Jodi. *Colonial Saints. Discovering the Holy in the Americas, 1500-1800* (Abingdon: Routledge, 2015).

Greyerz, Kaspar von. *Religion and Culture in Early Modern Europe, 1500-1800* (Oxford: Oxford University Press, 2008).

Groethuysen, Bernhard. *Die Entstehung der bürgerlichen Welt-und Lebensanschauung in Frankreich*, 2 vols. (Frankfurt: Suhrkamp, 1978).

Grosse, Sven. *Heilsungewissheit und Scrupulositas im späten Mittelalter. Studien zu Johannes Gerson und Gattungen der Frömmigkeitstheologie seiner Zeit* (Tübingen: JCB Mohr, 1994).

Gunnarsdóttir, Ellen. *Mexican Karismata. The Baroque Vocation of Francisca De Los Ángeles, 1674-1744* (Lincoln: University of Nebraska Press, 2004).

Hagemann, Eduard. "The Persecution of the Christians in Japan in the Middle of the Seventeenth Century," *Pacific Historical Review* 11 (1942): 151–160.

Haliczer, Stephen. *Sexuality in the Confessional. A Sacrament Profaned* (Oxford: Oxford University Press, 1996).

Hall, Marcia B., and Cooper, Tracy E. (eds.). *The Sensuous in the Counter-Reformation Church* (Cambridge: Cambridge University Press, 2013).

Hamm, Berndt. "Frömmigkeitstheologie als Gegenstand theologiegeschichtlicher Forschung," *Theologie und Kirche* 74 (1977): 464–497.

Hamm, Berndt. "Normative Zentrierung im 15. und 16. Jahrhundert," *Zeitschrift für Historische Forschung* 26 (1999): 163–202.

Hammel, Galvin. "Revolutionary Flagellants? Clerical Perceptions of Flagellant Brotherhoods in Late Medieval Flanders and Italy," in Nicholas Terpstra et al. (eds.), *Faith's Boundaries. Laity and Clergy in Early Modern Confraternities*, (Turnhout: Brepols, 2012), 303–330.

Hart, William B. "The Kindness of the Blessed Virgin. Faith, Succor, and the Cult of Mary among Christian Hurons and Iroquois in Seventeenth-Century New France," in Nicholas Griffiths and Fernando Cervantes (eds.), *Spiritual Encounters. Interactions between Christianity and Native Religions in Colonial America* (Lincoln: University of Nebraska Press, 1999), 65–90.

Hassing, Richard. *Cartesian Psychophysics and the Whole Nature of Man. On Descartes' Passions of the Soul* (London: Lexington Books, 2015).

Headley, John, and Tomaro, John. "Borromean Reform in the Empire? La Strada Rigorosa of Giovanni Francesco Bonomi," in Headley and Tomaro (eds.), *San Carlo Borromeo*, 228–249.

Headley, John, and Tomaro, John (eds.). *San Carlo Borromeo. Catholic Reform and Ecclesiastical Politics in the Second Half of the Sixteenth Century* (Washington: Folger Books, 1988).

Hecht, Christian. *Katholische Bildertheologie der frühen Neuzeit* (Berlin: Gebr. Mann, 2012).

Heinz, Andreas. "Das liturgische Leben der Trierischen Kirche zwischen Reformation und Säkularisation," in Bernhard Schneider (ed.), *Geschichte des Bistums Trier*, vol. 3 (Trier: Paulinus, 2010), 267–322.

Heinz, Andreas. "Die Feier der Firmung nach römischer Tradition. Etappen in der Geschichte eines abendländischen Sonderwegs," *Liturgisches Jahrbuch* 39 (1989): 67–88.

Heinz, Andreas. *Die sonn- und feiertägliche Pfarrmesse im Landkapitel Bitburg-Kyllburg der alten Erzdiözese Trier von der Mitte des achtzehnten bis zur Mitte des neunzehnten Jahrhunderts* (Trier: Paulinus-Verlag, 1978).

Helms, Chad. "Introduction," in idem (ed.), *Fenelon. Selected Writings. The Classics of Western Spirituality* (New York: Paulist Press, 2006), 1–113.

Henkel, Willi. *Die Konzilien in Lateinamerika. Vol. 1: Mexiko* (Paderborn Schöningh, 1984).

Henkel, Willi, and Saranyana, Josep-Ignasi. *Die Konzilien in Lateinamerika, Vol. 2: Lima* (Paderborn: Schöningh, 2010).

Henneberg, Josephine von. "Saint Francesca Romana and Guardian Angels in Baroque Art," *Religion and the Arts* 2 (1998): 467–487.

Hersche, Peter. "Die Marginalisierung der Universitäten im katholischen Europa des Barockzeitalters," in Rainer Schwinges (ed.), *Universität, Religion und Kirchen* (Basel: Schwabe, 2011), 267–276.

Hersche, Peter. *Muße und Verschwendung Europäische Gesellschaft und Kultur im Barockzeitalter*. 2 vols. (Freiburg: Herder, 2006).

Herzog, Urs. *Geistliche Wohlredenheit. Die katholische Barockpredigt* (Munich: CH. Beck, 1991).

Hillman, Jennifer. *Female Piety and the Catholic Reformation in France* (London: Pickering and Chatto, 2014).

Hippenmeyer, Immacolata S. "Der Pfarrer im Dienste seiner Gemeinde. Ein kommunales Kirchenmodell. Graubünden, 1400–1600," in Norbert Haag et al. (eds.), *Ländliche Frömmigkeit. Konfessionskulturen und Lebenswelten, 1500–1850* (Stuttgart: Thorbecke, 2002), 143–157.

Hoffman, Philip T. *Church and Community in the Diocese of Lyon, 1500–1789* (New Haven: Yale University Press, 1984).

Hoffmann, Anja. *Sakrale Emblematik in St. Michael in Bamberg. Lavabo hortum meum . . .* (Wiesbaden: Harrassowitz, 2001).

Hoffmann, Tobias. "Duns Scotus's Action Theory in the Context of His Angelology," *Archa Verbi. Subsidia* 5 (2010): 403–420.

Höfler, Max. *Die volksmedizinische Organotherapie und ihr Verhältnis zum Kultopfer* (Stuttgart: UDV, 1908).

Holler, Jacqueline. *Escogidas Plantas. Nuns and Beatas in Mexico City, 1531–1601* (New York: Columbia University Press, 2005).

Holzem, Andreas. "Kinder nicht um Gott betrügen–historisch, Andachtsbuch und religiöser Erziehungsrat in der frühen Neuzeit," in Reinhold Boschki et al. (eds.), *Religionspädagogische Grundoptionen. Elemente einer gelingenden Glaubenskommunikation. Feschrift Albert Biesinger* (Freiburg: Herder, 2008), 255–274.

Hoping, Helmut. *Für Euch hingegeben. Geschichte und Theologie der Eucharistie* (Freiburg: Herder, 2nd ed., 2015).

Hümmerich, Walther. *Anfänge des kapuzinischen Klosterbaues. Untersuchungen zur Kapuzinerarchitektur in den rheinischen Ordensprovinzen* (Mainz: Ges. für Mittelrhein. Kirchengeschichte, 1987).

Huovinen, Anja. "Zwischen Zölibat, Familie und Unzucht. Katholische Geistliche in Andalusien am Ende des Ancien Régime," *L'Homme* 9 (1998): 7–25.

Ivanič, Suzanna. *Cosmos and Materiality in Early Modern Prague* (Oxford: Oxford University Press, 2021).

Ivanič, Suzanna, and Laven, Mary (eds.). *Religious Materiality in the Early Modern World* (Amsterdam: Amsterdam University Press, 2020).

Jaffary, Nora. *False Mystics. Deviant Orthodoxy in Colonial Mexico* (Lincoln: University of Nebraska Press, 2008).

Jahn, Bernhard, and Schindler, Claudia (eds.), *Maria in den Konfessionen und Medien der Frühen Neuzeit* (Berlin: DeGruyter, 2020).

Jedin, Hubert. *Geschichte des Konzils von Trient*, 4 vols. (Darmstadt: WBG Reprint, 2017).

Johnson, Trevor. "Guardian Angels and the Society of Jesus," in Marshall and Walsham (eds.), *Angels*, 191–213.

Jones, Matthew L. *The Good Life in the Scientific Revolution. Descartes, Pascal, Leibniz and the Cultivation of Virtue* (Chicago: University of Chicago Press, 2006).

Jordan, Constance. *Renaissance Feminism* (Ithaca: Cornell University Press, 1990).

Jotischky, Andrew. *The Carmelites and Antiquity. Mendicants and Their Past in the Middle Ages* (Oxford: Oxford University Press, 2002).

Jubany, Narciso. "El Concilio de Trento y la renovación de las ordenes inferiores al presbiterado," *Estudios Eclesiásticos* 36 (1961): 127–143.

Kamen, Henry. *The Phoenix and the Flame. Catalonia and the Counter-Reformation* (New Haven: Yale University Press, 1993).

Kantola, Ilkka. *Probability and Moral Uncertainty in Late Medieval and Early Modern Times* (Helsinki: Luther-Agricola-Society, 1994).

Karant-Nunn, Susan C. *The Reformation of Feeling. Shaping the Religious Emotions in Early Modern Germany* (Oxford: Oxford University Press, 2010).

Karsten, Arne, and Thiessen, Hillard von (eds.). *Normenkonkurrenz in historischer Perspektive. Zeitschrift für historische Forschung, Beiheft 50* (Berlin: Duncker & Humblot, 2015).

Keitt, Andrew W. *Inventing the Sacred. Imposture, Inquisition, and the Boundaries of the Supernatural in Golden Age Spain* (Leiden and Boston: Brill, 2005).

Kiesler, Berta. *Die Struktur des Theozentrismus bei Pierre de Berulle und Charles de Condren* (Berlin: Triltsch & Huther, 1934).

Klieber, Rupert. *Bruderschaften und Liebesbünde nach Trient, Ihr Totendienst, Zuspruch und Stellenwert im kirchlichen und gesellschaftlichen Leben am Beispiel Salzburgs, 1600–1950* (Frankfurt: Peter Lang, 1999).

Kochuthara, Shaji George. *The Concept of Sexual Pleasure in the Catholic Moral Tradition* (Rome: Pontificia Università Gregoriana, 2007).

Körner, Reinhard. "Was ist 'inneres Beten'? Ein kurzer Gang durch die Begriffsgeschichte," *Communio* 26 (1997): 338–355.

Kraus, Johannes. "Fenelons Moraltheologisches Leitbild der Seelenführung nach den Lettres Spirituelles," in idem (ed.), *Fenelon. Persönlichkeit und Werk* (Baden-Baden: Verlag f. Kunst, 1953), 155–233.

Kugel, James L. *In Potiphar's House* (Cambridge: Harvard University Press, 1994).

Kurzmann, Frank A. *Die Rede vom Jüngsten Gericht in den Konfessionen der Frühen Neuzeit* (Berlin: DeGruyter, 2019).

Labno, Jeannie. *Commemorating the Polish Renaissance Child. Funeral Monuments and Their European Context* (London: Routledge, 2016).

Ladner, Gerhart. *The Idea of Reform. Its Impact on Christian Thought and Action in the Age of the Fathers* (Cambridge: Harvard University Press, 1959).

Ladner, Gerhart. "Terms and Ideals of Renewal," in Robert L. Benson and Giles Constable (eds.), *Renaissance and Renewal in the Twelfth Century* (Cambridge: Harvard University Press, 1982), 1–33.

Lajeunie, Etienne. *Saint Francis De Sales, the Man, the Thinker, His Influence* (Bangalore: S.F.S. Publications, 1986).

Lane, Christopher J. *Callings and Consequences. The Making of Catholic Vocational Culture in Early Modern France* (Montreal: McGill University Press, 2021).

Lang, Bernhard, and McDannell, Colleen. *Der Himmel. Eine Kulturgeschichte des ewigen Lebens* (Frankfurt: Insel, 1990).

Langmuir, Erika. *Imagining Childhood* (New Haven and London: Yale University Press, 2006).

Larkin, Brian. "Confraternities and Community. The Decline of the Communal Quest for Salvation in Eighteenth-Century Mexico City," in Martin Nesvig (ed.), *Local Religion in Colonial Mexico* (Albuquerque : University of New Mexico, 2006), 189–213.

Larkin, Brian. *The Very Nature of God. Baroque Catholicism and Religious Reform in Bourbon Mexico City* (Albuquerque: University of New Mexico Press, 2010).

Latasa, Pilar. "Tridentine Marriage Ritual in Sixteenth- to Eighteenth-Century Peru. From Global Procedures to American Idiosyncrasies," *Legal History* 27 (2019): 105–121.

Laun, Andreas. *Der Salesianische Liebesbegriff* (Eichstätt: Franz Sales Verlag, 1993).

Lavenia, Vincenzo. "The Catholic Theology of War. Law and Religion in an Eighteenth-Century Text," in Wim Decock (ed.), *Law and Religion. The Legal Teachings of the Protestant and Catholic Reformations* (Göttingen: Vandenhoeck & Ruprecht, 2014), 133–148.

Lavenia, Vincenzo. "Conscience and Catholic Discipline of War. Sins and Crimes," *Journal of Modern History* 18 (2014): 447–471.

Lavenia, Vincenzo. *L'infamia e il perdono. Tributi, pene e confessione nella teologia morale della prima eta moderna* (Bologna: Il Mulino, 2004).

Lavrin, Asuncion. "The Role of Nunneries in the Economy of New Spain in the Eighteenth Century," *American Historical Review* 46 (1966): 371–393.

Lazar, Lance Gabriel. *Working in the Vineyard of the Lord. Jesuit Confraternities in Early Modern Italy* (Toronto: University of Toronto Press, 2005).

Leavitt-Alcantara, Brianna. *Single Women and Devotion in Guatemala, 1670–1870* (Stanford: Stanford University Press, 2018).

Lebroc, Reynerio. "Proyección tridentina en América," *Missionalia Hispánica* 26 (1969): 129–207.

Leclercq, Jacques. *Saint François de Sales, docteur de la perfection* (Paris: Casterman, 1948).

Lehfeldt, Elizabeth A. "Discipline, Vocation and Patronage. Spanish Religious Women in a Tridentine Microclimate," *Sixteenth Century Journal* 30 (1999): 1009–1030.

Lehfeldt, Elizabeth A. "Ideal Men. Masculinity and Decline in Seventeenth-Century Spain," *Renaissance Quarterly* 61 (2008): 463–494.

Lehfeldt, Elizabeth A. *Religious Women in Golden Age Spain. The Permeable Cloister* (Aldershot: Ashgate, 2005).

Lehmann, Leonhard. "Sed sint minores. La minorita nella Regola non bollata," in Luigi Padovese (ed.), *Minores et subditi minores. Tratti caratterizzanti dell'identità Francescana* (Rome: Collegio S. Lorenzo, 2003), 129–147.

Lehner, Ulrich L. *The Catholic Enlightenment* (New York: Oxford University Press, 2016).

Lehner, Ulrich L. "De Moderatione in Sacra Theologia. Über die Grenzen theologischer Rede bei Ludovico Muratori," in George Augustin et al. (eds.), *Der dreifaltige Gott. Festschrift G.L. Müller* (Freiburg: Herder, 2017), 349–361.

Lehner, Ulrich L. *Enlightened Monks. The German Benedictines, 1740–1803* (Oxford: Oxford University Press, 2010).

Lehner, Ulrich L. *Im Klosterkerker der Mönche und Nonnen* (Kevaler: ToposPlus, 2015).

Lehner, Ulrich L. (ed.). *Innovation in Early Modern Catholicism* (New York: Routledge, 2022).

Lehner, Ulrich L. *On the Road to Vatican II. German Catholic Enlighteners and Reform of the Church* (Augsburg: Fortress Press, 2016).

Lehner, Ulrich L. (ed.). *Women, Enlightenment and Catholicism. A Transnational Biographical History* (New York: Routledge, 2018).

Lehner, Ulrich L., and Blanchard, Shaun. "Introduction," in Lehner and Blanchard (eds.), *The Catholic Enlightenment*, 1–20.

Lehner, Ulrich L., and Burson, Jeffrey (eds.). *Enlightenment and Catholicism in Europe* (Notre Dame: University of Notre Dame Press, 2014).

Lehner, Ulrich L., Roeber, A. G., and Muller, Richard (eds.). *Oxford Handbook of Early Modern Theology, 1600–1800* (Oxford: Oxford University Press, 2016).

Leone, Massimo. *Saints and Signs. A Semiotic Reading of Conversion in Early Modern Catholicism* (Berlin: De Gruyter, 2010).

Letourneau, George. *La méthode d'Oraison Mentale du Séminaire de Saint-Sulpice* (Paris: Libraire Victore Lecoffre, 1903).

Letter, P. De. "Two Concepts of Attrition and Contrition," *Theological Studies* 11 (1950): 3–33.

Levering, Matthew. *Predestination. Biblical and Theological Paths* (Oxford: Oxford University Press, 2011).

Levy, Ian Christopher. *Introducing Medieval Biblical Interpretation* (Grand Rapids: Baker Academic, 2018).

Lierheimer, Linda. *Female Eloquence and Maternal Ministry. The Apostolate of Ursuline Nuns in Seventeenth-Century France* (PhD Thesis: Princeton University, 1994).

Linden, Raymund. *Die Regelobservanz in der Rheinischen Kapuzinerprovinz von der Gründung bis zur Teilung 1611–1668* (Münster: Aschendorff, 1936).

Lisle-en-Rigault, Venantius a. *Monumenta ad Constitutiones Ordinis Fratrum Capuccinorum pertinentia* (Rome: Curia Generalia, 1916).

Livet, Georges, and Heinz, Iris (eds.). *Sensibilité religieuse et discipline ecclésiastique. Les visites pastorales en territoires protestants, pays rhénans, comté de Montbéliard, pays de Vaud, XVIe–XVIIIe siècles* (Strasbourg: Libr. Istra, 1973).

Lobenwein, Elisabeth, et al. (eds.). *Bruderschaften als multifunktionale Dienstleister der Frühen Neuzeit in Zentraleuropa* (Vienna: Böhlau, 2018).

Locker, Jesse M. "Rethinking Art after the Council of Trent," in idem (ed.), *Art and Reform in the late Renaissance. After Trent* (London and New York: Routledge, 2019), 1–19.

Loh, Maria H. "La Custodia Degli Occhi. Disciplining Desire in Post-Tridentine Italian Art," in Hall and Cooper (eds.), *The Sensuous*, 91–112.

Lohmann Villena, Guillermo. *La restitución por conquistadores y encomenderos. Un aspecto de la incidencia lascasiana en el Perú]* (Sevilla: Escuela de Estudios Hispanoamericanos, 1966).

Longhurst, John E. "Saint Ignatius at Alcala, 1526–1527," *Archivum Historicum Societatis Iesu* 26 (1957): 252–256.

Lorenz-Filograno, Maria Pia. "Das Inquisitionsverfahren beim Heiligen Offizium. Juristische Aspekte und Analyseperspektiven," *Zeitschrift der Savigny-Stiftung f. Rechtsgeschichte. Kanonistische Abteilung* 101 (2015): 317–372.

Losconzi, Peter. "Passionate Reason. Science, Theology and the Intellectual Passion of Wonder in Descartes' Meditations," in Willem Lemmens and Walter van Herck (eds.), *Religious Emotions. Some Philosophical Explorations* (Cambridge: Cambridge Scholars Publ., 2008), 131–144.

Lubac, Henri de. *Medieval Exegesis*, 3 vols. (Grand Rapids: Eerdmans, 1998ff).

Lundberg, Magnus. *Church Life between the Metropolitan and the Local. Parishes, Parishioners and Parish Priests in Seventeenth-Century Mexico* (Orlando, FL: Iberoamericana, 2011).

Luria, Keith P. *Sacred Boundaries. Religious Coexistence and Conflict in Early-Modern France* (Washington: Catholic University of America Press, 2005).

Lux-Sterritt, Laurence. *Redefining Female Religious Life. French Ursulines and English Ladies in Seventeenth-Century Catholicism* (Aldershot: Ashgate, 2005).

Lynch, Katherine A. *Individuals, Families, and Communities in Europe, 1200–1800. The Urban Foundations of Western Society* (Cambridge: Cambridge University Press, 2003).

MacCormack, Sabine. "The Heart Has Its Reasons. Predicaments of Missionary Christianity in Early Colonial Peru," *Hispanic American Historical Review* 65 (1985): 443–466.

Macek, Ellen A. "Advice Manuals and the Formation of English Protestant and Catholic identities, 1560–1660)," *Dutch Review of Church History* 85 (2005): 315–331.

Macek, Ellen A. "Devout Recusant Women, Advice Manuals, and the Creation of Holy Households 'Under Siege,'" in Weber (ed.), *Devout Laywomen in the Early Modern World*, 235–252.

MacLeod, Murdo J. "Confraternities in Colonial New Spain. Mexico and Central America," in Konrad Eisenbichler (ed.), *A Companion to Medieval and Early Modern Confraternities* (Leiden and Boston: Brill, 2019), 280–306.

Maher, Michael. "Confession and Consolation. The Society of Jesus and Its Promotion of the General Confession," in Katharine J. Lualdi and Anne T. Thayer (eds.), *Penitence in the Age of Reformations* (Aldershot: Ashgate, 2017), 184–200.

Maher, Michael. "Financing Reform. The Society of Jesus, the Congregation of the Assumption, and the Funding of the Exposition of the Sacrament in Early Modern Rome," *Archiv für Reformationsgeschichte—Archive for Reformation History* 93 (2002): 126–144.

Maher, Michael. "How the Jesuits Used Their Congregations to Promote Frequent Communion," in Patrick Donelly (ed.), *Confraternities and Catholic Reform in Italy, France and Spain* (Kirsville: Thomas Jefferson University Press, 1999), 75–95.

Mahlmann, Theodor. "Reformation," in *Historisches Wörterbuch der Philosophie*, vol. 8 (Basel: Schwabe, 1992), 416–442.

Maio, Romeo de. "L'ideale eroico nei processi di canonizzazione della Controriforma," in idem (ed.), *Riforme emiti nella Chiesa del cinquecento* (Naples: Guida, 1973), 257–278.

Maly, Tomas. "Early Modern Purgatory. Reformation Debates and Post-Tridentine Change," *Archiv für Reformationsgeschichte* 106 (2015): 242–272.

Mannarelli, María Emma. *Private Passions and Public Sins. Men and Women in Seventeenth-Century Lima, Diálogos* (Albuquerque: University of New Mexico Press, 2007).

Marceau, William C. *Stoicism and St. Francis de Sales* (Lewiston: Edwin Mellen Press, 1989).

Margerie, Bertrand de. "Theological and Pastoral Reflections on the History of Frequent Communion," in CIEL UK (ed.), *The Veneration and Administration of the Eucharist* (Southhampton: The Saint Austin Press, 1997), 146–157.

Margraf, Erik. *Die Hochzeitspredigt der frühen Neuzeit* (Munich: Utz, 2007).

Marschler, Thomas. "Providence, Predestination and Grace," in Lehner et al. (eds.), *Oxford Handbook of Early Modern Theology*, 89–103.

Marshall, Peter, and Walsham, Alexandra (eds.). *Angels in the Early Modern World* (Cambridge: Cambridge University Press, 2006).

Mayer, Adalbert. *Triebkräfte und Grundlinien der Entstehung des Meßstipendiums* (St. Ottilien: EOS, 1976).

Mazzonis, Querciolo. "The Company of St. Ursula in Counter-Reformation Italy," in Weber (ed.), *Devout Laywomen in the Early Modern World*, 48–68.

McClain, Lisa. *Divided Loyalties. Pushing the Boundaries of Gender and Lay Roles in the Catholic Church, 1534–1829* (Basingstoke: Palgrave Macmillan, 2018).

McClain, Lisa. *Lest We Be Damned. Practical Innovation and Lived Experience among Catholics in Protestant England, 1559–1642* (New York: Routledge, 2004).

McClain, Lisa. "Using What's at Hand. English Catholic Reinterpretations of the Rosary, 1559–1642," *Journal of Religious History* 27 (2003): 161–176.

McDonnell, Eunan. *The Concept of Freedom in the Writings of St. Francis de Sales* (Oxford et al.: Peter Lang, 2009).

McGinn, Bernard. *Mysticism in the Golden Age of Spain, 1500–1650* (New York: Herder, 2017).

McGinn, Bernard. *The Persistence of Mysticism in Catholic Europe. France, Italy and Germany, 1500–1675* (New York: Herder, 2020).

McGinness, Frederick J. *Right Thinking and Sacred Oratory in Counter-Reformation Rome* (Princeton: Princeton University Press, 1995).

McGinness, Frederick J. "Roma Sancta and the Saint. Eucharist, Chastity and the Logic of Catholic Reform," *Historical Reflections* 15 (1988): 99–116.

McGlone, Mary. "The King's Surprise. The Mission Methodology of Toribio de Mogrovejo," *The Americas* 50 (1993): 65–83.

McGrath-Merkle, Clare. *Berulle's Spiritual Theology of the Priesthood. A Study on Speculative Mysticism and Applied Metaphysics* (Munster: Aschendorff, 2018).

McKnight, Kathryn. *The Mystic of Tunja. The Writings of Madre Castillo, 1671–1742* (Amherst: University of Massachusetts Press, 1997).

McNamara, Celeste. *The Bishop's Burden. Reforming the Catholic Church in Early Modern Italy* (Washington, DC: Catholic University of America Press, 2020).

McNamara, Celeste. "Conceptualizing the Priest. Lay and Episcopal Expectations of Clerical Reform in Late Seventeenth-Century Padua," *Archiv für Reformationsgeschichte* 104 (2014): 297–320.

Meersseman, Gilles-Gérard. *Ordo fraternitatis confraternite e pieta dei Laici*, 3 vols. (Rome: Herder, 1977).

Mehr, Bonaventura von. *Das Predigtwesen in der kölnischen und rheinischen Kapuzinerprovinz im 17. und 18. Jahrhundert* (Rome: Istituto Storico Dei Fr. Min Cappuccini, 1945).

Meiwes, Relinde. *Von Ostpreussen in die Welt. Die Geschichte der ermländischen Katharinenschwestern (1772–1914)* (Paderborn: Ferdinand Schöningh, 2011).

Melion, Walter S. "Coemeterium Schola. The Emblematic Imagery of Death in Jan David's Veridicus Christianus," in idem et al., (eds.), *Quid est Sacramentum? Visual Representation of Sacred Mysteries in Early Modern Europe, 1400–1700* (Leiden and Boston: Brill, 2020), 533–579.

Menozzi, Daniele. "Prospettive sinodali nel Settecento," *Cristianesimo nella Storia* 8 (1987): 115–146.

Metzler, Josef. *Die Synoden in China, Japan und Korea, 1570–1931* (Paderborn: Schöningh, 1980).

Meyers, Albert, et al. (eds.), *Manipulating the Saints. Religious Brotherhoods and Social Integration in Postconquest Latin America* (Hamburg: Wayasbah, 1988).

Michalon, Pierre. *La Communion aux mystères de Jésus-Christ selon Jean-Jacques Olier* (Lyon: Éditions de l'Abeille, 1944).

Miele, Michele. *Die Provinzialkonzilien Süditaliens in der Neuzeit* (Paderborn: Schöningh, 1997).

Minnich, Nelson. "Concepts of Reform Proposed at the Fifth Lateran Council," *Archivum Historicum Pontificae* 7 (1969): 163–251.

Minor, Vernon Hyde. *The Death of the Baroque and the Rhetoric of Good Taste* (Cambridge: Cambridge University Press, 2006).

Mitchell, Nathan. *The Mystery of the Rosary. Marian Devotion and the Reinvention of Catholicism* (New York: New York University Press, 2009).

Molina, Michelle. *To Overcome Oneself. The Jesuit Ethic and Spirit of Global Expansion, 1520–1767* (Berkeley: University of California Press, 2013).

Molitor, Hansgeorg. "Mehr mit den Augen als mit den Ohren glauben. Frühneuzeitliche Volksfrömmigkeit in Köln und Jülich-Berg," in Klaus Ganzer et al. (eds.), *Volksfrömmigkeit in der frühen Neuzeit* (Münster: Aschendorff, 1994), 89–106.

Monson, Paul G. "Sub signis visibilibus. Visual Theology in Trent's Decrees on the Eucharist," *Logos. A Journal of Catholic Thought and Culture* 15 (2012): 145–158.

Monta, Susannah. "Uncommon Prayer? Robert Southwell's Short Rule for a Good Life and Catholic Domestic Devotion in Post-Reformation England," in Lowell Gallagher (ed.), *Redrawing the Map of Early Modern English Catholicism* (Toronto: University of Toronto Press, 2012), 245–271.

Mora, Adelina Sarrión. *Sexualidad y confesión. La solicitación ante el Tribunal del Santo Oficio* (Cuenca: Ediciones de la Universidad de Castilla-La Mancha, 2010).

Moriarty, Michael. *Fallen Nature, Fallen Selves. Early Modern French Thought*, vol. 2 (Oxford: Oxford University Press, 2006).

Mostaccio, Silvia. *Early Modern Jesuits. Between Obedience and Conscience during the Generalate of Claudio Acquaviva (1581–1615)* (Farnham: Ashgate, 2014).

Mostaccio, Silvia. "Shaping the Spiritual Exercises. The *Maisons de retraites* in Brittany during the Seventeenth Century as a Gendered Pastoral Tool," *Journal of Jesuit Studies* 2 (2015): 659–684.

Mostaza, Antonio. "Forum internum—forum externum. En torno a la naturaleza jurídica del fuero interno," *Revista Española de derecho Canónico* 23 (1967): 274–284; 24 (1968): 339–364; 24 (1968): 339–364.

Mujica Pinilla, Ramón. *Ángeles apócrifos en la América virreinal* (México: Fondo de Cultura Económica, 1996).

Mujica Pinilla, Ramón. "Angels and Demons in the Conquest of Peru," in Fernando Cervantes and Andrew Redden (eds.), *Angels, Demons and the New World* (Cambridge: Cambridge University Press, 2013), 171–211.

Muller, Aislinn. "The *agnus dei*, Catholic Devotion, and Confessional Politics in Early Modern England," *British Catholic History* 34 (2018): 1–28.

Müller, Gerhard Ludwig. *Maria—Die Frau im Heilsplan Gottes. Mariologische Studien XV* (Würzburg: Echter, 2002).

Müller, Joseph. *Der Heilige Joseph. Die dogmatischen Grundlagen seiner besonderen Verehrung* (Münster: Rauch, 1937).

Mullett, Michael A. *The Catholic Reformation* (London: Routledge, 1999).

Neumayr, Maximilian. *Die Schriftpredigt im Barock. Auf Grund der Theorie der katholischen Barockhomiletik* (Paderborn: Schöningh, 1937).

Neunheuser, Burkhard. *Taufe und Firmung. Handbuch der Dogmengeschichte*, vol. 4/2 (Freiburg: Herder, 2nd ed., 1983).

Newmark, Catherine. *Passion-Affekt-Gefühl Philosophische Theorien zwischen Aristoteles und Kant* (Hamburg: Meiner, 2008).

Newton, Hannah. "Holy Affections," in Susan Broomhall (ed.), *Early Modern Emotions. An Introduction* (London and New York: Routledge, 2017), 67–71.

Nordhues, Paul. *Der Kirchenbegriff des Louis de Thomassin. In seinem dogmatischen Zusammenhängen und in seiner lebensmässigen Bedeutung* (Leipzig: St. Benno-Verlag, 1958).

Noreen, Kirstin. "Ecclesiae militantis triumphi. Jesuit Iconography and the Counter-Reformation," *Sixteenth Century Journal* 29 (1998): 689–715.

O'Banion, Patrick. *The Sacrament of Penance and Religious Life in Golden Age Spain* (University Park: Pennsylvania State Press, 2012).

Ohlidal, Anna, and Samerski, Stefan (eds.). *Jesuitische Frömmigkeitskulturen. Konfessionelle Interaktion in Ostmitteleuropa 1570–1700* (Stuttgart: Steiner, 2006).

Olin, John C. *The Catholic Reformation. Savonarola to Ignatius Loyola. Reform in the Church, 1495–1540* (New York: Fordham University Press, 1992).

Olin, John C. *Catholic Reform. From Cardinal Ximenes to the Council of Trent 1495–1563* (New York: Fordham University Press, 1991).

O'Malley, John W. *Giles of Viterbo on Church and Reform* (Leiden and Boston: Brill, 1968).

O'Malley, John W. "The Hermeneutic of Reform. A Historical Analysis," *Theological Studies* 73 (2012): 517–546.

O'Malley, John W. *Trent and All That. Renaming Catholicism in the Early Modern Era* (Cambridge: Harvard University Press, 2002).

Onstenk, Nicolaus. "De constitutione S. Pii C. '*Circa Pastoralis*' super clausura monialium et tertiarium," *Periodica de re morali, canonica, liturgica* 39 (1950): 213–230; 317–363; 40 (1951): 210–255.

O'Reilly, Thomas. *From Ignatius of Loyola to John of the Cross. Spirituality and Literature in Sixteenth-Century Spain* (Aldershot: Variorum, 1995).

Oss, A. C. van. *Catholic Colonialism. A Parish History of Guatemala, 1524–1821* (Cambridge: Cambridge University Press, 2002).

Ott, Heinrich. *Eschatologie in der Scholastik. Handbuch der Dogmengeschichte*, vol. 4/7b (Freiburg: Herder, 1990).

Ottmann, Jennifer. *Models of Christian Identity in Sixteenth- and Early Seventeenth-Century Nahuatl Catechetical Literature* (PhD Thesis: Yale University, 2003).

Ozment, Steven. *The Age of Reform, 1250–1550. An Intellectual and Religious History of Late Medieval and Reformation Europe* (New Haven, CT: Yale University Press, 1980).

Paiva, Jose Pedro. "Pastoral Visitations in the First World Empires (Spain and Portugal in the 16th and 18th Centuries). A Comparative Approach," *Journal of Early Modern History* 24 (2020): 224–252.

Panzeri, Gianluigi. "Carlo Borromeo e la figura ideale del vescovo della chiesa tridentina," *Scuola eligion* 124 (1996): 685–731.

Pardo, Osvaldo F. *The Origins of Mexican Catholicism, Nahua Rituals and Christian Sacraments in Sixteenth-Century Mexico* (Ann Arbor: University of Michigan Press, 2004).

Paris, Charles B. *Marriage in XVIIth Century Catholicism* (Tournai and Montreal: Desclee, 1975).

Pascoe, Louis B. *Jean Gerson. Principles of Church Reform* (Leiden and Boston: Brill, 1973).

Pastor, Ludwig. *Geschichte der Päpste*, vol. 14/2 (Freiburg: Herder, 1930).

Patterson, Jonathan. *Representing Avarice in Late Renaissance France* (Oxford: Oxford University Press, 2015).

Pauls, Emil. "Zur Geschichte der Censur am Niederrhein bis zum Frühjahr 1816," *Beiträge zur Geschichte des Niederrheins* 15 (1900): 36–117.

Peñafiel Ramón, Antonio. *Mentalidad y religiosidad popular murciana en la primera mitad del siglo XVIII* (Murcia: Universidad de Murcia, 1988).

Pereira, Jose, and Fastiggi, Robert. *The Mystical Theology of the Catholic Reformation* (Washington, DC: Catholic University of America Press, 2006).

Pfülf, Otto. "Die Verehrung des hl. Joseph," *Stimmen aus Maria Laach* 38 (1890): 137–161; 282–302.

Poley, Jared. *The Devil's Riches. A Modern History of Greed* (New York: Berghahn, 2017).

Polleross, Friedrich. "Architektur und Panegyrik. Eine Allegorie der Jesuiten zur Geburt von Erzherzog Leopold Joseph 1682," in Martin Engel (ed.), *Barock in Mitteleuropa. Werke, Phänomene, Analysen.* (Vienna: Böhlau, 2007), 375–391.

Pomplun, Trent. "Catholic Sacramental Theology in the Baroque Age," in Lehner et al. (eds.), *Oxford Handbook of Early Modern Theology*, 135–149.

Poole, Stafford (ed.). *The Directory for Confessors, 1585. Implementing the Catholic Reformation in New Spain* (Norman: University of Oklahoma Press, 2015).

Poska, Allyson M. *Regulating the People. The Catholic Reformation in Seventeenth-Century Spain* (Leiden and Boston: Brill, 1998).

Poska, Allyson M. "When Love Goes Wrong. Getting Out of Marriage in Seventeenth-Century Spain," *Journal of Social History* 29 (1996): 871–882.

Praz, Mario. *Studies in Seventeenth Century Imagery*, vol. 1 (London: Arburg Institute, 1939).

Prien, Hans-Jürgen. *Francisco de Osuna—Mystik und Rechtfertigung ein Beitrag zur Erforschung der spanischen Theologie und Frömmigkeit in der ersten Hälfte des sechzehnten Jahrhunderts* (Hamburg: Kovač, 2014).

Prodi, Paolo. *The Papal Prince. One Body and Two Souls. The Papal Monarchy in Early Modern Europe* [orig.: *Il sovrano pontifice*, 1982] (Cambridge: Cambridge University Press, 1987).

Prodi, Paolo, and Wolfgang Reinhard (eds.). *Das Konzil von Trient und die Moderne* (Berlin: Duncker & Humblot, 2001).

Prosperi, Adriano. "Die Beichte und das Gericht des Gewissens," in Prodi and Reinhard (eds.), *Das Konzil von Trient und die Moderne*, 175–197.

Prosperi, Adriano. *Infanticide, Secular Justice, and Religious Debate in Early Modern Europe* (Turnhout: Brepols, 2016).

Prosperi, Adriano. *L' Inquisizione Romana. Letture e Ricerche* (Roma: Edizioni di storia e letteratura, 2003).

Prosperi, Adriano. *Tribunali della coscienza* (Turin: Einaudi, 1996).

Qu Yi & 藝 曲. "Song Nianzhu Guicheng (Die Anweisung zur Rezitation des Rosenkranzes). Ein illustriertes christliches Buch aus China vom Anfang des 17. Jahrhunderts," *Monumenta Serica* 60 (2012): 195–290.

Quantin, Jean-Louis. "Catholic Moral Theology, 1550–1800," in Lehner et al. (eds.), *Oxford Handbook to Early Modern Theology*, 119–134.

Rahner, Karl. "The Logic of Concrete Existential Knowledge in Ignatius Loyola," in idem, *The Dynamic Element in the Church* (London: Burns and Oates, 1964), 84–170.

Ramsey, Ann W. *Liturgy, Politics and Salvation. The Catholic League in Paris and the Nature of Catholic Reform, 1540–1630* (Rochester, NY: University of Rochester Press, 1999),

Rapley, Elizabeth. *The Dévotes. Women and Church in Seventeenth-Century France* (Montreal: McGill University Press, 1990).

Rapley, Elizabeth. "A New Approach. The filles séculières (1630–1660)," *Vincentian Heritage Journal* 16 (1995): 111–136.

Reinhard, Wolfgang. "Kirchendisziplin, Sozialdisziplinierung und Verfestigung der konfessionellen Fronten. Das katholische Reformprogramm und seine Auswirkungen," in Stefano Andretta et al. (eds.), *Das Papsttum, die Christenheit und die Staaten Europas, 1592–1605* (Tübingen: Niemeyer, 1994), 1–13.

Reinhard, Wolfgang. "Mythologie des Konzils von Trient," in Michela Catto and Adriano Prosperi (eds.), *Trent and Beyond. The Council, Other Powers, Other Cultures* (Turnhout: Brepols, 2018), 27–43.

Reinhard, Wolfgang, and Hersche, Peter. "Wie modern ist der Barockkatholizismus?," (Disputation), in Walter and Wassilowsky (eds.), *Das Konzil von Trient*, 489–518.

Reinhardt, Nicole. *Voices of Conscience. Royal Confessors and Political Counsel in Seventeenth-Century Spain and France* (Oxford: Oxford University Press, 2016).

Reitinger, Franz. "The Persuasiveness of Cartography. Michel le Nobletz and the School of Le Conquet," *Cartographica* 40 (2005): 79–103.

Repgen, Konrad. "Reform als Leitgedanke kirchlicher Vergangenheit und Gegenwart," *Römische Quartalsschrift* 85 (1989): 5–30.

Rey-Mermet, Théodule. *Un homme pour les sans-espoir. Alphonse de Liguori, 1696–1787* (Paris: Nouvelle Cité, 1987).

Ricard, Robert. *The Spiritual Conquest of Mexico. An Essay on the Apostolate and the Evangelizing Methods of the Mendicant Orders in New Spain, 1523–1572* (Berkeley: University of California Press, 1966).

Rifeser, Anna Elisabeth. *Die Frömmigkeitskultur der Maria Hueber (1653–1705) und der Tiroler Tertiarinnen. Institutionelle Prozesse, kommunikative Verflechtungen und spirituelle Praktiken* (Munster: Aschendorff, 2019).

Rincón, Manuel González. "La crítica sexual anticlerical en el Apókopos de Bergadís. La sollicitatio durante la confesión," *Byzantion Nea Hellas* 29 (2010): 113–133.

Robins, Nicholas A. *Priest-Indian Conflict in Upper Peru. The Generation of Rebellion, 1750–1780* (Syracuse, NY: Syracuse University Press, 2007).

Rödter, Gabriel. *Via piae animae. Grundlagenuntersuchung zur emblematischen Verknüpfung von Bild und Wort in den Pia desideria des Hermman Hugo SJ* (Frankfurt et al.: Peter Lang, 1992).

Roldan-Figueroa, Rady. *The Ascetic Spirituality of Juan de Avila, 1499–1569* (Leiden and Boston: Brill, 2010).

Roldan-Figueroa, Rady. "The Mystical Theology of Luis de la Puente," in Robert Maryks (ed.), *Brill's Companion to Jesuit Mysticism* (Leiden and Boston: Brill, 2017), 54–81.

Roling, Bernd. "Ein Anfang ohne Umkehr. Der Sündenfall und die Unmöglichkeit der Reue zwischen Mittelalter und Neuzeit," *Frühmittelalterliche Studien* 48 (2014): 389–412.

Roling, Bernd. *Locutio Angelica. Die Diskussion der Engelsprache als Antizipation einer Sprechakttheorie in Mittelalter und Früher Neuzeit* (Leiden and Boston: Brill, 2008).

Roling, Bernd. *Physica sacra. Wunder, Naturwissenschaft und historischer Schriftsinn zwischen Mittelalter und Früher Neuzeit* (Leiden and Boston: Brill, 2013).

Rossiaud, Jacques. "Fraternités de jeunesse et niveaux de culture dans les villes du Sud-Est à la fin du Moyen-Age," *Cahier d'histoire* 21 (1976): 67–102.

Rowe, Erin Kathleen. *Saint and Nation. Santiago, Teresa of Avila, and Plural Identities in Early Modern Spain* (University Park: Pennsylvania State Press, 2011).

Rowe, Erin. *Black Saints in Early Modern Catholicism* (Cambridge: Cambridge University Press, 2019).

Rubial García, Antonio. *Profetisas y eligions. Espacios y mensajes de una eligion dirigida por ermitaños y beatas laicos en las ciudades de Nueva España* (México: Universidad Nacional Autónoma de México, 2006).

Rudy, Kathryn. "A Guide to Mental Pilgrimage. Paris, Bibliothèque de L'Arsenal Ms. 212," *Zeitschrift für Kunstgeschichte* 63 (2000): 494–515.

Rutz, Andreas. *Bildung-Konfession-Geschlecht. Religiöse Frauengemeinschaften und die katholische Mädchenbildung im Rheinland* (Mainz: Zabern, 2006).

Ryan, Frances, and Rybolt, John E. (eds.). *Vincent de Paul and Louise de Marillac. Rules, Conferences, and Writings* (New York: Paulist Press, 1995).

Salomoni, David. *Educating the Catholic People. Religious Orders and Their Schools in Early Modern Italy (1500–1800)* (Leiden and Boston: Brill, 2021).

Sammer, Marianne. "Zur Volksläufigkeit aszetischer Literatur im 17. Und 18. Jahrhundert. Lorenzo Scupolis Geistlicher Kampf und sein literarischer Nachhall," in Andreas Solbach (ed.), *Aedificatio. Edification in the Intercultural Context of the Early Modern Age* (Berlin: DeGruyter, 2005), 319–332.

Sánchez, Álvaro Castro. *Franciscanos, místicos, herejes y alumbrados* (Córdoba: Servicio de Publicaciones, Universidad de Córdoba, 2010).

Sawicki, Diethard. *Leben mit den Toten. Geisterglauben und die Entstehung des Spiritismus in Deutschland 1770–1900* (Paderborn: Schöningh, 2nd ed., 2016).

Schäfer, Philipp. *Eschatologie. Trient und Gegenreformation. Handbuch der Dogmengeschichte*, vol. 4/7c (Freiburg: Herder, 1984).

Schlosser, Marianne. "Den Seelen helfen. Neues und Traditionelles in der Spiritualität des Ignatius von Loyola und der ersten Jesuiten," in Sigrid Müller and Cornelia Schweiger (eds.), *Between Creativity and Norm Making. Tensions in the Later Middle Ages and the Early Modern Era* (Leiden and Boston: Brill, 2013), 103–130.

Schnell, Rüdiger. "Concordia im Haus—Vielfalt der Diskurse (1300–1700)," in Christina Schaefer and Simon Zeisberg (eds.), *Das Haus schreiben. Bewegungen ökonomischen Wissens in der Literatur der Frühen Neuzeit* (Wiesbaden: Harrassowitz, 2018), 29–65.

Schnell, Rüdiger. "Die Frau als Gefährtin des Mannes. Eine Studie zur Interdependenz von Textsorte, Adressat und Aussage," in idem (ed.), *Geschlechterbeziehungen*, 119–170.

Schnell, Rüdiger. *Frauendiskurs, Männerdiskurs, Ehediskurs. Textsorten und Geschlechterkonzepte in Mittelalter und Früher Neuzeit* (Frankfurt/Main: Campus Verlag, 1998).

Schnell, Rüdiger. "Geschlechterbeziehungen und Textfunktionen. Probleme und Perspektiven eines Forschungsansatzes," in idem (ed.), *Geschlechterbeziehungen*, 1–58.

Schnell, Rüdiger (ed.). *Geschlechterbeziehungen und Textfunktionen. Studien zu Eheschriften der Frühen Neuzeit* (Tübingen: Niemeyer, 1998).

Schnell, Rüdiger. *Histories of Emotion. Premodern—Modern* (Berlin: DeGruyter, 2020).

Schnell, Rüdiger. *Sexualität und Emotionalität in der vormodernen Ehe* (Cologne: Böhlau, 2002).

Schultes, Reginald M. *Fides implicita. Geschichte der Lehre von der fides implicita und explicita in der katholischen Theologie* (Regensburg: F. Pustet, 1920).

Schulz, Susanne. "Der Diskurs über den welt-geistlichen Stand. Überlegungen zur rechtlichen Lage semireligioser Gemeinschaften," in Bergerfurt and Conrad (eds.), *Welt-geistliche Frauen*, 25–60.

Schüssler, Rudolf. *The Debate on Probable Opinions in the Scholastic Tradition* (Leiden and Boston: Brill, 2019).

Schutte, Anne Jacobson. *Aspiring Saints. Pretense of Holiness, Inquisition, and Gender in the Republic of Venice, 1618–1750* (Baltimore: Johns Hopkins University Press, 2003).

Schwaller, John. "Introduction," in Poole (ed.), *The Directory*, 3–28.

Seitz, Joseph. *Das Josephsfest in der lateinischen Kirche in seiner Entwicklung bis zum Konzil von Trient* (Freiburg: Herder, 1908).

Seitz, Joseph. *Die Verehrung des Hl. Joseph in seiner geschichtlichen Entwicklung bis zum Konzil von Trient* (Freiburg: Herder, 1908).

Sell, Barry D., et al. (eds.). *Nahua Confraternities in Early Colonial Mexico. The 1552 Nahuatl Ordinances of Fray Alonso de Molina, OFM* (Berkeley, CA: Academy of American Franciscan History, 2002).

Shagan, Ethan. *The Birth of Modern Belief. From the Middle Ages to the Enlightenment* (Princeton: Princeton University Press, 2018).

Shoemaker, Nancy. *Negotiators of Change. Historical Perspectives on Native American Women* (New York and London: Rutledge, 1995).

Siebenhüner, Kim. "Things That Matter. Zur Geschichte der materiellen Kultur in der Frühneuzeitforschung," *Zeitschrift für Historische Forschung* 42 (2015): 373–409.

Sigal, Pete. *From Moon Goddesses to Virgins. The Colonization of Maya Sexual Desire* (Austin: University of Texas Press, 2000).

Sigel, Andrea. *Der Vorhang der Sixtinischen Madonna. Herkunft und Motiv eines Motivs der Marienikonographie* (Zurich: Juris, 1977).

Sluhovsky, Moshe. *Becoming a New Self. Practices of Belief in Early Modern Catholicism* (Chicago: University of Chicago Press, 2017).

Sluhovsky, Moshe. *Believe Not Every Spirit. Possession, Mysticism, and Discernment in Early Modern Catholicism* (Chicago: University of Chicago Press, 2007).

Sluhovsky, Moshe. "Introduction," in idem (ed.), *Into the Dark Night and Back. The Mystical Writings of Jean-Joseph Surin* (Leiden and Boston: Brill, 2018), 1–18.

Sommervogel, Carlos. *Bibliotheque de Compagnie de Jesus* (Brussels and Paris: 1890ff).

Sousa, Ronald de. *The Rationality of Emotion* (Cambridge: Cambridge University Press, 1987).

Storey, Tessa. "English and Italian Health Advice. Protestant and Catholic Bodies," in Sandra Cavallo et al. (eds.), *Conserving Health in Early Modern Culture* (Manchester: Manchester University Press, 2017), 210–234.

Strauss, Gerald. "Reformatio and Renovatio from the Middle Ages to the Reformation," in Thomas Brady et al. (eds.), *Handbook of European History, 1400–1700*, vol. 2 (Leiden: Brill, 1995), 1–30.

Struthers, Sally A. *Donatelli's Putti. Their Genesis, Importance, and Influence on Quattrocento Sculpture and Painting* (PhD Thesis: Ohio State University, 1992).

Stump, Philipp. *The Reforms of the Council of Constance, 1414–1418* (Leiden and Boston: Brill, 1994).

Sudbrack, Josef. "Mystik und Methode. Ganzheitliches Beten bei Friedrich Spee von Langenfeld," in Michael Sievernich (ed.), *Friedrich von Spee. Priester-Poet-Prophet* (Frankfurt: Knecht, 1986), 107–118.

Svoboda, Rudolf. *Johann Prokop Schaffgotsch. Das Leben eines böhmischen Prälaten in der Zeit des Josephinismus* (Frankfurt: Peter Lang, 2015).

Talvacchia, Bette. "The Word Made Flesh. Spiritual Subjects and Carnal Depictions in Renaissance Art," in Hall and Cooper (eds.), *The Sensuous* (Cambridge: Cambridge University Press, 2013), 49–73.

Tausiet, Maria. "Patronage of Angels and Combat of Demons. Good versus Evil in Seventeenth-Century Spain," in Marshall and Walsham (eds.), *Angels*, 233–256.

Tavard, George. *Die Engel. Handbuch der Dogmengeschichte*, vol. 2/2b (Freiburg: Herder, 1968).

Tentler, Thomas. *Sin and Confession on the Eve of the Reformation* (Princeton: Princeton University Press, 1977).

Teuscher, Simon. *Lords' Rights and Peasant Stories. Writing and the Formation of Tradition in the Later Middle Ages* (Philadelphia: University of Pennsylvania Press, 2012).

Thalhofer, Franz Xaver. *Entwicklung des katholischen Katechismus in Deutschland von Canisius bis Deharbe* (Freiburg: 1899).

Thalhofer, Valentin. *Handbuch der katholischen Liturgik*, vol. 2 (Freiburg: 1890).

Thibodeau, François. *Saint Jean Eudes. Prêtre-missionnaire et l'Église en Nouvelle-France* (Quebec: L'Maison des Eudistes, 2014).

Thiessen, Hillard van. *Das Zeitalter der Ambiguität. Vom Umgang mit Werten und Normen in der Frühen Neuzeit* (Cologne: Böhlau, 2021).

Thiessen, Hillard van. *Die Kapuziner zwischen Konfessionalisierung und Alltagskultur. vergleichende Fallstudie am Beispiel Freiburgs und Hildesheims 1599–1750* (Freiburg im Breisgau: Rombach, 2002).

Thiessen, Hillard van. "Normenkonkurrenz. Handlungsspielraeume, Rollen, normativer Wandel und normative Kontinuität vom späten Mittelalter bis zum Übergang zur Moderne," in Karsten and von Thiessen (eds.), *Normenkonkurrenz in historischer Perspektive*, 241–286.

Thompson, Edward Healy. *The Life of Jean-Jacques Olier* (London: 1886).

Tietz, Manfred. *Saint François de Sales' Traité de l'amour de Dieu (1616) und seine spanischen Vorläufer. Cristóbal de Fonseca, Diego de Estella, Luis de Granada, Santa Teresa de Jesús und Juan de Jesús Maria* (Wiesbaden: F. Steiner, 1973).

Tingle, Elizabeth C. *Purgatory and Piety in Brittany, 1480–1720 (Catholic Christendom, 1300–1700)* (Aldershot: Ashgate, 2012).

Tomaro, John Butler. *The Papacy and the Implementation of the Council of Trent, 1564–1588* (PhD Thesis: University of North Carolina at Chapel Hill, 1974).

Tortorici, Zeb. "Masturbation, Salvation and Desire. Connecting Sexuality and Religiosity in Colonial Mexico," *Journal of the History of Sexuality* 16 (2007): 355–372.

Tortorici, Zeb. *Sins against Nature. Sex and Archives in Colonial New Spain* (Durham and London: Duke University Press, 2018).

Trémolières, François. "L'enseignement par l'image de Michel Le Nobletz," in Ralph Dekoninck and Agnès Guiderdoni-Bruslé (eds.), *Emblemata sacra. Rhétorique et herméneutique du discours sacré dans la littérature en images* (Turnhout: Brepols, 2007), 553–568.

Tricoire, Damien. *Mit Gott rechnen. Katholische Reform und politisches Kalkül in Frankreich, Bayern und Polen-Litauen* (Göttingen: Vandenhoeck & Ruprecht, 2013).

Tricoire, Damien. "What Was the Catholic Reformation? Marian Piety and the Universalization of Divine Love," *Catholic Historical Review* 103 (2017): 20–49.

Turchini, Angelo. "Die Visitation als Mittel zur Regierung des Territoriums," in Prodi and Reinhard (eds.), *Das Konzil von Trient und die Moderne*, 261–298.

Turley, Steven E. *Franciscan Spirituality and Mission in New Spain, 1524–1599* (Aldershot: Ashgate, 2014).

Tutino, Stefania. *Uncertainty in Post-Reformation Catholicism. A History of Probabilism* (New York: Oxford University Press, 2018).

Underwood, Lucy. *Childhood, Youth and Religious Dissent in Post-Reformation England* (Basingstoke, UK: Palgrave Macmillan, 2014).

Unterburger, Klaus. "Reform der ganzen Kirche. Konturen, Ursachen und Wirkungen einer Leitideee und Zwangsvorstellungen im Spätmittelalter," in Andreas Merkt et al. (eds.), *Reformen in der Kirche. Historische Perspektiven* (Freiburg: Herder, 2014), 109–137.

Vacher, Marguerite. *Des "régulières" dans le siècle. Les Soeurs de Saint-Joseph du Père Médaille aux XVIIe et XVIIIe siècles* (Clermont-Ferrand: Adosa, 1992).

Vacher, Marguerite. *Nuns without Cloister. Sisters of St. Joseph* (Lanham, MD: Rowman & Littlefield, 2010).

Vechtel, Klaus. "Das Priesterbild des Ignatius und die Priesterbildung heute," *Geist und Leben* 80 (2007): 94–108.

Veghel, Optat de. "Aux sources d'une spiritualité des laïcs. Le P. Benoit de Canfield et L'Exercice de la volonté de Dieu," *Etudes Franciscaines* 15 (1965): 33–44.

Vidal, Daniel. *Critique de la raison mystique—Benoît de Canfield. Possession et dépossession au XVIIe siècle* (Grenoble: Millon, 1990).

Vidal, Maurice. *Jean-Jacques Olier homme de talent, serviteur de l'Évangile, 1608–1657* (Paris: Desclée de Brouwer, 2009).

Visser t'Hooft, Willem A. *The Renewal of the Church* (London: Westminster Press, 1956).

Voekel, Pamela. *Alone before God. The Religious Origins of Modernity in Mexico* (Durham: Duke University Press, 2002).

Voorwelt, C. P. *De Amor Poenitens van Johannes van Neercassel, 1626–1686* (Zeist: Kerckebosch, 1984).

Vu Thanh, Hélène. *Devenir japonais. La mission jésuite au Japon, 1549–1614* (Paris: Pups, 2016).

Walsh, Aloysius. *The Priesthood in the Writings of the French School. Berulle, De Condren, Olier* (Washington, DC: Catholic University of America Press, 1949).

Walsham, Alexandra. *Catholic Reformation in Protestant Britain* (Aldershot: Ashgate, 2014).

Walter, Peter, and Wassilowsky, Günther (eds.). *Das Konzil von Trient und die katholische Konfessionskultur (1563–2013)* (Freiburg: Herder, 2016).

Ward, Haruko Nawata. "Women Apostles in Early Modern Japan, 1549–1650," in Weber (ed.), *Devout Laywomen in the Early Modern World*, 312–330.

Ward, Haruko Nawata. *Women Religious Leaders in Japan's Christian Century, 1549–1650* (Farnham: Ashgate, 2009).

Wassilowsky, Günther. "Das Konzil von Trient und die katholische Konfessionskultur," in Walter and Wassilowsky (eds.), *Das Konzil von Trient*, 1–30.

Wassilowsky, Günther. "'Wo die Messe fellet, so ligt das Bapstum.' Zur Kultur päpstlicher Repräsentation in der Frühen Neuzeit," in Birgit Emich et al. (eds.), *Kulturgeschichte des frühneuzeitlichen Papsttums. Zeitschrift für historische Forschung. Beiheft 48* (Berlin: Duncker & Humblot, 2013), 219–247.

Weber, Alison (ed.). *Devout Laywomen in the Early Modern World* (New York: Routledge, 2016).

Weber, Alison. "Devout Laywomen in the Early Modern World. The Historiographic Challenge," in idem (ed.), *Devout Laywomen in the Early Modern World*, 1–28.

Weber, Alison. *Teresa of Avila and the Rhetoric of Femininity* (Princeton, NJ: Princeton University Press, 1990).

Webster, Susan V. "Native Brotherhoods and Visual Culture in Colonial Quito (Ecuador). The Confraternity of the Rosary," in Nicholas Terpstra et al. (eds.), *Faith's Boundaries. Laity and Clergy in Early Modern Confraternities*, (Turnhout: Brepols, 2012), 277–302.

Wengel, Macarius. "Zur Frage der historischen Forschug über das Skapulier," *Münchener Theologische Zeitschrift* 2 (1951): 1–24.

Wengel, Macarius. "Zur Frage der Zeugnisse der Tradition des hl. Skapuliers," *Münchener Theologische Zeitschrift* 2 (1951): 251–262.

Werz, Joachim. "Die Kirche erklären. 'Der Layen Kirchen Spiegel' von Bartholomäus Wagner (ca. 1560–1629) als Beispiel jesuitischer Katechese in der Frühen Neuzeit," in

Veit Neumann et al. (eds.), *Glaube und Kirche in Zeiten des Umbruchs. Festschrift für Josef Kreiml* (Regensburg: Pustet, 2018), 529–543.

Werz, Joachim. "Predigten des Laien Bartholomäus Wagner," in Christian Bauer and Wilhelm Rees (eds.), *Laienpredigt—Neue pastorale Chancen* (Freiburg: Herder, 2021), 75–89.

Werz, Joachim. *Predigtmodi im frühneuzeitlichen Katholizismus. Die volkssprachliche Verkündigung von Leonhard Haller und Georg Scherer in Zeiten und Bedrohungen (1500–1605).* Reformationsgeschichtliche Studien und Texte 175 (Münster: 2020).

Westervelt, Benjamin. "The Prodigal Son at Santa Justina. The Homily in the Borromean Reform of Pastoral Preaching," *Sixteenth Century Journal* 32 (2001): 109–126.

Wicki, Josef. "Die unmittelbaren Auswirkungen des Konzils von Trient auf Indien," *Archivum Historiae Pontificae* 1 (1963): 241–263.

Winston-Allen, Anne. *Stories of the Rose. The Making of the Rosary in the Middle Ages* (University Park: University of Pennsylvania Press, 1997).

Wirbser, Rouven. "A Law Too Strict? The Cultural Translation of Catholic Marriage in the Jesuit Mission to Japan," in Antje Flüchter and Rouven Wirbser (eds.), *Translating Catechisms, Translating Cultures. The Expansion of Catholicism in the Early Modern World* (Leiden and Boston: Brill, 2014), 252–283.

Witko, Andrzej. *Jesús Nazareno Rescatado sobre la iconografía de la Orden de la Santísima Trinidad en los siglos XVII–XX* (Roma: Curia Generalizia dei Trinitari, 2004).

Witko, Andrzej. "The Trinitarian Iconography," *Folia Historica Cracoviensia* 13 (2007): 145–152.

Wogan, Peter. "Perceptions of European Literacy in Early Contact Situations," *Ethnohistory* 3 (1994): 407–429.

Wolf, Hubert. *Krypta. Unterdrückte Traditionen der Kirchengeschichte* (Munich: C.H. Beck, 2015).

Wolff, Lawrence. "Parents and Children in the Sermons of P. Bourdaloue. A Jesuit Perspective on the Early Modern Family," in Christopher Chapple (ed.), *The Jesuit Tradition in Education and Missions* (Scranton: Scranton University Press, 1993), 81–94.

Woodcock, Philippa. "The French Counter-Reformation. Patrons, Regional Styles, and Rural Art," *Church History and Religious Culture* 94 (2014): 22–49.

Worcester, Thomas. "The Classical Sermon," in Joris van Eijnatten (ed.), *Preaching, Sermon and Cultural Change in the Long Eighteenth Century* (Boston and Leiden: Brill, 2009), 133–172.

Worcester, Thomas. *Seventeenth-Century Cultural Discourse. France and the Preaching of Bishop Camus* (Berlin: DeGruyter, 1997).

Wright, Anthony D. *The Division of French Catholicism, 1629–1645* (Aldershot: Ashgate, 2011).

Wucherpfenning, Ansgar. *Josef der Gerechte. Eine exegetische Untersuchung zu Mt 1–12. Herders Biblische Studien* (Freiburg: Herder, 2008).

Zagorin, Perez. *Ways of Lying. Dissimulation, Persecution, and Conformity in Early Modern Europe* (Cambridge and London: Cambridge University Press, 1990).

Zeeden, Ernst Walter (ed.). *Die Visitation im Dienst der kirchlichen Reform* (Münster: Aschendorff, 1967).

Zwyssig, Philipp. *Täler voller Wunder. Eine katholische Verflechtungsgeschichte der Drei Bünde und des Veltlins (17. und 18. Jahrhundert)* (Affalterbach: Didymos, 2018).

# Index

*For the benefit of digital users, indexed terms that span two pages (e.g., 52–53) may, on occasion, appear on only one of those pages.*